Women and Credit

D0283388

Cross-Cultural Perspectives on Women

General Editors: Shirley Ardener and Jackie Waldren, for The Centre for Cross-Cultural Research on Women, University of Oxford

ISSN: 1068-8536

Recent titles include:

Women and Credit

Researching the Past, Refiguring the Future

Edited by
*Beverly Lemire,
Ruth Pearson and
Gail Campbell*

Oxford • New York

First published in 2001 by
Berg
Editorial offices:
150 Cowley Road, Oxford, OX4 1JJ, UK
838 Broadway, Third Floor, New York, NY 10003-4812, USA

Berg is the imprint of Oxford International Publishers Ltd.

Library of Congress Cataloging-in-Publication Data

A catalogue record for this book is available from the Library of Congress.

British Library Cataloguing-in-Publication Data

A catalogue record for this book is available from the British Library.

ISBN 1 85973 479 0 (Cloth)
        1 85973 484 7 (Paper)

Typeset by JS Typesetting, Wellingborough, Northants.
Printed in the United Kingdom by Antony Rowe Ltd, Chippenham, Wiltshire

Contents

Acknowledgements

In September 1999, women and men from many continents arrived in the small Maritime city of Fredericton, New Brunswick, Canada, to exchange information and ideas about women and credit. The participants brought expertise from many disciplines and life experiences. They came to learn from each other and to share perspectives on women's past, present and future economic opportunities. Organizing the conference was the work of several years; this volume is the expression of many of the papers presented over the three and a half days.

An interdisciplinary gathering of this type depends on shared visions and common interests. All who attended were committed to collective exchanges across cultures. Participants, funding agencies, institutions of various sorts and the many co-organizers assisted through their advice, encouragement and labour. Acknowledgment of their assistance is an inadequate expression of my debt to their perceptive comments and timely aid. From the genesis of the idea to the creation of this volume, Shirley Ardener has been a sounding board, a source of invaluable advice and persistent support. She and Cathy Lloyd, at the Centre for Cross Cultural Research on Women, Oxford University, showed what could be done. Rosemary Ommer, Director of the Calgary Institute for the Humanities, showed me a vision of interdisciplinary exchanges that I could only hope to emulate. She bolstered me when I flagged, gave advice when I called and lent her presence to the whole. My colleagues in the Department of History, especially the current Chair, Gillian Thompson, provided me with time, advice and support. She and Gail Campbell gave day-to-day help that cannot be repaid. Alice Taylor laboured with the nuts and bolts of conference organizing with style and panache, while balancing her own research agenda, remaining calm in crises, creative in application. Lisa Todd, Sarah Estabrooks and Laura Turner created the supplementary conference exhibit relating women's self-employment practices in New Brunswick over the last two hundred years. Their work was exemplary. Cathy Beck shared experiences and perspective from years of inter-disciplinary work in several continents and institutions. Jerri Dell, of the World Bank, shared her time, extraordinary energy and lifetime commitment to women's economic equality. Mary Coyle and Gord Cunningham, of the Cody International Institute, St Francis Xavier University, gave assistance and advice when it counted. Professor Barry Bisson, ACOA Chair in Technology Management and Entrepreneurship, University of New Brunswick, and Rhona Levine Reuben of the Business Development Bank of Canada, listened and contributed in important ways. Many others also provided timely aid: Wendy Johnston, Shannon Lemire, Lianne McTavish, Daphne Rae, Walter Schenkle and Marie-Andrée Somers. Conference participants who did not contribute to this volume were, nevertheless, instrumental in the success of the experience: Peter Baskerville, Maxine Berg, Rena Delacruz, Jerri Dell, Margot Finn, Brigid Grant, Jennifer Harold, Margaret Hunt, Daurene Lewis, Lynne Milgram, Josette Murphy, Colleen Neat, Rosemary Ommer, Joan Thirsk, Colleen Tobin and Roger Wehrell.

Funding for the Women & Credit Conference ensured that key participants could attend regardless of the cost of travel from various parts of the world. At the same time, financial support ensured that issues related to women's access to resources received wider regional attention in Canada. I would like to thank Rose-Marie Leblanc of the Atlantic Canada Opportunities Agency; her cogent comments and ACOA's support for this endeavour were invaluable. Warm thanks are also extended to Dr Elizabeth Parr-Johnston, President of the University of New Brunswick, for her personal support and advocacy. The Royal Bank of Canada showed their continuing interest in women's financial future through their financial backing; the individuals who reflected the commitment of The Royal Bank included Betty Wood, in Toronto, and Karen MacPherson, in the Halifax office. The Social Sciences and Humanities Research Council of Canada provided further financial assistance, as did the New Brunswick Department of Labour, the Canadian International Development Agency, the International Development Research Council and the York, College Hill, Capital and New Brunswick Teachers Association Credit Unions. The New Brunswick Department of Intergovernmental and Aboriginal Affairs ensured that translation services were available to facilitate communication.

My co-editors have taught me many lessons about interdisciplinary projects. Ruth Pearson's experience and vision created a contextual structure through which to render three and a half days of intense discussion into a reasoned volume. Gail Campbell's editorial expertise was invaluable in our decision to create a record of this event. Finally, from conference to collection, my husband, Morris, shared in the quotidian trials and joys. My thanks to all.

Beverly Lemire
Fredericton, New Brunswick

Notes on Contributors

Gail Campbell is Professor of History at the University of New Brunswick. She is a former editor of *Acadiensis: Journal of the History of the Atlantic Region*. A Canadian social and political historian, her recent research projects examine the experience of nineteenth-century New Brunswick women, viewed through the prism of their diaries and correspondence. She is also engaged in a detailed examination of the public career of Senator Muriel McQueen Fergusson and her contributions towards raising the status and profile of Canadian women.

Mary Coyle holds the positions of University Vice-President and Director of the Coady International Institute at St Francis Xavier University in Antigonish, Canada. Previously she was the Executive Director of Calmeadow, a Canadian NGO specializing in micro finance work in Canada and internationally. Her professional interests include sustainable livelihoods and economies, effective, democratic community-based approaches to development and the role of technology in global knowledge generation and dissemination.

Beatrice Craig is an Associate Professor in the Department of History at the University of Ottawa and has conducted research in the areas of migratory movements, nineteenth-century agricultural developments and women's work. Her recent publications include 'Inheritance and Property Transmission in Rural Canada in the 19th and 20th Century' in *Family Matters, Papers in Post-Confederation Canadian Family History* (1998).

Owuraku Sakyi-Dawson is a Lecturer at the Department of Agricultural Extension, University of Ghana, with teaching and research interests in agricultural economics and extension. Since completing his Ph.D. on 'Rural households' access to financial services in South-East Ghana' he has been involved in a number of research projects and consultancies in this field.

Joyce Bayande Endeley is the Head of the Department of Women and Gender Studies, as well as Vice-Dean of Students' Affairs and Records,

Faculty of Social and Management Sciences, University of Buea, Cameroon. Her current Interests include training in gender analysis and capacity-building; research on women and gender issues, with emphasis on women in agriculture, and women's empowerment; plus evaluation of the gender sensitivity of development projects and policy.

Laurence Fontaine is Director of Research at the *Centre national de recherches scientifiques*, attached to *l'Ecole des Hautes Etudes en Sciences Sociales* in Paris, and is a Professor at the European University Institute in Florence. She works on migration, pedlars, mountain communities and the economies of early modern Europe. Her recent publications include 'Antonio and Shylock: Credit and Trust in France, *c.*1680–1780', *Economic History Review* (2001).

Aidan Hollis is Assistant Professor in the Department of Economics at the University of Calgary. He has a wide set of research interests, ranging from historical Irish micro-credit institutions to the analysis of anti-competitive practices in the pharmaceutical industry.

Mary Houghton is President of Shorebank Corporation, a regulated bank holding company with a social purpose. It focuses on the economic development needs and opportunities in inner-city communities in the US and the economic and environmental needs and opportunities in rural communities, and advises internationally on small and micro business support.

J. Howard M. Jones is a Lecturer at the International and Rural Development Department, University of Reading, UK, with a long-term interest in the informal financial sector. He is leading a DFID-funded research project on 'Addressing attitudinal constraints in the provision of formal financial services to the rural poor in Madhya Pradesh, India' and will shortly undertake a re-study of a Rajasthan village as part of a DFID-funded research project on livelihood diversification in South Asia.

Abdoulaye Kane completed his doctorate and is now a Researcher at the Amsterdam School for Social Sciences Research. His research interests include popular financial arrangements, migration, women, transnational networks and community development.

Beverly Lemire is Professor of History at the University of New Brunswick and University Research Professor. A recent holder of a Killam Research

Fellowship, she has worked on gender and the informal and formal economic patterns during the rise of industrial capitalism. Her work on women and micro-credit will be included in her forthcoming book entitled *Disciplined Desires: Gender and the Politics of Consumer Culture in England*, c.1600–1900.

Hotze Lont is preparing a Ph.D. thesis at the Amsterdam School for Social Science Research on the subject of financial self-help organizations and social security in Indonesia. He is currently organizing an international conference on 'Livelihood, Savings and Debt in a Changing World', to be held in Wageningen, The Netherlands, May 2001.

Linda Mayoux is a Research Fellow at the Development Policy and Practice Centre for Complexity and Change, The Open University, Milton Keynes, England, as well as an independent consultant. She has worked in many regions of the world, including India, Nicaragua and Africa, with many agencies, including the UNIFEM, ILO, DANIDA, Hivos, ActionAid, CAFOD, and Oxfam (UK and Ireland). Her work focuses on achieving gender equity through development. Her publications include articles, books and collections in the field of women and development, with her most recent projects focusing on women's empowerment, micro-finance, enabling enterprise environments and impact assessment. She is currently a consultant for DFID working on impact assessment of enterprise development. Among her works are the collection *Microfinance and the Empowerment of Women: A Review of the Key Issues* (2000) and *Jobs, Gender and Small Enterprises: Getting the Environment Right* (2001).

Anne E. C. McCants is the William and Betsy Leitch Associate Professor of History in Residence at the Massachusetts Institute of Technology. She is the author of *Civic Charity in a Golden Age: Orphan Care in Early Modern Amsterdam*, and is currently studying the relationship between material culture, household structure, and the distribution of wealth in the urban environment of the Dutch Republic.

Ruth Pearson is Professor at the Centre for Development Studies at the University of Leeds, England. She was the Director of the Gender Analysis in Development MA programme and Chair of Graduate Studies at the University of East Anglia, and until March 1999 half-time Professor at the Institute of Development Studies, the Netherlands. Professor Pearson also has extensive consultancy experience for the British Council, DFID, the EU, SIDA (Sweden) DGIS (Holland), the Commonwealth Secretariat, Marie Stopes International, the North–South Institute, UNRIISD and the World Bank. She has written and edited extensively on topics related to women's employment, globalization, technological change and economic crisis, including the co-edited volume *Feminist Visions of Development : Gender Analysis and Policy* (1998).

Najma R. Sharif is Associate Professor of Economics at Saint Mary's University in Halifax, Nova Scotia. Her research interests are predominantly in the area of development economics and include, amongst other things, the determinants of the socio-economic status and livelihood opportunities of youth (especially females) in developing countries.

Grietjie Verhoef is Professor in Historical Studies at the Rand Afrikaans University, Johannesburg, South Africa. Her research centres around the role of informal financial organizations in mobilizing capital in the informal sector, as well as the empowerment and social security functions of such organizations in the informal sector.

Jayshree Vyas is the Managing Director of SHRI MAHILA SEWA SAHKARI BANK LTD. (a fully regulated cooperative bank organized by the Self Employed Women's Association in Ahmedabad, India) and a Board member of Women's World Banking. Her main professional interest is in developing innovative new financial products and services for poor self-employed women such as daily savings, financial counselling and insurance.

PART I

Exploring the Western History of Women and Credit

1

Introduction. Women, Credit and the Creation of Opportunity: A Historical Overview

Beverly Lemire

This collection of essays began from the premiss that a clear knowledge of past practice strengthens future initiatives. Thus, social policy initiatives affecting women can best be pursued with a clear understanding of women's historic experiences. In this context, the relevant history affecting women encompasses more than just the last dozen years. At the centre of this reassessment is the long history of the rise of industrial capitalism and the roles of women as both informal and formal economic agents. Although the geographic focus of my research is Britain, the site of the first industrial revolution, there are numerous comparative elements that find resonance in other societies and other times. The overview provided here has a Western focus; however, there is much to discover and more work to be done in comparative reassessments of women's practices.

The history of women's roles in past societies is more than a matter of passing curiosity. Their experiences, and the social and economic patterns revealed, speak to the evolving structures in a modernizing world. Recent research has also uncovered the persistent initiatives of generations of women, information that has been absent for too long in standard analyses. This oversight is now being remedied. At the same time, our understanding of industrial capitalism is being reformulated to include the full contributions of half the population.

Discovering the history of women's economic endeavours is not without challenges (Alexander *et al.* 1979; Hall 1992). Gender inequities ensured that many elements of women's work went unrecorded. At the same time, as the tenets of liberal economics were set in place, the creators of these theories systematically excluded women's activities from consideration. In theoretical discourses and in practical policies, ubiquitous female endeavours fell more and more into the shadows. Mainstream liberal and Marxist economic thought illuminated and defined the practice of male workers, institutions, investors, entrepreneurs. Ultimately, most things defined as economic were gendered male (Pujol 1992; Bodkin 1999). Marilyn Waring notes that economic theory constructs reality. Through the lense of theory, some elements of social activity come into sharp focus, while others are blurred or invisible on the margins. Waring states that 'Theory is used, first of all, in order to decide what facts are relevant to an analysis. . . . Overwhelmingly, those experiences that are economically visible can be summarized as *what men do*' (Waring 1988: 17). The repercussions of this historic invisibility have yet to be fully resolved.

Ester Boserup (1990: 14) finds that 'All contemporary societies are in transition between subsistence economies and fully specialized economies. Even in highly industrialized countries, production of goods and services in the family, mainly by women, accounts for a considerable share of total work hours.' Her observations apply as well to the experience of Western societies in transition to industrial capitalism. Home-based production of goods and services constituted many women's principal activities. Economists designated these activities as 'unproductive' domestic tasks, and therefore outside the market, because they took place within a home base and were undertaken by women. This selective exclusion warped perceptions of societal development. Over the twentieth century, feminist economists and economic historians asked questions and challenged categories of analysis that imperfectly define the full human experience (Lerner 1986; Folbre 1991; Pujol 1992; Honeyman 2000). What is now indisputable is that poor women, working women and wage-earning women creatively and productively marshalled resources to help sustain their households. In this context, they also organized credit for petty production, retail and domestic use as part of their habitual responsibilities. This recovered history is now entering the mainstream as a challenge to misperceptions and expectations surrounding women's roles.

Micro-credit, in various forms, was central to the experience of women in the Western world, particularly in the growing urban centres, from at least the sixteenth century onwards. The hunt for and use of credit formed part of their daily lives, a mechanism that enabled many to get by and a few to flourish. Recent research challenges the assumption that women only recently became active commercial agents, securing loans and lending money. It also refutes the claim that women were excluded from financial activities, except as servants or employees. A number of the contributors to this volume offer detailed accounts of women's experiences as borrowers, lenders and productive actors. The next section will introduce some common historical facets of western women's economic lives during the rise of industrial capitalism.

Women's Use of Credit before the Rise of Industrial Capitalism

Credit was indispensable to labouring men and women in pre-industrial and early industrial societies. The pressures of fluctuating employment and irregular pay meant that credit of various sorts was a necessity. Aside from shop credit, ordinary folk turned most commonly to formal and informal pawnbrokers and moneylenders to meet their credit needs. Among the labouring and lower middle ranks, the housewife's general responsibilities included the management of this household credit.

The trope of the thrifty housewife is well known. It is equally well known that women were disproportionately responsible for household functions. But these responsibilities included more than making soup from bones or mending worn socks. Arranging credit was particularly important at a time when households were the sites of retail, service and manufacturing activities. In this complex transitional period, household functions cannot be neatly compartmentalized into discrete economic categories labelled 'production' or 'consumption'. Garrets or cottages housed commercial activities along with explicitly domestic projects. At the same time, market exchanges were far more eclectic than a simple trade of cash for goods. Adaptive strategies, such as engagement with the second-hand clothing trade, enabled generations to balance household accounts. Linens and apparel could easily be turned into cash or commodities. Moreover, they were bought both for their practical and their investment features. Household wares represented some of the most important material disbursements for working families. Not only did they provide comfort and convenience, but these mutable items also functioned as a kind of currency. In this economic climate, formal and informal pawnbrokers flourished, turning goods into cash. The credit they provided was indispensable, offering ready sources of cash where there were limited options (Lemire 1997: 112–17; Wijngaarden 1998). This complex commercial environment produced dense networks of economic and social interaction where women played key roles.

Credit and Community

The nature of early modern communities varied, and women directed their commercial activities to match the economic niches available. Distinctive conditions permitted particular credit practices. Large ports like London, for example, created opportunities for enterprising women within the maritime community, as Margaret Hunt has shown. Seafaring men set the parameters for the women's experiences. Absent husbands, impermanent marriages and infrequent pay for husbands, brothers and fathers from naval or mercantile bureaucracies, offered opportunities as well as challenges to sailors' wives, sisters and neighbours. After a long voyage, a sailor's pay was calculated through the seaman's ticket; these chits circulated like currency in seaports. Women brokers discounted seamen's tickets for their neighbours and took seamen's tickets in exchange for goods and services. Some women also developed specialities as legal or financial counsels, assisting the holder of the ticket to secure payment from the Royal Navy or some other bureaucracy. Hunt illuminates an active commercial network, where married women used the powers of attorney assigned by their absent husbands to lend, borrow and secure loans for neighbours. Even without the legal sanction of a power of attorney, married women from the labouring classes did not relinquish their commercial ambitions, as once was thought (Hunt 1998, 1999). Hunt's insightful re-creation of the port community suggests the kind of comparable ventures that might be found in other seaports. Women in similar settings may well have followed corresponding paths, looking for ways to make ends meet.

Thus, throughout the cities of Europe from at least the sixteenth century onwards, generations of women arranged credit for productive and consumer needs (Lemire 1998; Wijngaarden 1998; Bogucka 1998; Muldrew 1998; Amián 1998). Most typically, they pawned household goods in a continuous counterpoise between income and outflow. The context of the pawnshop varied according to national and regional norms. Laurence Fontaine notes the importance of the *mont de pieta* – municipal or church-run charitable pawnshops, designed to provide low-cost credit to the poor. These institutions flourished throughout continental Europe from the fifteenth century onwards. Aidan Hollis recounts the features of the Irish Loan Fund, another regional mechanism to provide the poor with inexpensive credit options. England offered no successful ventures of these sorts. Nevertheless, the gender and social patterns of lending revealed in English documentation confirm some important norms in the credit process.

Common community patterns of lending and borrowing are revealed in the surviving records of a shopkeeper based in South London in the later seventeenth century. These records, in combination with a range of supporting materials, suggest the ubiquitous patterns of credit in which women predominated. John Pope kept a haberdasher's shop in a poor neighbourhood on the south bank of the River Thames, a neighbourhood filled with seafarers and recent immigrants to London (C108/34, PRO).

Few of Pope's customers boasted highly skilled occupations. Most survived making low-quality goods, selling cheap commodities in the bustling streets or providing essential services, like washing laundry. Pope served their credit needs, furnishing several sorts of credit for these small traders, artisans, servants and working poor. Moneylending comprised just under three-quarters of all his credit transactions; these loans were unsecured. Pope depended on community knowledge and the reputation of the borrower. Pawns provided a greater measure of security and comprised over a quarter of his surviving transactions. These records permit a reconstruction of the channels through which credit flowed and the social mechanisms that defined these exchanges.

Risk reduction was a priority for Pope, and the guarantor played a pivotal role in the lending process, bridging the gap between lender and borrower. New borrowers relied on introductions and endorsements from proven borrowers, after which began an independent credit relationship. Arranging and securing loans was evidently seen by established members of the community as an obligation to their dependants and to their neighbours. Men and women collaborated routinely in arranging credit. However, women were disproportionately active as intermediaries in the loan process.

Credit Networks and Gender

Intervention was often critical for both the lender and borrower. A partner or guarantor, with a sound reputation, offered security to the lender and spread credit to a wider circle, especially among the poor (Muldrew 1996: 926–31). Those without material collateral relied even more heavily on the weight of their reputations than did those with property to mortgage. Pope's ledgers contain a wealth of evidence of relationships established and sanctioned through credit. Commercial and social bonds were forged by men and women. Male borrowers depended equally on other male or female partners. Women, on the other hand, relied more commonly on other women. More than 70 per cent of women borrowers relied on other women to mediate the credit process. Women relied more on other women than on men to assist in the getting of credit; their reliance was not misplaced. Similar patterns have also been found in other ventures involving women in England, as well as in the Netherlands (Walker 1994: 83–5; McCants 2001). Networks of sociability contributed to this pattern. But, there were also significant gendered commercial links at the periphery of mainstream markets where women's informal trade abounded. Women bargained and haggled, bartered and sold, struggling to maintain a hold in the margins of the main market. Credit enabled them to get by.

The majority of urban women, from the labouring and lower middling classes, were familiar with facets of credit, with needs met through short-term loans, such as could be arranged by the pawning of apparel. My work on the second-hand trade (1997: 95–120) reveals that untold numbers of women functioned in informal commercial capacities, pawning and acting as brokers, accepting their neighbours' pledged clothing, sheets or cookware. Their often informal commerce was a vital facet of this economy. In John Pope's neighbourhood there is further evidence of the patterns typical of poor trading women. Some women attained prominence as organizers of credit. Roberta Jones stands out among those guaranteeing loans. Jones was a laundress and a widow. She was undoubtedly poor. Yet, in spite of these objective disadvantages, Roberta Jones was a woman of standing in her neighbourhood. Pope relied on her judgement; men and women sought her out for assistance in their affairs. Jones arranged more loans than any other man or woman in Pope's books. Wool spinners, a silk weaver, a pin maker, mop makers, and laundresses looked to her for assistance with loans. Pope relied on her discretion. These facts are confirmed by the note penned after a number of loans: Roberta Jones 'douth pase her word to se it payd' (C108/34, PRO). This humble woman typified the countless women, like her, who cultivated commercial niches in the as yet unregulated credit environments of the West's growing cities. Their agency left few tangible traces in formal records, yet their initiative and financial acumen was an important stimulus to the economy. In turn, others were assisted through a wider access to credit. In the Pope records, more than 84 per cent of pawns and 62 per cent of loans were arranged by women (see Figure 1.1). The predominance of women in all loan transactions underscores their pivotal function in the sphere of small-scale credit. In spite of the formal Common Law prohibition against married women entering into contracts, poor women could and did arrange credit for themselves. Moreover, their preponderance in this ubiquitous commercial sector persisted for generations.

Lending and the Regulation of Credit

Over the course of the eighteenth and nineteenth centuries legal and structural changes in the economy also affected the organization of small-scale credit. The context in which women secured loans also changed.

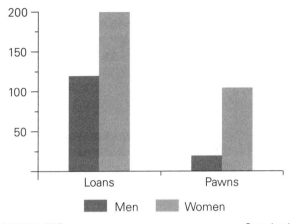

Source: C108/34, PRO   Sample: 440 loans

Figure 1.1 Male and female borrowers from John Pope, South London, 1667–71.

The provision of credit was being transformed even as credit requirements expanded and differentiated over this era. As enterprises grew and separated from the household, the organization of small loans also evolved. Governments passed legislation to regulate lending and the business of pawnbroking to mitigate usurious interest rates. They tried, as well, to eliminate informal money lenders and pawnbrokers (Tebbutt 1983: 73–5, 112–14). Even with these changes, some patterns persisted well into the nineteenth century.

Women continued to make the majority of pawn transactions. Figure 1.2 illustrates this point. The surviving documentation from pawnbrokers shows that an overwhelming majority of pawn transactions were organized by women. This is evident from the records of a late eighteenth-century pawnbroker from York, George Fettes. More than 60 per cent of pledges were undertaken by the women of York and surrounding neighbourhoods. This is consistent with the Pope records. Moreover, this pattern persists in records from the early nineteenth century. In the records of a Sheffield pawnbroker, we see a continuing predominance of female borrowers. Similarly, the sorts of goods offered as pledges were consistent across the centuries from London, to York, to Sheffield. The majority of articles brought to the pawnshop were everyday household items, such as textiles or clothing. These articles typically represented the most costly personal material goods bought by ordinary people. Women most frequently pledged these items. A mid-Victorian commentator (Anon. in

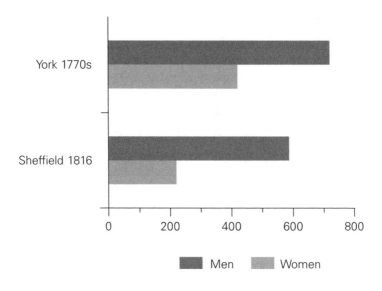

Source: Acc. 38, York City Archives; J90/1007 PRI.

Figure 1.2   Gender pattern of pawns, 1770s and 1816.

Ingestre 1852: 285) asserted that: 'Certainly women pawn the most; but where large sums are required, men generally transact the business – but I would say they number as seven of the former to one of the latter.'

As the volume of consumer products increased over the eighteenth and nineteenth centuries, the allocation of household resources also changed. Men were already distinguished as the principal owners and pawners of watches. Watches were an important new consumer item. Moreover, they could rival or exceed in value traditional household wares largely controlled by the women of the family. This suggests the new dynamic brought about by gendered patterns of consumption within the household, which in turn affected patterns of credit. Just as items like watches assume a greater importance as objects of personal investment, so too men were most frequently involved with larger transactions, even among those who continued to frequent pawnbrokers. While women pawned in greater numbers than men, the context of their role in the organization of petty credit had changed. At the very least, the popularity of new sorts of consumer wares among men, like watches, brought a new dynamic into the household economy and into the provision of credit.

Conclusion

For countless generations, pawning was one of the principal archetypes for small-scale loans. Pawning and pledging goods for ready cash was as commonplace over that long era as credit card transactions are for the contemporary population. Many elements of small-scale credit remain to be assessed. However, it is indisputable that the changes in production and consumption had ramifications for credit. These changes, in turn, had implications for the lives and experiences of women. I believe it is here that we can discern substantial changes in Western society. Credit from pawnbrokers for petty production persisted through the nineteenth century, but it held a different level of importance. For most of the working class, production was increasingly separated from the home; furthermore, credit needs for production and retail were larger than in the past and growing. By the mid-nineteenth century, pawning was a more socially marginalized activity, reviled by many reformers. They were appalled by the commercial practices of the lower orders, along with the economic burden of interest payments imposed by pawnbrokers. In addition, long lines of working-class women who formed outside the pawnshop on Monday mornings generated more critical comments. That the routine of arranging small household loans was gendered also coloured public perception of the phenomenon (Tebbutt 1983: 113; Hardaker 1892: 41–57). Nonetheless, it continued as an active trade, with an estimated 29 million transactions by metropolitan London pawnbrokers in 1866. As with women in previous periods, the skill of the working-class wife in balancing and contriving determined the relative comfort and security of many working-class families. The position and power of these women was certainly augmented by their control of daily credit. Pawning did provide late-nineteenth-century working-class women with a source of power within the household (Ross 1993: 81–3; Llewelyn Davies 1975 [1931]: 62–3). But this was a conditional power, the shape and context of which was measurably changed since the seventeenth century. Pawning was becoming marginalized by class and community; at the same time, opportunities for alternate sources of credit multiplied.

In the first half of the nineteenth century new lending opportunities were sanctioned by government. These new-style enterprises included loan societies: The London Equitable Loan Bank Company and The Tradesman's Economical Loan Company for granting Loans of £2 and upwards are only two of the approximately 550 private loan societies licensed by 1860. Business records survive for The Porto Bello Loan Society (J90/1007, PRO). And in these documents one can see both change and continuity in the patterns of borrowing. The Porto Bello Loan Society (1841–57) lent money in much the same way as did John Pope centuries before. A majority of borrowers were small traders of various sorts. The loans were predominantly for relatively small sums and they required the guarantee of another householder. However, there were very striking changes in the participation of women as borrowers and guarantors. Women still participated in both these functions, but at a greatly diminished level; only about 5 per cent of loans from the Porto Bello Loan Society were taken out by women – a startling transformation. Although the Irish Loan Funds presented wider opportunities for women, the few remaining records from other loan societies in England suggest significant declines in the number of women borrowers over the nineteenth century.

Regulation and greater capitalization changed the face of pawnbroking, just as surely as the collective economic and social pressures of the industrial era altered the functions within the household for which credit was obtained. This combination of dramatic economic and social change undoubtedly brought in its wake new patterns of household credit for the middle and respectable labouring classes. In the middling ranks and above, the growing credit needs of business, retailing and manufacturing were regularly handled through personal loans, mortgages and partnerships – formalized and separate from domestic budgeting (Mathias 1979: 92–3). The specialization of the credit markets offered alternative sources of credit to various classes of patrons (Tebbutt 1983: 101). Pawnbroking was increasingly restricted to the working poor, and the practice itself was derided. In working-class districts in major European cities, women routinely lined up to pawn and reclaim household goods. But this practice was no longer habitual among most classes. The persistence of pawning among working-class communities, the persistence of women as the organizers of these pawns, was viewed as a distinctively proletarian aberration. Moreover, the continuing commercial agency of women was increasingly rendered in broadly comedic strokes by satirists, or styled as an indication of profligacy.

Throughout this period it is clear that the reputation for thrift and prudence that accrued to a virtuous urban housewife included her capacity to employ credit, whether or not such skills were acknowledged in prescriptive literature. These norms cast a new light on the growth of the industrial economy and its relationship to the homely economy, for this economy of make-do included among its tasks borrowing and brokering loans for productive and consumption purposes. The formalization and regulation of credit came at the same time as most economic functions began to be seen as distinctively male prerogatives. Options narrowed for women, even as working-class mothers continued to shoulder the responsibilities for credit in their families.

Currently, social activists are working to expand economic opportunities for women, including access to credit. While recognizing the context of contemporary micro-credit initiatives, it is also important to recognize that women have a long history of working with credit of various sorts. Uncovering the history of women's credit activities, it is clear that their agency contributed directly to the wider economy. Kitchen and community were linked through adaptive credit practices that, in turn, were nurtured and sustained by generations of women as a critical adjunct to their domestic roles. This collection of essays bridges the divisions between women's past and present-day economic experiences. Highlighting persistent practices, it also suggests the need for future policies to secure women's full economic equality.

References

Unpublished Sources:
Public Record Office: C108/34, J90/1007.
York City Archives: Acc. 38.

Published Sources
Alexander, S., A. Davin and E. Hostettler (1979), 'Labouring Women: a Reply to Eric Hobsbawm', *History Workshop Journal*, 8: 174–82.

Amián, A. G. (1998), 'El credito informal realizado por las mujeres de Andalucia en el siglo XIX: una actividad mas urbana que rural', unpublished paper presented at the Twelfth International Economic History Congress, Madrid.

Anon. (1852), 'Truths from a Pawnbroker', in Viscount Ingestre (ed.), *Melioria: Or, Better Times to Come*, London.

Bodkin, R. G. (1999), 'Economic Thought: Adam Smith, Harriet Taylor Mill, and J. S. Mill', *Feminist Economics*, 5(1): 45–60.

Bogucka, M. (1998), 'Women and credit operations in Polish towns in the early modern period', unpublished paper presented at the Twelfth International Economic History Congress, Madrid.

Boserup, E. (1990), 'Economic Change and the Roles of Women', in I. Tinker (ed.), *Persistent Inequalities: Women and World Development*, Oxford: Oxford University Press.

Folbre, N. (1991), 'The Unproductive Housewife: Her Evolution in Nineteenth-Century Economic Thought', *Signs*, 16(31): 463–84.

Hall, C. (1992), *White, Male and Middle Class: Explorations in Feminism and History*, Cambridge: Polity.

Hardaker, A. (1892), *A Brief History of Pawnbroking*, London: Jackson, Ruston and Keeson.

Honeyman, K. (2000), *Women, Gender and Industrialisation in England, 1700–1870*, Basingstoke, Hampshire, England: Macmillan Press.

Hunt, M. (1998), 'Capital, Credit and the Family in Eighteenth-Century England', unpublished paper presented at the Twelfth International Economic History Congress, Madrid.

—— (1999), 'Women, Credit and the Seafaring Community in Early Eighteenth-Century London', unpublished paper presented at the Women & Credit Conference, Fredericton, New Brunswick, Canada.

Lemire, B. (1997), *Dress, Culture and Commerce: The English Clothing Trade before the Factory*, Basingstoke, Hampshire, England: Macmillan Press.

—— (1998), 'Petty Pawns and Informal Lending: Gender and the Transformation of Small-Scale Credit in England, *circa* 1600–1800', in K. Bruland and P. O'Brien (eds), *From Family Firms to Corporate Capitalism*, Oxford: Oxford University Press.

Lerner G. (1986), *The Creation of Patriarchy*, New York: Oxford University Press.

Llewelyn Davies, M. (ed.) (1975 [1931]), *Life as We Have Known It: by Co-operative Working Women*, New York: W. W. Norton & Co Ltd.

Mathias, P. (1979), 'Capital, Credit and Enterprise in the Industrial Revolution', in Peter Mathias (ed.), *The Transformation of England*, London: Methuen & Co Ltd.

McCants, A. (2001), 'Petty Debts and Family Networks: The Credit Markets of Widows and Wives in Eighteenth-Century Amsterdam', in B. Lemire, R. Pearson and G. Campbell (eds), *Women and Credit: Researching the Past, Refiguring the Future*, Oxford: Berg Publishers.

Muldrew, C. (1996), 'The Culture of Reconciliation: Community and the Settlement of Economic Disputes in Early Modern England', *The Historical Journal*, 39(4): 915–42.

—— (1998), 'Women, Household Credit and Debt Litigation in Early Modern England', unpublished paper presented at the Twelfth International Economic History Congress, Madrid.

Pujol, M. (1992), *Feminism and Anti-Feminism in Early Economic Thought*, Aldershot: E Elgar.

Ross, E. (1993), *Love and Toil: Motherhood in Outcast London, 1870–1918*, New York: Oxford University Press.

Tebbutt, M. (1983), *Making Ends Meet: Pawnbroking and Working-Class Credit*, London: Methuen & Co Ltd.

Walker, G. (1994), 'Women, Theft and the World of Stolen Goods', in J. Kermode and G. Walker (eds), *Women, Crime and the Courts in Early Modern England*, London: University College London Press.

Waring, M. (1988), *If Women Counted: A New Feminist Economics*, New York: Harper & Row Publishers.

Wijngaarden, H. Van. (1998), 'Credit as a Way to Make Ends Meet. The Use of Credit by Poor Women in Zwolle, 1650–1700', unpublished paper presented at the Twelfth International Economic History Congress, Madrid.

2

Women's Economic Spheres and Credit in Pre-industrial Europe

Laurence Fontaine

Women's experiences with credit in pre-industrial Europe were multi-dimensional. They varied according to social status, law, history and culture. Europe under the *ancien régime* was a status-based society. In this society women had two sets of allegiances, grounded in and dependent on both their sex and their social standing: an aristocratic woman did not have the same rights or fulfil the same roles as an ordinary woman. And this duality was itself subject to variations, so that we cannot talk of women in general, but must consider their status in the various orders of society.

Another factor contributing to the complexity of this subject was that, according to the available documentation, the legal framework of women's activities varied widely from one end of Europe to the other. For one thing, European law was a nuanced and fluid mix, based on at least three different sources: Germanic law, Roman law and canon law. For another, the law has its own history, the imprint of which can be found in its various codifications. Finally, the spirit of the law is very different in a democratic society than in a society based on social orders. In the former it standardizes the statutes, and in the latter it justifies special cases and exceptions.

A third complicating factor was that although each social status was defined by its legal capacities, the groups thus determined were not static; they possessed their own dynamic based on the need to survive and to reproduce – all in a changing world. The law evolved in a more-or-less parallel direction, revealing changes in the configurations of power involving women.

The final complicating factor derives from changes in perceptions and expectations of women and in their status, depending on their stage of life, whether they were married to a man or to God, and whether they were single or widowed. In certain circumstances, however, the pressing needs of husbands and families forced women to give up their traditional roles and become engaged in economic activities that opened up areas of freedom and authority to them.

Women's ability to juggle time, money and credit depended on the complex balance linking social institutions, women's roles within society, their cultural construction, and the powers surrounding them, which defined women's place and their access to resources, whether land, labour or capital. The relationships between these elements varied enormously across Europe. I must emphasize that to profit fully from juggling time and money, one had to have money in the first place. Having money meant not only earning or receiving it, but also having the freedom to spend it as one wished or give it away. In other words, it meant managing it freely, and hence being able to enter into legally binding arrangements; it also meant being able to safeguard it. In a period when private and public were largely interdependent and when economic success was dependent on the Prince who bestowed economic privileges, trading rights and monopolies, the ability to play a role in politics was essential for building up, holding on to and consolidating wealth. To understand the relationships women maintained with credit it is necessary to explore the wide range of legal capacities that defined women's autonomy, and finally determined what was a woman's word, a woman's honour.

I should like to stress the relationship between the rights of women in Europe, and the economic spheres that they created, and to emphasize three distinct cleavages that gave rise to change: (1) the linking of the law to a woman's life cycle; (2) the development of the market; and (3) the migration of men. After this, and very briefly, as it is an issue more fully developed in other contributions to this volume, I shall highlight the role of women as financial intermediaries and merchants; and finally, I shall pose some questions relating to the existence of specifically female financial practices and economic cultures.

The Law and Women's Economic Activities

Legal Frameworks

The three principal branches of law to be found in Europe were far from being internally consistent. Germanic laws varied. Canon law was a juxtaposition of elements, many of them contradictory, because it reflected the history and the ambivalence of the Church, always torn between a desire to see both sexes as equal and a wish to subjugate women (Metz

1962: 59–113). Law, despite its 'a-historical' appearance and like all social activities, is a product of the play of power and contradictory perceptions which cut across society. In other words, law is also something that is practised, that draws on complex and contradictory bodies of work and which thus allows a certain latitude to lawyers and judges to interpret it.

Three main tendencies are apparent within this diversity. The first followed the life cycle, and separated married women from unmarried women and from women who were no longer married. In northern France, Belgium, the Netherlands and Germany, a married woman was 'incompctent', and both she and her property came under her husband's authority. Everything – notarial records, the wording of rulings, memoirs, plays and novels – proves that this tradition of placing married women in a position of dependency grew stronger in the early modern period, starting in the sixteenth century (Portemer 1958: 441; 1962: 471). Between the sixteenth and eighteenth centuries, woman's legal incapacity became progressively more widespread, but, in return, her financial interests came to be more protected everywhere (Gilissen 1962: 255–6).

A married woman could not go to court, enter into legally binding contracts, or even act as a witness to a contract. She was allowed to have her own separate property, but her husband managed it and received income from it as though it were his own. He was not allowed to sell it, use it as collateral, divide it or initiate any legal action involving it without his wife's consent, however. In the seventeenth century, jurisprudence introduced the *hypothèque légale* or legal claim in favour of the wife, which was a characteristic of regions of written law, and applied it to the husband's real property and to jointly owned moveable property; but the woman could legitimately relinquish her claim. If, during their marriage, the woman feared her husband's financial ruin, she could request separate estates *(séparation des biens,* which came from Roman law). This right should not be overstated. It was refused to women under numerous *coutumes* (customary law), especially in Germanic regions (Portemer 1962: 460–5; Gerhard 1997; Petot 1962: 247).

The various Italian regions were divided between the mixed influences of Roman, canon and Germanic law. Despite the equality within the family proclaimed in principle by Christianity,[1] the Lombard invasion brought with it – as happens in all military societies – conditions that were even more restrictive for women. As they were not able to bear arms – a fundamental prerequisite for the status of legal subject – Lombard women were placed under the permanent guardianship of their father, relatives, husband, or, failing these, of the King, the ultimate guardian. As the various elements of Roman, Church and Germanic law converged, overlapped and merged, the trend was for these prejudices and restrictions to continue (Rossi 1962: 117).

In those territories exempt from Germanic law, such as Rome, Venice and Ravenna, women could engage in any legal action when they attained their majority. Yet here too the trend was to restrict women's autonomy. One of the first changes arose from the need for communes and families to control the circulation of capital. Women's freedom was restricted so as to prevent them taking their wealth elsewhere if they married outsiders. A second development was the strict reinforcement of lineage. A husband's permission was not always enough, and the consent of the relatives in charge of the family group might be required in a case of the alienation of a patrimony. In the same way, a woman's right to be the beneficiary of a will was limited, just as she herself was often obliged to draw up her own will according to the wishes of her protectors. This situation, which was sometimes imposed even when the law allowed otherwise, persisted in several regions of Italy to the end of the *ancien régime* (Rossi 1962: 122). But in places where Roman ideas remained strong, it was not unusual, especially in merchant circles, for women to have personal wealth not derived from their dowry, which they could dispose of as they saw fit, even though normally its administration would be the husband's responsibility.

In Poland and Russia, married women managed their own property except, in Poland, when it was a question of alienating real property. They even entered into contracts with their own husbands. The early modern era saw, in Poland as elsewhere, a limitation of the rights of women, who could no longer take cases to court alone, but had to be accompanied by their husbands (Roman 1962: 397–403).

Only in England was the trend in the opposite direction. Common law was undeniably one of the strictest in Europe, prohibiting the married woman from owning anything (all that she owned, including her moveable goods, was given to her husband who, in exchange, settled her debts), from entering into any contract and, of course, from making a will. It was not until the sixteenth century and the development of the concept of equity law (which had begun, hesitantly, to make an appearance in the ambit of the Chancery in the fourteenth century) that the severity of common law was mitigated. Secular Lords Chancellor, such as Francis Bacon (1561–1621), succeeded in extending women's legal capacities. They introduced the system of trusts, which meant that a woman handed over all that she owned to trustees – in most cases professionals – through whose mediation she had use of her property, and could sell, give or bequeath it, or otherwise dispose of it as she saw fit. Moreover, the Court of Chancery imposed the famous 'settlements' on recalcitrant husbands, whereby a woman was assured of the equivalent of a dower and income in keeping with her social standing during her lifetime. In the matter of property reserved for her in this way, the married woman had the legal rights of a single woman (des Longrais 1962: 145–6).

What can be said of these changes in the rights of married women? I should like to draw attention to two developments: on the one hand, the increasingly categorical affirmation that the role of women was in the private sphere (which strengthened the guardianship of husbands) para-doxically also opened up spheres of freedom for women by reshaping their economic roles. In effect, women's primary task was to find a way to match irregular income with the daily need to feed the family. A central concern nowadays, but one about which historical documents have very little to say, is to understand the extent of women's bargaining power within the family and the couple, and how income was brought in and parcelled out within the family. We know very little about everyday money management in the early modern era, even though the law allows us certain glimpses. So that she could provide for her family, in several regions of customary law – in Belgium (Gilissen 1962: 299), the northern Netherlands and England – the married woman had the right to make contracts and incur debts for the needs of the household, independently of the control of her husband, and in so doing she pledged the family's property (Bosch 1962: 334). In Poland, women who were responsible for the household could not be deprived of the freedom to manage it alone: alone they sold or bought dairy products, poultry, vegetables and so forth (Roman 1962: 397–8).

On the other hand, one of the consequences of hypothecation, which became widespread in the seventeenth century as a way of protecting women's rights despite poor management by husbands, was that those who had dealings with the husband, either over property that she owned or property that was acquired during marriage, now took the precaution of asking the wife to waive her legal right to the property in question. In consequence, the married woman, despite her legal incapacity, found her control over how her husband disposed of her property strengthened (Petot 1962: 251). But customary law that privileged lineage, such as that of Normandy and of numerous Germanic regions (Gerhard 1997), continued to restrict women's rights until the end of the eighteenth century (Perrot 1975: v. 2, 245).

Unmarried women, whether of the age of majority or widowed, in northern France, Belgium, the Netherlands and Germany, were not, in principle, legally incapacitated, even though constraints gradually appeared in these places too. If classical Roman law had got rid of the legal guardianship of women, in numerous regions of Germany the practice of *cura sexus* was very much alive (Portemer 1962: 453; Gerhard 1997). The law allowing the widow to relinquish the communal estate and thereby be released from household debts existed in many customary traditions in France, Belgium, in the Netherlands and elsewhere, but here too there were numerous exceptional cases in which the widow was not allowed to relinquish joint ownership of the estate (Bosch 1962: 336; Gilissen 1962: 317–18).

In Poland and Russia unmarried women with their own property enjoyed the right to enter into contracts and legally binding arrangements, to sell and bestow gifts and so forth, generally without restriction, except in the early modern era in Poland, when unmarried women could not act without the help of their guardian. Widows were *sui juris*, dependent upon no one, unless they were poor or had freely chosen a guardian. Here too the rights of widows were reduced in the early modern era in the matter of the management of property and children, and by the requirement that women be accompanied by a guardian if they wished to go to court (Roman 1962: 397–8).

Moves in the opposite direction were evident in certain Germanic regions, in particular in the Rhineland, where widows gradually acquired the right to manage the property coming from their dowry and their dower, on their own, only being required to have recourse to a male intermediary (in most cases a professional) in case of dispute or important agreements (Opitz 1991: 325).[2] Widows were also involved in providing surety. Finally, in England widows benefited from a dower provided by the husband, which had to correspond to their social standing as assessed by the legal authorities (des Longrais 1962: 184).

If, broadly speaking, widowhood bestowed freedom on women everywhere, once again we must be cautious. Young widows with their own property were likely to remarry, even against their wishes, and, in any case, many preferred to put themselves back under the protection of a man and to enjoy the material support he could provide, for, in too many cases, widowhood meant poverty. Official terminology makes the predominant attitude clear: it ranks widows among the groups characterized by structural poverty, on the same level as orphans, the infirm and the elderly.

Women, the Market and the Law

The second major area of change was the market-place, and this meant primarily the town. Everywhere since the Middle Ages the development of trading had been accompanied by an expansion of women's legal autonomy. For men, running a business had been a way of escaping paternal authority, and for women it also became a reason for acquiring the capacity to enter freely into legally binding agreements.

The rapid expansion of large towns in Flanders, Brabant and the region of Liège from the eleventh and twelfth centuries onwards had created a town law that was codified in the thirteenth century and remained in force until the end of the *ancien régime* and that was very favourable towards women. Town law abolished male privilege in matters of inheritance, bestowed upon widows full guardianship of their children, brought property acquired during the marriage into joint ownership and prevented the man from disposing of the most significant assets without the agreement of his wife. Finally, when a marriage ended, town law allowed the surviving spouse – male or female – to retain either full ownership of all jointly owned property or the use thereof. In addition, a woman had the right to make a will, to spend the household's money and to defend herself in the criminal courts. Naturally, there were subtle differences between established customary law and practices as they evolved, with coastal Flanders, which was more commercial, having the most liberal law, and eastern Flanders offering an example of how the law evolved in the other direction (Gilissen 1962: 256–8, 286).

Elsewhere the legal category of female trader was created. The female trader was usually a woman who 'kept shop'. Under the customary law of Belgium, the Netherlands and certain German towns, she had to run her business separately from that of her husband because, if she worked for him, it was he and not she who was legally responsible (Bosch 1962: 335–6). (But if she was involved in her husband's business, then she was jointly liable for his bankruptcy (Gilissen 1962: 297).) She did not need prior permission to do this; it was enough for her to conduct her business in the plain view and knowledge (*au vu et au su*) of her husband. His tacit permission was sufficient, as he had only to exercise his right of counteraction to bring the situation to an end. Thus, within the legal limits applying to her business, she was responsible for all contractual arrangements and all debts. As a consequence of the permission granted to her by her husband to engage in commerce, her property, their jointly owned property and also his property were at stake in her business. A woman trading publicly could be arrested for debt, whereas a married woman could not be.[3] If a woman suspected her husband of squandering her estate, she could request a legal division of property. In many traditions, a woman who had been granted a separation of property had full legal capacity, just as if she had been widowed (Gilissen 1962: 287–99).

Amongst urban artisans, women's autonomy was less widely accepted. French and Spanish women were excluded from professional organizations, such as the guilds. A widow could take over her husband's business, however. Conversely, there were many women active in small and large businesses in the Netherlands, Italy and certain German towns (such as Lübeck, Bremen and Cologne), where, until the sixteenth century, they had access to existing guilds or were organized in their own guilds (Bosch 1962: 347; Wiesner Wood 1981: 18 ff.). This century marked such a decline in the number of artisan women that, in 1688, the German jurist Adrian Beier could write: 'In accordance with the rule, no person of the female sex may enter into business as an artisan, even if she is just as skilled as a person of the male sex' (Opitz 1991: 316). This exclusion did not mean that women no longer worked as artisans, but that they were forced into working at home, or into subordinate roles.

Nor was business exempt from restrictive legislation. In sixteenth-century Nuremberg, widows could only take over their deceased husband's shop for one or two years. Their right to start up a business was likewise restricted (Opitz 1991: 317–19; Wiesner Wood 1981: 3–13). In Polish towns the situation was similar: excluded from the guilds, women of the lower orders bought and sold illegally at fairs and markets. They wove, made bread, brewed beer, sold the products they made and ran taverns, but if they had a business under their own name it remained strictly limited in scale because of women's reduced legal, political and social standing (Roman 1962: 403).

In England, retail business was the preserve of freemen of the towns. Country women who produced poultry and dairy products had the right to sell them at market, however, either in person or through a servant acting as an intermediary. Nonetheless, it should not be forgotten that here they faced competition from gardeners and the army of pedlars who traded in anything they could get their hands on – from baskets of fruit to left-over meat – and that the majority of these traders were also women (Thwaites 1984: 23–42).

A specific analysis of criminal offences in England shows, however, that large numbers of women did not respect the law, and that farmers' wives were skilled in treading the fine line between legal and illegal activities. They sold the produce of their own gardens quite legally, but added to this other produce that they had acquired, something they were not allowed to do. Other court cases demonstrate that some women set themselves up as grocers and bakers in town, in defiance of the prohibition, even though it meant paying a one shilling fine. The low rate of the fine was an indication of how representations on behalf of women and, consequently, the law had evolved. The type of discrimination described here was disappearing. It was not women who benefited, however. The movement toward the enclosure and sale of common land, together with the changes in the food industry, which required ever more capital, more professionalization and more access to credit to feed the towns, spelled the marginalization of women. These developments explain why, in England, the cheese-seller, who was a woman at the end of the seventeenth century, had become a man by the eighteenth century (Thwaites 1984: 30–4).

Thus, although the social and political hegemony of the husband continued, the economic importance of the wife was increased *nolens volens* by the growth of markets. Even if wives did nothing more than help, they gained sufficiently in importance that, at least in the artisan milieu, conflicts grew up within couples, as illustrated in innumerable bawdy and misogynistic farces and *fabliaux* on this theme. These were a product of the development of the market-place and the transformation of social roles in business and amongst urban artisans (Opitz 1991: 295).

Finding Spaces: Cultivating Economic Niches

The third area of change was women's replacement of men. The departure of the men, whether to go off to war or to go off to earn a living, meant that women gained a *de facto* autonomy during their absence. Thus, in the families of sailors and pedlars, husbands' long absences and their high mortality rate gave women an essential role, both in the organization of the family and in the decisions made within it. And the husband often bestowed power of attorney on the wife so that she could manage their affairs in his absence and have recourse to the law.

War also created trading opportunities around drinking, eating and men's sociability. During the Thirty Years' War, about a hundred outlets for selling brandy were authorized in Nuremberg. Almost all were run by elderly women (Wiesner Wood 1981); women were omnipresent in the food and spirits trade and ran most of the taverns. Jobs such as these allowed women to get round the general rule that if a woman wished to borrow more than five *livres* she had to have the consent of her husband. These women were free to lend and borrow money, and absolutely free to conduct their affairs as they saw fit. Their freedom was, in fact, greater than that enjoyed by rich widows. Gluckel Hamel's heroine, popularized by Bertolt Brecht in *Mother Courage*, came from this world of women who made their living from the movements of men.

We can draw two conclusions from this brief summary of the relationship between the law and women's economic spheres. First, we cannot talk about women in general, given the wide variations in law from region to region, and the equally wide gap in women's experience, determined by their social milieu and their business activities. Secondly, it should be emphasized that women's autonomy was doubtless promoted by the fact that Europe was a patchwork which juxtaposed very different legal traditions in territories which were very close to one another. It could be argued that the indecision and contradictions of the law allowed women to take advantage of new freedoms and to widen the horizon of their thoughts. Throughout Europe women lived surrounded by other women who, because they were widows, were in particular religious orders or were involved in running a business, had attained a great degree of autonomy. Moreover, they were aware that, over the course of their lives, they too might gain access to these areas of relative autonomy – although women still lacked too many rights, especially political and legal ones. Despite everything, this diversity of experience meant that women were able to hold on to ideas of what was possible. Reservoirs of reflection and encouragement to imitate other women helped them to sustain an imaginary horizon of the mind and to preserve other, freer and more independent ways of doing things, and this, perhaps, also explains why women had such little regard for the law.

Finally, to get round the legal proscriptions, married women also built up mutual support networks in town: they acted as one another's guarantors, borrowed money and pawned goods (Lemire 1998: 112–38; Jordan 1993: 93). But these networks of female solidarity, which were a response to women's legal exclusion, are very difficult to document. These networks and the financial experiences of women are the subject of the rest of this chapter.

Women as Financial and Trading Intermediaries

Women were faced with a challenge. On the one hand, they had limited political, administrative or legal capacities, which constrained them to staid and unimaginative management of their assets. But, on the other hand, in spite of being subject to guardianship and restrictive laws, they had to manage family expenditures and constantly juggle the regular need for money against an irregular income, and to do so with a budget that they rarely controlled. To help themselves square this circle, women operated at the centre of informal networks of urban credit, pawnbroking and second-hand markets.

Certain characteristics of the economy of the *ancien régime* should be stressed, beginning with the lack of cash. First, money did not circulate as freely as today, and a large proportion circulated in the form of goods. Salaries, pensions and loans were systematically paid at least partly in kind. The circulation of goods as money has been largely obscured in the work done on the economy of the *ancien régime*. Secondly, the economy of Europe at this time was based on credit. This credit was still largely between individuals, however, and the conventions governing it were very specific, depending on who was borrowing and who was lending. Everything depended on the amount of time granted or refused, and time was not available to all. The time allotted for repayment was a function of the social status of the borrower. The higher it was, the more time was on the side of the debtor and against the creditor. As a result, the majority, who were without social status and had no property with which to guarantee their loans, would only have access to credit (if we make an exception for credit between relatives) that was, in effect, a delayed sale. In other words, their only access to credit was the pawnshop, which was the financial tool *par excellence* of precarious economies.

These two characteristics explain why the market for second-hand clothes and all other objects produced by society was one of the most important in Europe at this time, and why the used clothes business was linked to pawnbroking. Alongside the more organized groups (the Jews, those from the Alps and the Auvergne) and the dealers' guilds, all sorts of petty merchants, both male and female – dressmakers, laundry men and women selling second-hand clothing – were involved in this market, the importance of which can be observed in Paris in the numbers involved in the clothing professions. In 1725, those making new clothes numbered 3,500 tailors and dressmakers, against 700 petty female second-hand clothes dealers, as many laundry women again, and between 6,000 and 7,000 second-hand dealers (Roche 1989: 328, 344). Women were at the heart of this mini-economy, where clothes circulated in place of money and could be rented or pawned as needed.

It is, however, extremely difficult to pick up the trail of the women who were active in pawnbroking and second-hand markets, since they were of no interest to the State and its various record-keepers (Boulton 1987). A few account books belonging to pawnbrokers in England reveal the role of women, who can also be glimpsed in some of the inventories drawn up after a death, when the debts owed to the dead person were disproportionately high and there was no sign of a workshop or shop to account for such financial claims (McCants 2001). Charitable organizations (*charités*) recorded the continual pawning of objects as soon as work was hard to come by (Gutton 1986: 62–9; Woolf 1986: 32–3). Finally, some of these women may occasionally be pinned down in the legal archives, and in the extremes of activity recorded the more ordinary practices can be deduced. The Archives de la Bastille contain details of a number of these ordinary women in eighteenth-century Paris, arrested because their demands exceeded the amounts they lent, because they charged exorbitant rates of interest, and because they sold pawned articles or rented them out to gain further profit.

The file on *dame* Bertrand, a pawnbroker arrested in 1735, contains all these elements, which is why I have chosen her as an example. She worked for herself, in association with *dame* Noret, and *sieur* Lafosse, who acted as a lender. Through them a man pawned an outfit with Lafosse, which, when he reclaimed it, he maintained showed signs of wear and had 'love letters in the pocket, and a bill for 444 £ made out to one Desarsis'. The man went to see Desarsis, who confirmed that he had rented the outfit from *dames* Bertrand and Noret. After her arrest, the complaints stacked up against *dame* Bertrand. A laundry worker told how *dame* Bertrand was demanding twelve *livres* in interest from her on a loan of twenty-one *livres* that she had contracted with another lender, even though, to help her parents, she had also pawned a dress and petticoat which she had bought with sixty-eight *livres* from her savings. Others complained of her habit of keeping the items pawned with her, and one Regnier, a captain of the Nanterre regiment, listed clothes and objects amounting to a total value of 700 *livres* that he had been unwise enough to pawn in order to borrow eighty-four *livres*, and that the moneylender refused to give back: a woollen suit with a jacket of silver cloth, a damask dressing gown, two embroidered shirts, a pair of silver-plated candlesticks, and two shell snuffboxes. Luckily for her, *dame* Bertrand had a sister in whom an aristocrat was interested, wrote the police superintendent, who for this reason rapidly signed her release papers (Archives de la Bastille, dossier 11273, 1735).

All of these women, whatever the scope of their business, also worked together. They represented one of the links in the business of finance and of resale that was a driving force in the urban economy, whereby money, goods, clothes and other objects changed hands in a long chain of intermediaries. These women knew whom to approach to borrow money or to sell second-hand goods, and shopkeepers came to them when one of their female customers needed money. It was not unusual for three or four intermediaries to be involved in a transaction. Lending money for day-to-day survival, or acting as an intermediary for a more important lender were thus typical urban roles for women, and there were many women to provide information on potential lenders and borrowers and to serve as intermediaries and sometimes as guarantors.

Women were central to the business of second-hand clothes and pawnbroking in both England (Lemire 1991, 1997) and in Germany (Wiesner Wood 1981; Boulton 1987; Hunt 1998). Servants, who were often given clothes as a form of bonus, were also at the heart of the redistribution networks (Meldrum forthcoming). In Nuremberg, in 1542, 111 *Keuflinnen* were involved in the second-hand market, dealing with clothes, shoes, furniture, arms and armour, household utensils, tools, and leather bottles and containers of all sizes. Most of them had a reserved pitch at the market; the rest had a special licence that allowed them to sell from door to door – with, however, a limit imposed on the times at which they could sell and the amount of profit they were allowed to make. They also acted as pawnbrokers. Their expertise was such that 95 per cent of those who valued goods for inventories after a death (*Unterkeuflin*) were women. They had numerous clashes with members of other guilds, who accused them of selling forbidden foodstuffs, such as bread and meat. Despite all such tensions, the town recognized the role they played and often ruled in their favour. As a group they stood together and there were few denunciations of one *Keuflin* by another, although they constantly attacked other professions in order to protect their own (Wiesner Wood 1981).

Specific Economic Practices?

Did the economic marginalization of women and the particular nature of their monetary worth, composed predominantly of letters of credit, cash and moveable goods, give rise to specific economic behaviour? Since they were often obliged to live on small, irregularly paid incomes, did they manage their money differently from men?

To be sure of having an income, widows and single women were accustomed to investing their money in annuities (*rentes*) arranged with individuals as well as with institutions such as hospitals, pious associations, churches, guilds and so forth. This entry into financial markets took place gradually across Europe as early as the sixteenth century (and doubtless before in Italy), in the seventeenth century in Poland and England, and probably not until the eighteenth century in France. This rough time-frame is approximate, and was largely dependent on social groups and phases of the life cycle.

Can we talk about specifically female money management? The first variation was social. Aristocratic and bourgeois women did not invest their money in the same places as women from the lower orders. For

France, if we compare the late eighteenth-century creditors of the hospitals and the *Mont de Piété* (pawnshop) of Marseilles, it is clear that women invested far more in the pawnshop than in the hospitals. A social divide is at work here: it was predominantly the widows of merchants or nobles who invested in the hospitals, as their husbands had done before them, whereas the pawnshop received deposits of money from the wives of sailors and day labourers, and from small-scale women traders and workers (Coudurie 1974: 188–9, 248). As in Marseilles, an analysis of the money received by the Barcelona pawnshop in the second half of the eighteenth century shows that the wives of poor folk liked to deposit their savings there – especially widows who were saving for their old age, or young women saving for their dowry (Corbonell i Esteller 1997).

Holderness's work on England confirms these social distinctions among women making financial investments. After 1680, the number of aristocratic and bourgeois *rentières* who lived comfortably from money invested in government loans increased, though, on the whole, the source of widows' income was not specified (Holderness 1984: 438–9). We should not forget that, in order to safeguard women's standard of living, the law required that families employ professionals to manage women's inheritances, and that husbands leave them the means to live out their life in a manner consistent with their social status. Otherwise, in less well-off milieux, widows and single women very often played a central role in loans within communities – to relatives, neighbours and other villagers. Between 1660 and 1799 all the widows without occupation who were creditors when they died had placed at least a third of their fortune on account with relatives. Single people, both male and female, manifested similar behaviour. Credit represented 64 per cent of the wealth of unemployed widows, and of single people. Amongst the gentry and the clergy this figure was 27 per cent, for the farmers and merchants 13 per cent (Holderness 1975: 100–1; 1984: 440–1).

Similarly, in Poland, in Gdansk in the first half of the seventeenth century, more than 70 per cent of loans were issued by women, who were responsible for a number of small loans within their neighbourhoods. As elsewhere, widows were very active in this sort of enterprise, but the wives of craftsmen working in the clothing trades also played a part (Bogucka 1998). In Italy, women invested their savings in *luoghi di monte* or with private companies: the *censi* and the *compagnie d'ufficio*, where returns were fixed from the outset for the duration of the investment (Ago 1998). These were no-risk investments.

Conclusion

I should like to conclude by posing some questions about the culture surrounding these experiences. It would be interesting to know whether the norms and practices peculiar to women were a product of their own economic cultures. Naturally, in this research one is constantly confronted with subtle differences in behaviour, depending on the country, the era, status and phases of life. It is difficult, too, to gauge female behaviour when the influence of men's advice cannot be gauged. Still, the case studies I have chosen allow us to identify two very different behaviours. That of the women of Nuremberg working on a small scale in the retail business was perfectly consistent with standard business practices, since they put prices up when products were in short supply, entered into contracts with farmers to ensure a constant supply of produce and were capable of finding new supply networks, thus demonstrating a truly entrepreneurial outlook. Was it the legal recognition of their economic role and of their status as workers that allowed these women to take part fully in the whys and hows of the market-place (Wiesner Wood 1981)?

At the other end of the spectrum, life on the margins of the law, and in the informal economy that accommodated numerous ordinary women in other parts of Europe, caused women to develop economic cultures based on subterfuge and secrecy, which served to hide and reinforce their illegal (or quasi-illegal) economic practices, and a culture of solidarity to compensate for the fact that they were legally less protected. These subterfuges had two aspects. The first involved exploiting all the possibilities of the system, such as hiring out clothes that had been pawned. We have an example of this in *dame* Bertrand in Paris. The same sorts of behaviour were observed among English laundresses, who took the clothes of their clients to the pawnshops and, with the money they got for them, bought a number of goods to resell, so that, with the money they made on the sale, they could complete the cycle, and reclaim the clothes and finally return them to their clients (Tebbutt 1984).

The second aspect demonstrates women's ability to twist the image which society assigned to them. This is clearly demonstrated in the criminal economy, where they became the main fences and dealers in stolen goods, exploiting not only their sewing skills, but also the fact that the law imposed more lenient punishments on them. It was in just such a case, in eighteenth-century Paris, that the famous crook Cartouche was accused of making use of women of the lower orders on a grand scale.

Of course, neither attitude is uniquely feminine, and other groups also learned the economic cultures of marginality and the subterfuges required by anyone who, in order to survive, had to break the rules. Finally, I should point out that women shared the financial gap with other minorities. Not having full political rights, it was equally difficult for foreigners to get into business or become established as craftsmen; like women, many of them had to turn to ventures in which their legal incapacity was not a hindrance: the world of moneylending and the informal economy.

Notes

1. Christianity imposed on all members of the family certain duties towards one another, recognizing in marriage 'a divine and indissoluble institution', and attributing to the father and to the mother reciprocal rights, shared duties and equal authority over the children. However, increasingly this equality was considered as pertaining to spiritual and moral status rather than seen on a practical level: Christian asceticism, which glorified celibacy, the tradition that placed women under the guardianship of men, and descriptions of woman that emphasized her physiological and psychological weakness explain why, despite the proclaimed equality, women were only allowed 'limited legal responsibility' (Rossi 1962).
2. In 1820, this type of guardianship was abolished in the Rhineland (Sabean 1990: 26).
3. In the Netherlands, imprisonment for debt was not implemented for women. In France, women trading publicly could be imprisoned for breaking legally binding arrangements between traders and in relation to merchandise, but people in their seventies and above – old people – minors, (ordinary) women and girls could not, unless they had committed fraud (Law of 15 Germinal, year IV; Portemer 1962: 493).

References

Unpublished Sources
Archives de la Bastille: dossier 11273, 24 January 1735.

Published Sources
Ago, R. (1998), 'Credit, Consumption and Women's Work: Rome in the XVIIth Century', unpublished paper presented at the Twelfth International Economic History Congress, Madrid.
Bogucka, M. (1998), 'Women and Credit Operations in Polish Towns in the Early Modern Period', unpublished paper presented at the Twelfth International Economic History Congress, Madrid.
Bosch, J. W. (1962), 'Le statut de la femme dans les anciens pays-bas septen- trionaux', *La Femme,* in *Recueils de la Société Jean Bodin pour l'histoire comparative des institutions,* 12: 325–50.

Boulton, J. (1987), *Neighbourhood and Society: A London Suburb in the Seventeenth Century*, Cambridge: Cambridge University Press.

Carbonell i Esteller, M. (1997), *Sobreviure a Barcelona. Dones, pobresa i assistència al segle XVIII*, Barcelona: Eumo Editorial.

Coudurie, Marcel (1974), *La Dette des collectivités publiques de Marseille au XVIIIe siècle. Du débat sur le prêt à interêt au financement par l'emprunt*, Marseilles.

Gerhard, U. (ed.) (1997), *Frauen in der Geschichte des Rechts. Von der Frühen Neuzeit bis zur Gegenwart*, Munich: Verlag C. H. Beck.

Gilissen, J. (1962), 'Le statut de la femme dans l'ancien droit belge', *La Femme*, in *Recueils de la Société Jean Bodin pour l'histoire comparative des institutions*, 12: 255–321.

Gutton, J.-P. (1986), *La Société et les pauvres en Europe XVI–XVIIIe siècle*, Paris: Presses universitaires de France.

Holderness, B. A. (1975), 'Credit in a Rural Community 1660–1800. Some Neglected Aspects of Probate Inventories', *Midland History*, 3: 94–115.

—— (1984), 'Widows in Pre-industrial Society: An Essay upon their Economic Functions', in R. M. Smith (ed.), *Land, Kinship and Life-Cycle*, Cambridge: Cambridge University Press.

Hunt, M. (1998), 'Capital, Credit and the Family in Eighteenth-Century England', unpublished paper presented at the Twelfth International Economic History Congress, Madrid.

Jordan, W. C. (1993), *Women and Credit in Pre-Industrial and Developing Societies*, Philadelphia: University of Pennsylvania Press.

Lemire, B. (1991), *Fashion's Favourite: The Cotton Trade and the Consumer in Britain, 1660–1800*, Oxford: Oxford University Press.

—— (1997), *Dress, Culture and Commerce: The English Clothing Trade before the Factory*, Basingstoke, Hampshire: Macmillan Press.

—— (1998), 'Petty Pawns and Informal Lending: Gender and the Transformation of Small-Scale Credit in England, *circa* 1600–1800', in K. Bruland and P. O'Brien (eds), *From Family Firms to Corporate Capitalism: Essays in Business and Industrial History in Honour of Peter Mathias*, Oxford: Oxford University Press.

des Longrais, F. J. (1962), 'Le statut de la femme en Angleterre dans le droit commun médiéval', *La Femme*, in *Recueils de la Société Jean Bodin pour l'histoire comparative des institutions*, 12: 135–241.

McCants, A. (2001), 'Petty Debts and Family Networks: The Credit Markets of Widows and Wives in Eighteenth-Century Amsterdam', in B. Lemire, R. Pearson and G. Campbell (eds), *Women and Credit: Researching the Past, Refiguring the Future*, Oxford: Berg Publishers.

Meldrum, T. (Forthcoming), *Domestic Service and Gender, 1660–1750: Life and Work in London Households*, London: Longman.

Metz, R. (1962), 'Le Status de la femme en droit canonique médiéval', *La Femme*, in *Recueils de la Société Jean Bodin pour l'histoire comparative des institutions*, 12: 59–113.

Opitz, C. (1991), 'Contraintes et libertés (1250–1500)', in C. Klapisch-Zuber (ed.), *Histoire des femmes en Occident*, vol 2, *Le Moyen Age*, Paris: Plon.

Perrot, J.-C. (1975), *Genèse d'une ville moderne Caen au XVIIIe siècle*, 2 vols, Paris: Mouton.

Petot, P. (1962), 'Le statut de la femme dans les pays coutumiers français du XIIIe au XVIIe siècles', *La Femme*, in *Recueils de la Société Jean Bodin pour l'histoire comparative des institutions*, 12: 243–54.

Portemer, J. (1958), 'La femme dans la législation royale aux XVIIe et XVIIIe siècles', in *Mélanges Petot*, Paris.

—— (1962), 'Le statut de la femme en France dupuis la Réformation des coutumes jusqu'à la rédaction du code civil', *La Femme*, in *Recueils de la Société Jean Bodin pour l'histoire comparative des institutions*, 12: 447–97.

Roche, D. (1989), *La culture des apparences. Une histoire du vêtement XVIIe–XVIIIe siècle*, Paris: Fayard.

Roman, S. (1962), 'Le statut de la femme dans l'Europe orientale (Pologne et Russie) au Moyen âge et aux temps modernes', *La Femme*, in *Recueils de la Société Jean Bodin pour l'histoire comparative des institutions*, 12: 389–403.

Rossi, G. (1962), 'Status juridique de la femme dans l'histoire du droit italien. Époque médiéval et moderne', *La Femme*, in *Recueils de la Société Jean Bodin pour l'histoire comparative des institutions*, 12: 115–34.

Sabean, D. W. (1990), *Property, Production and Family in Neckarhausen, 1700–1870*, Cambridge: Cambridge University Press.

Tebbutt, M. (1984), *Making Ends Meet. Pawnbroking and Working-Class Credit*, London: Methuen.

Thwaites, W. (1984), 'Women in the Market Place: Oxfordshire c.1690–1800', *Midland History*, 9: 23–42.

Wiesner Wood, M. (1981), 'Paltry Peddlers or Essential Merchants? Women in the Distributive Trades in Early Modern Nuremberg', *The Sixteenth Century Journal*, 12, 2: 3–13.

Woolf, S. (1986), *The Poor in Western Europe in the Eighteenth and Nineteenth Centuries*, London: Methuen.

3

Petty Debts and Family Networks: The Credit Markets of Widows and Wives in Eighteenth-Century Amsterdam

Anne E. C. McCants

Much has been written about the central role played by Amsterdam in organizing the first truly international credit market over the course of the late seventeenth and eighteenth centuries. And much of the success of this precocious market has been attributed, by contemporaries and historians alike, to the remarkable ability of Dutch financiers to tap into and centralize the (reportedly ubiquitous) savings of both the great and the small in the urban economy. A separate but related literature has likewise emphasized the important role played by widows in early modern rural economies in the centralization of financial resources so that they could be lent out again to spur on local productive enterprises. This research is an attempt to join these two themes by examining the role played by poor to middling citizen widows and wives in the credit markets of Amsterdam itself. In particular, it seeks to differentiate the activities and strategies of women who broke into the rarefied atmosphere of organized finance from those of women whose only credit dealings were local and informal. This research also examines the credit-market participation of men of similar social status, both married and widowers, in order to provide a context for a meaningful discussion of the female experience.

A Window on the Resources of Amsterdam's Citizens

This chapter is part of a larger ongoing project I am engaged in, dealing with the emergence of a consumer revolution in the Dutch Republic and especially with the economic developments that accompanied it. The results presented here are based on a collection of probate inventories drawn up in the eighteenth century by the regents of the Amsterdam Municipal Orphanage following the deaths of either former orphans or parents of newly admitted orphans. The regents of the orphanage required that inventories be drawn up for the estates of all citizen decedents leaving minor children to be cared for at municipal expense. They did this with a view to assessing the ability of those estates to contribute to the costs of maintaining the orphaned children in the institution. Thus, even the deceased parents of very poor children were evaluated, so long as they were citizens of the city and their children were eligible for residence in the city orphanage. As a result, this collection represents an unusually broad spectrum of the citizen working poor, middling artisans and shopkeepers of the city. While the total collection contains close to fifteen hundred inventories, the sample reported on here is composed of the 913 inventories that were drawn up between May 1740 and April 1782.[1]

On account of the atypical nature of the collection of these inventories, they offer an unusually complete source of information on the households under their purview. The orphanage made a complete accounting of families, including the names and ages of all children, even those grown and married, or those being sent to other orphanages in the city. Where applicable the presence of step-parents was noted as well. The orphanage was, after all, in the business of taking in the qualified minor children of the decedents, and because full orphanhood was a requirement for admission, the distinction between biological parents and step-parents was an especially critical one. Moreover, because all family members held potential claims on the inventory, each had to be taken into account in deciding whether to accept or repudiate any given estate and its debts. Thus, the inventories not only include the marital histories of the decedents, but also yield usually complete information on the size, composition, and stage in the life cycle of the households under consideration.

The orphanage regents also generated inventories upon the death of former orphans, at least those who had not yet bought the right to name their own heir, in the hope of recovering some of the costs associated with their earlier upbringing at municipal expense. This provision fortuitously ensured that some inventories were made for married women, even those with still living first husbands, and for both single men and women who were not yet household heads. In fact, women form a slight majority (55 per cent) of the total inventory population and, of those, nearly 70 per cent were widows. The unusually heavy representation of women in these records, combined with the presence of never-married individuals of both sexes, offers a rare opportunity to study a much more diverse population than is possible with the probate inventories found in notarial records.

It is worth noting that probate inventories are typically silent on the issue of claims against the estate of the deceased. Debts left unpaid at the time of death are not the property of the deceased – although they are often inextricably connected to that property – but of his or her creditors. We would expect them to show up only if a comparable inventory were to have been fortuitously drawn up at roughly the same time for the creditor. Admittedly, the omission of debts is not a serious defect for the study of material culture itself. But it is an unqualified disaster for those who wish to use probate inventories to map out wealth distributions or other economic and social hierarchies. The relationship between total assets and debt is a complex one. As both Margaret Spufford and Alice Hanson Jones have argued for early modern England and the American colonies respectively, debt can sometimes be an indication of poverty, but more often those who carried the largest debt burdens were also those with the greatest assets (Spufford 1990: 151–3; Jones 1980: 141–5). Thus, rank orderings made on the basis of assets alone do not approximate even roughly to rank orderings made on the basis of true net worth. Probate inventories alone cannot be used, then, as was once commonly supposed, to estimate wealth distributions, either within communities or across them. Nor can they say much about the existence of credit markets or the kind of people who participated in them as either debtors, or creditors, or both.

Assessing Estates: Gender, Credit and Debts

This problem is fortunately solved by the nature of the sources being used here. Because the orphanage was interested in the net cash value of an estate rather than in retrieving any particular possession or asset, their notaries and bookkeepers were meticulous in accounting for all moveable goods (almost always valued), real estate (only sometimes valued, but usually described in some detail), stocks, cash holdings and debts. Thus, the inventories drawn up by the orphanage are really a combination of what we would normally think of as the inventory proper and the administrative accounts of the estate, which might normally not be completed until well after the death of the decedent. Because the deceased's creditors had a stronger claim to the assets than did the municipal orphanage, the bookkeeper could only determine whether or not to repudiate an estate if he had meticulously sought out all other possible claimants and determined accurately the resulting net value. We can be especially confident that this was the guiding principle in the bookkeeper's work as a great many of the inventories actually contain in the margins a record of the later sale of goods and the final disbursement of cash to interested parties, including the orphanage itself.

Table 3.1 displays the basic characteristics of the inventoried population. As has already been noted above, the orphanage was slightly more likely to possess claims on the property of female decedents than on that of males. These women were much more likely to have been living as widows at their deaths than were their male counterparts as widowers. It

Table 3.1 Distribution of the Inventories (by demographic and other characteristics)

	All		No Possessions		Males		Females	
	N	%	N	%	N	%	N	%
Sex								
Male	410	45.0	50	37.6				
Female	502	55.0	83	62.4				
Marital Status								
(re)married	279	30.6	16	12.0	181	44.2	98	19.5
widow(er)	547	60.0	114	85.7	201	49.0	346	68.9
never married	86	9.4	3	2.3	28	6.8	58	11.6
Relationship to Orphanage								
left child(ren)	709	77.7	127	95.5	341	83.2	368	73.3
former orphan	148	16.2	5	3.8	55	13.4	93	18.5
relative of orphan	55	6.0	1	0.8	14	3.4	41	8.2
Shop on Premises								
no shop	773	84.8	134	100.0	323	78.8	449	89.6
shop	139	15.2	0	0.0	87	21.2	52	10.4
Net Value of Inventory								
debts > assets	527	57.7	0	0.0	251	61.2	276	55.0
debts < assets	252	27.6	0	0.0	109	26.6	143	28.5
no possessions	134	14.6	134	100.0	50	12.2	83	16.5

Source: Geemente Archief Amsterdam, particulier archief #367 (oud), ns 652–688.

is worth recalling that all of those who entered the orphanage records as parents of newly admitted orphan children had to have already lost a spouse in the past, because only full orphans were eligible for institutional care. Thus, the relatively higher rate of men in marital unions at their deaths is a reflection of higher remarriage rates for men, rather than any necessary differential mortality between the sexes. The men in this sample were also twice as likely to have been running retail shops or artisanal workshops at their deaths as were the women, while the latter were more likely to have died with no possessions at all. These are all signs that point towards an environment of relative female economic disadvantage. The only characteristic of the data that is seemingly incongruous with such a story is the higher incidence of males dying with negative net worth, that is, with outstanding debts that more than swamped their assets. If women, especially those living as widows or spinsters, were less well-off then men on average (as was in fact the case), we might expect them to have suffered more frequently from a negative net worth at death (see Table 3.2). The fact that they did not suggests that assets were a prerequisite for the acquisition of debt in this economy; either that or we have to suppose that women simply showed more self-restraint against excessive borrowing in the face of financial need. This would be a difficult argument to sustain, and it does not fit with the fact that wealthy women did rely on the credit market in the same ways as their male peers did. Thus it is most likely to have been the relative poverty of the women that prevented them from acquiring the debt burdens of some of their male contemporaries. This hypothesis will be explicitly tested in the remainder of this chapter, at least as it pertains to the acquisition of financial debts. Work I have done elsewhere suggests that other types of debts, such as those for burial, medical care, medicines, nursing care, child care, fuel, food and, to a lesser extent, unpaid rent, were not significantly different across gender and marital status lines, at least not after accounting for the expected impact of differential household size (McCants 1997).

Even a cursory overview of the financial profiles of the individuals who found their way into the orphanage's administration suggests that only a very few of them were involved in the borrowing or lending of money at all. While well over half the inventories showed at least some outstanding debts for the earlier delivery of food, goods or services, less than a quarter of them record cash debts (21 per cent), and even fewer (15 per cent) reveal debts of a formal variety. These latter were typically denoted in the inventories as *obligatien* or *handschriften*, and often the record also notes the date of issue and the prevailing rate of interest. By contrast, simple cash loans were only rarely recorded with a date of issue

Table 3.2 Value of Inventories in Guilders (sorted by demographic attributes)

					Only inventories with at least one asset or debt		
Panel A: All Inventories							
	N	Mean	Median	Max	N	Mean	Median
Debts	779	419.3	95.9	21,534	912	359.1	78.2
Moveables	779	106.1	60.0	1,012	912	90.6	46.0
Assets	779	259.1	69.5	8,127	912	222.2	52.8
Net Value	779	−159.4	−23.4	2,977	912	−136.1	−12.3
Panel B: By Sex							
	N	Mean	Median	Max	N	Mean	Median
Males							
Debts	360	509.7	114.7	12,886	410	447.5	98.5
Moveables	360	109.1	64.0	1,012	410	95.8	52.0
Assets	360	299.0	78.0	8,127	410	262.5	62.9
Net Value	360	−210.7	−31.9	2,339	410	−185.0	−21.8
Females							
Debts	419	341.7	80.0	21,534	502	286.9	67.0
Moveables	419	103.3	55.5	914	502	86.3	44.0
Assets	419	224.7	65.2	6,861	502	189.1	47.3
Net Value	419	−115.1	−16.5	2,977	502	−96.0	−7.9
Panel C: By Household Type							
	N	Mean	Median	Max	N	Mean	Median
Married Couples							
Debts	263	491.5	123.5	14,467	279	463.4	113.4
Moveables	263	123.5	73.0	1,012	279	116.5	69.0
Assets	263	254.7	88.0	3,691	279	240.1	82.5
Net Value	263	−236.9	−43.3	1,485	279	−223.3	−38.2
Widower							
Debts	163	630.4	122.1	12,886	201	511.3	92.2
Moveables	163	101.8	60.0	650	201	82.6	35.0
Assets	163	355.7	73.2	8,127	201	288.4	52.0
Net Value	163	−274.8	−30.0	2,218	201	−222.8	−11.0
Widow							
Debts	270	320.6	73.7	21,534	346	252.5	54.2
Moveables	270	101.8	47.5	914	346	79.4	29.5
Assets	270	240.7	52.5	6,861	346	190.1	31.0
Net Value	270	−77.3	−15.4	2,977	346	−60.3	−4.8

	N	Mean	Median	Max	N	Mean	Median
Single/Never Married							
Debts	83	97.1	62.3	1,353	86	93.8	59.0
Moveables	83	72.2	55.8	298	86	69.8	51.0
Assets	83	141.9	66.0	2,339	86	137.0	62.9
Net Value	83	49.0	9.2	2,339	86	47.3	5.7

Key: Moveables = Precious metals/Jewellery + Clothing + Bedding + Household Items
      + Perishables
      All Assets = Moveables + Securities + Shop Goods + Owed Debts;
      Net Value = All Assets – Debts

Source: Geemente Archief Amsterdam, particulier archief #367 (oud), ns 652–688.

or a specified rate of interest due on repayment. Even less common in this population was the lending of money in the formal credit markets – not even 3 per cent of the inventories overall showed this practice. Given the relatively poor nature of this population, as measured by both quantity and value of material possessions, especially as compared with other inventoried individuals from Amsterdam in this period (Faber 1980: 149–55), this latter finding cannot be much of a surprise.

Nonetheless, it is worth exploring further the characteristics of those who did engage in either the borrowing or lending of money in an effort to evaluate the nature of their financial dealings, as well as to determine those attributes that allowed them (or necessitated them?) to borrow. Men and women who were living in marital relationships at the time of death were the most likely to have outstanding financial debts, with widowers only slightly less likely, and widows falling much further behind (see Panel A of Table 3.3). The striking similarity of the debt profiles of married male and female decedents, despite the marked differences between men and women overall, suggests that the debts of married couples were, for all practical purposes, entered into jointly. Because the inventories record the total household property – with the expectation, of course, that the surviving spouses would retain their legally fair shares of the assets – it only makes sense that total household debt would also be accounted for, even if a debt may not have been specifically undertaken by the deceased as an individual. This point is most important for those cases where the deceased happens to be the wife, although it could matter for deceased husbands as well. For example, Gijsbert Vergouw died in April of 1745 leaving behind his second wife, Maria Widemans, and five children from his first marriage. A debt of thirty guilders is noted against the assets of his property, although the debt is explicitly recorded as a *Bank van Leening*

Table 3.3 Composition of the Debtor Sample

Panel A: Distribution of debts and debtors by demographic composition

	No. Debtors	% of pop.	No. Debts	Number of debtors with multiple debts: 2	3	4	5–9	% with pawns
Married Persons	119	42.8	236	24	16	7	7	17.6
(Male)	80	44.0	149	18	6	5	4	20.3
(Female)	39	40.6	87	6	10	2	3	12.5
Widowers	60	29.9	116	10	7	5	3	12.5
Widows	77	22.2	126	24	4	3	1	14.1
Single Males	6	21.4	11	2	0	1	0	3.6
Single Females	8	13.8	12	1	0	1	0	6.8
Total	270	29.6	501					14.0

Panel B: Type of debt – in row percentages by demographic composition

	Cash	Obligations	Notes	Schepening k.	Other
Married Persons	53.6	27.2	12.3	6.0	0.9
(Males)	51.4	23.4	12.8	6.8	0.7
(Females)	57.5	25.3	11.5	4.6	1.1
Widowers	43.1	36.2	12.9	6.9	0.9
Widows	55.6	31.5	9.7	0.8	2.4
Single Males	45.5	45.5	9.1	0.0	0.0
Single Females	83.3	16.7	0.0	0.0	0.0

Panel C: Gender and kin relationship of creditors – in row percentages by demographic composition

Debtor	Creditors: Male	Female	Couple	Related	Unrelated
Married Persons	70.3	27.9	1.7	17.9	82.1
(Males)	68.5	29.4	2.1	21.8	78.2
(Females)	73.3	25.6	1.2	11.5	88.5
Widowers	69.6	30.4	0.0	20.0	80.0
Widows	58.5	41.5	0.0	26.8	73.2
Single Males	77.8	22.2	0.0	27.3	72.7
Single Females	33.3	66.7	0.0	25.0	75.0

Panel D: Types of relationships – in absolute numbers of individual debts per category

Related Creditors

Debtors	Bro-in-law	Sis-in-law	Brother	Sister	Parent	Other male	Other female	Landlord or Neighbour
Married Males	9	9	1	4	2	3	4	0
Married Females	1	2	2	2	0	1	2	1
Widowers	5	2	2	3	1	8	2	1
Widows	8	1	5	7	1	4	6	1
Single Males	0	0	1	0	0	1	1	0
Single Females	0	1	0	2	0	0	0	2

Panel E: Assets and shop management of debtors – in row percentages by demographic composition

Assets (in guilders)

	< 15	15 - < 200	> 200	Shop	No Shop
Married Persons	2.5	52.9	44.5	31.9	68.1
(Males)	1.2	52.5	46.3	33.7	66.3
(Females)	5.1	53.9	41.0	28.2	71.8
Widowers	16.7	40.0	43.3	30.0	70.0
Widows	16.9	57.1	26.0	15.6	84.4
Single Males	16.7	50.0	33.3	16.7	83.3
Single Females	25.0	50.0	25.0	0.0	100.0

Source: Geemente Archief Amsterdam, particulier archief #367 (oud), ns 652–688.

(pawnshop) debt of Maria's dating from February of the same year. A gold chain was being held at the Bank in anticipation of the repayment of the debt. Although the item at pawn was well understood to belong to his wife, the debt was still recorded by the orphanage bookkeeper as a claim against the estate of the deceased. Thus, for much of this analysis the married men and women can be treated together, for, at least until the death of one partner, their economic experience was influenced as much by their marital status as by their gender.

What then were the factors that contributed to the ability of some to borrow and others not? While it might be tempting to ask the parallel question of why some needed to borrow and others did not, the data here suggest that this would point us in a false direction. Those who were at the margins of meeting basic subsistence were either able to receive credit from local shopkeepers for bread, shoes, clothing and other necessities (debts that appear in the inventories, but not as debts of money *per se*), made shift in ways that cannot be found in the inventory record, or were forced into dependence on the charitable resources that the city provided to its citizens. Those who actually borrowed money, especially in larger amounts via formal arrangements, were not the neediest of the sample population, but more often those with the greatest assets, as measured by both the quantity and the value of their material possessions and property. For example, while nearly 60 per cent of those who borrowed money in the formal markets (and thus did so in substantially larger amounts) had assets that put them into the highest wealth category for this population, only 25 per cent of those who borrowed petty cash were in that group. Instead, 15 per cent of the petty cash borrowers were in the poorest wealth category (with total assets of less than fifteen guilders), while only 2 per cent of the formal borrowers had such meagre assets.

To investigate the nature of these debts further detailed information for the 501 financial debts and 46 financial credits has been collected (representing 270 and 28 individuals respectively). Thus, of the 913 individual decedents in the larger data project, just under a third of them (29.6 per cent) left at least one monetary debt at their deaths. For each individual transaction there is information on the value and type of debt, the gender and relationship of the creditor (if one was explicitly mentioned or can be inferred by the surnames) and sometimes the date the debt was undertaken and the interest rate charged to it. In a few cases, the value of the original debt is known, in addition to the value that was still outstanding at the time the inventory was drawn up. The original loan values could be either higher or lower than the current debt burden, depending on whether interest charges had accumulated or the deceased had already begun paying off the principal.

But the incidence of indebtedness was not evenly distributed across households of differing compositions (see Panel Λ of Table 3.3). As we might expect, nearly half of all married persons had at least one financial debt, and often more. By comparison, not even a quarter, 21.4 per cent, of widows had such debts. Widowers fell in between, with 29.9 per cent having at least one financial debt at death. The widows were also the least likely to have large numbers of debts per person, aside from the few never-married individuals. Furthermore, widows were more dependent on their own kin for securing the limited debt they did carry than were any other group, as well as the most dependent on other women to be their creditors.[2] Over 40 per cent of all of their debts were to other women, despite the fact that women creditors were responsible for only one-third of all the debts (see Panel C of Table 3.3).

The relatively heavy dependence of widows on other women and kin to be their sources of either emergency cash or working capital is entirely consistent with the relatively lower value of their debts. The median size debt undertaken by all widows was 30 guilders, less than half as much as the median debt of widowers of 68 guilders. This differential is remarkably similar to the spread between the median loan made by women of 30 guilders with a mean of 150, versus that made by men of 60 guilders with a mean of 266. The median debt incurred by married persons falls in between that of the widows and widowers, despite the fact that they borrowed just as often from men as did the widowers. Even when widows borrowed from their immediate kin, most often from sisters, brothers or brothers-in-law, the median value of their debt was still less than the median debt of their married peers, especially those borrowing without the 'benefit' of kinship; and it was still substantially less than what a widowed male could expect to borrow (see Table 3.4).

The consistently lower values of the widows' debts should not be surprising in the context of their overall asset profiles. Recall that the widow debtors were only half as likely – that is, 15 per cent versus over 30 per cent of the married and widowers – to have been running shops, with all the collateral assets that that could have provided. And 17 per cent of them also fell into the lowest wealth category as denoted by those inventories, with assets totalling under fifteen guilders in value. By contrast, only 2 per cent of the married couple borrowers fell into this wealth category. Not surprisingly, the poor widows, and others from this lowest wealth group who did manage to borrow money, did so for only very small amounts. The median value of their debts was only 12 guilders as compared to 20 guilders and 150 guilders for the other two wealth groups respectively (see Table 3.5).

The importance of possessing an income-generating asset, such as that offered by a working shop, is especially evident in the material I have examined. A disproportionate share of all debtors who had undertaken larger loans, in the forms of *obligatien* or the *schepenning kennis*, were those running either an artisanal or a retail shop. Although only 15 per cent of the inventories suggest evidence of a shop, 42 per cent of those with formal debts could be so identified. This connection could work in

Table 3.4 Value of individual debts in guilders by demographic and relationship categories

	N	Mean	Median	1st Quartile	3rd Quartile
All Cases	501	221.6	50.0	12.0	200.0
Married (all)	236	219.4	50.0	13.3	183.0
(Related)	43	166.4	65.0	12.2	177.0
(Unrelated)	192	232.2	50.0	14.0	200.0
Widowers	116	346.4	68.0	20.0	287.5
(Related)	23	188.0	50.0	13.0	100.0
(Unrelated)	92	389.5	100.0	20.0	307.0
Widows	126	134.6	30.0	6.0	200.0
(Related)	32	134.6	30.0	12.0	165.0
(Unrelated)	92	133.6	26.5	5.0	219.0
Singles	23	91.7	25.0	4.3	94.0
(Related)	6	8.8	5.0	3.0	14.0
(Unrelated)	17	120.9	50.0	5.0	150.0

Source: Geemente Archief Amsterdam, particulier archief #367 (oud), ns 652–688.

either one or both of two ways. First, the established shop might serve as collateral for borrowing; or second, the loan could have been the foundation upon which a shop was built up in the first place. An example of how this latter process could work for a man can be found in the case of Gerrit Remmers, master carpenter, who died in September 1772. At his death he left five children ranging in age from seven and a half to fifteen and a half, assets valued at over 8,000 guilders (including outstanding shop credits worth nearly 3,000 guilders, and a house with a separate backhouse), and debts valued at nearly 6,000 guilders. A substantial part of that debt burden was for four loans all undertaken within a fairly short period of time. On 1 February 1765, Mr Remmers signed for an obligation of 300 guilders from one Hester Nieuwenhuis (unrelated as far as can be known) and an additional obligation of 500 guilders from the widow of Hester's brother. Nineteen days later he secured a further 1,700 guilders from one David Recker (also unrelated). Then two years later in February of 1767 he borrowed an additional sum of 1,000 guilders, again from a widow who appears to have been no relation. His was clearly a thriving

Table 3.5 Value of individual debts in guilders by type of debt, gender of creditor, wealth of debtor and shop management

	N	Mean	Median	1st Quartile	3rd Quartile
Debt Type					
Cash	260.0	38.1	14.0	5.0	34.5
Obligations	152.0	365.5	239.0	102.0	425.0
Notes	57.0	101.9	61.0	26.0	145.0
Schepening k	23.0	1,034.4	800.0	522.0	1,035.0
Gender of Creditor					
Male	324.0	268.6	60.0	15.8	260.5
Female	159.0	146.4	30.0	6.0	150.0
Wealth of Debtor					
Assets <15 guilders	37.0	31.3	12.0	6.0	25.0
Assets 15–200	225.0	82.2	20.0	5.0	60.0
Assets > = 200	237.0	389.5	150.0	50.0	408.0
Shop Management					
Ran shop	165.0	415.3	150.0	50.0	390.0
Did not run shop	334.0	130.0	26.0	8.0	101.0

Source: Geemente Archief Amsterdam, particulier archief #367 (oud), ns 652–688.

business, most likely built up as an independent shop in 1765 with the first large loans, when Gerrit would have been in his mid- to late thirties, with at least four children living at home. The fact that he was able to borrow again just two years later, and for such a large sum, is further evidence that the shop itself had become collateral for further borrowing.

Ownership of a shop might also facilitate borrowing among those widows who were well enough situated to be running one. However, even in these cases the size of the loans tended to be smaller than for their male peers. For example, Aaltje Hilberda died in July 1772 while running some sort of unspecified shop out of her dwelling. She had total assets worth nearly 600 guilders and debts of nearly 500 guilders. Three hundred guilders of that debt was in the form of two obligation notes, one for 200 guilders contracted with the widowed mother of her deceased husband, and the other 100 guilders borrowed from an unrelated male as recently as one month before her death. In this case we can be sure that the smaller debt was hers alone, because of its very recent vintage. But both the scale of her debts and her assets was well below the level of the typical male proprietor of a shop. Moreover, the larger of those debts had been contracted with kin and not in the market at large.

In fact, the one case where a widow seems to have managed to secure loans of a more substantial nature is probably misleading. Elisabeth van Ruijtenburgh, the widow of Pieter Altena, master glassmaker, died in March of 1746. At her death the orphanage figured her assets to total just over 600 guilders. But her debts were a substantial 2,474 guilders (of which 2,128 guilders were in obligations and accumulated interest payments), making her a very poor prospect indeed from the orphanage's point of view. It seems likely that her husband had not been dead all that long. We know he was still alive in 1742, as he had been recorded in the tax assessment undertaken by the city in the spring of that year. Moreover, his widow still owed money (fourteen and a half guilders) for his burial at the time of her death, suggesting that it had not been all that long before hers. It seems very likely, then, that the four outstanding obligations against her limited assets had, in fact, been undertaken while Pieter was still alive, particularly since one of them, for 800 guilders, was owed to his brother. His glassmaker's shop may once have been a thriving concern, but without a doubt it had fallen on hard times by the time of Elisabeth's death. This conclusion is further supported by the fact that the majority of the other debts Elisabeth left at her death were for a wide variety of household necessities, such as food, shoes and wages for household assistance, and not for items clearly associated with the running of the business. Far from being an example of a widow/proprietor active in the local credit market, Elisabeth is more likely to have been an economic casualty of the premature death of her craftsman husband.

And she was hardly alone in her predicament. The source of emergency credit of last resort was the local pawnshop; 14 per cent of all widows in this study died while still in its debt. While this fraction was not excessive compared to those shown by other demographic groups, it is noteworthy that the total value of widows' pawns (as well as the total number of items they had pawned) was much less than for all other groups. This reflects the relative material poverty in which widows lived. Yet despite the low value of their pawn debts, widows faced the most difficulty in recovering their possessions. The average number of days elapsed between the submission of a pawned item and death was in the low-to-mid two-hundreds for every demographic group except the widows. For them, it was substantially greater: 376 days.

Of course, not every widow was desperately poor. Twelve widows (out of the 347 in the total inventory population) were actually lenders of money in either the formal or informal markets for obligations and cash. In fact, widows were actually the single most frequent source of *obligatie* credit in the orphanage records, accounting for almost half of all the *obligatie* loans recorded as outstanding credits. The enormous disparity in the wealth profiles of the widows who lent money versus those who did not suggests that for the minority of widows with sizeable assets, money lending was far and away the most profitable use of those assets. It was certainly more secure than trying to keep up an artisanal shop in what was still clearly the domain of the crafts*man*.

Nevertheless, the conflict between money lending (as a substantial enterprise in its own right) and maintaining a shop was an issue for all the demographic categories examined here. While a substantial number (just over one half) of the total credits outstanding were owed to individuals who had also run shops, less than one-third of the individual creditors were actually shop-owners. This divergence suggests that, while those few shop-owners who lent out money did so with unusual frequency, most lenders were not in fact combining the two roles (see Panel A of Table 3.6). The consistently lower values of the loans made by shop-owners is also consistent with this story. Widows were the most severely affected of all by this financial bind. In fact, only two widows out of the twelve who died as creditors were simultaneously running shops. One, Joanna van Veen, who died in July of 1762, was continuing to run her deceased husband's shoemaker's shop. She also held two obligations from the provincial governments of Friesland, which one suspects were a more reliable source of revenue than the shop itself, given the regularity of interest disbursements on public debt at this time. These obligations may indeed have even been part of a 'dependant's package' left her by her husband for precisely this purpose. The only other widow who combined shop management with money lending was, on the other hand, clearly working in an independent fashion.

Grietje Grant, who died in October 1742, ran a tavern/boarding house. Her possessions at death included twelve beds or sleeping boards spread over five separate rooms in her dwelling. She was also in debt for 556 guilders' worth of wine and spirits. Her credits included nine separate loans all made to unrelated males, mostly of under twenty guilders apiece. For Grietje, lending money was not likely to have been a source of any real financial security in her widowhood. Rather it seems to have sprung naturally out of her occupation. Her customers, mostly poor to middling like herself, drank her wine, slept in her beds, and occasionally borrowed money from her as well. Grietje may well have been an entrepreneur, but only of the most precarious kind.

Table 3.6   Relationship between Shop Management and Money Lending

Panel A: Incidence of individual credits and creditors by shop management

	Credits		Creditors	
	N	Column %	N	% of tot pop
Ran shop	24	51.1	9	6.5
Did not run shop	22	48.9	19	2.5

Panel B: Value of credits in guilders by selected demographic and shop management categories

	N	Mean	Median	1st Quartile	3rd Quartile
All – Shop	24	225.5	40.0	14.0	200.0
All – No shop	22	392.0	232.5	200.0	515.5
Widow – Shop	11	132.4	18.0	10.0	150.0
Widow – No shop	11	401.0	200.0	103.0	515.5
Males – Shop	9	265.5	54.0	52.0	600.0
Males – No shop	10	414.7	300.0	202.0	600.0

Source: Geemente Archief Amsterdam, particulier archief #367 (oud), ns 652-688.

Conclusion

In general, this research finds that while middling widows did participate in the Amsterdam credit markets, they did so in only a very limited way. The wealthiest among them occasionally played the role of the capitalist, but only in an older usage of that word – they supplied *fonds*. Much more often these widows were petty debtors, or worse, victims of the local pawnshop. What they were not, however, was substantial entrepreneurs. They did not borrow money in sizeable amounts in order to make more money with it in productive enterprise the way at least some of their male counterparts from the same social milieu were able to do. Their limited access to credit reinforced the social and economic constraints under which they lived and died.

Notes

1. These 913 inventories include 49,920 separate enumerations of household goods, 6,266 separate listings of debts outstanding, 571 credits outstanding, and 948 notations for goods at pawn (*lombard briefjes*). The manuscript collection can be found in the *Geemente Archief Amsterdam, particulier archief* #367 (oud), ns 652–688.
2. The singles were too few to assess reliably.

References

Unpublished Sources:

Geemente Archief Amsterdam, particulier archief #367 (oud Burgerweeshuis), ns 652-688.

Published Sources:

Faber, J. A. (1980), 'Inhabitants of Amsterdam and their Possessions, 1701–1710', in A. van der Woude and A. Schuurman (eds), *Probate Inventories: A New Source for the Historical Study of Wealth, Material Culture and Agricultural Development*, Utrecht: Hes Publishers.

Jones, A. H. (1980), *Wealth of a Nation To Be: The American Colonies on the Eve of the Revolution*, New York: Columbia University Press.

McCants, A. (1997), *Civic Charity in a Golden Age: Orphan Care in Early Modern Amsterdam,* Urbana, IL: University of Illinois Press.

Spufford, M. (1990), 'The Limitations of the Probate Inventory', in J. Chartres and D. Hey (eds), *English Rural Society, 1500–1800: Essays in Honour of Joan Thirsk*, Cambridge: Cambridge University Press.

4

Lending Women, Borrowing Women: Middle-Class Women, Investments and Credit in Northern France in the Nineteenth Century

Beatrice Craig

In the nineteenth century the *département* du Nord was one of the most heavily industrialized regions of France. In the central part of the *département*, the ancient cloth-making cities of Lille, Roubaix, Tourcoing and Armentières became one of Europe's major textile production centres. Lille was also an administrative, educational and military centre, and its economy was diversified. The surrounding towns, like Tourcoing, fifteen kilometres to the north-east, focused almost exclusively on textiles, more particularly the production of material for the fashion industry. Consequently, the Tourcoing middle class was dominated by entrepreneurs, whereas in Lille it also included senior civil servants and professionals and a not negligible proportion of *rentiers* and proprietors (Trénard 1977; Hilaire 1984; Lottin 1986; Fohlen 1956; Pouchain 1980; Wolf 1972; Toulemonde 1966; Chanut 1956; Codaccioni 1976; Statistiques générales de la France 1847–52; ADN, Statistiques industrielles 1880–1890).

Entrepreneurial or not, middle-class families were enmeshed in extensive and complex credit networks. Raw material was purchased on short-term credit, and the finished product was sold under the same conditions. The cash-flow problems this could cause led to the establishment of counting houses, and later banks, which provided business people with short-term credit secured by commercial documentation. Business people also required capital to start, expand or modernize their businesses. They could not rely on public financing, which was extraordinarily difficult to obtain before 1867 (Hirsch 1991; Fohlen 1954; Gille 1954; Pouchain 1986; Decroix 1999). Yet personal fortunes were often inadequate for the purpose. Entrepreneurs therefore relied on partnerships with relatives or strangers to secure the necessary funds (Hirsch 1991: 312–18). Civil servants, professionals and proprietors experienced a different relationship to credit. They had much less reason to borrow, and usually had money to invest. They became providers of credit.

One might assume that this world of credit, investment and business was a male one. The historical literature on business or on women has had little to say about women as either providers or users of credit. The 'separate spheres' paradigm, which informed most of the work on nineteenth-century women, seemed to preclude women's active involvement in financial activities (Davidoff and Hall 1987; Smith 1981; Rabuzzi 1995). Yet, recent studies of women of the lower classes suggest that lending and borrowing were part of the economy of expediency that allowed them to survive (Lemire 1997; Finn 1996, 1998, 1999; Hunt 1999; Fontaine 2001). Current research on English middle- and upper-class women similarly indicates that they, too, were significant players in credit markets (Wiskins 1999; Todd 1997; Baskerville 1999).

In the Lille area, middle-class women were present, in varying proportions, in all the credit markets, as borrowers and lenders. Their role as providers and users of business capital is easy to document: women were active or sleeping partners, or ran their own businesses. This participation is, however, difficult to quantify because of a lack of adequate sources. Like English middle-class women, French women were also important in supplying mortgage loans, which not only fuelled town expansion, but also occasionally served as a source of business capital. Mortgages had to be registered, and the records suggest that women may have played a role in this market disproportionate to their demographic importance.

Legal Factors Affecting Women's Credit and Lending

Two factors reinforced each other and served to make women's participation in various credit markets possible. The first was the legal system. The default clauses of the Civil Code ensured the equality of children irrespective of sex and birth order and provided for community of property between spouses; this meant equal division of most family assets at the death of one of the spouses. Local practices in Northern France favoured widows and widowers at the expense of the heirs, and protected women's properties even beyond the requirements of the law (Hirsch 1991: 291–300). The second factor involved was the absence of strong cultural barriers to middle-class women's economic activities. On the contrary, both nineteenth-century amateur historians and legal theoreticians promoted the image of the wife as deputy husband, corner-stone of the region's historical economic prosperity (Lambert-Dansette 1954; Legrand 1852; Taillard 1849; Briet 1908). However, despite such recognition, married women were legally without power. Single and widowed women, on the other hand, were free to act as they saw fit, and could control considerable assets.

Most women first received assets on their marriage. The property, referred to as a 'dowry' in the marriage contract, was, in fact, an advance on inheritance. Unless the woman married in separation of property, which was highly unusual, her assets were administered by her husband. He could not alienate this 'dowry', however, nor any property she sub-sequently inherited. If he predeceased her, the value of those assets was returned to her before any distribution of estate took place. At widowhood, women not only regained control over their own assets, but, by law, women married in *communauté* received half the value of the *communauté,* of the goods jointly owned by the couple during marriage. As a rule, Lille marriage contracts also gave the survivor the usufruct of the other half of the *communauté*, and of the *assets* of the predeceased, (unless there were children, in which case the usufruct was reduced by half). Women from the middle and upper middle classes therefore became widows of means. They normally walked away from the *notaire*'s office in control of more than half the couple's assets, and benefiting from the usufruct of a good part of the remainder.

A few examples will show what this meant in practical terms. When Constant Vanderhaeghe, *propriétaire* in Lille, died in 1869, he and his wife were worth 436,543f. They had eight adult children. The deceased's *propres* were worth 3,324f; the widow's, 2,847f. Under the terms of their marriage contract, the widow received 271,121f in full ownership (or 62 per cent of the couple's assets), which she took in cash, stock, bonds, mortgage loans and one house, the one in which she lived. The children received 13,156f each in full ownership and 6,294f in *nue propriété* (ownership encumbered by a usufruct). The share of the married daughters was reduced by the amount of their dowries (ADN J 1472-237). François Philibert Vrau, a thread manufacturer in Lille, died a year later. He left a widow, two married daughters and a middle-aged son. The couple's real and personal estate (including a thread-making factory) amounted to 1,027,547f. Mme Vrau received the value of her *propres* (130,830f), half the *communauté* (448,359f), and a quarter of her husband's estate, 140,733f, for a total of 719,922f (70 per cent of the family assets), plus the usufruct of another 140,733f. The three children received 93,822f less their dowries, in full ownership, and 46,911f in *nue propriété*. Mme Vrau took the factory, the equipment, most of the working capital and most of the goods in stock. The children shared the rest of the working capital and goods in stock (ADN J 1022-59; J 1022-60).

These two widows thus received a considerable share of what had been the couple's property. The composition of their share was very different however: 85 per cent of Mme Vanderheaghe's share consisted of stock and bonds, loans and notes. In contrast, 39 per cent of Mme Vrau's share consisted in factory equipment and operating capital; another 22 per cent was represented by the factory building itself. She took all the stocks and bonds owned by the couple, but they represented only 8 per cent of her settlement. The two women were typical of widows of their class: they received most of the assets of their family, and their children had to cool their heels and wait for their mother's death not only to inherit those assets, but even to benefit from most of their inheritance from their father, encumbered as it was by the mother's usufruct.

In managing those assets, widows regularly entered the world of investments and credit, and in so doing, often demonstrated a considerable business acumen. A few examples can show the extent and composition of Lille middle-class women's assets. When Anne Marie Wossars, a widow, died in 1830, her husband, Eugène Gobert, a *marchand chaud-ronnier*, had been dead for at least ten years. She had continued his business, and in the inventory of her personal estate was described by the notary as a *marchande chaudronnière*. She left behind 973.50f worth of furniture, linen and clothing, 323.75f in cash, a perpetual annuity of 300 florins and six mortgage loans worth 12,200f, four houses and a piece of farm land (ADN, J 548-58).

The widow Dubar, who died the same year, was not a merchant craftsperson but a *propriétaire*. She left 974f worth of furniture and linen, 5,829f in cash, three mortgages worth 7,400f and five promissory notes worth 17,514f. Her real estate included a grist mill, three houses and some farm land (ADN, J 839-44). Both widows managed to increase their real estate holdings after the death of their husbands, and both lent money at interest. Both managed to keep their sources of income diversified: urban rents, rural rents, interests, annuities, and, in the case of the widow Gobert, a rather masculine business. Their experience was also typical.

Moreover, widows' abilities to earn a living from their properties, their investments and, less often, their involvement in trade or manufacturing did not really change in the course of the century. The twice-widowed Constance Geneviève Destombes left two sons from her first marriage with Philippe Delepoulle, and a son and two daughters from her union with Philippe Durif in 1869. She left 10,174f worth of furniture, linen and silverware, 45,465f in stocks and bonds and 63,846f in urban and rural properties. Before her husband's death, two of her sons and one of her daughters had formed a partnership, first to manufacture linen, and then to ret and spin flax. The children had borrowed money first from their parents, and later from their widowed mother. At the time of her death, they still owed her 33,865f (ADN 3Q 524-55). Sophie Constance Duthoit, a proprietor and merchant trader who died the same year, was the widow of Amable Crombez. She left six children, two sons and four daughters. Her furniture etc. was worth 6,200f; she left 56,179f worth of trade goods and twelve loans worth 72,000f. Her real estate, including a farm, a warehouse and half a merchant-manufacturer dwelling-business was worth 60,720f (ADN 3Q 527-57).

Although separated by a generation, these two widows shared some common characteristics with the widows Gobert and Dubar: they had resources at their disposal; they could stay in business; and they invested, in mortgage loans, in the market and in real estate. The last two characteristics were direct consequences of the first. And although the nature of her assets framed a widow's opportunities and informed her actions, individual women's decisions about how to use the assets they controlled differed considerably.

Business Women, Investments and Credit

Many widows simply took over the running of the family business when their husbands died. In Lille, according to the city directories, between 5 and 8 per cent of the listed manufacturing enterprises and wholesale trading houses were run by women between 1830 and 1880. In 1830, three-quarters of those were run by widows. In the second half of the century, this fell to half (*Almanach du commerce* 1831–1855; *Annuaire du commerce* 1855–1881). In Tourcoing, according to the censuses, 10.7 per cent of the entrepreneurs and merchant traders were female in 1796, and 10.4 per cent in 1886 (AMTg, Recensements, 1796, 1851, 1886; Table de population, 1821–36). The business tax rolls for the second half of the century document a progression in the proportion of businesswomen: 4 per cent of the textile firms were headed by a woman in 1852 and 1857; 9 per cent in 1882 and 1887; 13 per cent in 1892; 10 per cent in 1897. Female ownership of wholesale firms went from 7 per cent in 1852 to 12 per cent in 1897 (AMTg, Matrices de patentes G1C 3-46). Almost all the women on the tax rolls were widows; only a few were single. Almost none were married, because husbands paid the taxes on their wives' businesses, and therefore are the ones listed unless the couple was married in separation of property. A notch lower, the proportion of female shopkeepers and tavern-keepers went from 25 per cent in 1851 to 29 per cent in 1886; two-thirds of those women were married (Craig 2001).

Not all widows took over the family business. Some went into partnership with their children. In a region where banks were slow to develop and joint stock companies were rare, partnership was the most common way to secure additional capital for one's business (Hirsch 1991: 312). Widows may or may not have needed the financial assets of their children to continue the family business. The children, however, often had no choice but to pool their resources and rely on their mother's financial backing. Partnerships were also a way to secure an income. In many partnerships in Lille and its area, the partners not only received a share of the profits, but were also entitled to 5 per cent interest on the money they had put into the business. Partnerships, then, operated like savings banks.

Partnerships fell into one of three categories: share-holding societies, which were very difficult to set up before the 1867 legislation; *sociétés en commandite* (limited liability partnerships); and *sociétés en nom collectif* (unlimited liability partnerships). In a *société en commandite,* one or more parties (the sleeping partners) provided one or more others (the *commandités*) with funds. They played no managing role and their exposure was limited to their investments. They did not have to be named, and this is a pity, because one suspects that some of the *commanditaires* were women. The *commandités*, on the other hand, managed and had unlimited liability for the debts of the firm. The *société en nom collectif* (unlimited liability partnership), usually between close relatives (siblings, parents and children), was the preferred form of partnership. Slightly less than a quarter of those in Tourcoing involved women (see Table 4.1). The proportion varied throughout the century however: 31 per cent of the partnerships registered between 1800 and 1840 involved at least one woman; 12 per cent in 1851–70; and 28 per cent in 1871–90.

The 319 simple partnerships (*sociétés en nom collectif*) involved 422 males and sixty-nine females. One-third of the women were widows, 14 per cent were married (and duly authorized by their husbands) and half were single. Forty-four per cent of the single women had signing rights, against one-quarter of the widows and one-third of the married women. By contrast, 94 per cent of the male partners had signing rights. One can assume that women without signing rights were primarily investors, and did not take an active part in the running of the business. They lent their money for a fixed term of years, shared in the benefits and in the losses, and may have drawn interest on their investments.

Table 4.1 Types of partnerships in Tourcoing registered at the Tribunal de Commerce, 1800–1890

Years	Sociétés en nom collectif						Sociétés en commandite	Share-holding societies
	Male partners only		Male and female partners		Female partners only			
	N	%	N	%	N	%	N	N
1800–1830	15	62	8	33	1	4	1	0
1831–1840	21	72	8	28	0	0	0	0
1841–1850	16	59	11	41	0	0	5	0
1851–1860	43	86	7	14	0	0	11	0
1861–1870	77	89	9	10	1	1	44	1
1871–1880	29	74	9	23	1	3	11	1
1881–1890	43	68	20	32	0	0	13	6
Total	244	76	72	23	3	1	85	8

Sources: ADN, série U, Justice, Tribunaux de commerce de Lille et de Tourcoing, 1781–1890.

One common type of partnership involving women was between a widow and her children. And although widows were far more likely to be passive partners than were single, or even married women, one should not assume that they automatically exchanged one patriarch for another. The articles of association deposited at the *Tribunal de Commerce* suggest that the relationship between mother and children ran the entire possible range of arrangements. On the one hand was Mme Vrau, whom we have already met. Her partnership contract with her son and son-in-law stipulated that in case of disagreement between the partners, she would decide 'in all sovereignty' (ADN 6U2 653,1871). Other widows, although clearly not interested in merely cheering from the sidelines, showed no inclination to keep their sons on a tight leash. Some stayed long enough to ensure a smooth transition, and then retreated into the role of mentor. Adele Françoise Dubois and her son Charles Edouard Brice had been partners for seven years when they modified the articles of their association. Both partners retained signing rights, but Mme Brice would henceforth devote to the affairs of the firm only the time she judged appropriate, without being under any obligation to do so (ADN 6U2 650). The Brice and the Vrau partnerships were very similar in structure, but their meanings could not have been more different.

Partnerships between siblings were another common type of partnership involving women. In Tourcoing, single women were more likely to enter partnerships than widows, and they almost always entered a partnership with siblings. Although this might seem a good strategy to keep an inheritance intact, most sibling partnerships seem not to have been the direct continuation of a parental business. In the case of the Delepoulle–Durif partnership mentioned above, it may have been a means to achieve a modicum of economic independence – and it had required loans from the parents. In entering into a business partnership with her brothers, Mlle Durif had made a very different choice from that of her younger sister, who entered a convent. The partnership between the Baxter sisters in Lille was also a way to gain an income. Isabelle, Marguerite, Henriette and Charlotte Baxter, burlap spinners in Lille, set up a factory in rented quarters in 1868; they invested 50,000f each. The firm went by the name Baxter *fils* (Baxter sons). The four women granted signing rights to their aunt Henriette Drummont, and the management to their brother Drummond. If they married, their husbands would have no right to manage or sign for the firm. Drummond Baxter, who was also a partner in both a sugar-refining business and a burlap bag-making firm, set up a joint stock company two years later and raised a capital of two million francs (2,000 shares worth 1,000f). His aunt Henriette bought ten shares. His sisters bought none (ADN 6U2 656).

The Dervaux partnership, established forty-one years later, was of a different cloth. Cyrille, Henry and Catherine Dervaux, aged forty, thirty-five and fifty, all single, all traders in Tourcoing, joined to create a wool-trading concern under the name *Dervaux Coine fils*, and intended to continue it until 1888. All partners had signing rights. The firm appears in the city's business tax rolls from 1880 to 1897, with Catherine as its *associée principale,* meaning she was the one liable for the tax. Catherine apparently was the one who organized her brothers and used their capital to set up a firm that would support them all (ADN 6U5 3, AMTg, G1C 33-1882; G1C 37-1887; G1C 41-1892, 7F3D et 7F3F).

These women's experiences exemplify the range of partnership agreements and suggest the range of motivations that could lead single women to join others and go into business. Some were primarily investors looking for an income, and not minding the risks inherent in manufacturing or trade; others were gatherers of capital, looking for a way to finance their own ventures; Mlle Durif and many others may have gone into business to support themselves, augment their capital, help their brothers and learn how to run a business, in the event they should end up on their own. Occasionally, women went into partnership with their sisters or other women. This did not happen in Tourcoing, but in Lille female partnerships to run fashion or linen stores were fairly common. More surprising was the Van Imshoff partnership – two sisters trading in lumber, who opened credit lines secured by mortgages to local contractors (ADN 4Q 38-674).

Alongside intra-family partnerships were others where the women struck an association with unrelated males. Some widows became partners by default, upon the death of a husband in partnership. Articles of association usually gave the widows the choice of remaining in the partnership as a sleeping partner, or withdrawing. The latter option gave widows leverage; some used it to be given a more active role in the firm as a partner with signing rights.

Widows also entered partnerships with non-family members of their own free will. Such was the case with Eugénie Fidèline Vaneslande, *propriétaire*, and widow of Philippe Delepoulle. She entered a *société en commandite* with a J. B. Briquet, twister. Briquet provided his skills and time, and Eugénie Fidèline the necessary equipment and 10,000F. Adeline Pollet, widow Bouchard, *rentière*, established a similar association in 1883, eight years after her husband's death, with Pierre Delahousse to trade spun yarns and wines. They both had signing and managing rights. Delahousse was to do the travelling and Adeline was to keep the books and the cash box. Adeline Pollet-Bouchard was listed as a broker in the 1886 census. The division of labour between the two partners was also typical of male–female partnerships that spelled out the duties of each associate: women kept the books and the cash box and men travelled. Partnerships were often the means whereby a man with skills or special-ized knowledge, but no money, secured the capital required to start a firm. For his partner, it was a way to invest his – or her – money profitably. Married women were also known to become partners in firms that had nothing to do with their husbands, but this was rare.

Women were also rarely *commanditées*. While both men and women were sleeping partners, active partners, who often did not have to provide any capital of their own, were men – with only two exceptions in Tourcoing. In this case, the exceptions were two unmarried women who were bankrolled by sleeping partners to open or take over a fashion store. The case of Julie Allard exemplifies the difficulties inherent in such ventures. She was not allowed to marry for five years, and then, if she married, her husband under no circumstances was to involve himself in the business or engage in a similar branch of trade (ADN 6U2 652). From the investor's point of view, if a woman was given the funds to start or continue a business, there was always the risk that control over this capital would shift to a stranger not chosen by the investors. Women were not bad credit risks *per se,* but they were liable through marriage to lose their legal capacity. Thus partnership agreements usually stipulated that a woman would cease to be a partner when she married.

Although, as this discussion has shown, they could be entrepreneurs in their own right, women were much less visible as borrowers of capital. They did secure financial backers and did get credit, but seemingly in much lower proportion than men. Their competence, the appropriateness of their activities for women, were not called into question, and therefore such issues cannot be advanced as an explanation for this under-representation. But in one very important way women were bad credit risks; they could marry and overnight lose their right to run their business.

While women who sought to borrow money faced significant obstacles, it is nonetheless evident from the multiple examples provided that women from the merchant or industrial class controlled, through inheritance or widowhood, considerable assets they could use at will. This made them important sources of long-term business credit for entrepreneurs. They seem to have invested like the men of their class: in their own businesses, which they could run alone or in partnership, or in the businesses of family members, as a partner without signing authority, as a limited liability partner (*commanditaire*), or, like the widow Durif, merely as a provider of a loan.

Personal and family businesses were, however, not the only local form of investment open to well-to-do women. Proprietors as a rule avoided risky business investments. They preferred safe ones, generating predictable incomes. Real estate was one form of favoured investments. So were mortgages, described by Codaccioni as a proprietor's monopoly. Mortgages were also a source of capital. Lenders and borrowers included women – but not in the same proportion.

Women and Mortgages

There were different types of mortgages, only one of which interests us: loans secured with real estate. Mortgage agreements were drafted by notaries and publicly registered. Mortgage registers and notarial records provide information not only on lenders but on borrowers as well. Over the course of the nineteenth century, the role of mortgages in the economic strategies of lenders and borrowers evolved until, by the end of the century, the mortgage market had shrunk significantly: fewer people lent and borrowed, but those who did lent and borrowed much more than in the past. The occupational profile of the lenders changed little, but the profile of the borrower changed significantly. Finally, the participation of women in the mortgage market shifted profoundly. In the 1830s and before, they were practically absent. By the end of the century, they appeared to have played a role disproportionate to their numbers in the local society.

Based on the files of two notaries, for selected years over a sixty-year period, Table 4.2 shows the number of loans and the number of lenders by sex, the average value of each loan and the average amount of money lent by individuals over each two-year period under consideration. Some individuals were multiple lenders, and are counted as one person in the 'male lenders' and 'female lenders' columns.

Table 4.2 Loans and lenders – Two *notaires*, 1829–1890

	All loans		Loans by men		Male lenders		Loans by women		Female lenders	
Year	Number[1]	Value	N	Value	N	Value	N	Value	N	Value
1829–30	204	5221	151	5257	96	8269	47	4922	32	7230
1849–50	99	6736	58	7380	49	8735	40	5957	32	7446
1869–70	230	9629	121	10178	93	13242	95	5939	60	9403
1889–90	145	15522	94	11839	64	17665	42	17257	27	26844

[1] This number does not add to the total of loans by men and loans by women because a small number of loans were made by tutors on behalf of minors, by groups and by banks.

Sources: ADN serie J , Greffes de notaires.

The first striking feature is the drop in the number of loans in 1849–50. This is almost certainly a result of the devastating economic crisis of the late 1840s, and of the political uncertainty resulting from the revolution of 1848. The decline in 1889–90 is harder to explain. It is clearly not a sign that people are getting poorer, as the value of the loans and the amount lent surged upward. The decline in the number of loans may reflect competition from other forms of investments for people's money and from other sources of credit. But for the hypothesis to hold, lenders had to have more money, as the amount lent went up. According to Codaccioni, the average value of the assets left by members of the upper middle class, proprietors and professionals went from 190,224f in the 1850s to 261,072f in the 1870s and 319,516f in the 1890s (Codaccioni 1976: 65, 111, 171).

The greatest increase in wealth would have occurred before 1873 – and yet the greatest increase in per capita amount lent occurred after 1870. Alternatively, it is possible that, among this layer of the middle class, a group of people investing a larger than average proportion of their assets was emerging, distinct from people who preferred investing in the stock and bond market.

Equally striking is the repositioning of women on this market. The proportions of loans made by women and of female lenders are approximately the same (see Table 4.3).

Table 4.3   Lenders by sex

	Loans		Lenders	
	Males	Females	Males	Females
1829–30	74%	23%	72%	24%
1849–50	54%	40%	46%	36%
1869–70	53%	41%	59%	36%
1889–90	65%	29%	67%	28%

Source: ADN serie J , Greffes de notaires.

Women were not less likely to be multiple lenders than men in the 1830s and the 1890s, and just a little less in the intervening period. The proportion of female lenders increased in the first half of the century (a quick count in 1810 shows that there were almost no female lenders at that time), remained stable till the end of the Second Empire, and then declined. At all times, however, women were likely to be over-represented among the lenders. Married women normally could not administer their property (unless their husbands allowed them to do so). And, consequently, the female population able to lend was overwhelmingly made up of widows and spinsters. It is doubtful that one-third of the middle class in Lille was composed of unmarried women. In Tourcoing, in 1851, according to the census, only 24 per cent of the adults belonging to the socio-economic categories that lent money in Lille were females without husbands. Women, then, were more likely to be mortgage lenders than men. Until the end of the century, women lent smaller amounts of money than men, as shown in Table 4.2. The gap was particularly wide in 1869–70. By 1889, however, the situation had completely changed. Women were now lending much more than men. The behaviour of women seems to mirror that of the middle class at large; a group of females emerged among the mortgage lenders as heavy lenders in the same way as a group of individuals had emerged from the rank of the middle class as larger lenders.

Who were the lenders? Female lenders were almost exclusively drawn from the proprietor/*rentier* subclass. The rest were storekeepers, farmers, manufacturers or 'filles de confiance'. Significantly, except in 1829–30, female lending proprietors were always as numerous or almost as numerous as male ones. And yet, according to the 1855 city directory, there were two male proprietors for every female proprietor. Females were again over-represented.

Male lenders were, on the other hand, drawn from more varied backgrounds. Proprietors dominated their ranks. The composition of the rest changed with the period: professionals, storekeepers and employees came next in 1829–30; merchants and storekeepers in 1849–50; craftsmen and merchants twenty years later; and merchants, storekeepers, manufacturers and professionals rose proportionally at the end of the century. Codaccioni claimed that proprietors dominated the mortgage market. They did not in terms of number. Except in 1869–70, when male and female proprietors represented 53 per cent of lenders, their proportion never exceeded one-half. However, proprietors overall made larger loans than any other lender category. In this sense they dominated the mortgage market and, by 1890, a large proportion of mortgage money came from women proprietors.

Table 4.4   Average amounts lent by *propriétaires* (francs)

Year	Male	Female
1829–1830	7930	9126
1849–1850	14872	9538
1869–1870	16160	10887
1889–1890	20366	33016

Source: ADN serie J , Greffes de notaires.

The pattern of lending as shown in Table 4.4 represents a significant change in the level of resources controlled by women. Why did women lend less money than men for most of the century? There are different possible explanations. Women may have favoured other forms of investment. Women may have been more willing to diversify their investments, explaining why proportionally more women than men invested in mortgages, but invested less in value. Women may also have been poorer. This hypothesis is perhaps not very probable, as daughters inherited equally with their brothers and, under the community regime, widows received the same share of the *communauté* – of the couple's joint assets, as widowers. However, although single men, in the aggregate, were probably no richer than single women, married men had more assets at their disposal. They had the legal right to administer the *communauté*, and therefore could lend not only their share, but their wife's as well. This, of course, leaves the sharp increase in the value of female loans at the end of the century unexplained.

When we look at the mortgage market from the point of view of the borrowers, we get a different picture (see Table 4.5).

Table 4.5   Loans and borrowers – Two *notaires*, 1829–1890

	All loans		Loans to men		Male borrowers		Loans to women		Women borrowers	
Year	Number	Value	N	Value	N	Value	N	Value	N	Value
1829–30	204	5221	173	5410	148	6324	31	4164	26	4966
1849–50	99	6736	85	7077	75	8021	12	4608	11	5027
1869–70	230	9629	90	10286	109	19534	23	3713	14	6100
1889–90	145	15522	67	14287	77	17998	35	6280	27	8140

Source: ADN serie J , Greffes de notaires.

There are many fewer female borrowers than male ones, and fewer female borrowers than female lenders. The proportion of female borrowers, however, seems to reflect their proportion in the population 'at risk'. The increased proportion of female borrowers (Table 4.6) echoes the rise in the amount of money lent by women at the end of the century. By century's end, a quarter of the loans were made to women. This increased proportion may be a consequence of men turning to other sources of credit, whereas women continued to borrow against their real estate, but we must note that the absolute number of women borrowers also went up – by about 100 per cent. Women did borrow more frequently at the end of the century.

In terms of the amount of money borrowed, women were secondary players, however. At the beginning of our period, women borrowed almost as much as men. By the end of the century, they borrowed half as much,

Table 4.6 Borrowers by sex

Years	Loans		Lenders	
	Males	Females	Males	Females
1829–30	85%	15%	85%	15%
1849–50	86%	12%	87%	13%
1869–70	90%	10%	89%	11%
1889–90	67%	24%	74%	26%

Source: ADN serie J , Greffes de notaires.

largely because male borrowing had increased at a much faster rate then theirs.

Why women borrowed less, and particularly borrowed less often than men for most of the century, requires further investigation. One can dismiss the notion that lenders believed women were a greater risk, as mortgage loans are as close to being risk-free as possible. And marriage here was irrelevant; debts contracted before marriage had to be repaid just the same. Women may have been more cautious than their male counterparts. Female borrowers, like female lenders, were generally widows; widows tend to be older than average, and people's willingness to take risks tends to decrease with age. Like male lenders, married male borrowers also had more mortgageable assets at their disposal. They could mortgage property held jointly. They could also, as administrators of their wives' patrimony, mortgage this, provided they did the proper paper work. The notarial records indicate the origins of the mortgaged property. In the majority of the cases, it was a community property. Wives' properties came second, husbands' patrimony a distant third. Married men, then, were in a favoured position on the mortgage market, both as lenders and borrowers. But none of these explanations accounts for the changes that occurred during the period. The changing position of women at the end of the century, either as lenders or borrowers, needs further investigation. Perhaps a demographic shift occurred; there may have been proportionally more women without husbands.

The socio-economic composition of the borrowers did not change much over the period. In all periods two-thirds to four-fifths of the female borrowers were proprietors, *rentières*, or did not list an occupation. Yet, in the 1850s, the city directory listed more unmarried women in trade and industry than as proprietors. Proprietresses borrowed. Other women rarely did so. In contrast, male borrowers, like male lenders, were drawn from a much wider occupational spectrum: storekeepers, proprietors, wholesale merchants and the building trades were the leading categories.

Were the *notaires'* clients representative of other borrowers and lenders across the city? We can answer that question by comparing the mortgage deeds drawn up by the two *notaires* with the ones at the mortgage registry office in 1851 and 1870. On the whole, there were more similarities than differences.

Conclusion

The money market in the Lille area was not strictly a masculine world. Women lent and borrowed for business purposes or to gain an income. There are no signs that their activities elicited criticism or attempts to curb them, as was the case for the seventeenth-century female lenders investigated by Barbara Todd (Todd 1997). But married women's strict legal subordination to their husbands made all women secondary players. Married women could administer their property and run a business only with their husband's permission, and he could, of course, revoke that permission at any time. Only unmarried women could be independent economic agents. But they were also liable to marry and lose this autonomy. Unmarried women could be loaned money if the security was good enough; their husbands would be responsible for repayment from their *propres* or from the *communité* if they married. But they had fewer mortgageable assets at their disposal than married men, and thus could provide less security for loans. And they were poor risks for investors looking for a business to underwrite: what if they married an individual whose business sense left something to be desired? One could also plan the dissolution of a partnership if the female partner married – but the process may have entailed losses. Marriage and favourable phases in the business cycle may not have coincided.

As far as the mortgage market is concerned, the position of women evolved quite dramatically. From being very marginal participants during the Napoleonic period, they became significant players in terms of proportions of lenders and then borrowers, sums loaned and, at the end of the century, sums borrowed. The secondary place of women on the mortgage market for most of the century can be explained rather easily, but such is not the case for the end of the century shift. Three hypotheses are possible. The first suggests an increase in women's economic activities at the end of the century – and we have seen that this seems to have actually taken place. The second possibility is the withdrawal of men from the mortgage market as they found alternative sources of credit and shifted their investments in other directions. One wonders, however, why women would not have done the same. The third possibility is demographic; there may have been proportionally more women able to lend or borrow at the end of the century. The number of women in the 'deceased millionnaire's club' (people leaving at least one millions francs' worth of assets) identified by Codaccioni went from one in the 1850s (9 per cent) to four in 1870 and thirteen (28 per cent) in 1890. By 1908, they were twenty-eight or one-third of the deceased millionaires (Codaccioni 1976: 67–70, 112–22, 172–85, 335–44). But although we cannot completely explain the position of women on the mortgage market, one conclusion is undeniable: this was not a 'sphere' to which they did not belong. And neither was the financial sphere in general. Middle-class lending and borrowing were common facets of women's economic activity, contributing to the vitality of their families and community.

References

Unpublished Sources
Archives départementales du nord (ADN):

M653-46, Statistiques industrielles, arrondissement de Lille, 1880–1890.
Serie J, Greffes de notaires, J 548-58, 56-590; J 1442 30-34, 87-93, 179-187, 272, Etude de Me Lardenois et successeurs (Gruloy, Wesquin, Ducrocq); J 1472 76-84, 160-167, 237-243, 300-305, Etude de Me Coustenoble et successeur (J. Lefebvre); J 839-44 Etude de Me Musias, J 1022-59-60, Etude de Me E. Lefebvre.
Serie U, Justice, Tribunal de commerce, 6U2 9-16, 186, 190-97, 645-654, Tribunal de commerce de Lille, 1781–1870; 6U5 2-5 Tribunal de commerce de Tourcoing 1870–1890 (Tourcoing part of Lille before 1870).
Serie Q Enregistrement, 3Q Tables de successions Tourcoing.
4Q 38-679 Enregistrement des hypothèques.

Archives municipales de Tourcoing (AMTg):
Recensements Tourcoing 1796, 1851, 1886
Table de population de Tourcoing, 1821–1836
Matrices de patentes, G1C-3-46, 1852–1897
Dossiers d'entreprises, 7F3D to 7F3F

Published Sources
Almanach du commerce (1831, 1840, 1851, 1855*), Almanach du commerce des arts et métiers des villes de Lille, Armentières, Roubaix et Tourcoing,* Lille: Vanackère fils.

Annuaire du commerce (1855, 1860, 1870, 1881), *Annuaire du commerce, de l'industrie, de la magistrature et de l'administration de l'arrondissement de Lille,* Lille: Ravet-Anceau.

Baskerville, Peter (1999), 'Women and Investment in late Nineteenth Century Urban Canada: Victoria and Hamilton, 1880–1901', *Canadian Historical Review,* 80: 191–218.

Briet, H. (1908), *Le droit des gens mariés dans les coutumes de Lille,* Lille: Le Bigot.

Chanut, A. (1956), 'La crise économique à Tourcoing, 1846–1850', *Revue du Nord:* 38: 74–105.

Codaccioni, F.-P. (1976), *De l'inégalité sociale dans une grande ville industrielle, le drame de Lille de 1850 à 1914,* Lille: Presses de l'université de Lille III.

Craig, Beatrice (2001), 'Petites Bourgeoises and Penny Capitalists: Women in Retail in the Lille Area during the Nineteenth Century', *Enterprise and Society,* 2 (June 2001): 198–224.

Davidoff, L. and C. Hall (1987), *Family Fortunes, Men and Women of the English Middle Class, 1780–1850,* Chicago: University of Chicago Press.

Decroix, P. (1999), *La saga d'une grande banque du Nord de la France, 1846–1934,* Paris: Editions Christian.

Finn, M. C. (1996), 'Women, Consumption and Coverture in England, *c.*1760–1860', *Historical Journal,* 39: 703–22.

—— (1998), 'Working-class Women and the Contest for Consumer Control in Victorian County Courts', *Past and Present,* 161: 116–54.

—— (1999), 'Legal Restrictions and Actual Practice: Married Women's Access to Credit in Nineteenth Century Britain', unpublished paper presented at the Women & Credit Conference, Fredericton, New Brunswick, Canada.

Fohlen, C. (1954), 'Industrie et crédit dans la région Lilloise 1815–1870', *Revue du Nord,* 36: 361–8.

—— (1956), *L'industrie textile au temps du Second Empire,* Paris: Plon.

Fontaine, L. (2001), 'Women's Economic Spheres and Credit in Pre-industrial Europe', in B. Lemire, R. Pearson and G. Campbell (eds), *Women and Credit: Researching the Past, Refiguring the Future,* Oxford, Berg Publishers.

Gille, B. (1954), 'La banque de Lille et les premières grandes banques du Nord', *Revue du Nord,* 36: 369–76.

Hilaire, Y. M. (1984), *Histoire de Roubaix,* Westhoek: Edition des Beffrois.

Hirsch, J. P. (1991), *Les deux rêves du commerce, entreprise et institution dans la région lilloise, 1780–1860,* Paris: EHESS.

Hunt, M. (1999), 'Women, Credit and the Seafaring Community in Early 18th Century London, 1700–1740', unpublished paper presented at the Women & Credit Conference, Fredericton, New Brunswick, Canada.

Lambert-Dansette, J. (1954), *Quelques familles du patronat textile de Lille–Armentières, 1789–1914. Origines et évolution d'une bourgeoisie,* Lille: Raous.

Legrand, P. (1852), *La femme du bourgeois de Lille,* Lille: Lefebvre Ducrocq.

Lemire, B. (1997), 'Petty Pawns and Informal Lending: Gender and the Transformation of Small-Scale Credit in England, *c.*1600–1800', in P. K. O' Brien and K. Bruland (eds), *From Family Firms to Corporate Capitalism: Essays in Business and Industrial History in Honour of Peter Mathias,* Oxford: Oxford University Press.

Lottin, A. (ed.) (1986), *Histoire de Tourcoing,* Westhoekk: Edition des Beffrois.

Pouchain, P. (1980), 'L'industrialisation de la région lilloise de 1800 à 1860, contribution à l'étude des mécanismes de la croissance', Thèse de troisième cycle, université de Lille III, Lille.

—— (1986), 'Banque et crédit à Lille de 1800 à 1939', *Revue du Nord,* 68: 635–61.

Rabuzzi, D. (1995), 'Women as Merchants in Eighteenth Century Northern Germany: The Case of Stralsund, 1750–1830', *Central European History,* 28: 435–56.

Smith, Bonnie (1981), *Ladies of the Leisure Class, The Bourgeoises of Northern France in the Nineteenth Century,* Princeton, NJ: Princeton University Press.

Statistiques générales de la France (1847–1852), *Industries en 1840–45,* Imprimerie nationale, tome I: Nord Oriental.

Taillard (1849), *Recueil d'actes des XII et XIII siècles, en langue romano-wallonne du Nord de la France,* Douai.

Todd, Barbara J. (1997) '"For the Publick Service of the Nation": London Women's Investments in Crown Loans, 1660–1694', unpublished paper presented to the annual meeting of the Canadian Historical Association, St John's, Newfoundland.

Toulemonde, J. (1966). 'L'industrie de Roubaix Tourcoing', *Revue du Nord,* 321–36.

Trénard, L. (ed.) (1977), *Histoire d'une métropole, Lille, Roubaix, Tourcoing,* Toulouse: Privat.

Wiskins, C. (1999), 'Business Women and Entrepreneurial Networks in Late Eighteenth and Early Nineteenth Century England', unpublished paper presented to the annual conference of the Economic History Society; summary published in the conference's programme, pp. 36–41.

Wolf, M. (1972), 'Elements pour la construction d'un indice de la production industrielle dans le Nord, 1815–1914', *Revue du Nord,* LIV: 284–316.

PART II

Bridging Past and Present

5

Women and Micro-credit in History: Gender in the Irish Loan Funds

Aidan Hollis

Access to credit is one of the most useful financial tools available to the poor. Credit allows human capital to be leveraged with physical capital in order to increase income. It serves as an insurance mechanism, allowing consumption to be spread evenly across time. However, credit raises problems of adverse selection and moral hazard, and this requires that the lender be able to trust the borrower. This has, in many contexts, hindered poor people, and especially poor women, from accessing credit. This roadblock, of course, has arisen within a specific institutional framework. In many societies, as in nineteenth-century Ireland, ownership of property was vested in the husband, and hence married women were more or less effectively prevented from borrowing. Even unmarried women faced considerable obstacles in obtaining credit. Most nineteenth-century Irish unmarried women were poor: they were traders and dealers, or spinners, labourers and small-scale farmers. For these individuals, credit was unavailable from banks, since the loans that banks made were larger than could reasonably be made to such poor individuals. In this context of poor women unable to obtain credit from the major financial institutions, it is interesting to study institutions from which poor women *were* able to obtain credit.

In this chapter, I examine the role of women in the Irish Loan Funds, a charitable micro-credit institution that operated from the eighteenth to the twentieth centuries and made millions of loans to the 'industrious poor' of Ireland. After briefly summarizing the history and operations of the loan funds, I examine the role of women in this institution. Surprisingly, approximately one-quarter of all borrowers were women, a proportion much higher than for comparable European and American institutions. Women were also important as depositors, founders, and managers of these funds.

A Brief History of the Loan Funds[1]

The Irish Loan Funds started with the efforts of that notable Irish nationalist and author, Dean Jonathan Swift, who deplored the inability of honest but impoverished tradesmen to obtain credit to carry on their businesses in Dublin. Out of his own pocket, he set up a revolving loan fund of £500, which made loans to tradesmen who had fallen on hard times but whose standing was nevertheless good in the community. He evaluated a person's credit among his peers by requiring all borrowers to present a guarantee from two neighbours, 'for it was a maxim with him, that any one known by his neighbours to be an honest, sober, and industrious man, would readily find such security; while the idle and dissolute would by this means be excluded' (Sheridan 1787: 234). Essentially, Swift was drawing on what we might today call social capital in the same way as group lending schemes operated by micro-credit organizations such as the Grameen Bank. This lending charity was deemed very successful and effective at the time.

Swift's lending charity died with him, but it had an influence, and within a few years a new lending charity operating on the same basis as Swift's received the patronage of the Dublin Musical Society. This society organized concerts, with the money they generated being used for various charitable purposes; but lending to 'poor but industrious' tradesmen soon came to dominate its activities, and it was incorporated for the purpose of making loans. By 1768, it had made loans totalling £27,108 to 5,959 individuals 'who without some seasonable Relief (at the Time) must have sunk under their Misfortunes, and their Families probably become a Charge, and Incumbrance on the Publick' (*State of the Charitable Loan . . .* 1769: 13). Its successes in Dublin led to an attempt to replicate its activities in other cities. The society continued to operate in Dublin for almost one hundred years, and many other unconnected loan funds began operations in provincial cities in the late eighteenth and early nineteenth centuries.

Ireland was a very poor country in the first half of the nineteenth century. Comparisons in terms of income with modern countries can be misleading. However, some indicators of poverty are unmistakable: there were frequent small and occasionally severe famines; the physical infrastructure of the country was very poor compared to that of other European countries; and visitors were often shocked at the appalling state of Irish agriculture and the standard of living. The German traveller Kohl commented in 1844 that 'until one has seen the west of Ireland he has no idea that human beings can live in a state of greater misery than in the fertile environs of Dublin' (Mokyr 1985: 6). Ireland was also famous for its potato dependency, which provided a plentiful if monotonous source of food most years. The average adult labourer in most regions of Ireland is estimated to have consumed over twelve pounds of potatoes per day, implying a daily intake of over 3,800 calories (Bourke 1968: 76). The nutritional status of the Irish poor appears to have been relatively good thanks to the potato, but since potatoes could neither be stored for more than a year nor transported at reasonable cost, crop failure in a single year was disastrous.

The entire system of loan funds received a major boost in 1822 when a London committee 'for the relief of the distressed Irish' gave £55,000 to set up local loan funds in ten counties that had suffered in a recent famine caused by failure of the potato crop. The size of this donation prompted legislation that protected and regulated the operation of these loan funds, as well as affording 'encouragement to the formation of other Institutions of a like kind' (4 Geo. IV, c.32). This legislation included provisions that enabled funds to charge interest on loans, and which exempted them from the 'Stamp Tax', a fee normally required to make private contracts enforceable by a Justice of the Peace instead of the slower Quarter Sessions. This exemption made the loan funds preferred over creditors who had not paid the Stamp Tax, and thus gave them a small cost advantage over other lenders.

The new legislation, in turn, prompted considerable growth in loan funds. The ability to charge interest to borrowers enabled loan funds to attract interest-bearing deposits, thus turning them into very loosely regulated banks. Some funds were operated as profit-making ventures with large salaries paid to the manager, who was also the chief depositor. Other funds were established by local committees wishing to alleviate poverty by making credit available to the 'industrious poor'. By the 1830s, there were well over a hundred loan funds operating throughout the country, competing with the banks.

This growth in the number of barely regulated loan funds led to new legislation in 1836 and 1838 that established a regulatory body, the Central Loan Fund Board, which had the power to inspect and shut down funds. The Board, though it had some regulatory authority, gave no financial support to individual loan funds, all of which remained independent and locally managed. The legislation also reinforced the charitable nature of the loan funds by requiring them to give half their profits to other local charities.[2] The creation of the Board seems to have encouraged the establishment of even more loan funds, and by the early 1840s there were some 300 loan funds operating under the supervision of the Central Board, and perhaps another 50–100 unregulated funds. The funds under the Board together made approximately 500,000 loans annually to perhaps 330,000 different individuals and had become an important financial institution for the poorer two-thirds of the population.

The typical loan fund in the early 1840s was a small-scale operation. It had some capital, which was composed of donations and retained profits; and it accepted deposits at an interest rate of 5 or 6 per cent. Deposits were typically around ten times as large as capital. The official manager was unpaid, and supervised (often in a rather nominal way) a paid clerk who performed the daily operations of the fund. The chief business of the fund was making small loans of between £1 and £10, averaging about £4, to individuals who lived in the neighbourhood of the fund. These loans were repayable in twenty equal weekly instalments and carried an interest rate of between 8 and 13 per cent. The average fund made around 1,650 loans annually. Loans were intended to be 'reproductive' in the sense that the loan would finance an asset that would generate a stream of cash sufficient to pay the instalments. Borrowers were required to present two guarantors who were jointly liable for repayment, just as in Dean Swift's original scheme. Delays in repayment resulted in quite hefty fines; and, in the case of ongoing failure to repay, the goods of the borrower and his guarantors were seized. The weekly repayment assisted borrowers in disciplining themselves, and also provided timely information to the loan funds concerning borrowers with liquidity problems. Figure 5.1 shows a promissory note made by Nance

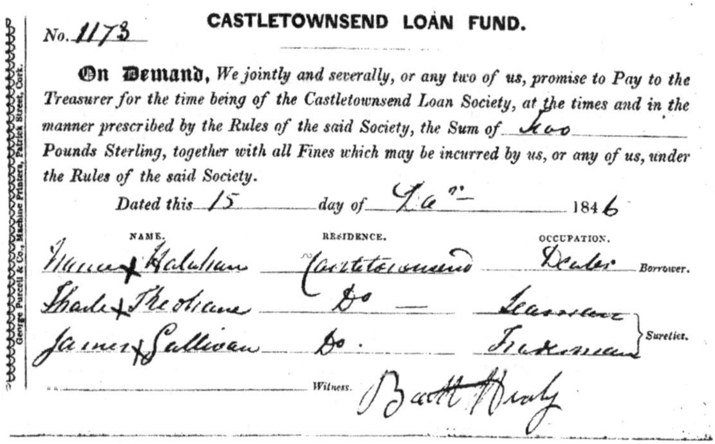
George Purcell & Co., Machine Printers, Patrick Street, Cork.

No. 1173 **CASTLETOWNSEND LOAN FUND.**

On Demand, *We jointly and severally, or any two of us, promise to Pay to the Treasurer for the time being of the Castletownsend Loan Society, at the times and in the manner prescribed by the Rules of the said Society, the Sum of* Two *Pounds Sterling, together with all Fines which may be incurred by us, or any of us, under the Rules of the said Society.*

Dated this 15 *day of* Jan. 1846

NAME.	RESIDENCE.	OCCUPATION.	
Nance + Halahan	Castletownsend	Dealer	*Borrower.*
Charles + Theohane	Do	Seaman	*Sureties.*
James + Sullivan	Do.	Tradesman	

Witness. Batt Healy

Source: PRO T/91/123 Castletownsend Loan Fund Loans Book.

Figure 5.1 Castletownsend Loan Fund Promissory Note, 1846.

Halahan, a dealer or small trader, to the Castletownsend Loan Fund in December 1846, for two pounds. Her two guarantors are a seaman and a tradesman, perhaps her supplier. Neither she nor her guarantors could sign their own names.

The banks, which were the chief competitors of the loan funds, were themselves quite new: only small private banks existed until 1824, when enabling legislation made it possible for joint-stock branch banks to be established and operate. The new joint-stock banks quickly set up branches in cities, but towns under 5,000 were largely without banks until the 1860s, when the banks began a new round of expansion. The banks were, until this time, fairly cautious in their lending, which did not include making loans under £10. In 1840 the average annual per capita income of the poorest 66 per cent of Irish households is estimated to have been approximately £4.30 (Mokyr 1985: 10–11). Thus most of the population was ineligible to obtain bank credit for small projects within their abilities but beyond their means, such as purchasing livestock, or stock for an artisan's shop.

The alternatives to banks consisted of the loan funds, private moneylenders and pawnshops. Private moneylenders performed a function similar to that of the loan funds, although their interest rates tended to be much higher than the legislated maximum of 13 per cent imposed on the loan funds. Moneylenders were also unable to perform financial intermediation – that is, accepting a deposit from one party and lending it to another – since they were unregulated, and people were unwilling to place deposits with them. Thus the amount of financing they were able to provide was limited to their own means. Pawnshops were ubiquitous, and allowed poor people to obtain small amounts of credit, almost always under £1. Agricultural labourers, small-scale farmers and dealers typically did not possess items of value greater than £1 that they could pawn, restricting considerably the scope of investments that could be financed through pawnshops.

Loan funds were thus the principal source of credit for loans in the range of £1 to £10 in the period of the 1830s to 1850s, and they became, by the early 1840s, the principal 'formal sector' source of credit for the poorer two-thirds of the population. Hollis and Sweetman (1998a) estimate that, at their peak in the early 1840s, the loan funds were lending to approximately 20 per cent of all Irish households.

There is substantial evidence that these households were primarily among the poorer part of the population. The extant lists of occupations from various loan funds, as well as evidence from commissions, indicate that borrowers were mainly small farmers, labourers, dealers and other poor people. In addition, almost all borrowers were illiterate. Extant promissory notes from the Baltimore Loan Fund in County Cork in the early 1840s show that, at most, 1 per cent of the borrowers could sign their names (PRO, T/91/109). This is a remarkably low rate in a barony in which around 20 per cent of the total population claimed to be able to read in the 1841 census, and adds to evidence presented elsewhere that the loan funds were lending almost exclusively to the poorer two-thirds of the population.

The advantage loan funds had in their operations was a familiarity with local conditions and sometimes personal knowledge of borrowers. Banks did not lend to poor people partly because of the lack of information on those borrowers. Typically, bank managers were not hired locally, and indeed, many managers were imported from Scotland because of a lack of managerial and technical expertise in Ireland. Such managers could not, of course, employ local knowledge about reputations and 'social capital'. In contrast, loan funds were local to the community and operated in a small area in which the loan fund manager, depositors and clerk had some familiarity with borrowers. An example of this local information in action is provided in the Tandragee Estate Loan Fund List of Applic- ations. This loan fund was mainly established to assist tenants on the estate, though loans were made to others also. The clerk operated the fund, but loans appear to have been vetted by the estate agent. The clerk and/ or agent inquired into each applicant's circumstances if they were not well known. When Patrick Flood applied for a £6 loan to purchase lime for his field, the notes from the agent instructed the clerk: 'Tell Robertson to enquire – give £3 in turn' (PRONI, D1248/LF/5A: 68). When Widow Gibson asked for a loan of £4, the loan was granted, although in the margins another hand had added 'improper conduct amongst members of the family' (PRONI, D1248/LF/5A: 59). When Samuel Ruddell requested £8 to put in his crop, the loan was refused and the marginalia include the comment 'is going to America' (PRONI, D1248/LF/5A: 41). Clearly the estate agent and/or the clerk were able to call on resources within their community to identify characteristics of borrowers to improve their lending risk, and it is exactly this kind of information that made the loan funds viable as lenders in a market that the banks avoided.

The loan funds reached their apex at an unlucky time, for they had no sooner grown into a substantial institution than Ireland was struck low by what the Loan Fund Board described as 'the fearful famine afflicting the country, which has disorganized the whole ramifications of society', or what is commonly known as the Potato Famine (*Ninth Annual Report of the Central Loan Fund Board* 1847: 5). The Great Famine of the period

1846–8 caused terrible destruction in Ireland: out of a population of approximately 8.5 million, excess mortality is commonly estimated to have been around 1 million people, and famine-induced emigration accounted for the loss of another 1 million. This was of course very traumatic for the loan funds, whose borrowers were mainly among those worst hit by the Famine. Loan funds contracted their operations, partly out of fear of making bad loans, partly because their clientele was so diminished, and partly because many deposits were withdrawn to finance consumption or emigration, and by 1850 about half the pre-Famine funds had closed. Those that remained in operation returned to their pre-Famine size, and the system overall saw little change in the following fifty years, although it gradually shrank as it failed to attract new deposits. At the same time, as the banking system grew, bank branches slowly became more entrenched in smaller communities after the 1860s and gradually displaced the loan funds in almost all areas. Loan funds nevertheless continued to operate throughout the country until at least 1961. At that time, the funds were still limited by the £10 maximum loan size that had been set by legislation in 1822.

Women and the Loan Funds

Women as Borrowers

In this section, I examine the position of women as borrowers from the loan funds. The evidence indicates that single women were accorded equal access to credit from the loan funds and that hundreds of thousands of poor Irish women obtained finance for investment and consumption through the funds. This credit was obtained at the same interest rate as that paid by men. Married women were largely excluded because of laws concerning the ownership of marital property.

While there is no evidence that the earliest loan funds lent to women, by the early 1800s women formed an important part of the borrowing clientele of the loan funds. This was clearly intentional: the standardized rules of funds clearly state, in most funds, that the purpose of the institution is for lending to 'industrious persons of either sex'.[3] Not all funds had this inclusive clause explicitly written into their rules, but no funds had a rule that explicitly required loans to be made only to men. Some funds, however, were limited to lending to women only. Thus the funds were intentionally open to female borrowers. Of course, intention is not everything, although it certainly demonstrates that the activists who established these funds recognized that female poverty was just as important as male poverty, and that the loan funds had a role to play in assisting women to obtain credit.

Despite their good intentions, loan funds faced a formidable obstacle in lending to married women: the husband was the owner of all property in a marriage, so that 'a married woman should not be accepted as the principal debtor' (INA, TIPP 27/1/1, No G 3828/16: Sept 1916). As the wife could not own property, the loan funds faced the problem that, in case of default, they were unlikely to be successful in claiming against the husband for a debt incurred by his wife. This did not stop funds from lending to married women, but certainly would have been a discouraging factor. Thus most funds, although theoretically able to lend to both women and men equally, did little lending to married women; though perhaps in some cases when married women wished to borrow, their husbands undertook to borrow for them.

Spinsters and widows, however, were able to hold property in their own names, and so it is not surprising that they figure more prominently in the extant records of borrowers, indeed, that about 90 per cent of women borrowers appear to have been unmarried. There are a number of ways of identifying this: the most common is that some lists of borrowers identify the occupations of borrowers. Spinsters and widows are, in some cases, listed as occupations, as though being husbandless was a job in the same way as being a farmer or labourer. For example, the reports from the Ballycastle Loan Fund for the period 1838–40 show that it made 1,992 loans, of which 1,407 were to men with occupations such as 'farmer' and 'labourer', while 585 were to women with occupations listed as 'spinster' (392 borrowers), 'widow' (163) and 'married woman' (30) (*Third Annual Report of the Loan Fund*: 12). However, some other lists do not include 'spinster' and 'widow' in their occupational breakdown, so that in those cases we cannot identify whether the spinsters and widows are not borrowers or whether they are considered to have other occupations.

It is instructive to examine what proportion of the female population was thus eligible to borrow from the loan funds. Anecdotal evidence suggests that the loan funds did not lend to minors, and that almost all borrowers would have been over twenty-five years of age. Thus we are interested in determining the percentages of single women over twenty-five. The percentage of unmarried women was 19 per cent in 1841, and the percentage of widows was also 19 per cent, so that 38 per cent of women over twenty-five were single. The proportion of single women increased over the nineteenth century as shown in Table 5.1, which shows the percentage of single women (spinsters and widows) aged twenty-six to thirty-five. Thus we infer that the proportion of unmarried women over twenty-five must also have increased.

Table 5.1 Percentage Single among Women aged
26–35 in Ireland, 1841–1901

1841	28
1851	39
1861	39
1871	38
1881	41
1891	48
1901	53

Source: (1954) *Commission on Emigration and Other
Population Problems,* Dublin: Government Publications: 72.

If the loan funds made loans without discriminating between men and
single women (and assuming equal demand from the two groups) we
would expect that men would be approximately three times as numerous
in the lists of borrowers, or that they would represent about 75 per cent
of borrowers. This is indeed what we observe in the extant records on
the numbers of male and female borrowers.

Data on the proportion of female borrowers comes from a variety of
sources. Table 5.2 shows the number of male and female borrowers, as
well as dates, based on all the available sources that identify males and
females. All but the data on the Roscrea fund are from the middle of the
nineteenth century.[4]

There is no reason to think that the proportion of women borrowers
was systematically different in funds for which there is no extant information. The reasons why data are extant for some funds only seem not
to be connected with how well the fund was run, but seem rather arbitrary.
All funds were required by law to maintain records, but most of these
records were destroyed as being of little interest after many years.
Archivists have preserved the records of only a few funds. Thus it appears
that the percentage of women borrowers is roughly proportional to the
ratio of single women to all men. While the earliest loans appear to have
been only for men, the loan funds grew to serve an increasingly female
clientele in their last years in the 1950s. The last recorded loan is for £10,
to a widow, in August 1961 (INA, TIPP 27/4/5). Since all borrowers from
the loan funds were required to have two co-signatories, it is not surprising
that many of the cosignatories were also women (INA, TIPP 27/1/1).
Given the proportion of female borrowers, of the 330,000 people who
borrowed from the loan funds annually in the early 1840s, about 80,000
would have been single women. As there were 630,000 single women

Table 5.2 Numbers of Male and Female Borrowers

Fund	Date	Males	Females	% Female
Ballycastle	1838–1840	1407	585	29
Ballygar	June 1835	34	9	21
Ballygar	June–October 1847	46	14	23
Baltimore	January 1842	59	7	11
Baltimore	1846	251	60	19
Baltimore	1847	11	8	42
Castle Hacket	1843	314	28	8
Elphin	January–March 1845	174	44	20
Elphin	1847	105	40	28
Roscrea	May–July 1949	46	14	23
Tandragee Estate	Jan., Feb., May 1846	117	29	20
Tandragee Castle	7 April 1847	123	18	13
Tandragee Castle	July–September 1847	10	7	41
Total		2697	863	24

Sources: INA TIPP27/3/8 Account book of Roscrea Loan Fund; PRO T/91/114 Loans Book of the Baltimore Fund, 1840–1847; PRO T/91/115 Loans Book of the Baltimore Loan Fund, 1846; PRO T/91/22 Elphin Loan Fund Loans Book; PRO T/91/77 Castle Hacket Loan Fund Issues Book, 1843–1846; PRO T/91/70 Loan Book of the Ballygar Co. Loan Fund; PRONI D1248/LF/3 Tandragee Estate Loan Fund Ledger; PRONI D.1248/LF/4 Tandragee Estate 'Castle' Loan Fund Account Book; Ballycastle, Third Annual Report of the Loan Fund Board: 12.

over twenty-five in Ireland according to the 1841 census, the implication is that approximately 13 per cent of all single women over twenty-five were borrowing from the loan funds at this time. To be sure, as the loan funds were weakened by the Famine and then suffered a steady decline in size, the numbers of women borrowers would have fallen.

One interesting point to draw from the data concerns the cases in which there is a repeated observation of borrowing from the same fund, with the second observation being during the Great Famine. The famine was growing steadily worse through 1846 and 1847, with repeated failures of the potato crop. Of the four funds with a repeated observation, in each case the proportion of women increases in the later period. It is interesting to speculate on the reasons for the apparent increased preference for female borrowers during the Famine: the most reasonable explanation is that women appeared to be more creditworthy during the Famine. This accords with the demographic data on famine mortality, which shows that men died and emigrated at a higher rate than women.[5]

The only pieces of extant evidence on female vs. male default rates come from the Tandragee Estate and Baltimore Loan Funds at the time of the Great Famine. At Tandragee, the bad debts as of 31 December 1850 show that of the 245 defaulters during the previous few years, forty-eight were female, a proportion of 20 per cent (PRONI, D1248/LF/5B). This is exactly the same proportion as women borrowers from the sampled period of 1846. The proportion of female defaulters in the Baltimore Loan Fund is also approximately the same as the proportion of female borrowers (PRO, T/91/114, 1840–7). It may not be useful to rely on famine default rates to establish whether women or men were, in general, better borrowers, since the Famine was not an ordinary time and starving people with no possessions must default whether they are honest or not. The descriptions of the situation of defaulting borrowers of these funds is very dismal: the account books note, after the borrowers have stopped repaying their loans, 'paupers' or in some cases 'all dead'. However, to the extent that we can draw any conclusions from this small sample during a very unusual time, the rates of male and female default appear to have been approximately the same.[6]

There is little evidence about how loans were used by women specifically. The Baltimore Loan Fund lists occupations, stated purpose of borrowing, and amount lent for the seventeen female borrowers in January and May 1842, summarized in Table 5.3.

Recognizing that this is a rather small sample, the impression given is that women used their loans for a variety of purposes. One might have expected that most of the loans would be for spinning or weaving, but that does not appear to have been the case. Rather, the records reflect the wide range of activities in which ordinary Irish women were involved. The table also shows the range of occupations that women held, which is comparable to the range of occupations undertaken by men.

Some of the stories told about borrowers in the reports of the individual loan funds to the Board testify to the utility of the loans made. For example, in an inspection of the Moate Loan Fund, the Secretary of the Loan Fund Board interviewed all the borrowers who came in to repay their instalments. He recorded summaries of the histories told him, including the following:

Mary Brenan, widow and farmer, borrows £5, buys pigs and lambs; 2 pigs at 30s., and four lambs at 10s. Her ground would be idle without the stock, and has no means but the Loan of stocking it (*Fourth Annual Report of the Central Loan Fund Board*, Appendix: 32).

Table 5.3 Occupation, Stated Purpose of Loan, and Amount: Baltimore Loan Fund Loans to Female Borrowers in January 1842

Occupation	Purpose	Amount (£)
Widow	Thatch	1
Dealer	Dealing	3
Spinner	Flax	1
Farmer	Timber for house	1
Farmer	Rent	1.5
Fisherwoman	Rent	1
Labourer	Spillars*	0.5
Farmer	Cow	3.5
Sailor's Wife	Potatoes	1
Carter's Wife	Cart	3
Dealer	Dealing	1
Widow	Potatoes	1
Dealer	Dealing	1
Labourer	Potatoes	1
Fisherwoman	Potatoes	0.5
Farmer	Nets	1

Source: PRO T/91/114 Loans Book of the Baltimore Fund, 1840–7.

* Trawl lines for fishing.

The Clones Loan Fund report to the Board recounted:

> A widow holding two acres of land, and having three children to support, incapable of affording her the slightest assistance, was accommodated with the Loan of £5; she bought a cow, and readily paid the 5s. a week from the proceeds of her milk and butter. From this cow she has reared two calves, one of which is now an excellent milch cow, the other just ready for the butcher. A week or two since she sold her first purchase for £9; and states that but for the assistance of the Society, she should have been a beggar (*Fourth Annual Report of the Central Loan Fund Board*, Appendix: 33).

The many accounts of how women were able to put money to good use suggests that they were in the same position as borrowers as men: they had human capital and perhaps even owned some land, and could increase the return on these assets considerably by augmenting them with physical capital – livestock or fishing nets or stock for dealing.

It is instructive to compare this evidence on the proportion of female borrowers at loan funds with the proportion of female borrowers in other institutions. Although data on individual borrowers from the Irish banks is lacking, the nature of their business would have precluded widespread lending to women. Pawnshops, on the other hand, would probably have been used extensively by women, and especially by married women, given the difficulty married women faced in providing security for loans. However, as was noted above, pawnshops rarely lent more than one pound. In France, Hoffman, Postel-Vinay, and Rosenthal (1992) show women constituted just 8 per cent of borrowers in their data set of credit contracts signed between 1690 and 1840. In Germany, the Schulze-Delitzsch, Raffeisen, and Haas credit cooperatives, with over two million members, were the principal small-scale credit institutions, and made millions of loans annually to poor and middle-class Germans in the period between 1850 and 1914. However, membership was restricted to men, and, though there might have been some borrowing on behalf of women, it could only be through a man.[7] In Italian credit cooperatives, or *casse rurali*, on the other hand, there is anecdotal evidence that women borrowed, but no statistics on what proportion of borrowers they constituted. In the antebellum United States, female borrowers appear to have been very rare, with extant records suggesting that only a tiny fraction, less than 1 per cent, of all borrowers from banks were women.[8] In the Canadian mortgage market in the period 1795 to 1850, Redish (1998) finds that 8 per cent of borrowers were women.

Thus the loan funds are a significant outlier in terms of the fraction of their clientele made up of women. It is not immediately apparent why they differed so much from other European and American institutions. One possibility is that their explicit focus on poverty relief made it natural for them to lend to single women, who were often among the most disadvantaged.

Women as Depositors

Women were, to be sure, involved in other aspects of the loan funds, such as depositing. For example, ten of seventeen depositors in the Baltimore Loan Fund in 1842 were women (PRO, T/91/112). At the Letterkenny Loan Fund in 1839, seventeen of forty-five depositors were women (*Second Annual Report of the Letterkenny Loan Fund Society*: 1839). Other data on the sex of depositors show similar proportions of women, who were not, of course, restricted to being single. Indeed, one witness before the 1855 Select Committee on Loan Fund Societies recalled that 'an old lady smuggled in a sum of money which she said she did not wish her husband to know she possessed' (*Annual Report of the Central Loan Fund Board*, PP, UK, 1855: 52). Data on the sex of depositors across the loan funds is unavailable, but in 1891, out of £113,401 in deposits, women owned £15,314, or 13.5 per cent. Since women tended to make smaller deposits than men, the proportion of female depositors was probably somewhat higher than this. The rates of female participation as depositors may reflect several characteristics of the loan funds. First, as 'charitable' institutions, the loan funds may have attracted deposits from middle-class women on whom the burden of charity rested most heavily. Second, as many women had only small resources, the loan funds may have attracted their deposits, since they were often located in many small towns far from banks. The costs of getting to the bank could be high if it involved a trip of twenty or thirty miles, and a small deposit would hardly justify such an expense.

Women as Founders and Managers

Women were also important in establishing and managing loan funds, again perhaps because charity was often the domain of women. Indeed, women were involved in the earliest loan funds. For example, the Derry Sermon Charity had operated from the 1770s making small loans to the poor. In the years 1809–1830 it made 12,600 small loans. It was founded in the 1770s by the ladies of the Pery family, who 'attended to it most closely and assiduously, and it prospered' (*Report from the Select Committee on the State of the Poor in Ireland*, PP, VII.1.,1830: Q. 1964). As the loan fund system grew, many women were involved as managers and committee members, which stemmed naturally from their position as depositors. For example, at the Letterkenny Loan Fund, seven of seventeen committee members were women (*Second Annual Report of the Letterkenny Loan Fund Society*, 1839). In the O'Brien's Bridge Association for Bettering the Condition of the Poor in the Adjoining Districts of Tipperary, Limerick and Clare, which operated a loan fund, all committee members including the manager were women (INA, Clare ID-41-3).

Many funds also received donations from women. Women made some of the earliest and most substantial donations to the loan fund supported by the Dublin Musical Society, including a legacy of £1,358 to the fund in 1766 (*State of the Charitable Loan for the Relief of the Poor . . .*, 1769). For example, in its first year the Sandymount Loan Fund received donations from forty-one different persons, of whom ten were women. It also received, like many loan funds, a donation of £20 from the 'British and Irish Ladies' Society, London' (*First Report . . . of the Sandymount Loan-Fund . . .*, 1832). The Letterkenny Loan Fund received a grant of £57 from the Letterkenny Ladies' Association.

The donations from Ladies' Societies appear to have been matched with donations to Ladies' Societies. For example, the Ladies' Society of Tyrrell's Pass, Co. Westmeath, was 'worked through the loan office' and assisted in 1840 '417 female presents, heads of families' (*Third Annual Report of the Central Loan Fund Board,* 1841: 23). The Moate Loan Fund donated some of its profits to help establish the Moate Ladies' Charitable Association, which employed forty poor females full-time (*Fourth Annual Report of the Central Loan Fund Board,* 1842: 83). Other funds made donations to widows and other impoverished women as part of their charitable activities (T/91/90, PRO). There is not, however, any evidence that loan funds were similarly involved in charitable activities specific to men, and most of the charitable donations made by loan funds were to non-gender-specific institutions such as schools and hospitals.

Conclusion

The Irish Loan Funds were the most important financial institution in Ireland for poor women in the 1840s and 1850s. They made about one-quarter of their loans to women, or about 125,000 loans per year before the Famine, and approximately 13 per cent of single women would have been clients in any given year. Since married women were hindered from offering security for their loans, almost all the female borrowers were single, and the proportion of female to male borrowers was at least as high as the proportion of single women to all men in the general popul-ation. It thus appears that the loan funds did not discriminate against or for single women in their lending. The proportion of women borrowers from the loan funds is much higher than that of comparable institutions or banks in other countries or in Ireland in the nineteenth century. It seems likely that, had the laws of the time allowed married women to hold property in their own name, the loan funds would have had an even larger market of potential borrowers.

Notes

1. Hollis and Sweetman 1998a, 1998b and 2001 provide greater detail on the operations and development of the loan funds.
2. It appears that this provision of the legislation was not enforced, although most loan funds did indeed make substantial donations to local charities such as schools and hospitals.
3. See, for example, Irish National Archives (hereafter INA) Clare ID-41-3 'Rules of the Kildysart Charitable Loan'. Founded July 2 1841; INA Kilkenny County

Court Records, 1D/58/76 *c*.1824. 'Resolutions of the Castle Comer Charitable Loan'; INA Clare ID-41-3 'Rules of the Knock Charitable Loan Fund', 1835.
4. I counted borrowers and obtained details on occupation and sex for several loan funds. The dates chosen are arbitrary, though I tried to include Famine and non-Famine samples for funds for which that was possible.
5. Ó Gráda 1999: 89, shows that reported deaths from famine-related causes were 21 per cent higher for men than women.
6. National Library of Ireland (hereafter NLI). The *Second Annual Report of the Letterkenny Loan Fund Society* (1839) lists 17 women among its 56 defaulters, but there is no corresponding evidence on the proportion of women among the borrowers.
7. I thank Timothy Guinnane for informing me of this.
8. See, for example, Bodenhorn 1997. His analysis of a private bank in Virginia shows that in the course of discounting approximately 2500 bills during the years 1847–55, it lent to exactly three women.

References

Unpublished Sources

Irish National Archive
Clare ID-41-3 - Rules of the Kildysart Charitable Loan; Rules of the Knock Charitable Loan Fund; Rules of the O'Brian Bridge Association for Bettering the Poor in the Adjoining Districts of Tipperary, Limerick and Clare.
TIPP 27/1/1 – Correspondence of Roscrea Loan Fund.
TIPP 27/4/5 – Weekly Loans Particularized List of Roscrea Loan Fund.
1D/58/76 – Kilkenny County Court Records. 'Resolutions of the Castle Comer Charitable Loan'.

Public Record Office (PRO)
T/91/90 – Minute Book, Clifden Loan Fund.
T/91/109 – Promissory Notes for the Baltimore Loan Fund.
T/91/112 – Account Book of the Baltimore Loan Fund.
T/91/114 – Loans Book of the Baltimore Fund.
T/91/123 – Loans Book of the Castletownsend Loan Fund.

Public Record Office of Northern Ireland
D1248/LF/5A – Tandragee Estate Loan Fund List of Applicants.
D1238/LF/5B – Tandragee Estate Loan Fund List of Arrears.

Published Sources
Annual Report of the Loan Fund (1841–1847, 1855), *Annual Report of the Central Loan Fund Board*. Parliamentary Papers, London.
Bodenhorn, H. (1997), 'Private Banking in Antebellum Virginia: Thomas Branch & Sons of Petersburg', *Business History Review*, 71(4): 513–42.

Bourke, P. M. A. (1968), 'The Use of the Potato Crop in Pre-famine Ireland', *Journal of the Statistical and Social Inquiry Society of Ireland*, 12(6): 72–96.

First Report . . . of the Sandymount Loan Fund . . . (1832), *First Report and Statement of Accounts of the Sandymount Loan-Fund Committee*, Dublin: William Underwood.

Hoffman, P. T., G. Postel-Vinay and J.-L. Rosenthal (1992), 'Private Credit Markets in Paris, 1690–1840', *Journal of Economic History*, 52 (2): 293–306.

Hollis, A. and A. Sweetman (1998a), 'Microcredit in Prefamine Ireland', *Explorations in Economic History*, 35(4): 347–80.

—— (1998b), 'Microcredit: What Can We Learn from the Past?' *World Development*, 26(10): 1875–91.

—— (2001), 'The Life-Cycle of a Microfinance Institution: The Irish Loan Funds', *Journal of Economic Behavior and Organization*, forthcoming.

Mokyr, J. (1985), *Why Ireland Starved*, London: George Allen and Unwin.

Ó Gráda, C. (1999), *Black '47 and Beyond: The Great Irish Famine in History, Economy, and Memory*, Princeton, NJ: Princeton University Press.

Redish, A. (1998), 'The Mortgage Market in Upper Canada: Window on a Primitive Capital Market', Mimeo, Vancouver: University of British Columbia.

Report from the Select Committee on the State of the Poor in Ireland (1830), *Report from the Select Committee on the State of the Poor in Ireland.* Parliamentary Papers VII.1., London.

Second Annual Report of the Letterkenny Loan Fund Society (1839), *Second Annual Report of the Letterkenny Loan Fund Society.*

Sheridan, T. (1787), *The Life of the Rev. Dr. Jonathan Swift.* 2nd edn, London: Rivington.

State of the Charitable Loan . . . (1769), *State of the Charitable Loan for the Relief of the Poor Industrious Tradesmen of the City of Dublin,* Dublin: John Abbot Husband.

6

Stokvels and Economic Empowerment: The Case of African Women in South Africa, *c.*1930–1998

Grietjie Verhoef

Women tend to be 'invisible' in many societies. In African communities women's participation in production and relative control over the means and fruits of production is often underestimated, leading to inadequate incorporation of women into macro-economic planning (Baerends 1998: 51). In the South African context particular attention is currently given to gender equality, specifically to women as the predominant financial managers of rural households in the informal sector (South African Government RP 38/1996: 4). Women have been creative in devising survival strategies in changing environments, sometimes through socio-economic innovation. This chapter addresses the transition of African women into the urban environment and investigates how informal savings organizations have been utilized to enhance economic survival and independence. The last part of the chapter focuses on strategies for the incorporation of women into the formal financial structure.

Women in the Traditional Economies

A basic understanding of the role of a woman in the traditional economy explains the entrepreneurial and managerial abilities illustrated by her adjustment into the urban environment. In traditional African societies, monogamous and polygamous marriages existed, but women were not allowed to have more than one husband. In the traditional household, women performed important economic roles. The household evolved around the woman. Households with more than one wife would take on a compound nature. Each marriage established a 'house' of the woman concerned, which centred around one wife and her children, rather than around the husband. The so-called 'house' (Nguni = *indlu*, Sotho=*lapa*) formed the centre of social and domestic arrangements (Preston-Whyte 1974: 179–80; Hoernlé 1950: 69–70; Bozzoli 1991: 40–2). The husband had specific responsibilities towards the woman and her children, providing dwellings and a means to maintain a livelihood (Preston-Whyte 1974: 180; Baerends 1998: 52). Livestock were usually attached to the 'house' and remained 'house' property – they were inviolable and were employed to benefit the children of that 'house'. The wife and her children worked the fields and cultivated the land. The 'house' thus revolved around her, although she was subordinate to the mother of the husband and to the husband. She did not own property privately; it belonged to her 'house'. The woman's right to live in a homestead thus depended on her relationship to some man, alive or dead (Mayer 1971: 233–4; Preston-Whyte 1974: 182–3). The woman's independence increased with the birth of children, but the subordination to the mother-in-law remained until the latter's death. Thus, rights over a woman passed from her father to her husband *and* his family. These rights included control over her activities, productive and reproductive. Her traditional household duties depended on her relationship to her husband. Should her husband die, she could not inherit the land – it was communal land. The property of the 'house' and the land devolved, by right of inheritance, to the children of that house, although the widow might retain the use of her deceased husband's fields. Under the rules of quitrent, theoretically nothing could prohibit a woman from acquiring land by purchase; but it was official policy to prevent such acquisition (Sansom 1974: 160–2; Mayer 1971: 233–4).

Given the structure of the rural system, urbanization was often the only strategy open to women who sought to move towards full economic independence. Men often preferred the rural environment, but the town environment was attractive to women. There they could earn an income independently from the 'house' and dispose of that income according to need. A woman could, moreover, conceal her income from the 'house' and her husband and live an independent life. Rapid urbanization occurred during the 1920s and 1930s in South Africa, when severe droughts and the impact of the depression reduced rural self-sufficiency. Industrialization provided the opportunity to men and women from rural African and white Afrikaner communities to earn a 'cash' income or to supplement rural subsistence with wage labour (Sansom 1974: 163–7; Mayer 1971: 234; Bozzoli 1991: 4, 129). A 'dual economy' emerged, as a life strategy for women to extend earnings beyond the traditional rural sector.

Women were not ill-equipped for economic independence in urban centres. In the traditional environment they organized the 'house', thus developing managerial abilities. They also showed initiative and independence from patriarchal control by moving to towns. Urbanization did not change the legal position of women, but created an environment where life skills could be utilized towards self-empowerment. The choice exercised by African women, to live in townships and to construct and maintain a household there, indicated a change in the nature and purpose of earning an income. To unmarried women, economic activity in urban areas meant breaking free, accumulating dowry and supplementing parental support. To married women it meant supplementing 'house' income as well as constructing and supporting their own households (Bozzoli 1991: 122, 134; Mayer 1971: 93, 234; Hellman 1950: 406, 409–10). African women in towns engaged in a variety of informal-sector activities to generate cash income. This chapter will not explore all these activities, and it is important to note that such activities were inadequate to maintain families. Women pioneered *stokvels* in their urban social environment to supplement income, to meet immediate and future needs.

Stokvels as Savings Institutions

Stokvels are typical informal rotating savings and credit associations (ROSCAs), as they are known in developing countries. These are community-based self-help organizations such as savings clubs and friendly societies that have emerged in economically deprived societies where formal means towards the alleviation of financial needs were either inaccessible or did not exist (Besley, Coate and Loury 1993: 792–3; Calomiris and Rajaraman 1998: 210–11; Smets 1996: 175). The name *stokvel* was derived from the nineteenth century Eastern Cape 'stock fairs' organized by the English-speaking settler stock farmers. The Black farmers and labourers who attended these fairs engaged in a lively interaction of ideas, socializing and gambling. Gatherings, which had their origins in the stock fairs, became regular meetings of people in Black communities, no longer exclusively associated with the stock fairs (Lukhele 1990: 4; Thomas 1991: 291; Schulze 1997a: 20–1). These largely social organizations soon developed an economic component, and became a common phenomenon in urban areas as Black people entered wage labour in the South African mining and industrial sectors. By 1920, *stokvels* were operating in the Western and Eastern Cape and the Witwatersrand, as well as in Natal and the Orange Free State. Generally a *stokvel* can be defined as a type of credit organization in which a group of people enter into an agreement to contribute a fixed amount of money to a common pool on a regular basis. Depending on the rules of that particular *stokvel,* the pool or a portion thereof is withdrawn by members, either in rotation, by bidding or in time of need (Lukhele 1990: 1; *Black Enterprise* 1990: 45; *Enterprise* 1996: 47; Burman and Lembete 1996: 23–4; Moodley 1996: 362). Black people mobilized savings through *stokvels* in order to provide loans to members. Small groups met regularly at the houses of individual members. Whoever served as host would be the recipient of the 'stock fair' of that particular meeting (Thomas 1991: 293). Over time changing social and economic relations in urban areas resulted in changes in the organization and functions of *stokvels.* People's funeral, consumption and credit needs paved the way for the emergence of dynamic informal organizations, such as micro-credit organizations, savings clubs, buying aids and burial societies.

Today *stokvel* is an umbrella term for a wide range of informal financial and social organizations that developed in South African Black communities. In different regions these organizations have different names. In the early days the different types of *stokvels* were essentially similar, but today stokvels display substantial differences. Stokvels are also known as *mahodisanas,* a word derived from the Sotho *hoda,* which means 'pay', *mahodisana* referring literally to the act 'to make pay back to each other' (Kuper and Kaplan 1944: 179). References to *stokvels* are sometimes corrupted into names such as *estokini* or *stokies.* In the Western Cape, *stokvels* are called *umgalelos,* which means 'to pour'. These groups had a strong religious inclination, commencing meetings with prayer. The more general term for *stokvels* in the Western Cape currently is *gooi-goois,* which is derived from the Afrikaans word *oorgooi* (to throw over), which, in the context of *stokvels,* means to lump money together (Thomas 1991: 291–2; Schulze 1997a: 21). In the Eastern Cape, speakers often refer to *amafella,* which refers to a number of *stokvel* groups (Franks and Shane 1989: 111–12; Lukhele 1990: 21). Amongst Sotho-speaking Africans in the Transvaal, *stokvels* are called *mogodisô,* from the Sotho word *gogodisô,* which means 'to grow' (Schulze 1997a: 21; Burman and Lembete 1996: 23). In Natal, informal rotating savings and credit associations are also found in the Indian community. The Hindi-speaking Indians refer to *chita* and the Tamil-speaking Indians speak of *chitu,* and these are similar to informal savings organizations in India (Ardener 1964: 207; Timbery and Aiyar 1984: 51; Thomas 1991: 292). *Stokvels* is used as an umbrella term that encompasses all these different types of savings and credit organizations.

The savings propensity has always been high in the Black communities (Mayer 1971: 249). Initially, savings took the form of hoarded cash. But the security risk of such a strategy, as well as the desire for social interaction, gave rise to the ROSCA type of savings through *stokvels*. Women were responsible for establishing *stokvels* on a regular basis in the urban environment and for integrating the practice into modern African society. Women met and drank tea together. As members of the *stokvel* they would also contribute a regularly agreed upon amount, which was allocated to the host member. These *stokvel* meetings were described as 'Christian tea parties' (*Black Enterprise* 1990: 45; Lukhele 1990: 6–7). In other cases *stokvel* gatherings were exclusively geared towards selling home-brewed African beer (Hellman 1950: 411). Although traditional African beer played an important role in *stokvels* from the beginning, it has never been the exclusive purpose of the gathering. *Stokvels* performed an important function in both generating and supplementing income, not only through the sale of beer, but also through the mobilization of savings, providing women as well as men with income they could dispose of independently.

Four categories of *stokvels* emerged in South African society:

1. *Savings clubs*. These consist of a relatively small membership meeting at regular intervals and making regular fixed contributions. The total contribution to a meeting can be paid out to the host after the meeting or is saved in a savings account at the Post Office or a bank. The latter approach is a more recent development and was not the practice initially (Lukhele 1990: 20; Kuper and Kaplan 1944: 179; Schulze 1997d: 105). Members receive the pool on rotation basis. The *gooi-goois*, *mahodisanas*, *umgalelos* and *mogodisôs* are all examples of savings club *stokvels*, characterized by regularity of meeting, compulsory contributions and rotation of benefit to members (Cross 1987: 87; Burman and Lembete 1996: 25; Moodley 1996: 361). Punctuality of attendance is non-negotiable, and only well-known and trusted friends, family or neighbours of long standing are invited to become members. It has been found that people joined more than one *stokvel* simultaneously.

2. *Investment clubs/syndicates*. These *stokvels* resemble cooperative societies. They do not pay out the total pool to members at the end of meetings. It is saved with a specific common goal of carrying out capital projects, purchasing an expensive large commodity in future, or investing in a business venture, equity or property (Franks and Shane 1989: 110; Thomas 1991: 277–99; Schulze 1997c: 79). These *stokvels* are also known as accumulating savings and credit associations, since the accumulated fund is often utilized for lending to members and non-members (Smets 1996: 179–80; Burman and Lembete 1996: 36–7).

These *stokvels* usually dissolve after loans have been repaid, and capital plus interest is divided amongst members (Lukhele 1990: 20–1). Capital mobilized via investment *stokvels* can be seen as 'seed capital', which is often supplemented by bank loans for larger investments, such as buying vehicles or property. The growth in affluence amongst urban Black people facilitated the emergence of investment *stokvels*, where regular contributions are relatively high. These investment *stokvels* have become increasingly popular with young upper income Black people. These *stokvels* resemble the Taiwanese *hui* ROSCAs, where participation by professional and technical workers, especially in the public sector, is above average. Participation in ROSCAs in Taiwan also increases as income brackets move upwards (Levenson and Besley 1996: 53–4). Investment *stokvels* move beyond the savings scheme towards investment in capital goods, property and financial instruments (*Sowetan* 1991; Schulze 1997a: 26).

3. *High-budget stokvels.* These associations consist of 100 members or more, of high social standing and credibility in the community. Members require high monthly contributions of between R200 and R2,000. Pay-outs vary between R7,000 and R15,000 per month. Regular pay-outs are not made on a rotational basis, but depend on the allocation of pay-out dates by the 'board'. The 'board' is the highest decision-making body in a high-budget *stokvel*. It consists of ten to twenty founder members, and has an elevated status. The board determines pay-outs, based on the creditworthiness or personal 'use' of the recipient to members of the 'board' (Schulze 1997a: 26; Burman and Lembete 1996: 25; Thomas 1991: 288–300). A definite opportunity for corruption and the misuse of power exists in this category of *stokvels,* but profitability is high. Interest rates on loans are also high. Pay-outs are always made during expensive parties, hosted by the recipient, who charges an entrance fee to defray expenses.

4. *Burial societies.* These are the most significant *stokvels* and women are exceptionally prominent here. Burial societies, or *makgotlas*, evolved from the African custom of bringing gifts of food and drink to the family of the deceased at a funeral. In traditional societies, the best ox was slaughtered for its skin to wrap the body and its meat to feed the funeral guests, because the deceased had to be buried in the most dignified manner possible (*Black Enterprise* 1989a: 54, 1989b: 12; Kuper and Kaplan 1944: 185; Bähre 1995: 26–8). Exceptional value is attached to being buried where one's forefathers were buried; but urbanization made this practice more expensive. *Stokvels* were formed to assist members with increasing funeral costs. Burial societies

ensured that the traditional practice of a dignified funeral was not eroded by the social and economic changes brought about by urbanization and industrialization. Burial societies generally consist of small groups of between five and twelve people, although in rare cases membership can reach as high as eighty people. Two types of burial societies have developed. The first has no written agreement or constitution, but functions on trust and loyalty. Members pay a fixed amount upon the death of a member or anyone in his immediate family. The total amount contributed is paid to the family of the deceased. This type of funeral provision does not involve regular savings or deposits in bank accounts (Schulze 1997c: 79–80; Bähre 1995: 24; Lukhele 1990: 17). The second type represents a more formal organization, with a written agreement, or constitution, stipulating the rules of the society. At regular meetings members contribute an agreed amount. These contributions are kept in bank accounts or, currently, invested in endowment policies with insurance companies (Schulze 1997a: 29; Kuper and Kaplan 1944: 185; Bähre 1995: 24).

Burial societies started in the Orange Free State in the 1930s, and were formed on the basis of tribal or ethnic loyalty; but this is no longer exclusively the case. Members often wear a distinctive uniform or badge and name their societies to identify a common heritage, such as the Great North Burial Society, which is a society of North Sothos of *Lebowa,* or the *Bopanang Bakgotla*, which is a society for *Batswana* people from the Rustenburg area (Lukhele 1990: 18). Membership is not restricted to one burial society alone. The high costs of funerals – between R250 and R20,000 (DRUM 1995; *Tribute* 1995) – have, in practice, resulted in multiple membership to ensure sufficient coverage on death. Burial societies' insurance policies have been taken out with burial society funds. In these matters, insurance and burial societies, women were conversant, since in the traditional society those matters were regarded as the 'affairs of women' (Kuper and Kaplan 1944: 185). In urban areas women were the conscientious savers, for funerals amongst other things. The woman paid insurance premiums and *stokvel*/burial society contributions from her own earnings (Mayer 1971: 248–9).

Stokvels: ROSCAs for African Communities

Stokvels closely resemble the international ROSCA phenomenon. *Stokvels* are formed on the basis of voluntary association of mutually trusted parties. The regular cash contributions are non-negotiable, and allocation of the lump sum can be in part, in total, on rotational basis or by bidding, according to prior mutual agreement. *Stokvels* have become savings mechanisms to meet life-cycle needs, and non-compliance with mutually agreed arrangements is harshly punished. Default control is exercised through social collateral and the demand for credit. These are general characteristics of ROSCAs, which also apply to the South African *stokvels* (Besley, Coate and Loury 1993: 792–4, 1994: 701–2; Ardener 1964: 201–2; World Bank 1989: 112–13; Moore and Schoombee 1995: 350–1; Loots 1991: 100; Memani 1996: 4).

The reasons for Black South Africans' participation in *stokvels* closely correlate with the experience in developing countries. People with low and irregular income find it difficult to establish creditworthiness and thus access to credit. Therefore they participate in ROSCAs as a mechanism of mobilizing savings that would otherwise lie idle under autarkic saving, to take advantage of the gains of inter-temporal trade (Besley *et al.* 1994: 702; Besley 1995: 2126, 2129; Srinivas and Higuchi 1996: 207–8; Smets 1996: 178–9; Ardener and Burman 1996: 4–5, 7–10). *Stokvels* were formed to augment meagre incomes and relieve poverty and, as such, are typical savings mechanisms aiming at the gains of inter-temporal trade. They have also developed into guarantees of access to credit (Cross 1987: 88–90; Dubb 1974: 466–7; Franks and Shane 1989: 110–12; Moore and Schoombee 1995: 350; Smets 1996: 178).

Stokvels emerged as savings organizations, first to supplement limited or no income in urban areas and later to mobilize income towards more substantial purchases or investments. In the traditional sector, women could not own property, but in urban areas they could, and *stokvel* activities were directed at the mobilization of savings to provide shelter (Mayer 1971: 248–9; Dubb 1974: 446). *Stokvels* also played a supportive role when Black people entered the cash economies of the towns. Women could make ends meet by pooling savings and selling beer at *stokvel* parties.

An important aspect of *stokvel* mutual support was moral support, resembling the close-knit tribal support structures in rural areas. *Stokvels* generated a strong sense of solidarity amongst members, taking on the functions of a provident society providing support to members in trouble or in need, as well as their families. Thus, for example, *stokvels* provided a safety net for families of women arrested (Hellman 1950: 411; Burman and Lembete 1996: 27, 39, 40; Thomas 1991: 292; *Black Enterprise* 1988a: 31, 1990: 45). Although African women traditionally brewed for their husbands, in urban areas women brewed beer to supplement cash income. Police often arrested women for not having licences to sell liquor, as required by the Liquor Act. When women were in jail, *stokvels* provided moral and material assistance to the families affected (Lukhele 1990: 7–13; Schulze 1997a: 23; Tager 1994). Furthermore, *stokvels* acted as an agent towards bridging tribal and ethnic divisions amongst Africans in urban areas and, as such, performed economic and social functions irrespective of traditional differences (Hellman 1950: 431).

On quite another level, *stokvels* transcended subsistence needs to facilitate purchases of durable commodities, or bulk buying, to improve living standards. *Stokvels* correlate with the Besley thesis that ROSCAs are primarily used to save up for the purchase of indivisible durable goods (Besley *et al.* 1993). The accumulated *stokvel* savings enabled members to buy durable consumer goods or to purchase bulk goods with cash, whereby discounts could be negotiated. 'One can afford things that one normally cannot afford', one *stokvel* member remarked (Franks and Shane 1989: 111; Moodley 1996: 363–4; Thomas 1991: 296; *Black Enterprise* 1988a: 22). There are examples of *stokvel* savings used to buy refrigerators, television sets, minibus vehicles used for taxi transport, etc. Accumulated savings are also used for special future events, such as to finance weddings or Christmas parties (Bähre 1995: 23); and recently, housing *stokvels* have gained in prominence following rapid urbanization during the 1990s.

Overall, *stokvels* played an important role as credit providers. Black people's access to credit had been compromised for different reasons, as, for example, a low and irregular income stream and a lack of collateral in the form of fixed property. Township dwellings were inappropriate as security to financial institutions and, until 1994, Blacks were prohibited from owning fixed property outside townships. Furthermore, as a rule, few Black people maintained bank accounts or savings accounts at the Post Office or building societies (Kuper and Kaplan 1944: 185). The majority of Black people were unfamiliar with Western banking procedures and requirements and the whole concept of banking. Consequently, they were also unfamiliar to the bank officials. Banks traditionally regarded lending to Black people as placing their fiduciary responsibility at risk. Moreover, the relatively small loans Blacks wanted were deemed too small for the banks. Bankers also considered the cost of administering micro-loans too high and unprofitable, given the lack of security. To illiterate Black people, banks were intimidating, and they sought other alternatives. *Stokvels* or *mahodisanas* offered them a more congenial and better-understood form of savings than Western-style banks (Tager 1994: 6; Moore and Schoombee 1995: 347; Moodley 1996: 363; Thomas 1991:

292, 301). As opposed to banks, *stokvels* provided security for a personal line of credit, amongst trusted friends. Non-default on loan repayments and on regular contributions would ensure future credit. It was observed that 'being too poor to borrow can be worse than net indebtedness'. Women would borrow, and therefore go into debt, in order to avoid default on *stokvel* commitments (Cross 1987:88).

Stokvels have thus emerged as 'hidden banks' or people's banks, generating savings for different purposes. *Stokvels* provided guaranteed access to credit (Preston-Whyte and Nene 1991: 240). Borrowing from a *stokvel* removed the impersonal and intimidating experience of applying for bank credit. The use of *stokvel* credit feeds back into savings: borrowing means repaying and wanting to borrow follows from previous savings discipline. Defaults on repayments are virtually non-existent, owing to the sanction of the loss of access to future credit. Evidence exists of women in informal business activities, like selling produce, or hand-made baskets, contributing a fixed amount from their earnings every week to a *stokvel*. Each woman took turns receiving the pool, but one woman initiated daily savings into their 'bank' to set some money aside for communal use. The daily savings were recorded in writing, and at the end of the week each woman got back in a lump sum what they had put in, minus a small amount for the 'kitty'. The common pool was saved for future use: for example, to improve the informal stalls, or for the acquisition of their own business property or perhaps their own transport. *Stokvels* perform a vital function as guaranteed providers of credit to members (Thomas 1991: 303; Cross 1987: 89; Kuper and Kaplan 1944: 183). The secured access to *stokvel* credit has enabled women to start their own informal businesses and generate collective funds to promote their common interests (Burman and Lembete 1996: 37–8; Mayer 1971: 250). This was undisputedly the case during the early years of African urbanization. It is still the case in rapidly mushrooming informal settlements around metropolitan centres in South Africa, as well as in more affluent Black urban townships. To women in informal settlements and rural areas, access to small unsecured loans, in most cases via *stokvels,* is the only way to increase their income to improve their family's welfare significantly (South African Government Printer RP 38/1996: 51; Höck 1996:1). The cost of this form of credit may not be the cheapest, but cost is not the most important consideration – access to credit is. Small loans can be obtained from *stokvels* at various interest rates: some charge 20 per cent monthly (Lukhele 1990: 22, 36), others between 50 per cent and 100 per cent per week (Thomas 1991: 302). Interest rates of between 25 per cent and 80 per cent have been recorded (Cross 1987: 90). Acceptance of the relatively high cost of informal lending highlights the vital insurance function of *stokvels* in the Black community.

Although *stokvels* have a basic monetary value to Black people, an equally important consideration for the formation of *stokvels* has been the desire for social interaction, moral support and leisure. Parties went hand in hand with meetings – be they Christian tea parties, parties serving traditional beer or parties consuming Western alcoholic beverages. A whole sub-culture developed around *stokvels*: lavish parties, flamboyant names, rhythmic music and sometimes violent criminal behaviour (Burnett 1996: 20–4; Thomas 1991: 302; Lukhele 1990: 7–15). The importance of these parties lay in their income-generating functions. Non-members attending such events paid an entrance fee, and food and drink were for sale at inflated prices, all accruing to the host. However, unacceptably noisy, violent, criminal or immoral behaviour that surfaced contributed to a rejection of *stokvels* by certain members of the Black community (Burnett 1996: 21–4: Burman and Lembete 1996: 35; Bozzoli 1991: 142–5; Lukhele 1990: 9). *Stokvels* have nevertheless remained a powerful informal financial network for the mobilization and allocation of informal savings.

Stokvels in the Modern Economy

The growth of the South African economy generated a rising demand for access to finance by people with limited collateral to offer as security for loans. This development contributed to a dramatic growth in the retail lending industry, of which *stokvels* make up the oldest and best-established associations. Since they operate in the informal sector, statistics on size and performance are not prolific. It is clear, however, that *stokvels* are the biggest generator of informal funds (*Financial Mail* 1998: 2–3). Moreover, *stokvel* activities have a multiplier effect in the economy by keeping money moving in the informal sector.

Markinor did the first comprehensive market research into the size of the *stokvel* industry in 1989. The following information was found:

- ± 24,000 *stokvels* existed in metropolitan areas.
- monthly contributions amounted to a turnover of ± R52 million.
- 41 per cent of *stokvels* were savings clubs, 29 per cent were burial societies and the rest were a mixture of other *stokvel* varieties.
- burial societies contributed 42 per cent of the monthly turnover.
- ± 25 per cent of the adult Black population belonged to a *stokvel* or communal buying group.
- 60 per cent of *stokvel* members were female (Lukhele 1990: 2–3).

These statistics did not reflect *stokvels* in rural areas, where more than 50 per cent of the Black population lived. Other sources have estimated 800,000 active *stokvels* countrywide (Schulze 1997a: 23; Cross 1987: 88–90). Another survey in November 1995 estimated that 29 per cent of the adult Black population participated in *stokvels* and that burial societies contributed 66 per cent towards total turnover. More than 33 per cent of the urban Black population over the age of sixteen was estimated to participate in *stokvels*. The number of people involved in *stokvels* was approximately eight million (Mills 1993). In 1996, it was estimated that the monthly cash flow through *stokvels* was R200 million, which represented roughly a 74 per cent growth in turnover between 1989 and 1996 (*Black Enterprise* 1990: 45; Burman and Lembete 1996: 24; Japp 1996: 3).

Market research undertaken by the Integrated Marketing Information Group in 1996 and 1998 provides a more comprehensive picture. This Group compiled a consumer scope, reflecting a Living Standards Measure (LSM), based on living standards, income levels, employment and *stokvel* (referring to the umbrella term) participation. The LSM is an indicator compiled from twenty-two candidate factors, including, amongst others, household size, ownership of durables, level of education, work status, occupation, household facilities and shopping habits. The 1996 survey is not identical to the 1998 survey, but provides useful categories for comparison.

Income of people in LSM1 to LSM3 varied from nothing to a maximum of R1,500 per month; those in LSM3 and LSM4 up to a maximum of R3,900; LSM5 up to a maximum of R5,900; LSM6 up to R8,000 and LSM7 and LSM8 more than R8,000 per month. The important observation is the significant presence of people with relatively low incomes (LSM1–LSM3) in *stokvels* and burial societies: 15 per cent of LSM1 belonged to *stokvels* and 0.2 per cent to burial societies, versus 24 per cent and 5 per cent respectively in the case of LSM3. Participation in these informal associations rose to 18 per cent and 9 per cent respectively in the case of LSM4, and 26 per cent and 13 per cent respectively in the case of LSM5. From LSM6 to LSM8 participation in *stokvels* declined, but in burial societies increased. The 1996 statistics use *stokvels* as the collective term, referring to all the types of savings clubs, including burial societies. The figures in column seven do not refer to the traditional African burial society membership, but to participation in any funeral arrangements that reflect funeral insurance. The strong *stokvel* participation in LSM5 (26 per cent), where 81 per cent of the population is Black, shows that *stokvel* participation is by no means restricted to poor people in rural areas. The

Table 6.1 Living Standards Measure, 1996

	1	2	3	4	5	6	7	8	9
LSM1	99.8	4358	20	43/57	–	19	0.2	15	3
LSM2	98	2875	13	41/59	–	33	1.3	14	10
LSM3	93	2993	12	52/48	–	40	5	24	23
LSM4	89	3343	13	53/47	–	44	9	18	36
LSM5	81	3314	14	51/49	–	41	13	26	44
LSM6	55	3247	13	48/52	–	46	21	14	64
LSM7	12	2987	11	51/49	–	55	26	3	93
LSM8	2	1423	5	41/59	–	62	26	3	97

Source: Integrated Marketing Information, *Consumer Scope*, 1996.

Categories: 1 = % Blacks; 2 = Number of Adults (16+ years), in 1,000s; 3 = % of total population; 4 = % men: % women; 5 = % no personal income (not recorded in 1996); 6 = % working (full-time & part-time); 7 = % members of burial societies or other funeral arrangements; 8 = % members of *stokvels* (collective term); 9 = % using any bank account.

drop to 14 per cent stokvel participation in LSM6 can be explained by the drastic decline in Black people as a portion of that LSM population.

It is also important to note that participation in *stokvels* is relatively high despite high levels of unemployment; in LSM1 only 19 per cent of the population engaged in waged work, but 15 per cent were still involved in *stokvels* of some sort. In LSM3, 24 per cent *stokvel* participation, plus 5 per cent burial society participation was noted, despite the fact that only 40 per cent of the population was engaged in formal employment; this ratio increased to 26 per cent *stokvel* and 13 per cent burial society participation in LSM5, despite only 41 per cent employment. Up to LSM5, participation in informal financial associations increased simultaneously with increased use of formal banking facilities.

People in LSM1 to LSM3 earn between nothing and R2,000 per month, people in LSM4 between R200 and R3,000, LSM5 and LSM6 between R500 and R4,000, LSM7 and LSM8 between R2,000 and R20,000 per month. The significant aspect of this study is that in 1998 about 25 per cent of people earning less than R2,000 per month belonged to burial societies and between 1 and 5 per cent to *stokvels* as well. These statistics do not show whether people belong to more than one society, but it is general knowledge that that is the case. As income rises, between 27 per cent and 37 per cent of LSM4 and LSM6's representatives belong to burial societies and between 6 and 7 per cent additionally to *stokvels*. Even amongst high-income earners, membership in burial societies and *stokvels*

Table 6.2   Living Standards Measure, 1998

	1	2	3	4	5	6	7	8	9
LSM1	99.7	2,808	13	39/61	32	22	21	1	0
LSM2	97	2,621	11	45/55	23	29	25	4	16
LSM3	96.3	3,208	13	44/56	25	40	25	5	18
LSM4	93	3,147	12	51/49	21	38	27	7	30
LSM5	88	3,831	15	51/49	19	41	33	4	34
LSM6	77	3,572	13	52/48	24	41	37	6	44
LSM7	35	3,274	11	49/51	17	54	31	3	74
LSM8	7	3,259	11	50/50	11	63.4	24	1	94

Source: Integrated Marketing Information, *Consumer Scope,* 1998.

Categories: 1 = % of Blacks; 2 = Number of Adults (16+ years), in 1,000s; 3 = % of population; 4 = % men: % women; 5 = % no personal income; 6 = % working (full-time & part-time); 7 = % members of burial society; 8 = % members of *stokvels* (collective term); 9 = % using any bank account.

remains at very much the same level as with lower income groups. Calculating column seven as a percentage of the number of adults in 1998, approximately 5.2 million people belonged to burial societies. The membership of *stokvels* is approximately 721,593, totalling about 5.9 million people in *stokvels*. Out of a total South African population of 25.8 million, 23.1 per cent belong to *stokvels,* and over 31 per cent out of a total of 18.9 million Black people belong to *stokvels*. It is problematic to do the same calculation for Table 6.1, owing to the inclusion of other funeral arrangements in the statistics reflected in column 7. Should the calculation nevertheless be made, ± 6.3 million people participated in *stokvels* in 1996. Providing for the inclusion of non-burial society funeral arrangements in the 1996 statistics, there is no dramatic declining trend observable in *stokvel* participation in South Africa in recent years. It remains important to note that there is a high correlation between people with no personal income in 1998 and *stokvel* participation. This reflects the importance of *stokvels* in Black communities. Even where Blacks make up only 35 per cent of LSM7, more than 34 per cent of the people belong to *stokvels*. The 1998 statistics underline the significance of *stokvels* in South Africa. In 1990, only 5 per cent of formal bank credit and hire purchase advances went to Blacks, whereas their income accounted for 36 per cent of total income and they made up 70 per cent of the total population (Lipschitz, Jaeger, Gordon, Doyled and Farah 1995: 129). This explains why approximately 40 per cent of the total credit advanced to

Blacks was provided by *stokvels* (du Plessis 1998: 39). The 1998 Consumer Scope shows that a larger percentage of the population belonged to *stokvels* than those using bank accounts. Only on the LSM7 and LSM8 levels did the use of bank accounts exceed the participation in *stokvels*. For the Black community *stokvels* still perform a vital financial intermediary role, despite the existence of a sophisticated financial structure. For Black women especially, the socio-cultural dimension of *stokvels* provides security and support no bank can provide.

Women and Stokvels in the Mainstream Economy

African women have adapted remarkably rapidly and successfully to urbanization and altered kinship relations. Baerends expressed concern about women's continuing responsibilities for the maintenance of their children without adequate means. Despite women's inferior legal position, they had managed substantial social and economic functions in traditional economies. In urban areas women continued to provide for the subsistence needs of their families despite having inadequate access to the means of production. Women remain largely outside the commercial sector and its benefits. Women need more and better opportunities that would enable them to cope independently (Baerends 1998: 74–6; Myburgh 1974: 303–4). This chapter illustrates how women have used *stokvels* to manipulate material and social factors at their disposal to sustain their managerial functions and achieve increased economic independence. The 1998 statistics prove substantial *stokvel* activities in all socio-economic strata, especially where Black people are prominent. Women's *stokvel* activities empowered them, both in rural and urban areas, by providing funds to start small informal businesses or simply to supplement limited earnings. The persistence of *stokvels* illustrates the transfer of women's traditional managerial skills and savings propensity into the non-traditional economic sector (South African Government Printer RP 108/1996: 25; Burman and Lembete 1996: 43; Mayer 1971: 248–9).

The volume of *stokvel* funds made them a target market for savings-strapped modern financial institutions. The growth of the *stokvel* industry prompted the establishment of an umbrella body in 1988, the National Stokvel Association of South Africa (NASASA).[1] NASASA aimed to mobilize *stokvel* savings, directing these towards Black economic empowerment and penetration into the mainstream economy. It also provides education and training to members to improve operational efficiency and consolidate *stokvel* muscle to negotiate bulk consumer concessions and services from financial institutions (Lukhele 1990: 52–3; Japp 1996: 4; Black Enterprise 1988a: 22, 1988b: 30). NASASA engineered two strategies towards increased penetration of its members into the mainstream economy. At first, it co-founded the Federation of African Business and Consumer Services (FABCOS), which immediately gave *stokvel* members access to FABCOS shopping and service discounts. The second level of penetration was the negotiation of investment opportunities for *stokvels* in the formal banking sector. Several savings products were jointly developed by banks and building societies to encourage savings in formal financial institutions in return for interest earnings, privileged access to funds and low cost structures. Financial institutions hoped to tap into the vast *stokvel* savings pool, and NASASA envisioned privileged access to credit and consumer goods. Not much of these visions materialized.

The first joint venture was the Perm Club Account, launched in 1988 by the Permanent Building Society. The Club Account provided for increased earnings on rising savings balances, no minimum balance requirements, no service charges, limitless withdrawals and a savings book to enable immediate knowledge of the account status (Lukhele 1990: 5–57; *Financial Mail* 1990a: 74; *Black Enterprise* 1990: 46). A positive response to this new savings account resulted in the mobilization of more than R96 million in 44,500 accounts within two years, but there is no proof that those deposits came from *stokvels* exclusively, since other clubs and associations could likewise use the facility. Since NASASA negotiated the product and marketed it as a *stokvel* benefit, it can be assumed that the bulk of the savings were of *stokvel* origin. The Club Account though, made no provision for loans.

Similar products were developed by other financial institutions. The Natal Building Society developed the Lifesaver Plan, Standard Bank the Society Scheme and First National Bank the People's Benefit Scheme (*Financial Mail* 1990b; *Enterprise* 1995: 38–9; Lukhele 1990: 27–9). All these products targeted the vast *stokvel* savings pool, without offering easy access to loans. The People's Benefit Scheme was a complex arrangement of savings, fixed deposits and participation in unit trusts on a group basis. Profits from the unit trust investments would provide collateral for loans to individuals and groups. In case of loans to individuals, the group would provide surety (*Enterprise* 1995: 39; Maheter 1999; Lukhele 1999: 29). No specific figures can be given for the use of this product by *stokvel* members, for the same reasons as stated above, but the product is currently mothballed, owing to insufficient returns. None of the attempts towards increased access to credit, via *stokvel* savings accounts, have notably increased women's access to credit. Banking institutions are caught up in traditional Western banking perceptions of what constitutes surety for loans. *Stokvels* have proven savings records and offer that as guarantee, but banks require conventional guarantees these *stokvel* members do not always have.

A more successful link between *stokvels* and the formal sector was the design of funeral schemes or policies for burial societies by insurance companies. In 1990, NASASA negotiated a funeral insurance scheme with African Life, a subsidiary of Southern Life Assurance Company. This policy provided for the payment of a small monthly premium up to the age of sixty-five years. On death a guaranteed amount is paid to the policy holder, or his/her family. This policy provided for the member and his/her spouse and children (Lukhele 1990: 57–8). Similar funeral policies were subsequently developed to provide for the whole family of the policy-holder and for multiple spouse benefits, with additional reduced premiums for children, excluding in-laws. Some policies also provided for disability and an educational trust for children. Special provision was also made for benefits to families of stillborn babies (Lukhele 1999: 30; *DRUM* 1992). These funeral policies operate via the existing burial societies, thus maintaining the common bond and mutual trust. Regular payments are made to the burial society, which pays premiums. Without such provisions, the risk of numerous simultaneous deaths exhausting a burial society's funds could render burial societies incapable of providing assistance to members.

The disappointing access to small loans via bank savings accounts led NASASA to negotiate a *stokvel* loan scheme with the Get Ahead Foundation, a Section 21 (not for gain) company. Established in 1987, it is funded by overseas agencies and local banks, primarily to address the high unemployment levels in Black townships. Micro-loans, in terms of the *stokvel* loan scheme, are provided to Black entrepreneurs who have been in business for at least six months and who belong to a *stokvel* of at least five members. The scheme was tailored along the lines of the loan facilities provided by the Grameen Bank in Bangladesh, to improve Get Ahead's bad debt ratio. *Stokvel* savings would thus provide collateral for the loan. This scheme has been extremely successful. Since its inception more than R33 million has been disbursed to more than 50,000 clients, with an annual recovery rate of 95 per cent. The programme operates in more than twenty-three townships around the country, with more than 90 per cent of the *stokvel* borrowers being women. Women entrepreneurs in urban areas have utilized the *stokvel* infrastructure to access loan capital (*Financial Mail* 1988: 33; *Enterprise* 1996: 84–5; *Finance Week* 1995:

20). The Get Ahead concept of micro-loans based on *stokvel* allegiance has proved more successful than formal banking loans, since it maintains the communal relationship of mutual trust.

Many micro-lending organizations have embarked on micro-lending in South Africa, because of the need for unsecured micro-loans, especially in the informal sector (du Plessis 1998). Women frequently utilize micro-loans (Cross 1987: 88; Höck 1996: 1, 3), but interest rates are excessively high, because those organizations are not regulated in terms of the banking legislation. One example of this is the Women's Development Banking, also a Section 21 company. It was established in 1991 with the aim of providing poor rural women with the necessary skills and resources to become financially independent. The average interest rate on loans is 40 per cent per annum (Women's Development Banking 1998: 5). A strong awareness exists within the government and development agencies that special attention needs to be given to women in rural areas who head households and are the financial managers of those households, since they have the greatest problems in accessing finance (RP 38/1996: 4; RP 108/1996: 25; Portous 1996: 2). Unfortunately, this has not yet translated into effective mechanisms to utilize the *stokvel* infrastructure towards that end.

NASASA set out to facilitate *stokvel* members' entrance into the mainstream economy, often in Black Economic Empowerment (BEE) ventures. (BEE refers to the initiatives since the early 1990s to give Black people more direct participation in the corporate sector of the South African economy through acquisitions of controlling shareholdings in large corporations. Various strategies towards Black control over corporations were implemented.) In 1994, when Southern Life sold its subsidiary African Life to BEE partners, NASASA, in collaboration with REAL (Real African Investment Company) took up 51 per cent of the Aflife equity (Lukhele 1999: 30; *Finance Week* 1995: 20; *Enterprise* 1996: 22). NASASA established the NASASA Investment Finance Company (Pty) Ltd in 1995 as a vehicle for participation in BEE initiatives. In March 1995 REAL was listed on the Johannesburg Stock Exchange (JSE). NASASA co-funded the listing and acquired 6 per cent of the issued share capital, but subsequently sold its equity to pursue more targeted business opportunities where 'on-the-ground' benefits could be achieved for members (Lukhele 1999:30). NASASA experienced participation in growing BEE corporate entities as an indirect and diluted avenue towards tangible practical benefits to *stokvel* members. NASASA utilized its investments in BEE corporations to negotiate discounts for members on the consumer level. NASASA also prefers *stokvel* members to be the owners of equity. However, the pyramid structure from *stokvels* up to

NASASA is not satisfactory. Listing on the JSE later in 1999 was being prepared in order to place share certificates directly with *stokvel* members, which would place *stokvels* directly into the mainstream economy.

In the course of BEE, several so-called Black Women's Economic Empowerment groups have emerged. All of them have raised capital from corporate and financial institutions internationally or domestically, to set up investment companies. Proceeds from investments, like dividends, were then used towards micro-finance for women in rural and urban areas. Only one such Black women's empowerment group, Women Investment Portfolio Holdings (Wiphold), has actively involved *stokvels* in their capital raising and investment strategies. The *stokvels* were approached to invest in Wiphold. Wiphold persuaded participating *stokvels* to change their savings pattern from a twelve-month cycle, after which funds would be withdrawn, to an investment action. Savings are now invested in long-term investments via Wiphold. At the same time the *stokvel* had to be transformed into a registered company in order to create transparent legal mechanisms through which problems could be addressed. These new '*stokvel* companies' then invested in Wiphold with the aim of long-term capital growth. In June 1997 Wiphold was listed on the JSE and raised R25 million. Wiphold was established in 1994 with loan capital of R500,000. By 1998 the value of Wiphold's investment portfolio was in excess of R1 billion, with the first dividends payable early in 1999 (*Financial Mail* 1998: 46–8). Wiphold has provided an effective vehicle for women savers to become investors and make their savings grow in long-term higher-risk instruments, rather than in savings pools. Many women's church savings groups *(mahodisanas)* have participated. One member from a Baptist Church women's group, now a Wiphold share-holder, remarked: 'We cannot talk about St Matthew or Luke on an empty stomach. We must preach the gospel of economic empowerment as well. One day we will be billionaires' (ibid.).

Conclusion

Stokvels are the biggest industry in the informal sector. They are vital in Black women's survival strategies in urban and rural areas. Although not exclusively a women's phenomenon, *stokvels* were introduced to Black urban life by women. Women used them skilfully to overcome the loss of means of production when moving into the urban environment, where they maintained the responsibility for family subsistence. Women have, moreover, not lost their managerial and planning skills when urbanizing. Kinship relations changed fundamentally, leaving women to seek alternative survival strategies. *Stokvels* represent one mechanism that evolved through Black urbanization, which women manipulated to generate funds for subsistence needs. *Stokvels* developed into a network of highly diversified savings organizations to suit the needs of low-income groups and middle-income groups as well as high-income groups. *Stokvels* have emerged as such a strong intermediary in the informal financial sector that the South African Reserve Bank included them in the regulatory framework of financial institutions in 1994. They described their activities as 'savings schemes' and, as such, excluded from the Banks Act (94 of 1990). Exclusion was on two grounds – the nature of the association and the type of activities performed. The SARB stated that 'the activities of a group of persons between the members of which exists a common bond, do not fall within the meaning of "the business of a bank"' (Schulze 1997b: 159; Tager 1994: 9–10). For *stokvels* to be exempted from the Banks Act, they had to be affiliated to NASASA or any representative body approved in writing by the SARB, and subscriptions from members might not exceed R9.9 million. Should they not meet these requirements, *stokvels* have to register as commercial or community banks. The regulation of *stokvels* acknowledges their powerful informal financial intermediary role without including them in formal financial regulation.

Stokvels are key informal financial intermediaries. They have become so integral to women's lives that more serious attention should be given to the savings discipline and managerial skills conveyed by women through these structures. The inclusion of *stokvel* savings in long-term higher-risk investments cannot be pursued by all *stokvels*, since some of them are formed to serve specific day-to-day needs. This chapter calls for acknowledgement of the contribution of *stokvels* towards improving access to credit. The high interest rates of micro-loans to the poorest of poor people need to be addressed. Gender awareness in South Africa must translate into actions to enhance the status of women, especially in financial matters. The prominence of women in *stokvels* justifies the utilization of *stokvels* towards improved access to credit.

Note

1. NASASA currently estimates monthly turnover at R1.3 billion, of which roughly 30 per cent (R400,000) is savings, not rotated (Japp Interview 30/5/99).

References

Unpublished Sources

du Plessis, G. (1998), 'The Micro Lending Industry in South Africa, 1997', Report compiled for the Micro Lending Association of South Africa, Stellenbosch: University of Stellenbosch.

Höck, C. (1996), 'The South African Microfinance Industry: The State of Play, the Potential and the Pitfalls', Unpublished paper presented to the South African Reserve Bank Seminar on Informal Financing.

Japp. S. (1996), 'The Role of Stokvels and Representative Bodies in the RSA', Unpublished paper presented to the South African Reserve Bank Seminar on Informal Finance.

Loots, A. E. (1991), 'Die Belangrikheid van die Informele Sektor in die Suid-Afrikaanse Ekonomie', M.Com. dissertation, Rand Afrikaans University, Johannesburg.

Lukhele, A. K. (1999), 'Stokvels Milestone, 1988–1998', unpublished NASASA Report, Johannesburg.

Maheter, C. (1999), First National Bank, Interview with G. Verhoef, Johannesburg.

Memani, K. (1996), 'Practical Issues Regarding Informal Financing', Unpublished paper presented to South African Reserve Bank Seminar on Informal Financing.

Mills, J. (1993), 'The People's Benefit Scheme – a generic financial instrument to enhance stokvel savings and provide access to geared loans', Unpublished report for the Development Bank of Southern Africa.

Porteous, D. (1996), 'Tears for the Unbanked/Tiers for the Unbanked', Unpublished paper presented to the South African Reserve Bank Seminar on Informal Financing.

Tager, L. (1994), 'Legal Aspects of Stokvels', Unpublished paper presented to the Center for Business Law, University of the Orange Free State.

Women's Development Banking (1998), 'Annual Report', Johannesburg.

Published Sources

Books

Ardener, S. and S. Burman (1996), *Money-go-rounds: The Importance of Rotating Savings and Credit Associations for Women*, Oxford: Berg Publishers.

Bozzoli, B. (1991), *Women of Phokeng: Consciousness, Life Strategy and Migrancy in South Africa, 1900–1983*, Johannesburg: Heinemann.

Lipschitz, L., A. Jaeger, J. Gordon, P. Doyled, and A. Farah, (1995), 'South Africa, Selected Economic Issues', IMF Staff Country Report, No. 95/21.

Lukhele, A. K. (1990), *Stokvels in South Africa: Informal Saving Schemes by Blacks for the Black Community,* Johannesburg: Amagi Books.

Mayer, P. (1971), *Townsmen or Tribesmen*, Capetown: Oxford University Press.

Preston-Whyte, E., and C. Rogerson (eds) (1991), *South Africa's Informal Economy.* Cape Town: Oxford University Press.

South African Government Printer. (1996), RP 108/1996, Final Report of the Commission of Inquiry into the Provision of Rural Financial Services, Pretoria.
—— (1996), RP 38/1996, Interim Report of the Commission of Inquiry into the Provision of Rural Financial Services, Pretoria.
World Bank (1989), *World Development Report.* Washington, DC.

Articles and Essays
Ardener, S. (1964), 'The Comparative Study of Rotating Credit Associations', *Journal of the Royal Anthropological Institute,* 94: 201–9.
Baerends, E. A. (1998), 'Changing Kinship, Family and Gender Relationships in Sub-Saharan Africa', in C. Risseeuw and K. Ganesh (eds), *Negotiation and Social Space: A Gendered Analysis of Changing Kin and Security Networks in South Asia and Sub-Saharan Africa,* pp. 47–86. New Delhi: Sage Publications.
Bähre, E. (1995), 'Wij Zullen Onze Beenderen in Waardigheid Begraven', *Cahier, jaargang,* 4, no. 1: 20–9.
Besley, T. (1995), 'Savings, Credit and Insurance', in J. Behrman and T. N. Srinivasan (eds), *Handbook of Development Economics,* vol. 3A, part 9, Amsterdam: 2123–207.
Besley, T., S. Coate and G. Loury (1993), 'The Economics of Rotating Savings and Credit Associations', *American Economic Review,* 83, no. 4: 792–810.
—— (1994), 'Rotating Savings and Credit Associations, Credit Markets and Efficiency', *Review of Economic Studies,* 6: 701–19.
Burman, S. and N. Lembete (1996 [1995]), 'Building New Realities, African Women and ROSCAs in Urban South Africa', in S. Ardener and S. Burman (eds), *Money-Go-Rounds: The Importance of Rotating Savings and Credit Associations for Women,* pp. 23–47. Oxford: Berg Publishers.
Burnett, C. (1996), '"Stokvel" as Rekreasie-Aktiwiteit in "n Gedepriveerde Gemeenskap"', *South African Journal for Research in Sport Physical Education and Recreation,* 19: 17–27.
Calomiris, C. W. and I. Rajaraman (1998), 'The Role of ROSCAs: Lumpy Durables or Event Insurance?', *Journal of Development Economics,* 56: 207–16.
Cross, C. (1987), 'Informal Lending', *Indicator SA,* 4, no. 3: 87–92.
Dubb, A. R. (1974), 'The Impact of the City', in W. D. Hammond-Tooke (ed.), *The Bantu-Speaking Peoples of Southern Africa,* 2nd edn. London: Routledge & Kegan Paul.
Franks, P. and S. Shane (1989), 'Building Commerce Through Co-operatives', *Indicator SA,* .6, no. 1/2: 109–12.
Hellman, E. (1950), 'The Native in the Towns', in I. Schapera (ed.), *The Bantu-Speaking Tribes of South Africa: An Ethnological Survey,* Cape Town: Maskew Miller.
Hoernlé, W. A. (1950), 'Social Organisation', in I. Schapera (ed.), *The Bantu-Speaking Tribes of South Africa,* Cape Town: Maskew Miller.
Kuper, H., and S. Kaplan (1944), 'Voluntary Associations in an Urban Township',

African Studies, 3: 178–86.

Levenson, A. R. and T. Besley (1996), 'The Anatomy of an Informal Financial Market, ROSCA Participation in Taiwan', *Journal of Development Economics,* 51: 45–68.

Moodley, L. (1996), 'Three Stokvels in the Urban Black Township of Kwa Ndangezi, Natal', *Development Southern Africa,* 12: 361–6.

Moore, B. J., and G. A. Schoombee (1995), 'Bank Credit to the Informal Sector: Challenge and Reward', *Development Southern Africa,* 12: 347–360.

Myburgh, A. C. (1974), 'Law and Justice', in W. D. Hammond-Tooke (ed.), *The Bantu-Speaking Peoples of Southern Africa,* 2nd edn, London: Routledge & Kegan Paul.

Preston-Whyte, E. (1974), 'Kinship and Marriage', in W. D. Hammond-Tooke (ed.), *The Bantu-Speaking Peoples of Southern Africa,* 2nd edn, London: Routledge & Kegan Paul.

Preston-Whyte, E. and S. Nene (1991), 'Black Women and the Rural Informal Sector', in E. Preston-Whyte and C. Rogerson (eds), *South Africa's Informal Economy,* Cape Town: Oxford University Press.

Sansom, B. (1974), 'Traditional Economic Systems', in W. D. Hammond-Tooke (ed.), *The Bantu-Speaking Peoples of Southern Africa,* 2nd edn. London: Routledge & Kegan Paul.

Schulze, W. G. (1997a), 'The Origin and Legal Nature of the Stokvel: Part 1', *South African Mercantile Law Journal,* 9: 18–29.

—— (1997b), 'The Origin and Legal Nature of the Stokvel: Part 2', *South African Mercantile Law Journal,* 9: 153–70.

—— (1997c), 'Stokvels. Part 1; People's Insurance', *Journal of Business Law,* 4, no. 2: 78–81.

—— (1997d), 'Stokvels. Part 2; People's Banking', *Journal of Business Law,* 4, no 3: 105–8.

Smets, P. (1996), 'Community-Based Finance Systems and Their Potential for Urban Self-Help in a New South Africa', *Development Southern Africa,* 13, no. 2: 173–87.

Srinivas, H. and Y. Higuchi (1996), 'A Continuum of Informality of Credit: What Can Informal Lenders Teach Us?', *Savings and Development,* 20, no. 2: 207–21.

Thomas, E. (1991), 'Rotating Credit Associations in Cape Town', in E. Preston-Whyte and C. Rogerson (eds), *South Africa's Informal Economy,* pp. 270–304. Cape Town: Oxford University Press.

Timbery, T. A. and C. V. Aiyar (1984), 'Informal Credit Markets in India', *Economic Development and Cultural Change,* Vol. 33.

Newspapers and Magazines
Black Enterprise, vol. 14, 1988a
——, vol. 15, 1988b
——, vol. 21, 1989a
——, vol. 27, 1989b

——, vol. 28, 1990
DRUM, October 1992
——, August 1995
Enterprise, vol. 88, 1995
——, vol. 100, 1996
Financial Mail, 30 September 1988
——, 26 September 1990a
——, 26 October 1990b
——, 5 September 1998
Finance Week, 9–15 March 1995
Sowetan, 12 September 1991
Tribute, January 1995

PART III

Pioneering Projects

7

Women, Institutional Roles and Economic Opportunity

Mary Houghton

Participation by women in the NGO-led micro-credit movement has been greater than could have been predicted when a few innovative organizations began creating large-scale micro-credit institutions in the 1970s. Energy that had, in the past, been spent in encouraging political participation or on organizing more traditional small business development was now spent on delivering short term credit to the self-employed.[1] It is a remarkable fact that the tool of micro-credit – a short-term loan for working capital – was very appropriate to the needs of women, enhancing self-employment opportunities in many places. Today, fifty high-performing institutions, which report on their performance annually to a peer review process, report that, on average, 65 per cent of their clients are women (*MicroBanking Bulletin* 1999, No. 3).

Yet even in the face of this remarkable participation by women in credit programmes for the self-employed, as I began to prepare this chapter, I worried a lot about the topic I had chosen: optimism and clarity about the future roles of women. I consulted with colleagues in the women's movement who gave me papers that identified relatively modest, highly conditioned but real positive impact on women's lives (Bauling 1999). I realized that I really knew very little about the effects on the lives of women borrowers at one organization in Chicago and at three large organizations in Bangladesh – Grameen, the Bangladesh Rural Action Committee and Proshika. I know a lot more about what is unique and necessary about the organizations delivering the credit than about what is unique about the outcome for the customer.

So, I am stuck with wanting us to celebrate the reality that women have taken the development world by storm – by dint of the fact that in many places many women borrow for self-employment and repay those loans, sometimes at a scale not previously seen in either an NGO or a banking environment. I am stuck because I cannot know with any certainty much more than that about the future economic roles of women in general. I am a feminist but not a specialist on women; I am a banker but not a programme evaluator; I am from Chicago, and only visit organizations elsewhere sporadically.

But because I am a banker who has tried to help create sustainable alternative development financial institutions, I do know about the institutional side of the equation. I know how often a good idea does not fly. Maybe it is because there are 'no takers' (in other words, no demand); or management's execution is poor; or subsidy is too limited. I do like to stick to reality, to things that have happened in the real world. So I am going to focus on the most important lessons I know about what works with credit, what kinds of permanent institutions are needed for women's economic roles to increase and what else women who care about creating institutions that build assets as an approach to poverty alleviation may need to achieve as they continue along the path so promisingly begun with micro-credit.

Credit Matters

On the most fundamental level, credit matters. It matters in all societies that have a need for new business formation that is not solely dependent on affluent and well-connected entrepreneurs who do not need loans. But why does so little credit get delivered to ignored sectors even when public and private grants are made to help banks and non-profit organizations with subsidy for the effort? Let me attack the traditional mind set of the banker. The banker is plagued with three debilitating attitudes when it comes to the small businessperson, male and, even more so, female.

- **Fit my convenience**
  Conventional lenders put portfolio needs first and customer needs second.
- **Small is simple and unimportant**
  Delivering small loans to small firms is more challenging than delivering large loans to large firms.
- **Bigger is better and community development is not business**
  Traditional bankers like big loans. They are transaction-oriented and have a short-term focus more on 'doing the deal' than on building a local economy. They believe too strongly in Adam Smith's 'invisible hand'. They avert risk instead of managing it.

These behaviours cause them to rely too much on the entrepreneur's asset base for collateral and too little on business analysis.

Even though a few large banks have recently figured out how to cream good loans to small businesses with credit-scoring and targeted mass mailings, most bankers are more than happy to palm off the responsibility of economic growth onto charity-type organizations. These organizations are far less well equipped to offer credit for enterprise development. This is a fatal flaw. These organizations are usually funded by third parties and are usually not paid for by the customer or on the basis of a value-added service to the customer. They are accountable not to the customer but to a third party. And the third party does not ask hard questions about what value was delivered to the customer. As a result, they do not deliver value.

It is time for some new truisms to guide us through the maze to successful economic interventions that try to improve local communities. I have come up with a list of ten.

New Truisms

- Small business formation feeds a region's growth.
- The poor repay.
- Scale matters.
- Match multiple types of unconventional and conventional credit to business needs.
- Capital without accurate information is useless.
- Talk is cheap.
- Small loans are more challenging than big ones.
- For-profit credit and information services are more powerful than subsidized credit and information services.
- Subsidize some credit and information services.
- Privately capitalized development finance institutions can do this work.

I will describe three successful interventions that demonstrate these principles, comment briefly on the progress of two women-led institutions, and come back to these principles.

Bangladesh Rural Advancement Committee (BRAC)

The world over, there are non-profit organizations that have evolved from political to social to economic to a comprehensive institutional approach to community development. Founded in 1972, BRAC – more formally called the Bangladesh Rural Advancement Committee – is the second largest non-government credit provider in Bangladesh, and one of the organizations that has achieved this transformation. Over the years it has been aggressively supported by CIDA.

BRAC extends credit to two million rural women for their micro-enterprises. BRAC's credit programme is operationally sustainable. This means that BRAC's credit programme covers all costs except the initial cost of capital. In June 1998, 90 per cent of BRAC's borrowers had not missed a single weekly payment (Shorebank Advisory Services, 1998). As an entrepreneurial organization, BRAC abandoned its original approach to credit when its performance paled compared to that of its friendly rival, Grameen Bank. Today, having adopted Grameen's method-ology, BRAC's credit programme is doing very well.

Some of the reasons why BRAC succeeded include:

- **It charges market interest rates.**
  Loans are not cheap. The entrepreneurs who run BRAC are more interested in being sustainable – covering their costs of operations from customers – than in being cheap. They found that most borrowers who need small loans can make a return on the capital that is higher than the rate of interest they charge to be sustainable.
- **It works on sound business principles.**
  The BRAC branch manager has incentives to manage the branch's cash flow. If, for example, a branch manager has a cash shortfall, he has to borrow from head office at a higher cost than if he collected 100 per cent of loans or had increased lower savings deposited at weekly meetings. This provides an incentive to the branch manager to 'collect hard' and encourage savings.
- **It provides incentives to perform.**
  Borrowers repay because they can get a bigger loan next time.
- **Success breeds success.**
  Staff know they are in the spotlight, so they perform well. They also feel motivated because of the high visibility of their organization. The transparent structure of the organization means that individual good performers are noticed and become candidates for promotion. Success thus becomes a self-fulfilling prophecy.
- **The geographic proximity of borrowers helps.**
  BRAC borrowers live in very close proximity to each other and their reputations are known to one another. They cannot escape seeing their neighbour when they neglect to make a payment. There is a *daily* pressure and shame.

This is a minimalist credit programme lodged within a broad development agenda that offers fee-based information services to grow *existing* firms. Credit is only one component of their development agenda. My data are dated but, for example, several years ago BRAC alone was employing 33,000 part-time teachers who covered 50,000 villages in sixty districts in Bangladesh. This programme has grown substantially since then. Although these businesses are managed separately, the impacts of their education and credit programmes, for example, are mutually reinforcing.

BRAC provides *and charges for* information services and technical support and training to borrowers who are already active in specific income-generating sectors, including fishing and poultry- and livestock-rearing, agriculture and sericulture. Service charges for borrowers were introduced in 1993. Staff hope to recover 100 per cent of all costs – including head office overhead and one-time staff training (Shorebank Advisory Services, 1998). And borrowers readily accept such policies. For example, chick-rearing borrowers whom Shorebank interviewed reported that they have no problem with paying for technical services, for such services enabled them to produce more, as well as better-quality, chicks. As one poultry-rearer told us: 'Just as there is no end to the benefits of education, so there is no end to the benefit of profit.'[2] BRAC focuses on providing technical assistance in a limited number of sectors to women *already* engaging in the sector-specific entrepreneurial activity.

Initial subsidization was necessary. BRAC would not have been able to get off the ground at scale if donors had not capitalized them up-front.

Northern Italy

My second example is a trade association. Twelve years ago I visited the town of Carpi in the region of Emilia-Romagna. This region had seen the creation of over 300,000 firms during the previous forty years, a time when labour strife had forced workers out of large industrial firms. With broad public support, a set of institutions was created to support the growth of small firms. Some say the strong civic culture of the region made this possible. Trade associations connected to political parties provide a broad range of specific management services to these firms. Unlike US trade associations, they relieve small firms of administrative costs and fill management gaps typical in small production firms. To this day, I have not seen as effective an example of small business technical assistance.

Initially these associations provided simple services on a fee basis, such as: payroll preparation, construction of industrial parks, technical and management courses, access to and representation at international trade fairs, assistance in the formation of cooperatives to solve problems such as bulk purchasing, product and process design, joint venturing on contracts and organization of guarantee cooperatives to get competitive rates from banks.

A second generation of intermediaries was started several decades later. These organizations provide specialized marketing and technical information to firms in a specific sector. It was one of these organizations – CITER – that I visited a decade ago. In Carpi, 12,000 of the 31,000 workers were engaged in the production of garments, mostly knitwear, in around 2,500 small firms or artisan shops. Together they produced 25 per cent of all Italian knitwear. CITER's technical assistance made this possible and, when we visited, over 80 per cent of operating costs of this technical assistance were self-financed.[3]

When we were there, a large group of tradespeople and buyers gathered at dusk at CITER for a party. It was an elegant Italian buffet. During dinner, there were two music videos displaying the 'neo-kitsch' fashion trend forecast to be 'hot' eighteen months hence. CITER also exhibited suppliers' yarns and a new CAD-CAM machine that members could rent by the hour. Towards the end of the evening, the band struck up some sentimental Italian music and everyone danced. CITER believes it can be most effective when it broadcasts valuable information to its members in large group meetings. There was no meeting that night; but technical assistance was delivered!

CITER solved a key problem for small firms: the problem of a lack of access to accurate and timely market information. Few small firms can afford it, but member groups like CITER can buy the same Paris and Milan fashion forecasts as large corporations can. Think of CITER as a 'connector', making a link between the entrepreneur and the market or, as Professor Sebastiano Brusco points out, carrying the innovation at the small firm to the larger outside equipment manufacturer and to the university (Brusco 1996: 115–19).

South Shore Bank's 'Rehabbers'

My third example is a bank, my own. Shorebank's only really successful enterprise support programme is in a highly unlikely sector – its multi-family mortgage loan programme, which finances residents in the business of rehabilitating apartment buildings in our target areas. This unconventional approach to entrepreneurial development created a profitable lending niche for South Shore Bank, successful businesses and visible development benefits. The local residents realized real estate appreciation, improved, secure, affordable rental housing and wealth formation for the primarily African-American building owners.

The 'rehabbers' operate in an informal sector; they acquire undervalued assets (apartment buildings in a neighbourhood that had undergone racial change), investing in their upgrade cost effectively through shrewd purchasing of materials and use of their own and other available labour. They also took advantage of strong market demand for safe and affordable housing. In sum: the market was right; the 'rehabbers' had the skills and drive; and they matched their motivation with a huge time commitment.

The way South Shore lenders tailored loans to meet customer needs was a critical success factor and a very different approach as compared to the technician-style asset-based approach that other commercial banks were taking to the same market. The loan programme operated simply, without construction escrows or much paperwork. This fits the pragmatic, blue-collar style of most borrowers.

Information was delivered through informal 'rehabber' networks started by a modest bank effort to aid information sharing. The local 'rehabbers' in South Shore knew of one another's skills and reputation but did not meet with one another on any structured basis. On the basis of the belief that entrepreneurs learn from other entrepreneurs, we offered them the bank's boardroom as a place to meet on Saturday mornings to talk about issues of common interest. They believe someone who has already done something that has worked. It is very different from the 'cheap talk' offered by the many trainers who have never set a foot on the ground, but who are used by many new entrepreneurs who are also in the 'just talking' stage.

In the beginning, we helped organize the meetings around specific topics. Boilers might be the topic. Half the attenders were proven operators; half were novices. The guys who had done well have credibility. So if one of them says 'Hey, don't get that type of boiler', or 'Use Jack's Boiler Company to fix that specific problem', or 'Get this particular part', the others listen and learn. In recent years, the 'rehabbers' have run their own meetings at a local McDonald's restaurant.

Our 'rehabbing' initiatives provide a good example of 'small is big', contradicting the banker's 'bigger is better' idea of business. Without a penny of subsidy, the finished product is a truly beautiful building that invites the typical tenant, a young woman with a child, to rent here for safe and affordable housing.

Since the early 1980s, the work of these entrepreneurs has affected well over a third of our first neighbourhood's 24,000 units of rental housing in South Shore. Demand remains strong in our initial neighbourhood twenty years later. The loss rate on these loans is low by bank industry standards, and the portfolio contributes substantially to the bank's profitability. In summary, the 'rehabbers' were successful because:

- of a strong market for affordable housing
- they bought under-valued assets
- they were skilled tradespeople with entrepreneurial flair
- they acquired loans that were structured to meet their cash flow needs
- they had easy access to information sharing and informal networks.

Women's Self-Employment Project

A second Chicago example is a Grameen Bank adaptation that I helped start about fifteen years ago. The lessons it conveys are more complex. Like several hundred other US efforts, it could not achieve a large-scale micro-credit programme. However, its commitment to participation by low-income African-American women in the economy in Chicago has had a massive and enduring effect on public policy thinking. Demand for information – both general and in specific lines of business – is extremely strong. And more of its clients are part-time employees today than ever before. Now, after twelve years in operation, it has very valuable market information about several sectors where women have skills, are active, and can make money.

Going forward, WSEP plans to develop depth of market knowledge in the sectors where it knows that profits can be made; and it knows enough about markets to deliver valuable information to women. It is going to plan on its clients having part-time jobs or part-time businesses. It is emphasizing savings and credit, because demand for assistance with savings planning seems as useful as or even more useful than access to credit.

When I compare how long it has taken WSEP to build its current expertise with how long it has taken another international women's organization to build a sophisticated credit support system, the conclusion is that women managers of credit and self-employment programmes began with a little expertise in two spheres of activity – banking and economic development. Skills in these spheres require decades of experience to build on lessons of 'what works' and where 'what works' is not intuitively obvious.

Conclusion: Common Threads

It is hard to imagine three places as dissimilar as BRAC in Bangladesh, Carpi in northern Italy and the south side of Chicago. In each place, an intervention has been attempted to increase the level of economic activity for the benefit of the ordinary citizen and the improvement of a community. What are the threads that tie these disparate experiences together? All these successful interventions were customer-driven, financially sustainable and operating at a scale to make a measurable impact. They also demonstrate the list of 'new truisms' that I outlined earlier.

First, small business formation feeds a region's growth. We saw it on a local scale in South Shore, on a regional scale in Emilia-Romagna and on a national scale in Bangladesh. None of the organizations 'bet the ranch' on one sector, but they did build deep knowledge of specific sectors in which some of their customers were already economically active. Diversified, locally-owned economies reduce dependence on any one sector. Diversification encourages economic growth through the more rapid deployment of innovation;[4] but specialization allows the intervention to be of more use to the firm.

Next, the poor repay. BRAC and Grameen repayment rates are phenomenal. South Shore Bank's repayment rates defy common stereotypes about blue-collar African-Americans. Moreover, small firms will pay for demand-driven information services in places as diverse as Bangladesh and northern Italy. SEWA in India also seeks full cost recovery for technical assistance.

Scale matters. Scale is only possible when programmes are sustainable: for example, BRAC, Carpi and South Shore. If growth requires subsidy for operations then growth is constrained by the availability of subsidy. If a programme can earn most of its revenues from its customers, then self-propelling and long-lasting growth is possible. Ordinary people would rather do business with an independent, growing, businesslike institution than with a short-lived programme.

Match multiple types of conventional and unconventional credit to business needs: for example, customer-driven credit. There is a broad spectrum of credit products that would be useful to firms of different sizes and stages of growth. It is not just micro or bankable, but much more complex.

Capital without accurate information is useless. It is more likely that a solid business idea will attract financing than that money will 'fix' a weak business idea.

Talk is cheap. The provision of general information by generalists is rarely truly helpful. Peers learn from their peers, as is evident among the

Chicago 'rehabbers' and in Carpi. Technical assistance should meet a 'market test' of being worth paying for. There are a lot of 'talkers' on both sides of the podium who take advantage of subsidy without being accountable for 'something happening'.

Small loans are more challenging than big ones. This being the case, there are implications for loan structure and risk management if companies have no credit histories or documented cash flows. Bank financing and non-bank, higher-risk financing is required to increase the pool of successful firms.

For-profit credit and information services are more powerful than subsidized credit and information services. Soft money has weak accountability mechanisms that work against sound business decisions. For-profit credit providers are permanent institutions and have the ability to act methodically over many years to reach 'scale'. People will pay for services they value, and these payments increase the relevance and permanence of the service provided.

Subsidize some credit and information services. This support may be essential. There was initial donor support of BRAC and regional and local government support of CITER.

Privately capitalized development finance institutions can do this work. Well-capitalized development finance institutions may be more accountable to their investors for development outcomes than non-profit and public agencies are to short-term, third-party payers. Because they are sustainable, they can retain people with the talent and ingenuity to envision and implement ambitious long-term goals or recognize an opportunity when it appears. The society makes a major error when it entrusts the work of intervention to short-term non-profit projects.

Institutions may need to specialize in women's economic development and be women-led to be sure that outcomes that meet women's interests are achieved.

We do a disservice to the places in which we live and work when we demand too much simplicity. We can find successes and draw lessons out of successes and failures. They will have to be greatly adapted from place to place. But if we cared, we could do it. Just because it has not been done much, or is challenging work, does not mean that it cannot be done. Women can do this work.

Notes

1. I was on the board of one such US organization that operated from 1948 to 1988 in developing countries.

2. Interview with BRAC manager during Shorebank Annual Review in December 1996.
3. Technology Institutes in Denmark, which also receive some public funding, are expected to earn approximately 70 per cent of their budgets from the firms they serve (Hatch 1988).
4. This has been argued by Jane Jacobs in 1984. The interplay between divers-ification of an economy and the benefits of specialization by sector, by both firms and public private enterprise support agencies, may be the complex core of effective economic development.

References

Bauling, T. (1999), 'Microcredit, Health and Empowerment. A Literature Review', unpublished paper.

Brusco, Sebastiano (1996), 'Trust, Social Capital and Local Development: Some Lessons from the Experience of the Italian Districts', in OECD *Networks of enterprises and local development : competing and co-operating in local productive systems*, Paris: Organisation for Economic Co-operation and Development.

Hatch, R. (1988), 'Building Manufacturing Networks' unpublished paper.

Jacobs, J. (1984), *Cities and the Wealth of Nations: Principles of Economic Life*, New York: Random House.

The MicroBanking Bulletin. Issue No. 3, July 1999.

Shorebank Advisory Services (1998)*, Annual Financial Review*, 18 December, Chicago.

8

A Personal Perspective on the Evolution of Micro-credit in the Late Twentieth Century

Mary Coyle

Micro-enterprise development and micro-credit have been central to my professional experience in development for the past twenty years. In this chapter, designed to offer some observations on micro-credit practice, I will use highlights of my own experience to illustrate the evolution of the sector. I will start with my earliest encounters with micro-enterprise development in Botswana in the early 1980s, proceed to my most significant micro-credit experiences during the 1986–1996 decade at Calmeadow, a specialized Canadian NGO, and complete the journey on Canada's East Coast at St Francis Xavier University's Coady International Institute.

Although micro-credit existed in traditional forms long before the early 1980s, and formal micro-credit efforts have certainly been identified early in the last century, I believe that my own experience working in the sector parallels fairly closely the widespread emergence of the sector in developing countries and in Canada.

1980 Botswana – Micro-enterprise and the Identification of the Demand for Micro-credit

In 1980, I was assigned to the post of Rural Industrial Officer, working for the Botswana Ministry of Commerce and Industry based in Kanye. The job entailed doing whatever it took to encourage the development of new enterprises and expand existing ones throughout the rural villages of the Southern District. It involved: organizing technical and business skills training; identifying, developing and promoting new technologies; providing infrastructure support; identifying markets for local products;

and putting people in touch with a variety of business support services. The one missing element was capital.

The purpose of the rural industrialization strategy was to improve employment opportunities for local people and increase their incomes in order to reduce poverty. These basic goals were common to many small enterprise development programmes of that time, and have endured to the present day.

The term 'micro-enterprise' was not yet in common use in Africa. In 1981 the United States Agency for International Development sponsored the 'Pisces Studies: Assisting the Smallest Economic Activities of the Urban Poor'. These studies were instrumental in drawing distinctions between the small enterprise sector and the micro-enterprise sector. 'Pisces' played a large role in starting to popularize the term 'micro-enterprise'. Prior to that the International Labour Office had officially approved the term 'informal sector'. The two are often used interchangeably. Micro-entrepreneurs are people who farm or fish or herd; who operate enterprises where goods are produced, recycled, repaired or traded; who provide services; who work for commissions; who gain income from renting out small amounts of land, vehicles, draft animals or machinery and tools on a very small scale in both rural and urban areas (Robinson 1995).

Other actors promoting micro-enterprise development in Botswana included local organizations, such as Brigades, and international non-governmental organizations (NGOs), such as Partnership for Productivity. The focus, again typical of the era, was the promotion of production enterprises rather than commercial or service sector businesses. It was believed that production enterprises had the greatest potential for growth and employment generation. This bias did end up being a great disadvantage to women, who were represented in large numbers in the service and market trade sectors. Also characteristic of the period was the tendency to refer to women's businesses as income-generating activities or projects. It was also fairly 'traditional' female productive activities, such as sewing, knitting, craft production, poultry raising, etc., that were promoted. Some exceptions to this practice were the support provided for women's involvement in small-scale mining ventures and for the gathering of desert plants for export to florists in Europe.

Important early subsector research was undertaken during this period by my colleague, Steve Hagglade, who was the Senior Rural Industrial Officer. In addition to carrying out his professional duties with the Ministry of Commerce and Industry, Steve was conducting his doctoral research on Botswana women and the small-scale beer-brewing industry.

His work was part of a larger research initiative, focused on the African Rural Economy, headed by Carl Liedholm at Michigan State University. These studies played a critical role in exposing the nature and extent of the small and micro-enterprise sector in Africa.

One final comment on the Botswana experience is that the lack of any financing mechanism was identified as a genuine hindrance to the rural enterprise development efforts. In response to this, the Financial Assistance Program (FAP) was introduced by the government of Botswana in 1984. Typical of many early financial interventions, FAP had significant grant and subsidized credit elements. It was designed based on the assumption that small and micro-enterprises required capital to invest in assets or to use as working capital, but that they could not possibly have the capacity to repay loans at commercial rates of interest. The FAP was therefore clearly not designed to be self-sustaining.

1983 CIDA – A State of the Art Review of Donor Assistance to the Sector

In 1983/4 the Canadian International Development Agency (CIDA) undertook a worldwide review of what donors, the multilateral agencies, such as the United Nations and the World Bank, the regional development banks, the bilateral agencies like USAID, Swedish SIDA, Norwegian NORAD, British ODA and other non-government agencies (for example, Ford Foundation, ACCION International, Catholic Relief Services) were developing or supporting in the small-scale enterprise sector. I had the good fortune to be a research associate on the study, and conducted most of the interviews in the United States, Canada and a sample of countries in Africa, including Egypt, Tanzania, Kenya, Ivory Coast and Burkina Faso.

The Americans were very actively promoting micro-enterprise development and micro-credit by this stage. USAID supported the sector through research and financing their own bilateral programmes as well as those developed by NGOs. One such NGO, ACCION International, had converted itself from a multipurpose NGO to one that focused exclusively on micro-credit. ACCION was one of the first to experiment with group lending in Latin America.

Grameen Bank in Bangladesh was also identified as an up-and-coming micro-credit initiative, and had started to use groups as the basis for lending.

A lot of what was happening in the sector was fuelled and/or shaped by the donors. Micro-enterprise and micro-credit projects started to proliferate. In many cases they were components of a larger development intervention. Africa did not have successful examples of micro-credit emerging in the way that Asia did with Grameen, BRAC and Proshika and Latin America did with the ACCION network of partners.

This was a period of discovery and legitimization for the micro-enterprise sector and an exciting early time of experimentation in credit and other small and micro-business services.

1984 Indonesia – Observations on ROSCAS

Although Indonesia is well known in the micro-finance world for its Bank Rakyat, Indonesia (BRI) and its BadanKredit Kecamatan (BKK) initiatives, I had very limited exposure to these rural, large-scale, state initiatives. The BRI and BKK are examples of large-scale, profitable financial institutions that were tremendously successful in capturing people's savings. Unlike the experience of their NGO counterparts in other parts of the world, in their case, credit followed savings.

The micro-finance activities I did witness on a regular basis in Sulawesi, where I was a rural development advisor from 1984 to 1986, were like the BRI and BKK, in that savings came first. What I am referring to are the *arisan*s, the indigenous savings and credit groups prevalent in villages, neighbourhoods and among office workers. My office, for example, had several *arisan*s going. This simple system involves members of a group contributing a set sum of money on a weekly or monthly basis to a common pot and then each member taking turns in receiving the pot for investment or consumption purposes. The generic name for systems such as *arisan*s is ROSCA – rotating savings and credit associations. These are very common throughout the world, and come under a variety of names: *hui* (Vietnam), *partner* (Jamaica), *pasanaku* (Bolivia), *susu* (Ghana), *tontine* (Mali), *chikola* (Kenya), *stokvel* (South Africa), to name a few. The other common source of credit in Indonesia was the money-lender. In our local area moneylenders tended to be shopkeepers or senior government officials. Again this informal credit source is in evidence in most countries.

1986 Calmeadow – Breakthroughs in the South and the South Instructs the North on Micro-credit Practices

From 1986 to 1996 I worked for an organization called Calmeadow based in Toronto. This decade truly was the golden age of micro-credit development in the south and in Canada. Calmeadow was a leader in the sector. In 1985, Calmeadow was a new foundation with a modest endowment and one central idea. Most people in the world earned a living from a micro-enterprise of one type or another. With limited access to credit, their ability to improve their income and employment opportunities was limited. Calmeadow was dedicated to promoting the proliferation of successful micro-credit facilities throughout the developing world. To this end, Calmeadow sponsored a conference at the Couchiching Conference Centre, north of Toronto, which brought together all the micro-credit gurus of the mid-1980s, including Muhammed Yunus of Grameen Bank, Mary Houghton of the South Shore Bank in Chicago, representatives from ACCION International in Latin America and others. There were no Canadian gurus in the mix, but the audience was primarily Canadian NGOs. Calmeadow's intention was to get these Canadian NGOs excited about micro-credit and then offer small grants as an incentive to become involved in micro-credit programming in developing countries.

The Canadian NGOs did not embrace the concept. On the contrary, many expressed concerns, on ideological grounds, that micro-credit and micro-enterprise development were counter-developmental because they were supporting petty capitalism and perpetuating the marginalization of poor people. Calmeadow's response was to get into the business directly by transforming itself from a funding organization into an operational one. If the other Canadian NGOs were not interested in micro-credit, Calmeadow would have to get involved directly.

In 1986, Calmeadow was busy learning everything it could about micro-credit practice by informally apprenticing itself to ACCION International and co-sponsoring micro-projects in Latin America. In that same year, Martin Connell, the President and co-founder of Calmeadow, decided that it was time for the organization to get involved in its own backyard. This is where I came in. I was hired in 1986 to help Calmeadow design and deliver a micro-credit programme for Canada's First Nations Communities. Over the years I worked in both domestic and international programming and ultimately became its first executive director. For clarity and ease of comprehension, I will start with the evolution of Calmeadow's involvement in micro-credit internationally and then follow with a description of how the domestic programming developed and why.

In its first decade of operations internationally, Calmeadow's understanding of the micro-finance sector grew tremendously, and its niche became very clearly focused and defined. It made the journey, through experience, from subsidized credit to commercial intermediation. On the heels of the Couchiching Conference and the First Latin American

Workshop of Solidarity Group Programs in 1985 in Bogota, Colombia, Calmeadow plunged into partnerships with ACCION in Brazil, Colombia, Peru and Mexico. Calmeadow's role was learning, co-funding (also attracting CIDA funding) and trying to stay one step ahead in order to be able to offer advice and, in some cases, a vision. The partners in all cases were local NGOs.

Calmeadow was always pushing its partners to improve the participation rate of women. Calmeadow was keen on women's participation for three reasons: women are more credit-disadvantaged than men (equity), women tend to share the benefits of an improved income with family and the community (impact) and women have proved to be better credit risks (good business).

Although Calmeadow did have a bias in favour of solidarity group lending (one loan shared by a mutually responsible small group), or peer group lending (individuals in a group each receive a loan, but are responsible to each other for repayment), other forms of credit delivery, such as village banking and individual/direct lending, were practised by some partners.

As Calmeadow matured and developed its own expertise, it expanded its partnerships to Africa and Asia. Dr Yunus of the Grameen Bank joined the Calmeadow Advisory Council. He was demonstrating in Bangladesh that lending to poor people could be done on a large-scale basis, that poor people could reliably repay loans, and that a permanent banking institution for the poor could supplant the earlier NGO credit projects. Dr Salehuddin Ahmed of BRAC in Bangladesh was advising that 'small is beautiful', but 'large is necessary', because the need and the demand for credit are so vast. He also preached institutional self-reliance, stating that reliance on donors could leave an organization vulnerable and subject to other whims.

In the late 1980s, Calmeadow was evolving into a much more technically sophisticated organization. It had identified its three goals for partnership development. Partners would need to be committed to having a significant *impact* on the poorest of the economically active population. They would also have to have the vision and desire to achieve *scale* – reach large numbers of people – and *sustainability* – be able to cover costs with revenues from products and services.

Calmeadow started to take partners from other parts of the world to Bangladesh to see the Grameen Bank, both to inspire them and to learn what it takes to scale up and institutionalize while still focusing on lending to the poor, and to women in particular. On one trip we took Pancho Otero of PRODEM, Bolivia, Carlos Costello of ACCION, Colombia and Oscar

Giraldo of Actuar, Bogota. Pancho and Oscar ran very large, successful NGO micro-credit programmes. They had adopted the conventional wisdom of the day as promoted by ACCION and Calmeadow. They believed in 'minimalist credit'; that is to say that they focused efforts largely on credit delivery without providing many other business services. This minimalist approach is based on the assumption that micro-entrepreneurs know what they are doing and also on the need to keep delivery costs down. They believed in charging rates of interest that incorporate the full costs of operating and financing the lending operation. They also agreed that strict discipline and strict repayment enforcement were essential for the health of the loan programme. What their organizations were lacking were the vision and the mechanisms for creating large-scale, sustainable, permanent micro-finance institutions.

Calmeadow then entered a new phase that saw it define itself as an organization that assisted micro-lending initiatives to scale up their operations in significant ways and transform themselves into permanent, sustainable and ultimately profitable financial institutions. This involved playing a technical consulting role, an investment role and a broad information-dissemination role. New staff were required, with finance and banking backgrounds. New investment vehicles were needed; and new mechanisms for disseminating lessons learned to the sector had to be developed. This was a completely new approach, and it did not develop overnight.

The first and best example of this was Calmeadow's role in the creation of Banco Sol in Bolivia. PRODEM, a highly successful micro-lending NGO, founded in 1984, and a member of the ACCION network in Latin America, was inspired to create a bank for a number of reasons. There was tremendous demand for its services; but its growth was constrained owing to the limited donor capital available and the regulatory restrictions that prevented it from capturing local savings to finance its growth. It needed capital and it needed a new structure. Calmeadow, in cooperation with ACCION, came in with financial and technical support for a two-year transformation project called COBANCO (1990–1992). This project involved conducting a feasibility study, creating a business plan for the bank, working through the regulatory issues with the government and raising the investment capital to finance the new bank.

In February 1992 I attended the official opening of Banco Sol in La Paz, Bolivia. This truly marked a new era in micro-finance. It was the first time a fully commercial micro-finance institution was created. It was not simple, and there have been growing pains as it struggled with management issues, its lack of experience in capturing savings and the challenge of defining an appropriate governance structure. Overall, however, Banco Sol has been a tremendous success, with 73,073 active clients as of 31 December 1999. It has been an inspiration to many others. Calmeadow now had a position on the board of the bank, along with the other investors. PRODEM became the largest shareholder in the bank it had created, and turned its attention to developing an innovative model of reaching out to rural areas, leaving the urban sites to Banco Sol. Calmeadow also remained a partner with the NGO, PRODEM.

Calmeadow became involved in other 'transformations'; but none were as complete or as successful as Banco Sol.

To complement its technical role, Calmeadow helped to establish an innovative mechanism for raising equity capital for ventures such as Banco Sol. PROFUND, a new equity investment company, was created to focus on newly developing or expanding commercial micro-finance institutions. It was financed by Calmeadow, ACCION, private business interests and donor agencies.

The Micro-Finance Network (MFN) was also created at around the same time. It is an association of the elite micro-finance institutions committed to the large-scale expansion and commercialization of micro-lending. The purpose of the MFN is to exchange information on best practices. Like Calmeadow and Banco Sol, all members of the Network believed that it is critical to attract private sector capital in order to be able to meet the enormous, unsatisfied demand for micro-finance services in all regions of the world. Donor resources were fickle and insufficient. Issues such as effective savings mobilization and institutional grievance were explored by the network. Calmeadow became the institutional home for the Micro-Finance Network.

As Calmeadow was learning and leading over the past decade, the micro-finance sector was growing at a tremendous rate. In 1995, the World Bank undertook a survey to attempt to enumerate and characterize what was happening in the sector. The results, as of mid-1996, indicate that there are more than 1,000 micro-finance institutions in over 100 countries, each reaching a minimum of 1,000 clients with at least three years of experience. Of the 206 that responded to a survey, 73 per cent were NGOs, 13.6 per cent were Credit Unions, 7.8 per cent commercial banks and the rest savings banks. The total outstanding loan balance reported by the survey respondents was US$4 billion, with 14 million loans to individuals and groups and US$19 billion in deposits, comprising approximately 46 million savings accounts.

Commercial banks accounted for 78 per cent of the total outstanding micro-loans, Credit Unions for 11 per cent, NGOs for 9 per cent and

Savings Banks for 2 per cent. Of the Institutions surveyed, 69 per cent were created after 1980, the majority of them NGOs (CGAP 1995).

The February 1997 Micro-credit Summit gathered many of these institutions from around the world to commit to an even greater push for growth over the next few years. The Summit's goal was to reach 100 million of the world's poorest families, especially women, with credit for self-employment and other financial and business services by 2005. It was estimated that an investment of US$21.6 billion would be required.

Most of this activity will take place in developing countries, where the demand and the need are greatest and where there is a proliferation of organizations involved. There is, however, a growing micro-enterprise sector in Canada that warrants some discussion.

In 1986, when Calmeadow was still early on in its international partnerships, the board decided it was time to initiate programming in Canada. The term 'micro-enterprise' was not yet in common use in the Canadian context. 'Self-employment' and 'home-based business' were commonly used, although the instances of these were not all small in scale. A recent study conducted by Calmeadow for the Department of Finance on 'The State of Microcredit in Canada' spells out a number of interesting facts on the nature and extent of the micro-enterprise/self-employed sector in Canada (Calmeadow Research 1999). Micro-enterprises:

1. are, in the majority of cases, run by women;
2. typically earn less than the waged employment sector;
3. are found in large numbers in large cities with heavy immigrant representation;
4. gross, as an average from all sources, a monthly income of $2,400;
5. have very little collateral, few personal assets;
6. are very young businesses, with 30 per cent created in the last twelve months and an average overall age of two years.

By 1996 there were 850,000 micro-entrepreneurs in Canada, 47 per cent of the 1.8 million self-employed.

Since 1989, 17 per cent of all Canadian workers are self-employed and three-quarters of all job growth has been in self-employment.

- The self-employed sector grows on an average of 5.5 per cent per year.
- The micro-credit providers (business loans below $25,000) are:
  - private financial institutions – 405,000 clients;
  - government loan programmes – 19,000 clients; and
  - micro-loan funds – 1,200 clients.

The study identified thirty-four non-profit loan funds, and the five largest serve 80 per cent of the 1,200 clients.

None of these non-profit initiatives were in place in 1986, and there was very little information available on the sector at that time. Calmeadow decided to start with a programme for First Nations communities. They were chosen because they were economically disadvantaged. People living on reserves had legal impediments to accessing capital, because they could not use their land as collateral on loans, as it was legally held it in trust by the Crown. To prepare for this initiative Calmeadow undertook two different kinds of research: one that delved into the nature and extent of the micro-enterprise sector on three Ontario reserves, and one that looked at micro-credit models.

The research on the micro-enterprise sector was illuminating. Gord Cunningham did a thorough study of the economy of the Wikwemikong First Nation on Manitoulin Island (Cunningham 1990). His study uncovered a far more vibrant micro-enterprise economy than was expected. One in three households was involved in some form of micro-enterprise activity. Most such activities were part-time. Lynn Convery found a similar situation in Sachigo Lake, a fly-in community in north-western Ontario (Convery 1990). People were earning a living through 'income patching'. They were involved in some seasonal employment, some received social assistance and many were engaged in a whole variety of micro-enterprises. One man in Sachigo had ten different micro-enterprises, including completing tax returns, cutting firewood, delivering water and setting up a hot dog stand at outdoor religious revival functions.

For research on micro-credit models, Calmeadow turned to its international experience. The pilot Native Self-Employment Loan Program (NSELP) was launched in 1986, drawing heavily on the Grameen Bank and ACCION models of group lending. At the time there were a number of other similar loan funds in the design phase in the United States. In October 1987, Calmeadow became the first organization in North America to issue a micro-loan using the peer group lending method imported from the South. Wikwemikong established the OssGobWehTodWin Loan Fund. The name meant 'to witness' or 'to stand beside' in Ojibway.

The NSELP pilot initiative was successful in many ways. Micro-loans were made with the participation of the local commercial banks through a guarantee scheme. Most loans were repaid. Calmeadow learned a lot about the communities and how to improve the lending model. The program was able to demonstrate that there is significant potential for micro-enterprise development in First Nations Communities and, most importantly, demonstrated to the sceptical Canadian public that First Nations people are bankable and could be good credit risks.

Buoyed by this early success, and fuelled also by its experience internationally, Calmeadow decided to expand its Canadian operations. It created a national programme for First Nations communities called the First Peoples Fund. It also created other loan funds in Nova Scotia and Vancouver, and then in Toronto. Funding for these initiatives did not come from government. Calmeadow wanted to keep the funds free from government or political influence and also wanted the borrowers to take repayment responsibilities seriously. Instead, the funding came from foundations and the private sector. The Royal Bank of Canada was a large supporter, providing operating grants, and allowing some of the loan funds to piggyback on their lending infrastructure.

The First Peoples Fund worked with any First Nations community that wanted to establish and manage its own loan fund. Calmeadow provided the basic model, training and technical assistance for the community members responsible for the local fund and a partial guarantee with the banks. In Nova Scotia, Calmeadow started with a pilot fund in Lockeport called PARD. After some initial success that model was modified and incorporated into a province-wide initiative. Calmeadow Nova Scotia became a separate non-profit organization with its own board of directors and separate charitable status. The PAL fund in Vancouver that originally partnered with the small CCEC Credit Union went through a phase of expansion under the Calmeadow West name with a new partnership with the Royal Bank. In 1996, in a move to ensure long-term sustainability, it was taken over by Van City Credit Union, one of Canada's largest Credit Unions. Calmeadow Metrofund in Toronto was Calmeadow's last fund to be initiated directly. In this case, Calmeadow did the lending itself.

All Calmeadow funds used the peer group lending model, whereby groups of four to seven individuals came together to guarantee each other's loans and provide support to one another. People started off with loans of up to $1,000 and, over time, if they repaid their loans and the other members of their group did the same, they could work their way up to loans of $5,000. Individual loans of higher value were built into the business plans for subsequent phases of Calmeadow Nova Scotia, Calmeadow West and Calmeadow Metrofund.

There were efforts in all funds to attract women. The goal was to reach at least 50 per cent women. In each of the First Peoples Fund communities, Calmeadow imposed the rule that the first group had to be female. The intention was to send a message to the community and to the women that the fund was for them.

As awareness of the self-employed sector grew, as word of Calmeadow's early successes spread and as the Grameen Bank gained a higher international profile, other groups and communities expressed an interest in starting up micro-loan funds. Calmeadow responded by creating a special unit called the Technical Support Group to provide training, technical advice and materials to other Canadian communities.

At the same time as this was happening in Canada, loan funds were springing up all over the United States. Out of these, a close-knit group formed that included Calmeadow, ACCION, Working Capital based in Boston, The Women's Self Employment Project in Chicago, the Good Faith Fund in Arkansas, the Lakota Fund on the Pine Ridge Reservation in South Dakota, Nebraska Micro-enterprise and the three pilot funds of the North Carolina Rural Centre. With the support of the Ford Foundation, the group assembled in 1993 at the Couchwood Centre in Hot Springs, Arkansas, with their Bangladeshi counterparts/gurus from BRAC, Proshika and Grameen. The Group took stock of their accomplishments to date and their challenges for the future.

Introducing micro-credit into Canada and the United States was not easy. The three goals of impact, scale and sustainability were elusive, and much more difficult to achieve in this North American context. The movement, which was largely inspired by the success of their overseas counterparts, was struggling to sustain its credibility. At the Micro-credit Summit in 1997, I made a presentation on sustainability of micro-credit initiatives in industrialized countries. I spoke about there being a number of internal and external factors that contribute to or detract from a micro-credit organization's ability to attain sustainability.

Although impossible to generalize, the following external preconditions are often present in the developing country context. There the micro-enterprise market is large. It is often more than 50 per cent of the population. It is concentrated. It is visible and often experienced. You can see the micro-entrepreneurs and see what they are doing, in market-places, on sidewalks, in front of their homes, etc. Economies of scale are possible in this context. Survival is often solely an individual and family responsibility. There is no social safety net. There is a large, unsatiated demand for credit.

There is information available on the sector now, and it is relatively well understood. With fifteen to twenty years of experience there are successful models such as Banco Sol and Grameen Bank to learn from. There is relative freedom in setting interest rates. Rates of 2 to 4 per cent per month are not uncommon. This is critical to generating the revenue required to cover costs. Delivery costs are relatively low as a result of local wage structures, and there are relatively few regulatory impediments to micro-enterprise development. Someone wanting to start up a micro-enterprise can just hang their sign out and do it.

In industrialized countries attaining scale and self-sufficiency is much more difficult. First of all, the micro-enterprise market is much smaller. The micro-entrepreneurs are not necessarily poor or low-income. More entrepreneurs are better educated, but less experienced in business. They are often home-based, and therefore invisible. The market is not so well understood. Businesses are often more complex, and are operating in a more complex market-place. Demand for credit is not as great, as people may have other options, such as credit cards. Both micro-enterprise and micro-credit are relatively new concepts. Market demand is both latent and suppressed, because:

- there is a regulatory environment that discourages micro and, in particular, home-based businesses;
- there are often disincentives built into the social assistance system.

For some, other needs may be greater than their need for credit. Delivery costs are higher, owing to greater human resource expenses, and there is less latitude on interest rates. This is a result of usury laws, public attitudes and conflicting public perceptions – resistance to the idea of charitable organizations supported through donations charging high rates. In spite of more than ten years of micro-lending experience in North America, there are no relevant, fully self-sufficient models to look to.

In addition to these external factors, there are also a number of internal factors that have impeded the attainment of self-sufficiency in the case of North American micro-credit initiatives. First, they may not have self-sufficiency as a goal. Many were not and still are not striving for self-sufficiency. Many, like early overseas initiatives, take a short-term project or programme approach instead of a more long-term institutional approach. Finally, many suffer from a confusion or lack of clarity about who the client is. Does one use a broader definition of credit-disadvantaged or a more strict low-income definition of the client group?

These factors and the small numbers identified in the recent Calmeadow study on the State of MicroCredit in Canada are discouraging for the people involved.

There are, however, some positive opportunities. It is clear from the recent statistics that the sector is growing rapidly and that awareness of its importance is increasing. There is a large amount of capital in North America and a growing interest within the financial sector in this emerging market. New technologies, such as credit cards and Internet banking, have the potential to improve efficiency and effectiveness. It will be up to the innovators, be they in the private, government or non-profit sectors, to come up with the next breakthrough in this area.

The goal of creating a large-scale sustainable micro-lending venture in Canada is still elusive even for Calmeadow, which has been the leader in this field.

1997 The Coady International Institute – The Member-based Solution to Sustainability

I was appointed Director of the Coady International Institute at St Francis Xavier University in January 1997. The Institute was named to honour Rev. Dr Moses M. Coady, first director of the StFX Extension Department and a leader in the Antigonish Movement. The Movement combined a popular approach to adult education and economic cooperation to solve the severe economic and social problems facing the people of the Maritime region in the late 1920s. It became well known for its promotion of successful cooperative ventures in communities. It was influenced by the social encyclicals of the Catholic Church, the Rochdale principles in England, Alphonse Desjardins and the Caisse Populaire movement in Quebec and Roy Bergengren and the US Credit Union movement. Many of the credit unions in existence in English-speaking Canada today can trace their origins back to Antigonish and the work of Moses Coady. A number of the credit union systems around the world can also trace their origins or their development to Coady.

The Coady International Institute was created in 1959 to extend the message and practice of community-based cooperation worldwide. It has done that through training community leaders at the Institute and working on the ground around the world. Coady's involvement in micro-credit is vast. It trains students from overseas in successful micro-finance methodologies. It works or has worked on the ground with partners such as SEWA Bank in India, ASA in Bangladesh, SANASA in Sri Lanka and the Micro-credit Project for women in Nepal. It assists other training organizations in developing countries to establish their own programmes in micro-finance. Recently, Coady has been involved in research on poverty targeting in micro-finance programmes, through CGAP, the World Bank-sponsored Consultative Group to Assist the Poor.

In all of these activities, the Coady Institute has a bias. It promotes a member-based model of micro-finance. Like the early model promoted by Moses Coady, in his book, *Masters of Their Own Destiny*, this model involves the ownership of community-based institutions by the people (Coady 1939). For Coady, sustainable, member-owned institutions are essential to achieving the important goals of economic, social and political democracy.

The credit union/financial cooperative model has been criticized for being slow to expand; but with the right combination of leadership, technical know-how and innovative capital injections and partnerships, this approach can foster both growth and sustainability. It also has tremendous potential for empowerment. The SEWA Bank serves and is owned by 26,271 poor women in Gujarat State, India. It has grown successfully without injections of external donor financing.

Conclusion

Looking back, the past twenty years have been an exciting period of action-based research in the micro-finance sector. Internationally, the emphasis has changed from enterprise development to micro-finance or financial intermediation that includes credit, savings and insurance services and products. A number of large-scale, successful micro-finance institutions have been developed. A much larger number of smaller programmes are emerging at a rapid rate worldwide. In spite of this, most people in the world still do not have access to institutional financial services. Although a large amount of NGO lending is targeted at women, they are still disproportionately underserved overall. No one has come up with the magic solution, achieving that elusive goal of creating large-scale, sustainable mechanisms for providing these services. This is because there probably is not any one solution. Hege Gulli, in *Microfinance and Poverty: Questioning the Conventional Wisdom*, states that 'the best route for poverty reduction through microfinance may be to combine narrowly targeted programs to assist the poor with broad steps to build a competitive, sustainable finance system that provides a wide range of small scale transactions' (Gulli 1998).

Innovation at home and abroad, fuelled by commitment to reaching the hardest to reach, must remain the priority as we go forward into the new millennium.

References

Calmeadow Research (1999), *The State of Microcredit in Canada*, Report presented to the Department of Finance, Economic Development Policy Branch, Toronto.

CGAP (1995), *Maximizing the Outreach of Microenterprise Finance: The Emerging Lessons of Successful Programs*, Focus Note No. 2., http://www. cgap.org/html/ p_focus_notes02.html.

Coady, M. (1939), *Masters of Their Own Destiny: The Story of the Antigonish Movement of Adult Education Through Economic Cooperation,* New York: Harper.

Convery, L. (1990), 'The Support of Micro-Enterprises in Remote Northern Canadian Native Communities: Issues, Constraints and Opportunities', unpublished MA thesis, University School of Rural Planning and Development, University of Guelph.

Cunningham, G. (1990), 'The Local Economy and Micro-Enterprise Sector of A Native Community: A Case Study of Wikwemikong (Unceded) Indian Reserve #26', unpublished MA thesis, University of Guelph.

Gulli, H. (1998), *Microfinance and Poverty: Questioning the Conventional Wisdom*, Washington, DC: Inter-American Development Bank.

Robinson, M. (1995), *Microfinance: The Paradigm Shift from Credit Delivery to Sustainable Financial Intermediation*, Cambridge, MA: Harvard Institute for International Development.

9

Banking with Poor Self-employed Women

Jayshree Vyas

In India about 93 per cent of all workers are self-employed. Women constitute more than half this workforce; more than 96 per cent of women workers are self-employed. Self-employed workers are those who earn a living through their own small businesses or through their own labour. Unlike workers in the organized sector, they do not obtain a regular salary. These workers are characterized by insecure employment, low incomes, lack of capital assets, lack of access to institutional support and no social security benefits, leading to an extreme level of poverty and vulnerability. They can be broadly divided into three categories: hawkers and vendors; home-based workers, such as weavers, garment-makers, food processors and craftspeople; and manual labour and service providers, such as agricultural labourers, construction workers, rag-pickers, domestic workers, and cart-pullers.

A small number of self-employed poor women formed their own organization in 1972 when the Self Employed Women's Association (SEWA) was registered as a trade union in Gujarat, Western India. Its main objective was to strengthen its members' bargaining power to improve their income, employment and access to social security.

Self-employed women are caught in the vicious circle of poverty, indebtedness, no government assistance and low income. A possible solution to free these women from this vicious circle involves linking them with registered banks. But attempts to link self-employed women with national banks through SEWA as an intermediary met with many practical difficulties. Bridging the gap between sophisticated bank staff and women in shabby clothes accompanied by noisy children was not achieved, because the banks were not able to relate to these women.

In 1973 the members of SEWA came forward with an answer: a bank of their own where they would be accepted in their own right and not made to feel inferior. Four thousand women contributed share capital of Rs.10 each to establish a Women's Co-operative Bank. In May 1974, the SEWA Bank was registered. Since then, it has provided banking services to poor, illiterate, self-employed women and has become a viable financial venture.

The main objective of SEWA Bank is to help poor women reverse the process of decapitalization at the micro-level and to begin the process of capitalization. This is accomplished by providing financial services like savings, credit and insurance which help women:

- to escape the clutches of moneylenders;
- to rescue their mortgaged/pledged assets, such as land, ornaments and cattle;
- to create their own assets, such as a house, savings and equipment;
- to expand their business through productive credit;
- to cope with losses due to sickness, accidents, death, floods and riots;
- to increase their bargaining power;
- to improve their living conditions; and
- ultimately, to empower them.

Main Features of SEWA Bank

A woman needs different types of financial services throughout her life. Savings schemes can greatly assist lifetime planning for the education and marriage of children or for old age. Credit is used to repay old debts, to fund working capital for business, for buying equipment, and for repairing, extending or buying a new house. Credit and savings also act as insurance against the risks of sickness, accidents, death, floods and cyclones.

Poor, illiterate women find it useful to deal with a bank only if its service is suitable for them. SEWA Bank meets their criterion through simple procedures, door-to-door service, and credit based on savings performance or loan repayment instead of collateral. SEWA Bank's integrated financial services respond to members by offering different types of suitable products under four categories of financial services: savings, credit, insurance and financial counselling. Since the majority of the women are illiterate, various banking procedures have to be adapted, such as using thumb prints or photographs and helping them fill in forms.

Poor people welcome credit, but they also want many other kinds of financial services. Savings, credit, insurance and financial counselling are integrated financial services offered by SEWA Bank. SEWA Bank also mobilizes linkages with other support services such as training, health care, childcare, legal aid, marketing, housing, technical services and other business development services.

The poor are vulnerable to all types of crises. Each threatens to put them deeper into the spiral of increasing poverty and vulnerability. To support members in these crises, SEWA Bank has designed its own integrated insurance scheme, which covers 3,200 women against loss of house, household goods and tools in case of flood, fire, riots or cyclones, and death, sickness, widowhood and maternity expenses. The Bank's experience is that insurance for the poor members can be contributory and linked with savings.

SEWA Bank received Government permission in 1994 to extend its activities to rural areas. More than 1,000 savings and credit groups have been formed, which are owned and managed by 23,000 poor women. Total savings received exceed Rs. 5 million, while 2,381 women have received loans totalling more than Rs. 9 million. These groups remain unregistered, but have formed into registered district-level savings and credit federations. SEWA Bank conducts training for village-level and district-level organizations.

© John M. Berridge.

Figure 9.1 Jayshree Vyas: Adapting Banking Services to Clients' Needs.

SEWA Bank collaborates with the Reserve Bank of India (RBI), State governments, insurance companies, apex institutions such as the National Bank for Agriculture and Rural Development (NABARD) and national housing finance organizations.

Since its inception, the Bank has been able to meet its operational costs, provide for bad debts and earn a surplus. The Bank's financial resources come almost entirely from its own members. As of 31 March 1998, the Bank was funded by share capital from members, 6 per cent; deposits owned by women, 82 per cent; ploughed back profits, 8 per cent; and borrowing from outside, 4 per cent. Income from net interest meets operating expenses and provides for non-performing assets. Part of the surplus earned from banking activity is used to provide support services, such as social security and education and the training of members. The remaining part is ploughed back into the capital of the bank after distributing dividends to members.

SEWA is a bank where women are users, owners and managers. Through identified leaders and organizers, continuous personal contact in the field is maintained with members. As owners, the members elect their own executive committee, make policies, decide on interest rates and share profits. They have a right to ask for accounts, and to change the by-laws of the bank. They give the Bank its direction. The Bank is accountable to members as well as depositors, and subject to audit by the Reserve Bank of India and by the Co-operative Department of the State government of Gujarat.

Approach to Banking with Poor Women

Banking for development with poor women requires an approach that meets their particular needs and draws on their capabilities. In its twenty years of experience SEWA Bank has formulated the following approach:

Priority for Savings

The worldwide interest in poor women's finance has restricted itself to micro-credit programmes. For SEWA Bank, however, savings are as important. Savings are used as a financial product for poor women's future planning. Most women would like to save even from their meagre earnings, but they have nowhere they can deposit their money, as it is much too time-consuming and too expensive to go to a bank for tiny savings amounts. However, once they are provided with an easily accessible savings facility, they are able to save small surpluses regularly. Saving has many important implications:

- It is a method of ensuring financial discipline, which results in improved repayment rates.
- It expands the total pool of resources available to the poorest, so that she has more options for her work and her life.
- Her bank balance is an asset that raises her capacity to borrow as well as her status as a bread earner and within her community.
- Savings are an autonomous means of economic growth for the woman.
- Growth of her business is within her control and can be supplemented by loans.
- Savings are a fall-back, a form of social security, in time of crises. Whenever she urgently needs cash in times of sickness or death, she has her savings to fall back on.

Women need to 'hide' their savings in a 'safe' place. Like other women, Savitaben, a rag picker, used to save a little every day and hide it in her trunk. The savings rose to Rs. 300. Once, on returning from her work, she saw the money gone. 'My husband had taken the money. I cried and cried. Because of this incident, I stopped saving in my home, but gave it to "good" neighbour to keep "safe". The amount Rs. 1,000 when I demanded from him, he showed the face as if I was a stranger!' Such experiences are all too common amongst poor women, rural and urban.

Once they are motivated, the members are ready to save; however they need the necessary financial services provided in forms suitable to them, such as collection at their home and/or in the market-place and with their photo on the pass book instead of a signature. About 70,000 savings boxes are provided by the Bank for their daily savings. Very often, the members want the Bank to maintain confidentiality from the men of their families. In villages, they invariably wanted first to test the reliability of SEWA Bank by depositing very small amounts. Now they have learned to invest their savings into long-term Bank securities.

Savings in any micro-credit scheme are the most crucial component, both for the provision of benefits to the poor and for sustainability. Local savings deposits help to provide a capital base from which to begin operations, and then, thanks to interest paid to savers and the increasing availability of loans, they help to maintain the members' commitment, which is, of course, vital to the growth of the banking programme. They provide for poor women a secure place in which to store and build up their cash assets and at the same time ensure the continuing viability of the bank.

Integrated Approach

SEWA Bank's integrated approach distinguishes it from other micro-credit efforts. Credit, though very important, is not adequate for sustained and substantial employment. It is becoming increasingly clear that access to financial services alone is not enough for poor people to transform their economic activities into profitable economic enterprises. Access to markets, information, technical know-how and social support services is as important as money if the poor are to share in economic growth. If poor people are going to build incomes, assets and livelihood in substantial ways, they need access to:

- market information and commercial linkages;
- technology and methods to improve productivity;
- market infrastructure;
- health and social security services;
- information, know-how to develop entrepreneurial ability; and
- representation on decision-making bodies.

SEWA Bank works closely with SEWA, the trade union, and with other economic organizations of the SEWA members, such as the Women's Co-operative Federation and the Women's District DWCRA (producer groups) Associations. At the same time the bank itself provides financial services and has set up a contributory work security or insurance fund and a housing services section.

Appropriate Mechanisms

Banking with the poor and illiterate requires special procedures and mechanisms suited to their culture, their needs and their economy. This requires adopting procedures and designing schemes suitable to them, like collecting daily savings from their places of business or houses or providing savings boxes or photos on their pass books. They require special loan procedures and rules that take into account their level of economy (for example, the repayment schedule has to be based on their cash flow). They require saving and credit schemes that allow for small amounts of major savings and banking policies that adapt to their crisis situations. They also require training and assistance in understanding and dealing with banking procedures.

Any self-employed woman can open an account with the SEWA Bank. As the majority of account holders are illiterate, the SEWA Bank has evolved a unique system of identification cards. Each individual's card has a photograph showing her holding a slate with her account number written on it. Her name and account number are thus associated with her photograph and not with her signature, as is the usual banking custom. Over a period of time, the illiterate account holders have learned to sign and read their pass books.

Asset Creation

Perhaps the one single factor that most often leads self-employed producers into the cycle of poverty is lack of assets. For women the condition is worse when the family does acquire an asset on which she has no claim. Asset creation under the ownership of women has been the priority of SEWA Bank. This includes transfers of agricultural land and houses in women's names, the acquisition of implements, tools, shops, handcarts, and livestock in their own names, their own capital, bank accounts, shares, and savings certificates. This also includes rescuing or releasing mortgaged houses and land, or pawned silver and gold.

Growth of SEWA Bank

In the beginning, SEWA Bank concentrated on mobilizing self-employed women to save with it, and acted as an intermediary to enable its depositors to get loans from the nationalized banks. Subsequently, the

© John M. Berridge.

Figure 9.2 Delivering Financial Services.

bank began advancing money from its own funds to its depositors; and since that time it has developed into a viable financial unit. The governing body is the Board of Directors, which has elected representation of major trade groups from SEWA Bank's membership. All the major decisions about the Bank are taken by the Board, which meets once a month. It sanctions all the loans advanced, and, in the wake of the recent liberalization of interest rates, the board decides the interest to be charged for different categories of loans. The illiteracy of the members has rarely stood in the way of taking decisions or finding solutions. Since its inception, SEWA Bank has consistently been given 'A' grade by the auditors.

As Table 9.1 below shows, SEWA Bank has grown slowly but steadily over the last twenty years, with a spurt in growth after the liberalization policies of the last five years. SEWA Bank started as an urban bank, but in recent years has expanded to the rural areas, serving a growing rural population of self-employed women. Along with offering savings, credit, financial services and financial counselling, SEWA Bank has expanded to offering deposit-linked work insurance schemes and housing services.

Table 9.1 Growth of SEWA Bank

Year	Share-holders	Share Capital Rs.	Depositors Rs.	Deposits Rs.	Working Capital Rs.	Profits Rs.
1975–6	6,631	75,990	10,459	950,388	1,660,431	30,016
1980–1	7,507	80,690	14,022	2,728,876	3,194,930	54,192
1985–6	9,825	538,130	22,208	11,278,886	13,537,252	222,267
1990–1	13,151	1,460,000	27,923	24,466,000	34,417,000	741,000
1995–6	17,485	4,259,000	44,841	72,165,000	98,206,000	1,001,000

Source: SEWA Bank Annual Reports, 1975–6, 1980–1, 1985–6, 1990–1, 1995–6.

Savings Services

All banking activities in SEWA Bank start with savings. Women are encouraged to save, and all the necessary facilities to allow them to do so are provided. Usually, a woman is considered eligible for a loan if she has saved regularly. SEWA Bank relates to its members in two ways, as individuals and as groups. Generally, the group approach is used in the rural areas and the individual in the urban areas, although, as the bank grows, the group approach is being encouraged in the urban areas, too. In the rural areas, savings services are provided by mobile vans, which service each area at particular times. Each area has its 'group leader' who

© John M. Berridge.

Figure 9.3   SEWA Bank, my mother!

maintains contact with the bank, motivates and creates awareness among members and serves as a link between the bank and the women.

In rural areas, women in each village form their own savings group. The size of the group varies from ten to fifty women, and the monthly savings amount varies between Rs.10 and Rs. 25 per woman, depending on the size and economy of the village and the needs of the group members. The women are trained in banking procedures, each woman having her own pass book, and the group pass book being maintained by the two or three women leaders of the group. In the initial stages, the bank field workers collect the savings; but as the management capacity of the group grows, the women leaders come to the bank to deposit their periodic savings.

Like savings, 'consumption' loans are also badly needed by poor women. SEWA Bank has never distinguished between consumption loans and productive loans. Actually, consumption loans lead to work security in the case of the poor, and of the poorest in particular. Like savings, they provide security by reducing vulnerability and contributing to income. Living at such a precarious level, the poor are constantly vulnerable to a multiplicity of disasters: illness (and medical expense), death (and funeral expense), crop failure (and therefore extra food expenses, as well as the need to buy seeds for the next season), and rapid price rises, as well as the loss of assets like livestock (disease) or sewing machines (riots). They are faced with foreseeable but unmanageable expenditures, such as the need to replace or repair domestic items or their house, and to pay school fees, as well as needing to fulfil the various social obligations arising from events such as marriages. Consumption loans can assist the poor in coping with these needs without their having to reduce what few assets they have to raise cash, or to risk the traditional moneylenders' crippling rates of interest.

Consumption loans contribute to income of the poor because of the inseparability of their productive and consumption activities. 'Consumption' expenditures for food, health or even housing help to maintain their key productive asset, their labour, while paying school fees is an investment in the future. Or obtaining a cash loan rather than selling an animal could enable a family to have income – and surplus – later when the animal produces its young. Experience shows that the production-consumption dichotomy is, in fact, false for the poorest, and suggests that micro-banking should make provision for both.

Credit and Repayment

SEWA Bank first started advancing loans to its members in a modest way. The growth of the loans was slow at first, as SEWA bank learned about the credit needs of the self-employed women and how to deal with them. There was no blueprint for banking with the poor, and there were many problems, such as the non-availability of any collateral or security. The women did not have any banking track record on the basis of which financial decisions could be made. Written information on their businesses was absent, because no books of accounts were maintained by them. Women were illiterate and their work was labour intensive, and hence different kinds of mechanisms, such as door-to-door service and simple procedures, were required. Of course, there was high lending risk because of the financial vulnerability of the poor women and their groups.

However, with experience and with the active cooperation of SEWA union and its members and group leaders, SEWA Bank was able to come up with creative solutions to the problems and to develop its own blueprint for lending to the poor. Some solutions to the problems described above involved assessing their credibility on financial behaviour rather than depending on collateral or security. An emphasis was placed on group pressure from their trade group. Providing extensive credit-related extension services was made an integral part of all loans. Creating the

© John M. Berridge.

Figure 9.4 Women form their own Savings Groups.

bank's own track record on women banking with it and designing simple and suitable procedures was the real challenge. Constantly linking with other much-needed supportive services such as insurance, health care, child care, legal aid and training has worked effectively to reduce women's vulnerability. Establishing a continuous and personal relationship and maintaining interactive contact with the clients has earned for the Bank a definite place in the heart of the SEWA women. They exclaim 'SEWA Bank, my mother!'

As Table 9.2 below shows, credit has expanded rapidly, and the repayment rate has been excellent. Every year about 50 per cent of the funds advanced have been repaid by the members. These repaid funds then become available for further advances. Interest is charged at rates ranging from 12 per cent to 17.5 per cent per annum, and most of the loans have to be repaid in thirty-six monthly instalments. Technical assistance is provided to the borrowers where needed, to enable them to use their credit money productively by identifying direct sources of purchase of raw materials, better tools and equipment, links with the market for their goods and services and also ways to acquire skills for making new products and finding opportunities for work. There is a close monitoring of the loans to ensure that the money is spent for economic activities and hence to facilitate repayment. The facts that loans are advanced, in most cases, to members of SEWA union, and also that SEWA encourages and assists its members in becoming economically viable, have a significant bearing on the repayment of advances made by the SEWA Bank. In the case of rural groups, the groups themselves decide about loans to their members. They also decide about the interest rates to be charged. This helps the groups to capitalize and manage their own growing funds.

Perhaps the important indicator of sustainability is the repayment rate, which, as can be seen from Table 9.2, is more than 95 per cent. This could be achieved because the credit advanced from SEWA bank leads to a real growth of economic enterprise among the women, to higher incomes and to the ownership of assets. The improved economic conditions translate into high repayments because of close monitoring by the bank, links between the group leaders and the borrowers, and constant communication between the bank, SEWA, cooperatives and village groups. Repayment for the poor is a complex process, as they lead such vulnerable lives, and so are often in the grip of a crisis. At such times, the bank attempts to understand their problems, reschedule their loans and link with SEWA to provide supportive services. The Bank has also started its own work insurance scheme, which supports borrowers in times of crises.

Table 9.2 Advances and Repayment of Funds of SEWA Bank

Year	No. of Women	Advances Rs.	Repayments Rs.	Repayment Rate
1975–6	5	680	0	0%
1980–1	163	248,975	262,738	96%
1985–6	3,366	4,312,237	3,492,911	93%
1990–1	9,132	12,015,000	9,324,070	95%
1995–6	11,522	23,020,000	15,525,000	96%

Source: SEWA Bank Annual Reports.

SEWA Bank is also involved with banking activities in 'Parivartan', a World Bank Project of Slum Networking in collaboration with Ahmedabad Municipal Corporation covering 100 slums, in upgrading slum infrastructure under the leadership and management of local women. SEWA Bank also has special schemes for rehabilitating the families of mill workers in recently closed mills in Ahmedabad city through their women. The effects of these innovations on the lives of poor women can be illustrated through the history of Hanifa Ramjanbhai Baloch, a client who banks with SEWA Bank.

Business Life Story of Hanifa

Name: Hanifa Ramjanbhai Baloch
Age: 45
Occupation: Tea Vendor
Address: On Sabarmati river bank
Children: Two Sons

Hanifa's husband was a daily-paid wage-labourer in a private factory. His work was not regular, so Hanifa took up tea-vending on a rented cart, paying a rent of Rs. 10 per day, her day's total income being Rs. 20. In 1978, Hanifa was introduced to SEWA Bank by Sushila, a rag-picker, and a member of SEWA. Hanifa opened her savings account with Rs. 5 and then saved every day. Soon she applied for a loan.

a. The first loan of Rs. 1,500 was utilized to buy a cart of her own, and to repair the roof of her hut with a waterproof sheet. As a result of the loan, she saved the cost of the rent, thus saving about Rs. 300 per month and coming to own her own means of production.
b. A second loan of Rs. 5,000 was utilized for buying her stocks from the wholesaler on cash payment. Earlier she bought the stock on credit from a local retailer, the interest being paid at 10 per cent per month. This loan allowed her to save Rs. 450 every month on the interest previously paid on borrowing.
c. The third loan of Rs. 5,000 was utilized to buy her neighbour's hut, by which means her earlier domestic space of six feet by five feet was more than doubled.
d. A fourth loan of Rs. 10,000 was utilized to buy tin sheets for the roof (the former roof was of jute bags). It was also used to pay tuition fees for autorickshaw driving for her husband. This loan saved periodic recurring expenditures.
e. A fifth loan of Rs. 10,000 was utilized to install an electricity connection in her house, costing Rs. 7,500; the rest was spent to connect the drainage to drain off the storm water during the monsoon.
f. The sixth loan of Rs. 15,000 was utilized to build up the cart into a 'cabin', adding more room and a wider variety of stock, such as biscuits, snack packets, and chocolates, in addition to the tea she sold. Rs. 2,000 was also spent for water connection in the house.
g. A seventh loan is planned for
    i.   buying another cart to be managed by her son;
    ii. another cart for herself to serve a hot lunch of 'dal roti'; and
    iii. a toilet.

The impact:

- Through these loans her income and assets have increased. She has also improved her family's living conditions, created employment for her son and saved Rs. 16,000, which remains in her name in her bank account.
- Her family eats three times a day now. Her husband earns Rs. 50 per day from his rented rickshaw. She intends to buy an autorickshaw for him.
- She paid fees for another son to learn auto repair in a roadside garage.
- She linked another 100 to 120 neighbouring women and relatives to SEWA bank.
- Twice her hospitalization was covered under the Work Security Insurance Scheme of the Bank.
- She is one of the gold card holders of SEWA bank, and hence entitled to quick personalized service.

Problems and Constraints

- A constant threat of her cabin's being demolished at any time by the city authorities for want of a licence that the authorities will not give her.
- Regular payment of protection money to the police.
- The unstable mentality of her husband.
- A sickly mother.

The Growth of Rural Banking

SEWA started organizing rural agricultural labourers in 1977 as a union, but soon discovered that in the rural areas there is more need for developmental activities. Women needed credit, as the rates asked by private moneylenders were exorbitant, and the women had no access to banks. Unfortunately, Reserve Bank of India rules did not allow SEWA bank to extend its activities to rural members. So, while rural women continued to organize into cooperatives, producer groups and the union, their activities could not be supported by credit. Finally, after years of pushing at the policy level, only in 1994 was SEWA bank allowed to extend its activities to five rural districts, thanks to the Maranthe Committee Report of 1992.

Expansion in the districts was through village-level groups. These groups were unregistered, but have formed a district-level registered

Savings and Credit Association. SEWA Bank, while lending, also carries out ongoing training of village-level groups as well as district-level organizations in the five districts.

Housing

In response to demand from members, SEWA Bank has been gradually increasing its share of loans for housing. To date, more than one-third of its portfolio is housing loans. For self-employed women, their home plays a central role in their economic and earning activities. This is true for all: urban and rural; producers and workers; vendors as well as cultivators; artisans as well as rag-pickers – all working women. Their home is their workplace. Their home is a workshop, a store, a warehouse and a source of inputs such as water and electricity. For these women, the home is the productive heart of their enterprises, however modest. Housing loans for poor women range from loans to repair a wall or a door, to 'monsoon proofing', to adding a room, to deposits for rent, to buying a new house. They also include loans for water or electricity connection or installing a toilet. To date, SEWA Bank has provided loans totalling Rs. 50 million to 6,000 women for housing purposes. Dr Monique Cohen writes in her field note as follows:

> SEWA Bank estimates that nearly half of its loan portfolio is invested in housing. These funds are used for incremental improvements in housing, new construction as well as home repairs. Given the objective of micro- finance to enable the poor to improve the quality of their lives, it is clear that this kind of investment can achieve dramatic results. The impact is visible not only in the increased asset value of the house but also in the improvement in the quality of the environment in which the poor live.
>
> Poor people do not view their houses as passive investments. Rather home improvements are seen as an investment which will generate both short- and long-term returns. Borrowing for home improvements enables changes that can raise the earning capacity of those living in slums and substandard urban neighbourhoods.
>
> For many SEWA members, their homes are their workplaces. For a vegetable seller it may be her market stall; for others who carry inventory it is a storage place; for piece rate workers, including those involved in textiles, *bidi* rolling and incense making, their home is their workplace. A home improvement may include the installation of a lock on a door, a new roof, a level floor, or a space where one can store two weeks' rather than a day's worth of recyclables. All such investments can make a difference to the returns from one's business. In addition, borrowing for an electricity connection permits a micro-enterprise to shift technologies and possibly raise labour productivity.

For SEWA's members who are in the unorganized trades, earnings are low and vulnerability to crisis is high. Protection against risk is a high priority. Borrowing to install a lock on a door provides security. This not only translates into a safeguard against theft but also means that one can safely leave an adolescent daughter at home to continue production while a SEWA member goes to market, a meeting or to purchase inputs. In an uncertain environment, such small investments can be viewed as risk mitigation strategies, enabling a woman to minimize losses by enabling the working woman to increase her control over her production or other work.

Upgrading is an important use of a SEWA housing loan. Prior to taking a housing loan most SEWA members are primarily home owners or long-term renters with secure occupancy who live in substandard dwellings in slum neighbourhoods. These dwellings are usually 'temporary' structures with walls of un-nailed planks or made from mud mixed with straw. Roofs may be made of a variety of scrap materials and dirt floors are the rule. Dark and damp houses make for low productivity and insecure work environments. Dampness during the rainy season and lack of ventilation year round have negative health implications for residents. A loan of Rs. 10,000 to 25,000 permits the borrowers to gradually transform such homes into brick structures with plaster-covered walls and tiled floors. Windows are installed, providing light and the circulation of air. Scrap roofs are replaced with corrugated sheets.

In the area of Khodiyarnagar, a part of Behrampura which is a ward of the city where there are about 2,500 SEWA Bank clients, housing loans have been important. They enable the borrowers to replace their temporary shacks by three-room permanent houses. The incremental process of transformation seems to follow a consistent sequence beginning with reconstruction of one room, rebuilding the walls and levelling the floor. For example, a paper-picker, now into her second loan of Rs. 10,000, had completed the walls (brick construction followed by plastering) and tiled the floors of two rooms. Upon repayment of this loan, probably within 18 months, she intends to borrow again for housing. She will complete the final phase of upgrading the house: the side wall or outer wall of the third room and the roof will be completed. A 'rangati' cloth dyer is now into her second housing loan. The first loan was of Rs. 5,000, the second for Rs. 15,000. She has now completed the upgrading of her house. She has installed a floor, another asset, in a room in which she sleeps and cooks.

SEWA has only one loan product regardless of the stated purpose of the loan or whether it is secured or unsecured. Terms are

- 3 year term;
- loans up to a ceiling of Rs. 25,000;
- interest rate: 17 per cent per annum;
- repayments are made monthly;
- interest is paid on outstanding balance; and
- 1 guarantor required if loan under Rs. 2,000; otherwise 2 guarantors are needed for each loan.

Among the clients visited in Behrampura, three had received housing loans, two were on their second loans. Many of the loans were in excess of Rs. 10,000. With monthly instalments levels of between Rs. 500 and Rs. 1,000, these loans represent significant payments for women whose daily incomes vary between Rs. 60–100 per day. Yet two had paid off their loan in under the three years, one within 18 months.

While a review of the individuals' earnings level does not suggest such a strong ability to pay, the question is: how are such loans affordable? Part of the answer lies in the savings criteria used by SEWA in assessing loan eligibility of the client. A regular pattern of savings must first be demonstrated. The passbook of one borrower with a Rs. 25,000 housing loan indicated that she had opened a recurrent savings account in September 1993 and deposits Rs. 50 monthly. Currently her savings balance totals Rs. 39,393. A second factor confirmed from findings from other countries is that the poor are often willing to pay as much as 60 % of their income on housing when they have title to this asset. It would appear that SEWA members are no different. Thirdly, in many households visited, housing loans are seen as the responsibility of all the members. With a husband who is a former mill worker and two sons who are garment workers, a paper picker indicated that it is the family that together pays the instalments; everyone contributes to the cost of the house (Cohen 1998).

Integrated Work Security Scheme

As was mentioned earlier while arguing for so-called consumption loans, poor women are vulnerable to all manner of crises. They are continuously subject to individual crises such as sickness, social crises such as riots, natural crises such as floods and economic crises such as the unavailability of raw materials and the collapse of markets. Each crisis threatens to take them into the spiral of increasing poverty and vulnerability. In order to support its members in times of crisis, SEWA Bank has started its own scheme, and has demonstrated that insurance for SEWA members can be run in a self-reliant and financially viable way.

Twenty thousand members were covered in 1996 in a scheme run by SEWA Bank in collaboration with the Life Insurance Corporation and The United India Assurance Corporation. It covers the events of death, accidental death, sickness, widowhood, and loss of household goods and work tools in case of flood, fire, riot or storm. There is also coverage for maternity benefit as a special case, in view of the high rate of maternal mortality amongst poor women. In respect of maternity protection insurance, members availed themselves of the benefit of Rs. 82,800 in 1996.

Table 9.3   Premiums Paid vs Claims Paid

	Life Insurance Corporation		United India Assurance	
Year	Premium Paid	Claims Paid	Premium Paid	Claims Paid
1992–3	750,000	570,000	150,000	127,517
1993–4	150,000	960,000	210,000	370,420
1994–5	180,000	1,161,000	300,000	480,639
Total	1,080,000	2,691,000	660,000	978,576

Source: SEWA Bank Reports.

In 1995, Dr Helzi Noponen undertook a study of crises, setbacks and chronic problems – focusing on both the determinants and the impact of economic stress among SEWA women. The study analysed the incidence of economic stress that disrupts the household economy, considering frequency, costs and subsequent coping strategies. The analysis revealed that women who had been members of SEWA for longer periods, who had savings accounts in SEWA bank, and who contributed a greater earnings share to total family income had fewer stresses. The analysis underscores the positive effect of SEWA programmes in financial services, social security, and cooperative and trade union activities. The conclusions lend support to arguments in favour of the efficacy of credit-plus rather than minimalist credit programmes for poor women.

Performance of SEWA Bank

The real performance of the Bank is the impact on the lives of its depositors and borrowers. The following life history is a case in point. Nanuben started life as an agricultural labourer in the village Mehsana in the District of Gujarat. She and her husband were both earning Rs. 3 per day but, owing to irregular work in the village, decided to migrate to Ahmedabad city in search of work. They entered the city, in 1978, with Rs. 7 in their pockets. Luckily, her grandfather had one small hut in a slum on the river bank, which he rented to them at a rate of Rs. 5 per month. Nanuben joined her grandmother in the business of trading old clothes, going from house to house with a basket of new utensils that they exchanged for old clothes from housewives. Nanuben and her husband also took lessons in sewing so that they could repair the clothes exchanged for utensils and sell them at a good price. They learned this skill from their neighbour by paying fees of Rs. 125 for six months.

At that point, Nanuben was introduced to SEWA Bank by Chandaben, one of the leaders of their community and a long-time SEWA member. Nanuben took a loan of Rs. 500 in the year 1978, out of which she bought a basket at Rs. 125, some aluminium utensils worth Rs. 125 and also some food grains and oil for consumption. She made a profit of Rs. 400 out of this small investment, which she employed in business along with a second loan of Rs. 1,500. Thereafter she kept on repaying one loan and taking another loan, using the loan money and profit from business to buy a house and household furniture, investing in gold and silver, marrying her daughter and saving in the Bank. Nanuben recalls that: 'We were living in a hut and were eating only once a day, sleeping on floor, when we came to Ahmedabad; now we have a pukka house, with bed and fan, stock of food grains, groundnut oil, spices and soaps and match boxes. Earlier, I was myself washing and repairing all the clothes. Now we have employed one tailor who repairs clothes and a washerman comes daily to my house for collecting clothes for washing.'

SEWA Bank has demonstrated that it is not only possible but also profitable to run a bank of and for poor women. When poor women themselves own the bank, they take a keen interest in its management, ensuring high repayment rates, maximum surpluses, and efficient use of resources. Table 9.4 below shows the performance of SEWA Bank as compared to the Public and Private Sector banks in India.

The figures show that SEWA Bank has a high degree of stability, as its ratio of own to borrowed funds is higher; capital adequacy ratio and debt–equity ratio are the two major indicators of the financial health of any

Table 9.4 Comparative Performance Criteria among Indian Banks, 1994

Financial Ratios	Public Sector Banks	Private Sector Banks	SEWA Bank
Stability: Capital + Reserves/Deposits	0.07	0.03	0.13
Profitability:			
Profit/Deposits	0.02	0.007	0.01
Profits/Advances	0.03	0.01	0.03
Liquidity:			
Loans/Deposits	0.46	0.49	0.34

Source: SEWA Bank Annual Reports.

bank. SEWA bank has achieved the above prescribed norms even by international standards, and definitely at a higher standard than the Public Sector Banks and Private Sector Banks of our country. The performance figures also show that poor women contribute towards capital formation, thus calling into question the common perception of the poor as a 'burden' or case for 'expenditure'. When they are stakeholders in the enterprise they put forth their best efforts to make it viable. In spite of their poverty, the board members of SEWA Bank are very concerned to ensure that the profitability of SEWA Bank remains high.

Conclusion

From the point of view of the sustainability of the micro-credit programme itself, if the people own the institution and participate in its management, the benefit of the small guarantee group approach will extend to the operation as a whole. That is, the collective responsibility covers not merely agreeing to loan proposals and ensuring repayment for a small group but also raising and maintaining capital, including setting interest rates on savings and credits. Thus they ensure the viability of the entire banking operation. This active participation of the members and the Board is critical to the success of SEWA Bank. In other words, banking should be driven by those who save and borrow, not by the rules or the rule-keepers.

From the point of view of the poor women themselves, their involvement in and ownership of a successful institution enhances the collective strength and empowerment that come with organization. Poverty is characterized by vulnerability, powerlessness and dependency, as well as lack of income. Collective organization and ownership of wealth – the capital fund – and thus of a significant economic and social structure both address the psychological consequences of being poor and help challenge the wider structure of society.

From a still broader point of view, the democratic structures and functioning of member-owned or controlled micro-credit institutions can help to strengthen the democratic systems of the country. Democracy and development require active and informed participation from the grass roots. Democratic people's organizations and institutions can provide a valuable learning environment for the poor, leading to their proper participation in wider democratic structures. That is, just as in building a democratic society the political process contributes in expressing the wishes of the voters, so the economic process must also express the wishes of the majority. When this happens, the political economy of nation building becomes a constructive process.

I will close with the words of another SEWA customer. In Zebunissa's words:

> Riots are our worst enemies. A mob attacked our houses. I picked up my children, my little plastic box and ran to the police station for protection. We stayed in a relief camp for a few weeks. While the police and the minister visited us our houses were burnt and looted. The first thing that I did after being relieved from the camp, was to go to the SEWA bank.

Zebunissa appeared at the bank counter with her pass book with Rs. 700 deposits and Rs. 1,500 loan outstanding. The bank lent her further to rehabilitate her life and livelihood. Her precious little plastic box contained her deceased husband's photograph and her SEWA bank pass book! For SEWA bank, Zebunissa is not a 'defaulter', but a partner. Development finance must develop people, not only their financial status.

References

Cohen, M. (1998), *Housing, a Key Component of SEWA Bank's Loan Activity: Observations from a Field Visit*. Washington: Microenterprise Development USAID, and CGAP, member of the World Bank.

SEWA Bank (1975–6, 1980–1, 1985–6, 1990–1, 1995–6), *Annual Reports*, Ahmedabad, India.

10

Micro-credit as a Path from Welfare to Work: The Experience of the Full Circle Project, UK

Ruth Pearson

Women have long been economic agents in their own right, and their entrepreneurial activities have involved accessing financial credit for production, for trade and for reproductive and domestic activities. What is new in the present time is the way in which national and international policy makers have seized the policy tool of micro-credit and focused it on poor and low-income women in many different parts of the world, as a poverty alleviation tool as much as as an initiative to enhance women's entrepreneurial capacities and opportunities. Development agencies, as well as women's organizations and NGOs, have actively promoted credit as a missing link in the increasingly monetarized global market we inhabit today. But this is not only happening in developing countries. Ever since micro-credit programmes were embraced by the indefatigable Hillary Clinton, micro-credit has also been promoted as a path for North American and European countries, particularly in the context of debates about social exclusion and about reform and modernization of welfare regimes in the North (Rogaly, Fisher and Mayo 1999).

Developments in the UK – Following the US – Micro-credit as Tool Against Social Exclusion

This chapter is based on my political activism as well as my academic experience. In Norwich, where I used to work at the University of East Anglia, I was the chair of a women's organization called WEETU (the Women's Employment, Enterprise and Training Unit). This is an NGO (not-for-profit) organization that was set up, in 1988, with the objective of lobbying and influencing policy and also providing a service to women in the locality to enhance their opportunities in employment, enterprise and training. This region of the eastern UK, of which Norwich is one of the principal cities, has a significant population of rural low-income women with a distinct set of challenges. Activists there were inspired by examples from the South, particularly by SEWA in India and the Grameen Bank in Bangladesh. We were also conscious of the pioneering efforts in North America by South Shore Bank and WSEP (the Women's Self Employment Project in Chicago). With these models in mind, we set about developing and launching the first peer collateral micro-credit project for low-income women in the UK: The Full Circle Fund.

New Labour – New Approach

The start of this project coincided (more or less) with the General Election in May 1997 and the coming to power of the New Labour government of Prime Minister Tony Blair. This government had set the regeneration of Britain at the heart of its national policy – a regeneration that was badly needed. Central to this major initiative was its pledge to reorganize employment and welfare policies within a specific set of objectives. As one of its new goals, the new Labour government signalled, in 1997, that it intended to combat social exclusion. Social exclusion arose from the economic and social dynamics that continually re-created the situation whereby important segments of the population remained outside key institutions, including the labour market, the housing market, and the various opportunities for education and training. This situation was re-creating, in certain localities and groups, generations of people who were welfare-dependent, who had no expectation of getting paid employment and, in many cases, had no experience in two or three generations of people within their families of being in regular paid employment. Indeed, by the late twentieth century, certain areas of distinct geographical exclusion had been spawned in the UK. These regions were typified by being badly maintained and resourced areas of social housing (called estates) where households with multiple deprivation were concentrated. All the elements of social exclusion converged in these locales.

Such geographic concentrations occurred partly because of the devastation of particular manufacturing or heavy industries located in regional towns and cities. The coal-mining sector, the iron and steel industries and the textile industry had laid off tens of thousands of workers, most of whom were men, except in the textile trades, where women predominated. Men and women were made redundant and, because of their age and lack of experience in new technologies and work practices, had never been able to find alternative employment since being laid off by old industries. These concentrated areas of social exclusion also contained an increasing number of young people who, in previous generations, would have left school and entered industrial apprenticeships or unskilled jobs. This younger cohort also swelled the ranks of the unemployed, creating a new category of never-employed. In addition, their difficult situation was made worse by changes in social attitudes, particularly the rise of divorce and the reduction of prejudice against unmarried mothers, together with the espousal of consumerist rather than social values. This resulted in the growth of a particular section of welfare-dependent people, including a significant number of single (unsupported) women, the majority of whom are solely responsible for their children.

Against this background, the new Labour government set up a Social Exclusion Unit and created a series of policy initiatives – the so-called New Deal. The aim of the New Deal was to provide work experience for different groups of people currently outside the labour market and ultimately to equip them with skills and attitudes likely to facilitate their chances of finding a job in the fast-changing new economy. This was an ambitious undertaking. There were initially New Deals for young people (those less than twenty-five years of age) and, subsequently, New Deals for the long-term unemployed, the disabled and those over fifty years old. There is also a New Deal for lone parents, which encourages single parents to return to paid employment after their youngest child is enrolled in primary school.

These initiatives were squarely focused on the employed labour market. The options available for participants in the schemes comprised subsidies, employment with participating companies, voluntary work in environmental projects, and training, as well as basic education. However, in 1997–8 there was no consideration given to self-employment as a route out of welfare dependency. Indeed, as Prime Minister Blair said in 1998, 'There will be no fifth option'. He was referring to the insistence by government that young people, in particular, should not be permitted to receive income support without participating in one of the four options specified.

With echoes of welfare reform in the United States of America, New Labour was committed to reorganize welfare benefits so that they would be accessed primarily through work rather than only through unemployment – hence the Family Tax Credit. This national programme gives monetary benefits and child-care subsidies to parents in low-paying employment. And, finally, New Labour expressed a concern for the promotion of small and medium enterprises and a commitment to reverse the financial exclusion of poor communities. Financial exclusion is a significant hindrance to regional redevelopment as a result of the continuing withdrawal of banks and financial institutions from low-income communities over two decades. In some of these areas, one in ten households are without bank accounts and with no access to financial services.

A glaring absence from the consideration of government at that time was the option of support finance and training to allow any of these labour-market-excluded groups to pursue self-employment as a long-term means to support themselves and their families. In spite of the dissemination of micro-credit and its apparent link to the creation of micro-enterprises in the developing world and in North America (as Houghton and Coyle attest in this volume) micro-credit and enterprise support for the unemployed and socially excluded in the UK were very slow to make their way onto the government agenda.

Credit for Low-income Women: The Story of Full Circle

The brief contextual summary of policies towards the unemployed and those in receipt of welfare benefits in the UK in the late 1990s indicates that the possibility that the unemployed and socially excluded might be assisted to become successful self-employed entrepreneurs was not at the centre of policy. This oversight occurred in spite of the demonstrated success of such an approach in other parts of the world, North and South. Nor was there much recognition in government circles that low-income women might be particularly successful targets for credit and enterprise assistance, despite the documented evidence of the proficiency of women in financial and business activities in previous eras.

In this context, it was understandably difficult to persuade local business, banking and policy-makers in Norfolk, a conservative, risk-averse corner of rural England, that banking for the poor was possible or even desirable. But the burgeoning new social banking movement at a national and international level had already taken on many of the lessons of micro-credit development in the South. The dynamism of this broader social / financial movement provided a positive background against which we worked for change at the local level. And, in 1997, after three years' hard work, we found ourselves with funding for a pilot project. This support was forthcoming from the European Union's New Opportunities for Women Fund and the National Lottery Charities Board, with a loan fund from CAF (the Charities Aid Foundation) and a Loan Guarantee Fund from the National Westminster Bank. While this initiative was not part of a national programme, we were able to secure funds aimed at supporting low-income women into self-employment via a training and micro-credit scheme, becoming something of a laboratory for testing out training and lending methodologies to this specific project group.

Why Target Low-income Women?

The Full Circle Project – which is currently beginning its second phase of funded activity – was specifically focused on the political concerns about social exclusion discussed above. But, in addition, we were also concerned with the more gendered aspects of this issue, since women had been too often marginalized in previous policies aimed at supporting self-employment in the UK.

In spite of women's active roles as entrepreneurs at different times of the UK's history, there is significant research indicating that women in the UK are less likely to be able to access credit and other resources to support new or existing small business (Westall, Ramsden and Foley 2000). Partly this is the result of women's particular working history, at once both interrupted because of caring responsibilities and concentrated in low-income, low-skill jobs as married women. These employment patterns were exacerbated as mothers increasingly took up paid employment in order to make a necessary contribution to family survival. When women from these backgrounds apply to conventional financial institutions for loans, their relatively low income and lack of assets in their own name are negative factors that exclude them from any serious consideration by most financial institutions; while, for professional women, so-called 'career breaks' mean that they have less professional experience and smaller networks which are essential in successful business start-ups. Given that women's businesses are concentrated in the service sector – including many new personal services such as therapies – they are part-time and do not fit traditional lending perceptions of sound business opportunities. And, perversely, because women have tended to be more risk-averse and ask for smaller loans, these are seen as unprofitable by traditional lenders, who can easily dismiss them. As Mary Houghton notes (Chapter 7): '[t]raditional bankers like big loans'.

In addition, the policy context in which women operate in labour markets has also changed. The growth of two-earner households reflects both the inability to support families from a single adult's income and also a changing official attitude to the appropriateness of 'dependence' even for mothers of small children. There is an increasing insistence that paid work, rather than welfare dependency, should be the route out of poverty and social exclusion. The UK has, like the US, withdrawn from a position that excepted mothers, particularly single mothers, from this position. Government is currently encouraging single (though not explicitly married) mothers to enter paid work, supported by a raft of so-called 'family friendly' policies including subsidized child care and earned family tax credits that 'top up' the wage packets of those on low incomes.

Our project, therefore, aimed at enhancing opportunities for female self-employment seemed to be located in the centre of these concerns. We proceeded to develop an integrated training, credit and business support programme that has so far proved very successful. Norfolk is, as I noted, a very risk-averse area of the country with a very immobile population, very little in-migration apart from professionals and civil servants, and a significant level of ethnic homogeneity. By all traditional criteria, this did not seem like a very fruitful location for an innovation based on practices from the other side of the world. However, in spite of all kinds of gloomy predictions from sideline critics, we have succeeded beyond even our own expectations. At the present stage of growth there are about one hundred participants in the programme, thirty-five new 'front-room' micro-businesses, ten lending circles and a growing portfolio of micro-credit loans. And, so far, we can boast a 100 per cent repayment record.

We are justly proud of this programme. A recent EU evaluation report stated that 'the project . . . operates as an integrated support structure and the training and support measures are examples of best practice in working with women entrepreneurs . . . with the post business start-up support, including the lending circles and micro-credit, the project provides an example of excellence rarely found in self employment projects.' The project has been particularly successful in accessing the target group of low-income women, with a high proportion of lone parents and women from minority ethnic groups enrolling for the training. Women with disabilities are also being encouraged to participate, with positive results.

Women's Participation in the Full Circle Project

After three years of operation the Full Circle project has met its targets. We have developed a robust and viable model of peer lending, piloted training programmes and manuals and, in its second funding phase, we are working with a number of local and national partners to adapt the Full Circle model to different target groups. To date, more than forty loans have been taken out by members, of which over thirty have been to new start-up businesses, with the rest to already existing trading activities. As I mentioned previously, the repayment rate has been maintained at 100 per cent. The businesses involved are primarily in the personal and business service sectors, including office services, training, massage, children's clothing and party wear, knitwear and gardening board games.

The key aim of reaching low-income women, particularly those currently dependent on welfare support, has been achieved. A recent evaluation indicates that of those joining the training and support programme 27 per cent are lone parents, 10 per cent are disabled, 5 per cent are ethnic minorities (compared to less than 1 per cent in the local population) and 56 per cent are claiming benefits. Of those taking out loans, 41 per cent are lone parents, 59 per cent are claiming benefits and 9 per cent are from ethnic minorities.

Participants in the different stages in the project have also increased their participation in other sectors of the economy. A recent follow-up survey indicated that, of 180 women joining the programme in a two-year period, 37 per cent are currently self-employed, 24 per cent have moved into formal sector jobs, 9 per cent have moved into further education and 19 per cent have moved off income support benefit (Watson 2001).

In the current phase, the Full Circle Project is working with a community-based central government initiative (New Deal for Communities) to provide support in the training of both women and men to build up small local initiatives both individually and as community enterprises. We are also collaborating with the Small Business Service of the Department of Trade and Industry to deliver business training to a wide range of clients in Great Yarmouth, a depressed town in East Norfolk. Also, the project is working with commercial lenders to provide business services for this previously financially excluded group of women. In total, the Full Circle Project has introduced a number of key initiatives to tackle critical problems arising from years of social exclusion.

Lessons from the Project

However, the very success in accessing these clearly 'socially excluded' groups points to the contradictions and problems involved in transferring models of micro-credit from one social and economic context to another. In many of the areas where micro-credit for women has been developed – both in the global South and in the emergent countries of Eastern Europe and the former Soviet Union – participants are drawn from groups who have no social security entitlements through an organized non-contributory welfare system. In the UK, however, many low-income people, and particularly women with children, have a right to income support payments and to other benefits, including some housing costs and child benefits. These people stood to lose these benefits if they initiated a small business. The welfare state system has long assumed that any monies entering a household are available for household consumption purposes, so that it is also possible that credit itself could be seen as household income. This entrenched perspective in government circles had the potential to jeopardize micro-credit initiatives. This issue could not go unaddressed.

We have engaged in a long dialogue with various departments of the British governments to try to get them to create a regulatory space for women to pursue self-employment, with the support of training and micro-credit, without endangering the livelihood support for themselves and their families. There are two issues involved here. First, it must be acknowledged that it takes time to grow a micro-business. It is not something that can be done from one day to the next, and it is important that as well as credit being available there is a welfare shelter that would allow women to try out trading. And, providing their surplus is re-invested in the small but growing business, there should be no loss of entitlement to welfare support. Secondly, just as our training programme enables participants to separate out the family budget from the financial flows connected with their mini-enterprises – an achievement that, typically, the women see as a major feat and a tool to gain control over the household management as well as their businesses – so the welfare and tax regime need to understand the importance of this separation. In feminist theory we have emphasized the importance of the public–private divide. This is perhaps a rare example of the central importance of feminist concepts to public policy.

There are other examples of such welfare waivers in Northern regions and countries. The proposal we submitted to the UK Treasury is based on the waiver operated by the State of Illinois. There the promotion of micro-enterprise for welfare recipients is generally accepted, and projects such as WSEP (the Women's Self Employment Project, based in Chicago) are advertised on the welfare cheques given to welfare recipients. However, the UK, and, in particular, the eastern rural county of Norfolk, is not a society that is friendly to the idea of giving credit and support for small businesses amongst socially excluded groups. In addition, the traditional Left is reluctant to give up the idea of full employment; they consider anything less than a salaried post with full state entitlements to be an exploitation of marginal groups. On the other hand, the Right is wedded to the view that people on benefits are really welfare cheats, claiming welfare payments but working for cash in the unregulated grey economy. And, in spite of publicized examples of entrepreneurship and small business success, the UK is not generally considered to be a melting-pot where entrepreneurship is either widespread or normal. These cultural perceptions make it a more difficult environment to work in than North America, and make general policy changes quite complicated and long-winded. Moreover, the existence of a – however truncated – universal safety-net system of social security benefits, including income support for the non-employed as well as unemployment benefit for the unemployed, makes the situation very different from the context of the emergent economies of the Former Soviet Union and Eastern Europe, where coverage and entitlement are patchy, especially as regards domestically-based low-income women.

We have observed one other important distinction in this experience of North/South learning, as we have sought to adapt the lessons from the South to the policy context of the North. That is, if micro-credit is to be included as part of a welfare-to-work programme, it has to be understood that micro-enterprise is not a route out of social and financial exclusion for all those who are currently, or potentially, on the welfare rolls.

First, not all people have the personal qualities, skills, domestic circumstances, or aspirations to become self-employed. Programmes should be developed with a view to providing opportunities for those who want to participate, rather than as an alternative to unemployment or non-employment benefits for all claimants. In other words, such programmes should be part of a welfare-to-work strategy, rather than being the major welfare-to-work strategy.

Second, authorities must appreciate that many people move in and out of self-employment at different points in their working lives. Regulatory systems, particularly around micro-credit and income support, must facilitate rather than obstruct such movement.

Third, it must be recognized that skills in money management and access, plus a knowledge of financial products and systems, are fast becoming part of a necessary *financial literacy* essential for full social participation and survival. The skills obtained in a micro-credit programme have transferability into the mainstream labour market and other aspects of modern life. In this regard, the micro-credit initiatives, such as the Full Circle Project, serve an essential educative function invaluable to both the individual and her wider community.

Fourth, the programmes designed to address local needs must be framed according to the circumstances and needs of the target group of participants. For example, while group collateral structures have been successful in our particular target group of low-income women in Norfolk, there are other groups for whom different combinations of individual loan responsibility, combined with group support, might be more appropriate: for instance, with emergent entrepreneurs amongst the increasing number of urban homeless.

Fifth, it is important to recognize that some communities are, quite rationally, risk-averse, and do not embrace the idea of taking on financial responsibilities for repayment of micro-loans. This is particularly true among groups with high levels of historic labour-market exclusion, long-term welfare dependency and restricted mobility. Moreover, it would be ill-advised to assume that the local market can absorb an ever-extending range of new businesses, however original and niche-market-focused they may be. Projects designed for such groups, in places as far apart as urban Buenos Aires and rural Arkansas, have, as a result, combined credit and support for micro-enterprises with job training for low formal-skill activities, such as care of the elderly or home-care work. For this reason national programmes need to provide overall facilitating frameworks and funding, but they must also allow local communities to customize programmes to suit the characteristics of local communities and target groups. In this context, partnership between the national and local government offices, the financial institutions, including the banks, and not-for-profit organizations / NGOs can be extremely important.

And, lastly, we must beware of unthinking adaptations. Just as Full Circle, inspired by SEWA and Grameen, has learned from projects such as WSEP or the Good Faith Project in Michigan, we have produced a blueprint that perhaps none of them would recognize. Although Mohammed Yunis regularly refers to the Norwich adaptation as an example of the spread of micro-credit to the UK, it is not sensible for a project developed in Poland (like the USAID-supported Credit Mikros) to be adopted as the national model in the UK. Nevertheless, a proposal such as this was being actively considered until recently, even though the vexed issue of benefit entitlement and tax liability does not arise in Poland in the same way as it does in the UK (see Pearson 1998 for longer discussions of the dangers of de-contextualized replications). Adaptations must take into account the local and national conditions.

Micro credit and Sustainability in the North: A Caution

International donors have invested a lot in micro-credit programmes for the poor, as other chapters in this volume attest, and particularly as a tool to provide low-income women with the missing link needed for them to initiate or make profitable labour-intensive low-tech businesses (McKee 1989). These programmes have had varying successes, and there is a highly charged debate in the literature arguing the advantages and disadvantages of this approach and the extent to which they empower women, in terms of economic activity, within the family or the community (Mayoux 1999, this volume, Chapter 14; Rogaly 1996). However, experience in the UK, as in the US, has indicated that it is difficult if not impossible for community-level micro-credit projects targeted at socially excluded groups, such as low-income women, to achieve self-sufficiency through income-generating activities. Working Capital, a project set up in the New England states of the US, aimed to replicate the FINCA and ACCION models developed in Latin America. But the New England project was able to cover only a fraction of its operating costs through income and fees. Small projects in the UK, such as Full Circle, are similarly not able to sustain their operations from income generated within the project. Geoffrey Ashe (2000: 30) reports from the US that: 'Carrying out a substantial micro enterprise program in this country has proved to be an exceedingly difficult undertaking as evidenced by the fact that only five programs across the United States make more than one hundred loans a year, . . . After years of tinkering with the model Working Capital has accepted that it is unlikely to cover as much as half its operating costs though interest and fees and still serve the population it seeks to reach with the range of services it believes necessary.' Full Circle certainly continues to rely on grants to deliver its programme in a form that is appropriate for low-income women in the UK. Much like the Chicago-based Women's Self Employment project, Full Circle is insisting on the need to customize programmes to the particular profile of the women in the target group (Pearson 2000).

Conclusion

The provision of micro-credit to support women's businesses is a very exciting avenue through which to promote women's entrepreneurial activities, to enhance women's financial literacy and management skills, and to extend the range of possibilities open to women in the coming century. But it also needs to be remembered that there is a stratification among potential women entrepreneurs. While all women face a gendered market-place, those with connections and access to business circles and finance will require different kinds of support from those on low incomes on the margins of the low-paid labour market who juggle family and income-generating opportunities with minimum support and resources. It is essential, therefore, that programmes for the latter group are developed with women's organizations and others who have a real understanding of the gendered realities of low-income women's survival strategies.

There remains, as well, another danger. In celebrating the hitherto under-recognized role of women as entrepreneurs and, by extension, the desirability of credit programmes to support their micro-enterprises, it would be easy to support a simplistic notion that women can 'naturally' find a route out of welfare dependency through self-reliance and small business. It is important, instead, to stress that credit programmes for low-income women proto-entrepreneurs should be delivered by communities integrated at the local level, but with an appreciation of national and international policy initiatives. We should not take a universal position that a single micro-credit approach is appropriate for women occupying different spaces in an increasingly globalized world.

References

Unpublished Sources:
Watson, E. (2001) 'The Full Circle Fund', Presentation by Chief Executive of FCF to Conference on Poverty and Social Exclusion in North and South.

Published Sources
Ashe, G. (2000), 'Microfinance in the United States: The Working Capital Experience : Ten Years of Lending and Learning', *Journal of Microfinance: Practitioner and Development Perspectives*, 2: 22–60.
Mayoux, L. (1999), 'Questioning Virtuous Spirals: Micro-finance and Women's Empowerment in Africa', *Journal of International Development*, 11: 957–84.
McKee, K. (1989), 'Credit the Missing Link', *World Development*, July.
Pearson, R. (1998), 'MicroCredit Meets Social Exclusion: Learning with Difficulty from International Experience', *Journal of International Development,* 10: 811–22.
—— (2000), 'Think Globally, Act Locally: Translating International Micro-Credit Experience in the United Kingdom Context', in D. Lewis and T. Wallace (eds), *New Roles and Relevance: Development NGOs and the Challenge of Change*, Bloomfield, NJ: Kumarian Press.
Rogaly, B. (1996), 'Micro-finance Evangelism, 'Destitute Women', and the Hard Selling of a New Anti-poverty Formula', *Development in Practice*, 6: 100–12.
Rogaly, B., T. Fisher and E. Mayo (1999), *Poverty, Social Exclusion and Microfinance in Britain*, London: Oxfam and New Economics Foundation.
Westall, A., P. Ramsden and J. Foley (2000), *Micro Entrepreneurs: Creating Enterprising Communities,* London: New Economics Foundation and IPPR.

PART IV

Impacts and Issues

11

Credit Options, Human Resource Development and the Sustainability of Women's Projects: Case Study of the 'Association of Creative Teaching – Women in Development Projects' in the South-West Province, Cameroon

Joyce Bayande Endeley

In the light of a precarious economy since the early 1980s and the inability of governments to ensure equity in the distribution of entitlements and development benefits in many Third World countries, Human Resource Development (HRD) projects have gained in importance as a way to build up the capabilities of the poor. With an enhanced capacity, the belief is that many poor people, particularly women, will have the primary weapon to fight against poverty. Armed with this weapon, combined with other resources, such as credit and land, which are often the responsibility of the poor to obtain, they will engage in activities that would enable them to secure the well-being of themselves and their families, the sum total of the multiplier effects of these activities being a general reduction in poverty (UNDP 1993 and Engberg 1990).

In line with this thinking, HRD projects have continued to spring up like mushrooms in the rural areas, and are the common type of poverty-reduction projects in Cameroon. With women forming a larger portion of the poor and rural population in Cameroon, as expected, many projects for women (whether women-specific or integrated or components of rural development projects) are centred on HRD. Rejecting the welfare model, government and non-governmental organizations combine aspects of the anti-poverty, efficiency and empowerment models of the Women in Development policy approach[1] in the design of HRD projects for women.

The aim is to arm poor women with the capability necessary to understand and address issues of inequalities and inequities, which exacerbate their subordination.

However, many problems are known to plague women's projects. Among the many problems are meagre capital, inadequate financial credit and staff supports, the lack of women's participation in the project cycle and the lack of a strong policy commitment. The result is that women's projects are likely to be short-lived and non-sustainable (Rogers 1980 and Moser 1993).

It is within this context that this chapter examines the effects of credit options on human resource development and the sustainability of the 'Association of Creative Teaching – Women in Development' (ACT-WID) Project in Cameroon. The assumption is that poor women will participate actively in and ensure the sustainability of Human Resource Development Projects when there are possibilities to gain access to credit and when women can make use of this credit for income generation. Thus, HRD projects, which have a credit component and/or are able to create viable credit options, are more likely to achieve success in developing the human resource of their members and to be sustainable than ones without credit options. Without credit options, and despite other factors such as good leadership and relevant behavioural changes, the project will remain precarious, or will cease to exist, becoming history with the end of external funding.

The data used in analysing these assumptions, or hypotheses, come from four case studies of the Association of Creative Teaching – Women in Development (ACT-WID) project in four of the five Divisions of the South-West Province, Cameroon.[2] These Divisions comprise Manyu, Meme, Mundemba and Fako. While the case studies examined the sustainability of ACT-WID projects in the different Divisions following the end of external funding and projects' contributions to the improvement of members' (women's) human resource capacity, this chapter will focus on credit options for the projects.

For the purposes of this article: (i) Credit options are defined as a group's ability to access formal credit sources (e.g. banks, credit union cooperatives, poverty focused credit programmes, etc.) and informal credit sources (e.g. rotating savings and credit schemes such as *Njangis and Esusu,* moneylenders, pawnbrokers, friends, relatives etc.); (ii) Human resource development is defined as the ability of ACT-WID groups to provide non-formal education to their members to provide them with an enhanced capacity not only to carry out their present roles effectively, but also to perform a wider task. This non-formal education is mainly training for self-reliance and empowerment in the areas of agriculture, business, education, health, networking and project design, etc.; and (iii) Sustainability of the project is defined to include the ability of an ACT-WID group to (a) continue to function effectively and efficiently, (b) generate its own resources and sources of income to fund and sustain, and (c) expand its efforts and means of meeting its stated objectives following the withdrawal of external funding.

Literature Review

To carry out this assessment it is necessary to examine literature on the links between credit options, human resource development and the sustainability of projects, particularly projects for poor women. According to Mayoux (1995:35), credit provision of various forms has become a major feature in women's programmes, and is of interest to many development agencies. The reason for this is that credit is considered a cost-effective means by which development programmes can respond to women's demands. It is also a means of increasing women's income, because it creates opportunities for women to begin new market investments, keeping afloat their enterprises, reducing their dependency on exploitative moneylending sources, and putting into practice acquired capabilities from HRD projects.

Notwithstanding these advantages and benefits, evidence in the literature today shows that credit is still a 'missing ingredient' in many programmes and projects for poor women in Third World countries. While this statement is not necessarily true for projects supported by governments (national and international), it is true for activities and projects initiated by common initiative groups (CIGs). Many women-specific projects aimed at developing women's human resources and capabilities are either ineffective or have failed because they lack access to sources of credit as well as adequate amounts of credit. Unable to raise funds from credit sources to add to groups' meagre resources, many women's projects remain a disappointment to women in particular and a reminder of how time and energy (scarce resources for women) that could have been invested in other productive ways have been wasted. Evidence points to the fact that this type of project, rather than those centred on income generation and enterprise development, tends to omit credit as a component. Other plausible explanations why credit remains a missing 'ingredient' in and an acute problem to women-specific HRD projects include the following:

- Target beneficiaries, usually poor women, are unable to raise adequate funds either as individuals or as a group to carry out project activities. They have meagre capital that cannot be used as collateral to access credit from formal financial institutions such as banks and credit union cooperatives (Sirisena 1998). Even though women may be able to access informal credit sources, the amount of money raised is usually too small for business ventures. In the case of rotating savings associations, borrowers must be members of the association in order to gain access to its credit (Niger-Thomas 1995).

- Projects tend to receive token support from donor agencies, whether government or non-governmental organizations (Moser 1993). Often the budget allocation is not sufficient to execute project activities effectively, yet nonetheless projects commence. The hope is that group members will solicit additional funds from an unknown source. With little or no credit options or capability to raise funds, group members and leaders are left to shoulder the consequences of poor planning or planner's error.

- Concern for a group's access to credit institutions is usually an after-thought when imparted skills and knowledge are not being transformed into income generation, acquired behaviour is being wasted and becoming obsolete, members are becoming increasingly dissatisfied and group disintegration is imminent. This is the 'add-on and stir' approach, which is often used in a vain attempt to salvage women's integration into the development process. If it succeeds at all, imparted behaviour tends to support the creation of micro- and small enterprises, needing small-size loans. These scales of enterprises are considered high-risk ventures because the transaction cost of lending to small ventures is considered high by formal credit institutions, and so projects get hardly any attention from formal sources (Sirisena 1998).

- Donors and planners tend to overestimate poor women's capacity to generate or raise funds for project activities. Group leaders are often not willing, and rightly so, to seek out credit options or to act as the transaction person to secure a loan for the group. This is so because, in case of default, the leader would have to shoulder the burden. Yet group leaders may be able to provide the collateral or facilitate the process for gaining access to credit.

- On a general note, whether applying to formal or informal credit institutions, the process of gaining access to credit is not gender-neutral. Men have better access to credit institutions than women because they have a higher level of education and a better understanding of the lending process; do not require permission from their spouses, as women do, to gain access to credit; and have the necessary collateral for borrowing money from credit sources and users of credit institutions (Howald and Wyckoff-Baird 1998 and FAO 1995).

The evidence shows that where groups have had adequate financial support and access to credit options, projects have been successful in achieving their objectives. However, other evidence points to the fact that small producer groups can be successful without a significant amount of support – that extensive training, credit and marketing facilities have often caused serious problems because of an overly ambitious organizational plan. Whatever the case may be, the alternative is not to have no credit option. Basic access to adequate amounts of credit is of the essence. As Mayoux argues (1995: 46), women should be provided with a range of possible credit options so that they can, themselves, discuss and work out what they want; credit support to women should be context-specific and dependent on the needs and priorities of the concerned women.

But access to credit options cannot, by itself, ensure sustainability. Where the content of training programmes is not both challenging and within the capacity of poor women, project sustainability will be difficult. Mayoux further argued that programmes should take into account the delicate balance between building on women's own knowledge and experience and introducing (rather than imposing) new ideas and perspectives for change, taking cognizance of the differences and potential conflicts of interest between women. Projects should build on and strengthen initiatives that are already occurring.

The issue of cost sharing is another concern raised in the literature. The question is, to what extent can poor women be made to or expected to bear or share the cost of welfare and poverty alleviation projects? Because poor women are often ill-prepared for cost sharing, it is necessary to work out what proportion of the budget can be shared with them without damping their enthusiasm for participating in projects. For, according to Howald and Wyckoff-Baird (1998), women in Cameroon are among the most famous organizers of informal credit schemes, demonstrating that even the poor, if adequately prepared, can contribute to cost sharing.

Study Methodology

The study was a descriptive case study survey. A total of 132 accessible ACT-WID women's groups in the four Divisions constituted the population of the study. Using a stratified random selection procedure, 54 women's groups with a membership of 215 women made up the sample, distributed as follows: Meme–47, Manyu–60, Mundemba–66 and Fako–42 women. Because group members tended to be similar in terms of their participation and experience of the ACT-WID project, the sample size per stratum was small, ranging between three to seven persons per stratum (group). In addition, a total of 54 group leaders, all women, were interviewed using an interview guide. A questionnaire and interview guide were developed and used in collecting data from the 215 randomly selected women members and 54 group leaders respectively. The instruments collected data on women's awareness and perception of, and participation in, the ACT-WID project; the sustainability or non-sustainability of the ACT-WID project after withdrawal of external support; and the characteristics of the ACT-WID members.

Besides interviewing respondents, the following data collection methods were also employed: informal discussions and field visits to sites of business or funded projects. The latter method was useful for the verification of how project funds and other support, especially from external sources, were put to use by members. Researchers also had informal discussions with members and non-members regarding their perceptions of project contributions to family welfare and the development of the village/community at large. The period of field data collection, which lasted between three and four weeks, depended on the accessibility of the sites studied and the location of respondents.

Major Findings

In this section, relevant findings that are helpful in examining the effect of credit options on human resource development and the sustainability or non-sustainability of the ACT-WID projects will be presented and discussed. However, a brief description of the ACT-WID project in terms of the goals, objectives, activities and outcome, and the characteristics of members who were studied will precede the presentation of the major findings. This latter information provides the context necessary to facilitate the reader's comprehension of the article.

Project Origin

As has been mentioned previously, ACT-WID is an acronym for the 'Association of Creative Teaching – Women in Development' project. The project is a direct outgrowth of an earlier ACT project that operated in Cameroon between 1981 and 1989. The ACT project was a joint venture of the University of Guelph (Canada) and the University of Yaounde, funded by the Canadian Agency for International Development (CIDA). As a formal educational programme, the ACT collected and recorded oral literature of Cameroon so as to create culturally appropriate supplementary reading material for Cameroonian students in primary and secondary schools (University of Guelph 1995).

Through the ACT, not only did many teachers become exposed to the development needs and issues of women in rural community work, but it was thought that teachers of the ACT, through non-formal education, could train women group leaders using the creative teaching methods. Thus, through training of trainers, the ACT will contribute to the development of women's human resources and their capacity to provide leadership and to mobilize themselves to take up the challenges of defining their needs and pace of development.

This was the birth of the ACT-WID, initiated in 1989, as a five-year project from 1989 to 1993. Owing to the delay in starting, the project lasted until August 1994. While ACT is an acknowledgement of the origin, WID represents the specific interest, challenges and issues of women in development that the project aimed to address. The project evolved over the years as a broadly based multi-occupational coalition project, with support (resource persons, finance, material, time, etc.) from ACT leaders, the provincial Delegation of the Ministry of Women and Social Affairs (which has now split into two Ministries), resource persons from different disciplines, from the South-West (SW) Province, women's groups in villages and communities in four Divisions of the SW province and the University of Guelph, Canada. The project became operational in the divisions from 1991 (Martin 1998).

Project Aims

The original aims of the project included: to train teachers of ACT South-West in content related to women's issues in agriculture, business, education and health; to develop field-tested indigenous learning materials (the backpack) in Women and Development; to develop a para-professional cadre of women facilitators capable of using those materials creatively to improve the lot of the grassroots women's organizations that they represent; and to share these materials with women's groups throughout Cameroon and in other countries in Africa (University of Guelph 1995: 3).

A core group of six women in each of the six Divisions constituted the Divisional ACT-WID team. The team held workshops and organized activities with women's groups in line with the project objectives in their respective Divisions. Workshops were organized on themes of agriculture, education, health, small business and skills in motivating and mobilizing women at the rural community level.

Project Outcomes

The evidence from annual work plans and the report on women's training programmes in human resource development of the Buea – Guelph project (1995) showed the following project outcomes as per project objectives:

Training of teachers[3] *successfully*: Trained a substantial number of 'facilitators' in the South-West Province in content related to women's issues in agriculture, business, education and health (1995: 8).

Development of indigenous learning materials:[4] This objective was only met in part through the use of local trainers, and proved limited in terms of making a major contribution in the form of printed resource materials. It did assist in providing access to four publications for use by practitioners and met its objectives of basic training in video material production and provision of video resources to support workshop-training activities (1995: 10).

Development of a cadre of facilitators:[5] The project did achieve this objective through the dynamic empowerment of local women leaders using a range of human, printed and video resources, and less so through the use of 'backpack'[6] materials (1995: 11).

Sharing of materials with women's groups throughout Cameroon:[7] The objective was not met within the time-frame of the project. Lack of funds seemed to have compromised this goal. The test of time will determine whether lessons from the project will be broadened.

On the basis of the above analysis, *vis-à-vis* the project objectives, it is not an overstatement to conclude that the ACT-WID pilot-project in the South-West was relatively successful. By 1994 ACT-WID affiliated groups totalled 289, with an estimated membership of between a minimum of 1,445 and a maximum of 8,670. A total of 254 groups registered with ACT-WID and, of this number, one-third had paid their adherence fee of 100 Frs. CFA (about 17 per cent at 600 Frs. CFA per U$ 1) for the affiliation. Each woman in a registered group pays the 100 Frs. ACT-WID project fee on acceptance.

Findings and discussions in the following sections of this chapter will reveal the part played by credit in determining project outcomes and the effect and implications of outcomes on members and the larger community.

Case Studies Findings

Characteristics of Members

As is shown in Table 11.1, the majority of the women were forty years old or younger, the youngest being between the ages of fifteen and nineteen years. However, the women in ACT-WID Fako tended to be older, with more than half above forty years old. The mode was forty to forty-nine years. Even though the majority of women in the Meme and Manyu samples were not married, the larger proportion in the sampled population was married. This, in addition to patriarchy, might explain why husbands and male relatives are reported as heads of household, irrespective of the marital status of the women reporting. While the majority of women had some years of formal education, the women in ACT-WID Manyu and Fako Divisions tended to be more educated. A larger portion of these women could be said to be literate, since they had received some years of secondary education. Women in ACT-WID Meme constituted the largest proportion (21 per cent) of those with no formal education, as well as the largest proportion of women without University education (Eseme 1997: 23). The main occupation of the women was food-crop farming and processing, especially for ACT-WID Manyu women. In the case of ACT-WID Fako Division, analysis of the activities undertaken by members can be used as indication of the occupations of the women. There, many of the women practise and earn a living from fish smoking (for market and home consumption) and farming (Mokwe 1999). A few of the women are retired civil servants, petty traders and civil servants such as teachers.

The average household size was large (between six and fifteen persons) and much higher for women in Manyu ACT-WID. However, the average range for the number of children (one to five children) was below the fertility rate for Cameroon (six children), the exception being Fako ACT-WID women, who had up to eight children.

From the above characteristics, it is clear that the project targeted the category of women who are likely to benefit from human resource development training. While these women may not be the poorest of the poor, data on their occupations, level of education and size of household indicate that they may be poor. These variables have implications for women's ability to save and accumulate financial capital, and even more obvious implications regarding their likelihood of having the collateral necessary to exploit credit options for investment in income generation or to secure the well-being of their families. It is unlikely that projects that do not include income generation can hold the attention of this category of

Table 11.1 Findings Based on The Four Case Studies (1997)

Variable	Response by Division			
	Meme (n = 47)	Mundemba (n = 60)	Manyu (n = 66)	Fako (n = 42)
1. Demographic Characteristics				
a) Age range	20 to 40 years old – 74.5% (M = 21–40 yrs.)	19 to 39 years old – 70% (M = 30–39 years)	19 to 39 years old – 66.5% (M = 30–39 years)	20 to 39 years old – 42.7% (M = 30–39 years)
b) Marital status	Unmarried – 51% (M = married)	Married – 65% (M = married)	Unmarried – 64% (M = married)	Married – 71% (M = married)
c) Head of Household status	Self and joint (self and husband) – 60% (M = same as above)	Husband and Male Relatives – 68% (M = Husband)	Husband and Male Relatives – 71% (M = Husband)	Husband – 52% (M = Husband)
d) Education level	Some or completed primary school – 53% (M = some primary school)	Some or completed primary school – About 67% (M = some primary school)	Completed primary school and some secondary – 73% (M = some secondary school)	Some primary to University – 100% (M = some secondary school)
e) Occupation	Farming – 53% (M = farming)	Farming – 58% (M = farming)	Farm and some food processing – 64% (M = food processing)	Fish smoking and farming
f) Household size	6–10 persons – 63% (M = 6–10 persons)	6–10 persons – 63% (M = 6–10 persons)	6–15 persons – 79% (M = 11–15 persons)	6–10 persons – 59.5% (M = 6–10 persons)
g) No. of children	1–4 children – 55% (M = 1–4)	1–5 children – 47% (M = 1–5)	1–5 children – 47% (M = 1–5)	1–8 children – 84% (M = 5–8)
h) Age of children	5 years and below – 67%			
2. Awareness of ACT – WID	Aware – 57%	Aware – 100%	Aware – 74%	Aware – 88%

Variable	Response by Division			
	Meme (n = 47)	Mundemba (n = 60)	Manyu (n = 66)	Fako (n = 42)
3. Perception of ACT – WID	A training project – 49% No idea – 43%	Training project – 83% Funding project – 33%	Funding project – 100% Training project – 43%	Training project – 88% No idea – 17%
4. Participated in ACT – WID	Never – 83%	Participated – 100%	Participated – 74%	Participated – 88%
5. Benefit/assistance from ACT – WID	None – 83% Acquire knowledge/skills – 17%	Training – 100% Increased productivity of food and cash earning from sales of food	In-kind and training – 100% All said, they would have preferred cash Cash – 9%	Training/workshop Construction of Chakor oven for fish drying Sales of smoked fish and income generation
6. Change in group's activity	No change in group's activities – 81% Reason: lack of finance, adequate land, time and innovation	—	Reduction in no. of seminars End of Njangi i.e. thrift and loan Seek alternative funding sources; e.g. banks, financial houses, foreign donors/grants Involvement of men Implement credit programme on behalf of UNFPA/MINASCOF	Still earn income from fish drying Reduction in the no. of organized seminars Seek other sources of funding Reduce interest in group activities
7. Level of satisfaction with ACT – WID	Not satisfied – 83%; Reason: did not like approach (66%); programme (17%), etc.	Satisfied – 100%	Satisfied – 67%	Poor leadership Generally satisfied

Table 11.1 Findings Based on The Four Case Studies (1997) *(continued)*

Variable	Response by Division			
	Meme (n = 47)	Mundemba (n = 60)	Manyu (n = 66)	Fako (n = 42)
8. If ACT – WID was a success or failure	Failure – 83%	Success	Success	Success
9. Opinion on continuity of ACT – WID	Want a change in orientation of ACT – WID – 55% Want continuity – 38%	—	Want continuity Want expansion *Reinstitute revolving fund*	Want continuity but leadership issue should be addressed.
10. Leader's opirion of problems that affect group success	Lack of funds to carry out training for members Group is unable to raise funds to sponsor leaders in training of trainer sessions Failure by ACT – WID initiators to make available short-term loans at low interest rate so as to enable group to 'practicalise' acquired knowledge and skills Mismanagement and disagreement among group members *Lack of adequate financial support and follow-up by sponsor are held responsible for failure.		Administrators expected payment – a practice during the existence of the ACT – WID project.	

Variable	Response by Division			
	Meme (n = 47)	Mundemba (n = 60)	Manyu (n = 66)	Fako (n = 42)
11. Change in source of funding with end of ACT – WID	—	Experienced decline in availability of funding for project; seek funding from other sources.	Now generate funds from membership and other sources Reduced funding for projects but generate funds from other sources	Project's income-generating activities Group contributions and savings
12. Source of funding with end of ACT – WID	—	NGOs – 48% (Korup project, PAMOL, FIMAC) Others – 52% (USAID, British Council, Commonwealth, UNDP, Africa 2000)	Members – 100% (Njangies) Guelph Canada – 8% Others – 4% (Canadian Embassy)	—
13. Perceived factors affecting the continuity of project	—	Credit – 100%, among other factors, such as transportation market, land and labour in rank order.	Project continuity is assured only the scope might change.	Continuity ensured as long as Chokor oven functions
14. Satisfaction with leader's management of project	—	Satisfied – 87% (M = very satisfied)	Yes, but some express wish that Guelph Canada return and take control of project	General satisfaction

Source: Adapted from findings in Case Studies by Ako (1997), Eseme (1997), Itoe (1997) and Mokwe (1999) Univesity of Buea, Buea Cameroon.
M = Mode

women for long, especially in the case of Meme and Mundemba members. The low level of literacy also has implications for the ability of participants to understand the content of the training. Hopefully the facilitators have been trained in creative teaching and have the necessary support materials to teach women with low literacy skills.

Members' Access to Credit Options

The documents on ACT-WID indicated that the preoccupation of the project was to provide training and not funding for project activities. Therefore, besides the original project budget to execute ACT-WID, the responsibility for financing income-generating activities or projects that arise from training rests on the group members. While many women saw ACT-WID in this light, that is, as a training/educational project, nonetheless, variation existed in how members perceived the project. As is indicated in Table 11.1, about a third of ACT-WID members in Mundemba and all the members in Manyu considered it a funding project. The variation in perception is a clear indication that members were not adequately informed about the original agreement set out in the project aims. Besides, it is only normal and logical that participants should expect some form of credit support. This is especially true considering the nature of project activities, which focus on the practical aspects of agriculture, business, enterprise, education and health, and the participants' low socio-economic status, indicated by a high level of illiteracy, meagre capital and limited or no access to production resources. Anything contrary to this expectation raises ethical issues. For example, should not project planners anticipate and bear the responsibility for addressing the consequences of project outcomes, good or bad?

While ACT-WID was not a funding project, it was expected at least to provide credit support for activities resulting from the training it offered. This was made clear by the Provincial Coordinator of ACT-WID, who, in a meeting of the project management team, stated that 'it was Guelph's responsibility to find outside funding for projects that have developed through the training programme'. The lack of credit support, she said, 'has put the Divisional Coordinators on the line because expectations have been raised among women that if they came for training and organized themselves they would receive funds to realize their projects' (Minutes, BGPMT meeting, 23–25 February 1994: University of Guelph 1995: 14). Not only did the coordinator accept the blame for the poor conceptualization and planning of ACT-WID, but the projects were seen as ineffective by the participants, especially by those, like the Meme ACT-WID members, who could not secure external funding for group activities from donor agencies (Eseme 1997).

Many project leaders had to console or deal with members whose raised expectations were dashed when group project proposals did not get financial support. For example, none of the approximately sixty project proposals sent to the Canadian Coordinator who was acting as a broker received funding. A handful of other projects, like the Chokor Oven Fish Drying project, received funding from the Canadian Rotary Club; ACT-WID Manyu received funding from the Canadian Embassy; and ACT-WID Mundemba received funding from USAID, the British Council, UNDP-Africa 2000 and the Korup project. On the other hand, ACT-WID Meme, in addition to its acute leadership problem, lacked funds to carry out training for members and for income-generation projects.

Analysis of possible sources of project funding for ACT-WID revealed high dependency on external and bilateral donor agencies. Very little funding could be raised among members, and what there was came mainly from membership fees and groups that practised the rotating savings and loan schemes. These latter sources can hardly provide the amount needed to implement projects of a reasonable scale (Niger-Thomas 1995; Rowlands 1995).

Other than commercial banks, alternative formal funding sources that are more woman-friendly are available in Cameroon, for example, credit schemes for poverty reduction such as the agriculture and micro-projects fund (FIMAC[8]) and Credit Unions.[9] But these sources were not fully exploited. Only ACT-WID Mundemba had indicated that it was able to get credit from FIMAC. Attempts at establishing revolving credit schemes in Fako and Manyu were not sustainable. Yet these sources of credit, if integrated as a component in HRD and poverty-reduction projects, will go a long way towards ensuring the well-being and empowerment of poor women. Of necessity, training programmes on how to access national credit options and raise funds, besides the technical aspects of credit management, should be part of all HRD programmes and projects. Likewise, a credit information package will facilitate individual and group efforts to search for funding.

Effects of Access to Credit on HRD of ACT-WID Members

A major and important contribution to HRD is the achievement of ACT-WID in training teachers, as well as in developing a cadre of facilitators who are expected to train other members. Despite these achievements, findings from the case studies revealed a decline in the number of training workshops organized in the different Divisions because of inadequate funding or lack of it (see Table 11.1). The truth is that most groups are unable to generate or get funding support for HRD training workshops, to pay the transport fares of participants/members to attend workshops, or to be resource persons and provide workshop materials.

Analysis of the different case studies showed that groups faced difficulties holding workshops or conducting training owing to a lack of funding. The decline in the number of training workshops was reported for all the active ACT-WID projects in Manyu, Mundemba and Fako. However, they were the ones who continued with HRD. For example, with funding from Africa 2000 and the Korup project, training workshops were organized on environmental sanitation and for the training of agents to facilitate access to FIMAC credit in Mundemba. Fako organized training workshops on fish drying and the construction and management of Chokor ovens. ACT-WID Manyu seems to be the most dynamic of them all, probably because it does not receive funding from external sources (including national sources), but its members are able to raise funds for group activities. With the end of external funding, it has organized training in fish farming, making groundnut oil, processing salt from salt brine and starting and managing a small business, to name but a few (Ako 1997).

In contrast, Meme ACT-WID never succeeded in organizing any training in project areas for its members. According to the leaders, group members could not even raise a sufficient amount of money to sponsor their leaders in training trainer workshops, let alone organize one for themselves. This notwithstanding, there were some group leaders who had been sponsored by ACT-WID or themselves to conduct training for them. According to the leaders, the lack of funds and time and the fact that nothing new was learnt were reasons why further training workshops were not conducted. Nevertheless, these leaders were not willing to share acquired knowledge. Since only leaders participated in ACT-WID training, they alone enjoyed the benefits of training, as they were able to produce soap and process soyabean, milk and other items for sale. This produced considerable ill feeling between leader and group members, with consequences for the sustainability of ACT-WID Meme. Members, however, held the opinion that access to credit would have made a lot of difference. ACT-WID as a broker could have facilitated women's access to FIMAC or credit unions for short-term loans at low interest rates, which would have enabled members to invest in income-generation activities/

projects. It should be noted that ACT-WID projects worked with already existing groups who had some basic skills that could easily be exploited. Many of these groups had joined ACT-WID hoping that funds and/or credit would be available to exploit their skills.

In general, the lesson is that when credit options are available and groups are able to access the different sources or raise funds, the continuous provision of HRD training is not only guaranteed but the outcomes are broadened. This tenet is true for the case of ACT-WID Manyu. According to Ako (1997), the dynamic leadership and consistency in acquiring funds made ACT-WID a beneficial project for women. Through funds from revolving funds, and contributions by members, the Canadian Embassy, NGOs, SNV of the Netherlands and the United Nations Fund for Population and Development (UNFPA), several non-formal educational activities were held. The activities, which included seminars, workshops, round-table discussions, demonstrations and lectures on issues ranging from family planning, through managing small businesses, and salt production from brine, to strategies for dealing with aggressive husbands, were either provided as sponsored assistance or funded with ACT-WID grants. With funds and assistance, the project could make use of resource persons who are not ACT-WID members and hold regular educational and training activities aimed at human resource development. For ACT-WID Manyu, access to credit made HRD a means to an end, not just an end.

Effects of Access to Credit on the Sustainability of ACT-WID Projects

Evidence from the case studies reveals that three of the four ACT-WID projects have continued to exist four years after external support was withdrawn. The three successful projects are ACT-WID Manyu, Mundemba and Fako. The Meme project did not successfully take off; thus it was a total failure.

Of the three successful projects, Fako project retained the appellation of ACT-WID, while Manyu and Mundemba, under new sponsorship and management, are known respectively as the 'Association for Women in Development Experts Cameroon' (AWIDEC) and 'Association of Ndian Women in Economics and Environmental Development' (ANWEED). Irrespective of the appellation, over 80 per cent of the members are former ACT-WID members. The project activities are similar to those of ACT-WID, emphasizing agriculture, health, education and business. However,

ACT-WID Manyu and Mundemba have a new dimension to their project activities that reflects the aims of the new donor agencies. For example, because UNFPA funds AWIDEC, from May 1995, in addition to other ACT-WID activities, AWIDEC has focused on promoting women, population and development activities through a credit scheme for rural women's groups. Likewise ANWEED, with funding from Korup and other NGOs, carries out additional activities in environmental sanitation; trains group members to act as liaison agents for the group to assist members; accesses credit from the 'Investment Fund for Agricultural and Communal Micro-Projects', popularly known by its French acronym FIMAC; and has created a centre at Kumbe Balondo for skills development. In all three projects, the former ACT-WID project coordinators have been retained.

With the exception of the backpack (an objective which was not fully achieved in 1994), the projects have continued to implement or carry out training in the development of members' human resources through activities such as imparting income generation and basic welfare knowledge and skills in diverse areas (see Table 11.1). Groups have continued to implement the ACT-WID policy of educating women on issues relating to their needs and rights. They tend to address practical as well as strategic needs, fostering women's empowerment by carrying out sensitization campaigns on the importance of sending female children to school, of letting female children inherit property and questioning the present division of labour by gender in the various areas of women's triple role.

On the whole, most members (except those of Meme) were satisfied with ACT-WID and believed it was a success, particularly members of ACT-WID Mundemba, Manyu and Fako. The benefit to the community was such that Manyu under AWIDEC now has men members. With the exception of Meme, members were generally satisfied with the leaders' management of group projects. However, some women expressed the view that they would like Guelph to return and take control of the project – for reasons not known.

Nevertheless, all was not rosy with the end of the Guelph-Buea project in 1994. The period after the end of donor funding from Guelph under CIDA and during the transition when new sponsorship (e.g. UNFPA) was obtained saw a cessation or reduction in tempo of activities in all three successful projects, mainly due to the lack of savings from previous activities and inconsistency in the acquisition of funds. For example, in Fako ACT-WID, the second incomplete fish-drying oven in 1994 remains uncompleted to date. Training projects were halted or were irregular. Another concern, particularly for ACT-WID Meme, was the inability of groups to come up with challenging HRD activities of interest to members. For most groups, it was easy to identify suitable donor agencies who could fund projects. Yet most of the submitted proposals received no funding.

Conclusion

Analysis undertaken for this chapter suggests that a number of common factors contributed to the successes experienced in the project areas of Manyu, Fako and Mundemba Divisions. Above all, their success can be attributed to the ability to access funds on a continuous basis, since, for a while, an ACT-WID revolving scheme existed in Manyu and Mundemba ACT-WID. Also, leaders were personalities, political leaders and activists in their respective divisions and at the national level, who knew how and where to get funding and could, therefore, design projects that attracted funding (like the Chokor fish drying oven) from both national and external donor agencies. The ACT-WID coordinator in Fako, Mrs Gwendoline Burnley, was the first Anglophone woman member in parliament and is a retired civil servant; the ACT-WID coordinator in Manyu, Mrs Mary Chu, is currently one of the mayors from Manyu Division; and the ACT-WID coordinator in Mundemba, Agnes Mambe, is a former bank worker and political activist. The women participants, particularly from Mundemba, with a matrilineal culture, seemed to have access to and control over their resources, and some groups proved particularly skilled in fund-raising. In contrast, the failure of ACT-WID Meme can be attributed to a lack of funds, poor leadership, poor project design and poor management.

Irrespective of the success attained so far, the lack of a steady source of credit, short-term loans at low interest and personal savings that can be used for investment were cited as real threats to the continuity of human resource development in all the divisions. Without funds to enable women to apply newly acquired skills and knowledge training, the development of human resources becomes an end instead of a means to an end. Clearly, such a project will have little meaning for poor rural women who want to ensure the well-being of themselves and their families in a monetary economy where cash is needed to purchase basic services and goods.

Looking at the design and the implementation of the project one cannot but question its conceptualization. It is clear that the project designers underestimated and had a myopic view of the difficulties faced by rural poor women in accessing, managing or creating credit, especially as most rural areas do not have economic institutions. By any standards, it is essential and crucial that human resource development projects for the poor must not only have credit as a component of the project but must also exploit all possible opportunities to gain access to national credit facilities, both formal and informal. Women's capacity to generate credit can be enhanced if projects assist in strengthening local ROSCA schemes such as Njangis. Another weakness in the design of ACT-WID was that the time allotted (five years) was not adequate for the groups to attain maturity and independence. A well organized, experienced and effective group will barely take off in five years, let alone a group that is poorly organized with poor leadership – as was the case with ACT-WID Meme. Also questionable was the strategy used in identifying project coordinators, especially in ACT-WID Meme. The active participation of members in the selection of the project coordinator might have saved the project.

Notes

1. The Women in Development policy approaches include welfare, equity and anti-poverty, as categorized by Buvinic (1983) and efficiency and empowerment as categorized by Moser (1993). The policy approaches are used to analyse the appropriateness of interventions in meeting the gender needs of women.
2. The studies were carried out under the supervison of the author of this article, by Ako (1997) in Manyu, Eseme (1997) in Meme, Itoe (1997) in Mundemba and Mokwe (1999) in Fako Divisions.
3. Training of teachers: the actual achievements, in terms of number of planned workshops, were 50 per cent more than estimated (34 instead of 21), while the number of women trained increased substantially (1,269 instead of 324). According to the Guelph-Buea project of 1995, the fourfold increase was due partly to the shift from teachers as the training target to women's group leaders and from a provincial to a divisional level of activity.
4. The achievements were: four publications, titled *Deforestation, Afforestation and Bush Burning in Cameroon* (1991), *Methodology of Fieldwork for Teachers* (1992), *Modern Bee Keeping in Cameroon* (1992) and *World-Wide Effects of the Disappearing Rainforest* (1991); and video documentation of women's activities in Fako, Manyu and Meme by the University of Guelph/ Dschang team, with additional funding from Cameroon and Rotary Clubs. A total of 108 minutes of edited video material was produced.
5. Through the training in the workshops, group leaders were trained, who, in turn, returned to train their members in the dynamics of group involvement in development on related issues in health, education, agriculture and business. In the end, the trained leaders constituted a para-professional cadre of women facilitators capable of using the 'backpack' and other resource materials.

6. 'Backpack' is an information and programme resource to be used by para-professional women facilitators to improve the lot of grassroots women.

7. Project emphasis shifted from material production to mobilizing and training local women, using the core of experiences from workshop programmes. ACT-WID project resources and experiences seem to have been considered as exclusively for South-West ACT-WID. Even though ACT-North-West existed then, no conscious effort was made to invite other Cameroonian women's groups, even as observers, to major workshops. This is the outcome of local politics, which tends to support rivalry, especially between those of South-West and North-West origins.

8. Investment fund for agricultural and communal micro-projects (FIMAC). The aim is to fund micro-projects identified and prepared by rural communities. Priority is given to groups with women and women's groups (MINAGRI 1990).

9. Credit Unions can help women to gain economic independence and self-esteem. They have distinguished themselves from other financial cooperatives because they are owned by their members and operate on sound business principles. For example, the Cameroon Cooperative Credit Union League (CAMCCULL), which is the apex organization for all credit unions in Cameroon, has recently created a Women's Department and committees to ensure that women's issues in the operation and management of CAMCCULL are addressed.

References

Ako, I. M. (1997), 'The Sustainability of Women's Projects and Human Resource Development: The Case of ACT/WID Manyu', Unpublished research report. Buea, Cameroon: University of Buea.

Buvinic, M. (1983), 'Women's Issues in Third World Poverty: A Policy Analysis', in M. Buvinic, M. Lycette and W. McGreevery, (eds), *Women and Poverty in the Third World*, Baltimore, MD: Johns Hopkins University Press.

Engberg, L. E. (1990), *Rural Household and Resource Allocation for Development: An Ecosystem Perspective*, Rome: FAO.

Eseme, G. B. (1997), 'The Sustainability of Women's Projects and Human Resource Development: The Case of ACT/WID Meme Division, South West Province', Unpublished research report. Buea, Cameroon: University of Buea.

FAO (1995), *Development Policy and Strategy for the Benefit of Rural Women*, Rome: FAO.

Howald, Barbara and Barbara Wyckoff-Baird (1998), *A Profile of Training Opportunities for Women in Cameroon*, Washington: DAI (Development Alternative Inc.).

Itoe, N. N. (1997), 'Sustainability of Women's Projects and Human Resource Development: The Case of ACT/WID Ndian', Unpublished research report. Buea, Cameroon: University of Buea.

Martin, P. M. (1998), 'Women in Development: Women in Development Back-pack Handbook' (draft copy), Unpublished report, Yaounde and Guelph: Yaounde Project ACT.

Mayoux, L. (1995), 'From Vicious to Virtuous Circles? Gender and Micro-Enterprise Development', Occasional paper. Geneva: UNRISD/UNDP.

MINAGRI (Ministry of Agriculture), (1990), *Cameroon's New Agricultural Policy*, Cameroon: Ministry of Agriculture, Division of Agricultural Projects.

Mokwe, I. P. (1999), 'The Sustainability of Women's Projects and Human Resource Development: The Case of ACT/WID Fako Division', Unpublished research report. Buea, Cameroon: University of Buea.

Moser, C. (1993), *Gender Planning and Development: Theory, Practice and Training*, London: Routledge.

Niger-Thomas, M. (1995), 'Women's Access to and the Control of Credit in Cameroon: The Mamfe Case', in S. Ardener and S. Burman (eds), *Money-Go-Rounds: The Importance of Rotating Savings and Credit Associations for Women*, pp. 95–110. Oxford: Berg Publishers.

Rogers, B. (1980), *The Domestication of Women: Discrimination in Developing Societies*, London: Tavistock Publications.

Rowlands, M. (1995), 'Looking at Financial Landscapes: A Contextual Analysis of ROSCAs in Cameroon', in S. Ardener and S. Burman (eds), *Money-Go-Rounds: The Importance of Rotating Savings and Credit Associations for Women*. Oxford: Berg Publishers.

Sirisena, N. L. (1998), 'Credit Guarantee Schemes in Sri Lanka', *Small Enterprise*, Vol. 9, Number 4: 23–31.

UNDP. (1993), *Human Development Report in Cameroon – 1993,* Yaounde: UNDP. University of Guelph.

University of Guelph (1995), *Buea – Guelph Project: Women's Training Pro-gramme in Human Resource Development: A Pilot Project.* Guelph, Ontario, Canada: Department of Rural extension Studies, University of Guelph.

12

Negotiating Financial Autonomy: Women, Income and Credit in Urban Java[1]

Hotze Lont

On a sunny afternoon in July, I meet Parman in a foodstall on the main road close to his home. Parman is a labourer whom I have come to know very well. He just arrived on a truck that came to Yogyakarta to deliver building material and needed help to unload. Now he is tired and hungry. Parman orders a large plate of rice and vegetables, together with tea and some snacks and, after the meal, he buys a cigarette. For this food and for the breakfast, which he had taken in the morning, he has to pay Rp.4,000.

Then I offer Parman a ride to his house and so we leave. At his house, his wife is waiting; he tells about his job and orders her to fix a cup of tea for the guest. She prepares the drink and asks her husband for the money he earned. Parman throws a wrinkled Rp.500 note down in front of her. Her face turns grey and there is a grimace. For a moment it is unclear whether she wants to rail at him or cry. In the end she just sighed, 'Is that all!?' (Lont 1997–9).

This incident between Parman and his wife may seem to provide an image of the defenceless housewife waiting at home for what her husband is willing to give her. In fact, Parman's wife has two jobs herself, working in the morning and the evening, but that income is not enough to support her family. She remains dependent on the uncertain income of her husband. In that sense, the incident is directly relevant to an ongoing debate between social anthropologists working in Southeast Asia. This debate focuses on the position of the wife in the household, her status, power and room for manoeuvre *vis-à-vis* her husband. On both sides of this debate, the notion is prevalent that women in Southeast Asia have a particularly strong decision-making power with regard to financial affairs. This chapter challenges that notion and argues, moreover, that access to credit does not always enhance financial autonomy.[2]

It is particularly interesting to look at the position of women in relation to credit, since it is a commonplace assumption that one of the main drawbacks for poor women is their lack of access to so-called 'formal' credit. Many have advocated credit programmes specially targeted at women, usually with women's 'empowerment' as a final objective. Advocates believe that access to credit increases women's independence and improves their position within and outside the household (Hashemi *et al.* 1996). Critics of such policies have argued, however, that the idea that credit can create 'empowerment' is overly simplistic, and that, in many cases, the provision of credit (or debt) worsens the position of women rather than improving it (Rahman 1999; Adams 1999; Mayoux 2000). Therefore it is important to look at how women go about obtaining credit in their struggle for more autonomy in the financial sphere. This chapter thus deals with a number of questions. What is the position of Javanese women when it comes to domestic financial affairs? And what are the limitations that they have to deal with? What are the most important and decisive considerations for women when balancing money and the household budget? Many women in Bujung are not destitute, but, under the current economic crisis, most of them do experience considerable hardship.

Before going into detail about these issues, I will give an introduction to Bujung, in particular to the social divisions that play a crucial role in this ward, and also a short clarification of the fieldwork activities that provided the information on which this chapter is based.

Bujung, Yogyarkarta, Java

Bujung is a ward on the outskirts of the city of Yogyakarta, with around 6,000 inhabitants, divided over sixteen RTs (the smallest neighbourhood unit, consisting of around forty households). The central part of the ward is dominated by the well-cared-for houses of local businessmen, civil servants and teachers, more or less pushing away the more humble dwellings of labourers and pedicab drivers, whose houses are concentrated on the slopes of the two small rivers that border the ward. The ward is the home of a community where contacts between neighbours are strong, and voluntary work projects and funerals are well attended. The inhabitants of Bujung can be roughly divided into two categories: one with decent, relatively stable incomes (the upper section) and the other with low and relatively unstable incomes (the lower section).

The first category consists of the descendants of the original families who own much of the land in the ward, plus families of migrants with office jobs. Most members of the original families have junior high school education, and the often own small enterprises or work in the lower ranks of the civil service. The upper section migrants are slightly richer, and usually have a senior high school or even university education. Most of them arrived shortly after 1965,[3] and they have built good-quality houses on land bought from the original inhabitants. Most of these households depend, in large measure, on the monthly salary of one or more office workers, or on the revenues of a well-established enterprise. Although these incomes are too modest to allow for the lifestyle aspired to by the higher middle-class – the car, mobile phone and satellite dish – the important thing is that they are fairly stable. In addition to this stable basic income, they have access to all kinds of larger or smaller sources of additional income.

The second category is that of the poor migrants living on the slopes of the rivers. Most of them came in the 1970s from the dry agricultural district of Gunung Kidul, Yogyakarta Province. Few have more than an elementary education. They depend heavily on daily incomes, which are not only irregular in size, but also disappear when a person is ill or cannot work. Typical occupations for men are pedicab driver, labourer, construction worker or carpark attendant. Women have irregular incomes as traders or home producers; but a large number of women in this category also find regular employment as housemaids or laundresses, which makes for a very low but stable monthly income.

Methodological Issues – Uncovering Daily Budgets, Monthly Expenditures and Debt

This chapter is based on fieldwork conducted in Bujung between October 1997 and August 1998, later followed by a shorter visit in July and August 1999. In the first research period I lived in the ward, where I rented a house with a former head of RW (a cluster of RTs), in the upper section of the ward. I tried to participate in daily life as much as possible to observe daily activities and social interaction, engage in informal conversations with a wide variety of people and eavesdrop on all kinds of gossip. In the meantime I conducted a large number of more or less structured interviews with both women and men. For more quantitative date, I organized a structured questionnaire among 156 households, while ten women filled in booklets with daily income and expenditure.

The issues discussed in the chapter were not easy to investigate. I believe that there is hardly any society where people will readily discuss their financial problems and strategies with relative strangers, but in

Javanese society there is a particularly strong taboo on debts. This created significant difficulties during formal interviews, although the subject was a frequent topic for informal gossip. At the same time, while a number of moneylenders traversed the ward daily, hardly anybody was willing to admit that he or she borrowed money from them. But they were quick to say all their neighbours did.

Another initial problem was the fact that for me, as a male researcher, it was not easy to interview women; both class and gender constraints were inhibiting factors. In the first months, I was usually more or less forced to conduct interviews with the husband, with his wife as a silent witness. He would normally answer the questions, often incorrectly, even though they clearly related to the competency of his wife. Only in the second half of my fieldwork did it become possible to interview women on their own, although this was clearly less problematic in the lower section than in the upper section of the ward. In the first place, it was easier to approach the women in the lower section, who spent more time outside the houses because their kitchens were too small for cooking and laundering. Moreover, their lower status within the community allowed them to disregard general rules of conduct (see also Keeler 1990).

The Position of Women within the Javanese Household

In the ongoing debate about the position of Javanese women in the household, it is commonly agreed that their position is relatively strong, in common with the situation in most other societies in Southeast Asia. The main evidence offered in support of this notion is that Javanese women have no cultural restrictions on their mobility, in the sense that they are free to go out by themselves. Thus, they have ample opportunities to work and earn an income. These factors, it is assumed, suggest that Javanese women make most, or all, of the decisions over the household budget (Jay 1969: 92–3; Manderson 1983: 6). However, there are also a number of more balanced perspectives. Hildred Geertz (1961: 125), for example, observes that there are differences between one household and another, although the balance is usually in favour of the wife: 'household management ranges from dominance by the wife to a point of almost complete equality'. Keeler (1990: 129) also makes it clear that the decision-making power of women is sometimes restricted, especially when it comes to large expenditures. Papanek and Schwede present quantitative figures from urban Jakarta on this issue, and these data confirm the traditional opinion (1988: 89–91). In two out of three households the wife is dominant in the household; in one in five households decisions are taken jointly; and in only one in twenty households is the husband dominant. Wolf (1992: 65), however, questions these research findings and argues that answers can be considerably different if the question is asked in a more direct and less abstract way. Wolf also emphasizes, and this argument is supported by Keeler (1990: 128), that a high economic status is not necessarily accompanied by a high cultural status. Even more significant, when women are given autonomy as economic actors, performing roles that require handling money, taking loans and negotiating over small amounts of money at the market, this, in fact, signifies an inferior social position. Such roles force women to undertake activities that are considered demeaning, and thus have very low value within the Javanese cultural context (Wolf 1992: 66).

The New Order government has taken an active interest in the position of women in Indonesia. This becomes clear in a policy orientation that in the literature has often been labelled 'Ibuism'.[4] Although these policies are presented as aimed at improving women's position in Indonesian society, in reality they clearly try to force women to return to perceived traditional roles. This means that their main task is to care for their children and concentrate on the household, or reproduction instead of production. This message is promoted through various government activities and, in particular, the Family Welfare Programme (PKK). The groups arising from this programme exist at every level of Indonesian society; each mother must participate in local neighbourhood meetings, filled with speeches and activities that celebrate the role of women as mothers. Although many women in Bujung take these activities with a pinch of salt, and hardly any of them puts the main idea of 'Ibuism' into practice, on a discursive level most women have internalized the notion that the place for women is at home.

The majority of households in Bujung consist of two parents and a few (mostly two) children. Typical exceptions are households where elderly parents live with their children and grandchildren, or single mothers with one or more children. In a few cases, other relatives or friends join the household for short periods.[5]

In almost every household in Bujung both the husband and the wife provide income. It proved to be very hard to quantify the size of the contributions of women, because there is a strong tendency among both women and men to disqualify the income-earning activities of the wife as 'just helping the husband' (*bantu-bantu suami*). The general observation is that in most households the income of both partners is substantial, but that the husband earns a little bit more. However, in many households, especially among the labourers of the lower section of the ward, the wife may earn more than the husband.[6] In cases where unmarried youngsters earn income of their own, they are generally free to spend it on themselves. With a few exceptions, they are only asked to contribute in case of deficiencies.

In principle, the household budget is divided into three different kinds of money. Central is the shopping money (*uang belanja*), which is used to cover the daily household expenses. This money is controlled by the wife, and only a few husbands keep a close eye on how she is spending this. Apart from that, there is pocket money (*uang jajan*), which individual members of the household can use for private purposes. There is pocket money for husbands, children and the elderly, while wives have to manage with their shopping money. The third category of monies is that of pooled savings, money set aside for future expenditures. This money can be kept in a special jar in the house, at the bank, in an *arisan* or in the form of durable goods. Whether and when this money is used is usually the responsibility of husband and wife together. Which of them has the major influence in this is mostly a matter of personalities. The difference between these different kinds of money is ultimately determined by who is designated to manage it. In some households the money designated as shopping money may be wholly insufficient, so that pooled savings or pocket money are regularly used for shopping. In other households the shopping money may be more than enough, so that the wife is even able to save part of it for future needs.

Even though the wife has the responsibility for the shopping money, it is the husband who decides on the actual quantity available. A husband can influence financial matters by deciding which part of the household budget is earmarked as shopping money. Most husbands take a small amount from their own income before they give it to their wives, using it for cigarettes, an occasional snack and for gambling. A few 'meek' husbands simply hand over all their income and ask for money every time they want to buy cigarettes. Their wives are often able to save relatively large amounts of shopping money, sometimes in secret jars, thereby expanding their own financial room for manoeuvre. However, tough husbands make a conservative calculation of the shopping money needed and keep the rest as pocket money. In these households, there are frequent quarrels about money, and wives have to negotiate and 'cheat' in order to get a more realistic budget.[7] Although the factors assumed to favour women in the household are also in place in Bujung, their decision-making power is always contested.

Juggling Household Budgets

In the households of Bujung, occupational multiplicity is commonplace. Not only does the household income come from various household members, but each person generally derives an income from several sources. This way, households experience a complex mix of income cycles, where part of the money may arrive on a daily basis, another part on a monthly basis, and the rest only once in a while.

In the eyes of people in Bujung, a monthly income is most desirable. It gives more certainty and makes monthly payments, like those related to education, easier. It also makes a person more eligible for credit. A monthly income is normally associated with civil servants and with employees of private companies; but the many housekeepers and laundresses in the ward also get their wages once a month. The problem with a monthly income is that one has to be very careful with spending, so that one does not live the last days of the month with an empty wallet. Wives of civil servants regularly complained that they were stressed during these final days, and a woman who sold breakfast snacks door-to-door each morning told me that her turnover was significantly less at the end of the month.

People with a weekly income have similar problems of financial planning. They may also find it more difficult to deal with the larger expenditures. A weekly income is typical for labourers in small enterprises, such as workshops and retail shops. However, most people in Bujung earn a daily income, which is more or less uncertain. There are daily incomes for small food traders, home producers, pedicab drivers, construction workers, carpark attendants, taxi drivers, labourers, scavengers and shop-owners, for example. These people have to find ways to deal with days on which there is no income, or only very little. It is also very difficult for them to deal with the larger expenditures.

Some special attention should also be paid to *rezeki*. In Bujung, the word *rezeki* has a connotation of luck, and is used to refer to a windfall, a sudden income, relatively large and more or less unexpected. It is a special element in the fluctuation of incomes. Civil servants regularly receive special bonuses, which they consider *rezeki*. Pedicab drivers may have many customers on one day, or just one tourist who pays exceptionally well. Labourers can suddenly have a heavy, but well-paid, job. The group of housewives who once a year go to the North Javanese town of Pekalongan to wrap *Idul Fitri* presents, also considers this income as *rezeki*. And, of course, winning the lottery is also *rezeki*. People in Bujung like to use their *rezeki* for something special, like buying new clothes or a present for the grandchildren. However, many people are forced to use part to repay their debts, as a way to balance the money cycles. Without *rezeki* few people would dare borrow to deal with unexpected costs.

This situation of unreliable income is accompanied by irregular cycles of expenditures. In parallel with a basis of regular income there is also a basis of regular expenditures. Most of the household budget is spent on food. Most families every day spent similar amounts of money on rice, vegetables, meat or soybean cake, snacks and sweets. Other daily purchases are soap, cigarettes and school fees for primary school. In some longer cycles people are confronted with other costs. Each month there are the electricity and water bills, monthly school fees at high school, and contributions to financial self-help organizations. Each year the rent has to be paid (for those who do not own their own house or land), as well as the costs involved with *Idul Fitri* (the Islamic feast at the end of Ramadan) and also certain high annual school fees. On an irregular basis, people are confronted with costs of illness, and of family rituals – such as marriages, funerals, circumcisions, or reciprocal contributions to other households – as well as housing costs.

Unexpected or not, expenses do not always tally with income. When, for one reason or another, it is not possible or not desirable to mobilize either one's own savings or financial help from others, the only possible solution is to borrow. Shipton (1992: 27) defines credit or loans as 'any transfer of goods or services by one person or group to another, or to any of its members, with the expectation of compensation at a later time'. For the people in Bujung, a number of credit options are available, each with its own advantages and disadvantages. They are presented below roughly in order of importance.

Sources of Credit

A *boss* is one of the most appreciated sources of credit. The option is open to labourers in factories and shops and to housekeepers and laundresses. Most bosses are willing to pay wages up front, and these loans can be repaid through deductions on the future wage, minimizing the risk of default. No interest is charged, and in some cases it is possible to renew the loan before it is fully repaid. Some women like to borrow from their bosses, or even save a part of their wage with them, in order to acquire larger amounts of shopping money. Similar arrangements exist between traders and suppliers.[8] Office workers can often borrow from an office co-operative or even from the financial reserves of their department.

Credit is also often obtained from the small food stores, which can be found all over the ward. In many of these shops it is possible to buy your food on credit when you run short of cash. Immediate repayment is essential, in most cases on pay-day, otherwise you will not be allowed to borrow again. This is called *bon warung*, and it is only an available option for those people who have a weekly or monthly income. Because it is closely connected with shopping, it is a loan taken out by women, but it is often the wage of the husband that functions as collateral. Wives usually take the loan because the available shopping money is insufficient. Later, they will have to repay with shopping money as well, eventually creating another shortage that makes it necessary to buy on credit again. Women in the lower-income groups, in particular, tend to fall into such a credit cycle.[9]

Many women also participate in *ROSCAs* (Rotating Savings and Credit Associations), locally known as *arisan*. ROSCAs have been defined by Ardener (1995: 1) as 'an association formed upon a core of participants who make regular contributions to a fund which is given in whole or in part to each contributor in turn'. The participant who receives the fund early in the cycle has, in fact, received a loan from all others, which is to be repaid during the remaining rotation period. Smaller and bigger ROSCAs (in terms of money) exist inside and outside the ward. Most women in Bujung, including the poor, participate in one or more ROSCAs that provide substantial lump sums.

Relatives are another source of credit. Whether this is an option depends on the family wealth. But even if one has wealthy relatives, they do not automatically become an important source of credit. In Bujung, there are many stories of people who have succeeded in life and have then tried to minimize their contact with poorer relatives. In general, people do not like to lend money to their relatives, because it is highly uncertain that you will ever get your money back. However, it is difficult to deny close relatives a favour.[10] Repayment is, then, usually requested only when the lender is in need of money. In a sense, these loans are often repaid in kind. That is to say, the borrower will always be ready to provide help or practical support in case this is needed. In fact, relatives are most often an option when a woman needs just another Rp.1,000 to buy vegetables or to pay the moneylender. In such a situation it is easier to turn to a sister than to an unrelated neighbour.

In general terms, the borrowing conditions are similar with *neighbours and friends*. In these cases it is also difficult to deny a personal favour; but here, too, the risk is high that the money will not be repaid. The rule of thumb is that when you want your money back, you have to ask three times in advance. In that way, the borrower is given some time to find money for repayment. In some cases people ask for interest on loans to their neighbours, but this is considered inappropriate. These typically small and unsecured loans from relatives, neighbours and friends are much more common in the lower section than in the upper section of the ward and, although men do make similar arrangements, it is most often women who arrange these loans.

One of the least popular options is the *moneylender*. The people in Bujung distinguish among different types of moneylenders. The *Bank plecit* (chasing bank) is a moneylender from whom you can borrow small amounts. The *Bank plecit* is usually a small company, which sends employees around to the houses of the debtors to collect daily instalments. A second type is the *rentenir*. The *rentenir* are single women who live in the ward, give big loans and ask for collateral. Repayment is on a monthly basis. With these two types,[11] the interest is about 20 per cent per month. These moneylenders may allow a borrower to suspend repayments for some time, but when they get impatient they may enter a house and take away any asset that approximates to the value of the debt.

A slightly different lender is called the *tukang kredit*. This is also, like the *bank plecit*, a person who goes around to the houses. From him you can buy all kinds of things, such as plates, rice cookers and bicycle tyres, and pay for them in daily instalments. There is no explicit interest rate, but the interest is calculated into the higher price charged for the goods purchased. Both women and men borrow from these moneylenders, although they mainly cater to women. It is also more practical for them to deal with people who are at home most of the time. Most women in the lower section of the neighbourhood make use of the *bank plecit*; the daily repayments clearly target the income situation in households of labourers instead of office workers.

Another source for credit is the *pawnshop*. The Indonesian government runs a network of pawnshops all over the country, where valuable goods can be pawned. Jewellery, televisions and computers are especially favoured by these pawnshops. The interest rate is around 3 per cent per month. People who can afford these luxury items often use them to deal with unexpected costs. Apart from when they pawn their gold, the poor in Yogyakarta usually go to the illegal pawnshops run by Chinese people. They charge a much higher interest rate than the government pawnshops (around 20 per cent) and give less money for the same article. On the other hand, they accept goods that the government pawnshops reject, such as clothes and household utensils, and so they are more popular with the poor. However, if the loan is not repaid within three months, the assets are sold.

Other sources are the *simpan pinjam*, which is synonymous with an ASCRA (Accumulating Savings and Credit Association). In an ASCRA 'the pooled savings are not instantly redistributed [as in ROSCAs] but kept in custody and allowed to accumulate by lending parts of the fund to members or outsiders for interest' (Bouman 1994: 376). In Bujung these institutions are much more the domain of men. The women in Bujung do participate in the *simpan pinjam* of their RT, but in these associations the loans are often very small and meaningless. In the RTs of the lower section it is common practice not to pay instalments but to wait for a few months, and then borrow from a friend or relative in order to repay the whole loan at once. A new loan, which can then be acquired, is used almost completely to repay that friend or relative. The women themselves call this speculation, as they speculate that the loan they will be able to acquire is bigger than the debt they already have. The small 'profit' they make can then be used to fill holes in their shopping budget. Only a few women participate in *simpan pinjam* with larger loans, but the women come from all social levels. Most of them tend to borrow as much as they can, pay their instalments, and borrow again as soon as possible, disregarding specific financial needs. Before they can take out a new loan, they have to repay the old one. Thus, loans from *sinpan pinjam* are often not immediately available.[12]

Only a few people borrow from the *bank*. Civil servants can borrow money at low interest rates with their income as collateral. All other people need to have land as collateral, and those who have land often consider the risk of losing their land to be too high. The bank is hardly ever a source of credit accessible to a woman on her own, because the necessary collateral is usually in the name of her husband. In general, the bank is only an option for the lower middle class living in the upper section of the ward.

Women and Credit in the Upper and the Lower Section

Even though the financial strategies of women in Bujung differ from person to person, it is possible to distinguish patterns depending on the socio-economic position of a woman and her household. This can best be explained through the cases of Yani and Gunem, and their families, who represent different social categories.

Yani and Sartono. Yani is the daughter of a civil servants from Bantul. In the 1980s she married Sartono, who is the son of a civil servant from Madiun. While Sartono was pursuing education in Yogyakarta, his father bought a small house for Sartono and his brother in Bujung's upper section. After their marriage, Sortono's brother moved out and Yani came to stay with her husband. Now the couple have three children, one in junior high school and two in primary school. Sartono works at the provincial labour department as an instructor, earning Rp.450,000 per month. Formerly, from July to October he could usually make extra money through special projects at his work; but since the economic crisis this has stopped. In the evenings Sartono takes on jobs for acquaintances who want to have their car or motorcycle painted. Sartono hopes that after his retirement he can open a repair shop for cars. A few years ago Sartono borrowed money from his office cooperative so that Yani could open a small shop at their house. The shop was not a success, and they eventually abandoned the idea. Recently, however, they borrowed again, from Yani's sister and from a moneylender, this time to produce snacks and sell them at the market. Each time Sartono receives his wage, he deposits it in the bank and, whenever the shopping money of his wife is spent, they withdraw money from their bank account. Lately, the bank account has often been empty, and in those cases they borrow from the office cooperative or from the bank, where Sartono can borrow without collateral. However, they also have to be careful, because the instalments are automatically deducted from Sartono's wage, and the amount left each month has already become quite small. Altogether, the loans taken out by Sartono and Yani are relatively large, and the decisions about them are taken together.

Not all the women in the upper section are in a position like Yani's. For example, there are many women who participate in more *simpan pinjam* and manage their working capital on their own. Other women do not at all know how much their husband earns, and just accept whatever shopping money they are given.[13] On the whole, women in Bujung's upper section seem to exercise considerable control over the household budget, not only over the shopping money but also over pooled savings, in spite of the fact that they earn a relatively small proportion of the household income. These women themselves seldom borrow money, because their husbands have access to the most attractive sources of credit at their disposal – loans from banks and office cooperatives.

Gunem and Slamet. Gunem is the daughter of a landless peasant from Gunung Kidul. Her husband Slamet was born in Gunung Kidul as well. He came to Yogyakarta to work as a pedicab driver, but gradually he became a construction worker specializing in digging wells. Now they live in the lower section of Bujung, with three of their four children, the husband of their oldest daughter and a grandchild. Slamet can only dig wells in the dry season, but when he has a job Slamet can make Rp. 100,000 in three days. In construction, he can earn Rp.10,000 per day. The wage is not bad, but the problem is that he has many days without work. Gunem has also found a job as a housemaid for a Chinese family with a basic income of Rp.120,000 per month. She irregularly receives extra money for odd jobs, and there are special bonuses for the religious holidays. The two oldest children also have paid work, but they spend their earnings as they please, and only contribute to the household budget when money is short. Slamet and Gunem regularly borrow money from a variety of sources, including moneylenders, *simpan pinjam*, neighbours, Gunem's boss and colleague, and from the pawnshop. The reason for these loans is mostly that Slamet's income is unreliable. When sudden costs arise, such as school fees or the wedding of their daughter, but also for daily food, Gunem's shopping money is often not enough. In that respect, Gunem herself says that she cannot always rely on her husband.

> Slamet often does not have a job and when he does have a job he just gives me so and so much money. That is not enough to take care of the family and therefore I went to work. Almost all the women in this neighbourhood work because they cannot manage with what their husbands give them. If I can, I try to keep some money apart. If Slamet has a good job I can bring some money to the bank, or I buy some gold. Each month I save money with my boss, so that not all that I earn is spent on food. Slamet does not know. He thinks I only earn Rp.75,000 (Lont 1997–9).

Even though she has set some savings aside, Gunem prefers to borrow money when she is out of shopping money. 'I want to keep these savings as long as possible.'

Also, in the lower section of Bujung, not every woman is like Gunem. Some women never borrow, and discuss financial problems openly with their husbands. Other women, like Giyem, distrust their husbands, and are forced to have more secret savings. Giyem is the wife of an often-unemployed electrician. Before the economic crisis, she used to have three different places to save money: one box for shopping, one for business capital and one for circumcision of her son. She kept these last two boxes hidden, and her husband did not even know that the third existed. Eventually, when the son needed to be circumcised, the husband came to his wife to discuss the problem, suggesting 'maybe we should borrow some money'. Then she presented the box saying, 'See, I have saved some money.'

I kept it a secret because otherwise it may happen that he wants to buy cigarettes and he does not have the money. He might easily take from the savings box. Or he is alone and wants to watch TV. He asks me whether I have any money to buy cigarettes; I say: no, there is no money, you will have to do without. Of course he could be very angry when it turns out that there has been money all the time, but he will not. He has been lied to, but it was a good lie. In the end he is also happy that we do not have to borrow (Lont 1997–9).

Another woman said that she did not have a secret box, but 'if I had a husband who like to gamble and hang around [as Giyem's husband does], I would probably have a secret box too' (Lont 1997–9).

In the lower section, most women earn a considerable part of the household income, in some cases more than half, and take out more loans than their husbands do. The major reason for this is that these households depend on loans that are typically linked to the house (itinerant money-lenders and neighbours) and to shopping (*bon warung*). Nonetheless, in this part of the neighbourhood, the conflicts about money between husband and wife are more frequent and intense, and more women feel that they tend to draw the short straw financially. It also happens that in this neighbourhood incomes tend to be lower and more unreliable, and money is therefore more fiercely negotiated. Husbands like to assume that their wives, since they earn their own income, can take care of themselves.

Conclusion

It is too easy to say that women's contribution to the household income and their access to credit determine their autonomy and decision-making power within the household. In other circumstances this might very well be the case, but the situation in urban Java turns out to be much more complex. These households are social arenas where the role division between individual members is negotiated with reference to specific economic, gender and cultural constraints. The positive or negative consequences of access to credit for women can only be ascertained if the question of where these women stand within their households is taken into account.

The social and cultural factors that have been put forward by social anthropologists to explain the strong position of Southeast Asian women in the household are also in place in Bujung. Nevertheless, the decision-making power of these women is always contested. In general, one can say that in Bujung the wife is the manager of the household budget.

However, it is more precise to say that she is in charge of one of the household budgets. Shopping money is the responsibility of the wife, while pooled savings are managed by husband and wife. The relative sizes of both budgets and, thereby, the financial autonomy of the wife, are determined by how much the husband is willing to contribute to the household budget. If the husband is willing to contribute a substantial amount, then the wife has sufficient financial space to determine how much money she wants to have for shopping and how much she wants to save. If the husband is not willing, or simply unable, to contribute enough, then the wife faces financial problems. She can be forced to cut back on expenditures, but most of the time she will look for other solutions: cheating, begging or convincing her husband, or looking for an income for herself. However, this latter option may have an adverse effect when husbands decide they can have more money for themselves and contribute less to the household. Whatever women do, the allocation of money within the household is always subject to a continuous negotiating process, and women seldom hold the most powerful position.

Moreover, the various members of the household are positioned differently in the financial negotiating process, because they have different objectives. Wives are not as much concerned with their own consumption needs. Even though it sounds very much like a cliché, their prime concern lies with providing food for their families, avoiding embarrassing scenes with screaming children and ensuring that they can sustain the reciprocal payments to neighbours, friends and relatives. Balancing the household budget is the search for an optimal or correct allocation of financial means over time. To achieve that, a wife has to deal with the demands of her husband and children, with the demands of her neighbours, with her own consumer desires and with unpredictable circumstances. Husbands and adult children are generally not interested at all in the financial matters of the household. They just want to make sure that there is enough money to fulfil their personal needs, enough money to buy cigarettes, to go gambling and to buy the things they want to buy.

The observations presented here do suggest that the financial autonomy of women in Bujung is, in the first place, related to the actual size of the household income, not only the shopping budget under the direct authority of the wife, but also the household budget as a whole. The less there is available, the greater the tendency of members of a household to compete for control over household money. Thus, women in the lower section of the ward, in spite of their relatively larger contribution to the household and their relatively greater access to credit, enjoy less financial autonomy compared to women in the upper section. This leads us to the remarkable conclusion that when women earn a relatively smaller part of an expanding household income, this may, in fact, increase their financial autonomy. However, this greater independence comes as a result of income from their husbands.

The observations also suggest that credit does not necessarily contribute to female autonomy, or to empowerment in the terms of the 'financial self-sustainability paradigm' and the 'poverty alleviation paradigm' (Mayoux 2000: 2–3). If credit is used as an addition to the shopping money, as is mostly the case in Bujung, not much may be gained. Loans generally have to be repaid, and instalments tend to come from the same budget, in this case, the shopping money. If credit is used for productive purposes, as is hoped for by most micro-finance organizations, this also means more responsibilities and tasks for the wife, and not necessarily more financial room for manoeuvre. The increased income of the wife can also result in smaller contributions by the husband, especially in low-income households, where money is scarce.

Notes

1. An earlier version of this text was published in *Indonesia* 70 (October 2000). My thanks to Frans Hüsken, Gerben Nooteboom, and the participants in the 1999 Women and Credit Conference at UNB in Fredericton. I am also grateful to the Royal Netherlands Academy of Arts and Sciences (KNAW) for sponsoring my research.
2. According to Stoler (1977: 74), 'female autonomy' refers to 'the extent to which women exercise economic control over their own lives *vis-à-vis* men (e.g., in disposing of the fruits of their labour)' and 'social power' refers to the 'extent to which women exercise control over the lives of others outside the domestic sphere'. This chapter concentrates on the financial autonomy of Bujung women, meaning the ability of women to spend money according to their own wishes and insights.
3. The year 1965 is a turning-point, both in national Indonesian history and in local history, the year of the massive crackdown on the Indonesian Communist Party, in which hundreds of thousands were killed. This marked the beginning of the New Order regime. Bujung in those days was the centre of the Communist Party in Yogyakarta. Many local leaders were killed or imprisoned, leaving space for others to rise to prominence within the community.
4. *Ibu* is the Indonesian word for woman/mother. For a critique of PKK see, among others, Sullivan (1983) and Wolf (1992: 69–72).
5. In the two RTs where I concentrated my fieldwork, more than half the households consisted of two parents and one or more children. One in seven households consisted of two parents, one or more children and one or more

grandparents, and one in ten households consisted of a single mother and one or more children. The remaining households fell into various other smaller categories.

6. When one day Panut, a pedicab driver, was found guilty of adultery and banned from the neighbourhood for three years by a popular tribunal, his wife was dancing and singing in front of her house. The reason was not so much his promiscuous behaviour, of which she had been aware for several years, but mainly because Panut was a 'pain in the neck' and cost more than he contributed to the household. A neighbouring woman says: 'He is just lying around each day, only begging for food and money for cigarettes. She is working hard and I really feel pity for her.'

7. Zelizer (1989) has already considered the existence of different kinds of money. She describes the special status of household money for housewives in the United States. She argues that 'culture and social structure mark the quality of money by institutionalizing controls, restrictions, and distinctions in the source, uses, modes of allocation, and even the quantity of money' (p. 342).

8. Traders are often reluctant to ask for such loans from their suppliers, as they are concerned about the negative effects this might have on their business relationship. That risk is not perceived to be as high between labourers and their bosses, although I came across one case where a labourer was fired because he was taking too many loans.

9. This is a good example of why the poor pay more. The need to shop on credit forces poor housewives to buy in the local shops instead of in the market, where prices are cheaper. However, the owners of these neighbourhood shops are not able to charge interest or higher prices to those who want to buy on credit, even though this practice threatens the survival of their business.

10. A solution for this problem is frequently found in the informal pawning of assets; if you lend money to your sister, you can use her television until the money is paid back.

11. Some people distinguished the *lintah darat* (leech) as a third type, similar to the *rentenir* but without the collateral.

12. An interesting typology on the various sources of credit in Indonesia can be found in Bouman and Moll (1992).

13. An example is Wanti, the wife of a civil servant, who told me: 'In the households in this neighbourhood it is the wife who knows what is going on with the money. When there is a need for money, it is the wife who looks for a loan. Today I took a loan and I am certainly not going to tell my husband because he will be angry with me. I am forced to borrow because the money he gives me is not enough. He says, "Here is the money, it is up to you." I just have to manage with what he gives. On the other hand, he also has secrets from me. I saw on his payroll that he himself took a loan from the office. I asked him what it was for and he answered that it was for some necessity. Well, what can I do about that!?'

References

Unpublished Sources

Lont, H. (1997–9), 'Financial Self-help Organizations and Social Security in Urban Yogyakarta', unpublished fieldwork material, Amsterdam: ASSR

Published Sources

Adams, D. W. (1999), 'Inflated Expectations', *Devfinance* (September 27), available by email: devfinance@lists.acs.ohio-state.edu.

Ardener, S. (1995), 'Women Making Money Go Round: ROSCAs Revisited', in S. Ardener and S. Burman (eds), *Money-Go-Rounds*, Oxford: Berg Publishers.

Bouman, F. J. A. (1994), 'ROSCA and ASCRA: Beyond the Financial Landscape', in F. J. A. Bouman and O. Hospes (eds), *Financial Landscapes Reconstructed*, Boulder, CO: Westview Press.

—— and H. A. J. Moll (1992), 'Informal Finance in Indonesia', in D. W. Adams and D. A. Fitchett (eds), *Informal Finance in Low-Income Countries*, Boulder, CO. Westview Press.

Geertz, H. (1961), *The Javanese Family: A Study of Kinship and Socialization*, New York: The Free Press of Glencoe.

Hashemi, S. M., S. R. Schuler and A. P. Riley (1996), 'Rural Credit Programs and Women's Empowerment in Bangladesh', *World Development*, 24(4): 635–53.

Jay, R. R. (1969), *Javanese Villagers: Social Relations in Rural Modjokuto*, Cambridge, MA: The MIT Press.

Keeler, W. (1990), 'Speaking of Gender in Java', in J. M. Atkinson and S. Errington (eds), *Power and Difference*, Stanford, CA: Stanford University Press.

Manderson, L. (1983), 'Introduction', in L. Manderson (ed.), *Women's Work and Roles*, Canberra: ANU, Development Studies Center, Monograph No. 32.

Mayoux, L. (2000), *Micro-finance and the Empowerment of Women: A Review of the Key Issues*, The Social Finance Unit, Working Paper No. 22, Geneva, ILO.

Papanek, H. and L. Schwede (1988), 'Women Are Good With Money: Earning and Managing in an Indonesian City', in J. Bruce and D. Dwyer (eds), *A Home Divided*, Stanford, CA: Stanford University Press.

Rahman, A. (1999), 'Micro-Credit Initiatives for Equitable and Sustainable Development: Who Pays?', *World Development*, 27(1): 67–82.

Shipton, P. (1992), 'The Rope and the Box: Group Savings in the Gambia', in D. W. Adams and D. A. Fitchett (eds), *Informal Finance in Low-Income Countries*, Boulder, CO: Westview Press.

Stoler, A. (1977), 'Class Structure and Female Autonomy in Rural Java', *Signs*, 3: 74–89.

Sullivan, N. (1983), 'Indonesian Women in Development: State Theory and Kampung Practice', in L. Manderson (ed.), *Women's Work and Women's Roles*, Canberra: ANU, Development Studies Center, Monograph No. 32.

Wolf, D. L. (1992), *Factory Daughters: Gender, Household Dynamics, and Rural Industrialization in Java*, Berkeley, CA: University of California Press.

Zelizer, V. (1989), 'The Social Meaning of Money: "Special Monies"', *American Journal of Sociology*, 95(2): 342–77.

13

Poor Female Youth and Human Capital Development in Bangladesh: What Role for Micro-credit Programmes?[1]

Najma R. Sharif

Interventions by government and non-governmental organizations to help poor women in Bangladesh have increased enormously over the past two decades. Many of these organizations have chosen to stress the importance of micro-credit for setting up micro-enterprises, in the expectation that this would fight poverty and promote gender equity by empowering women. Indeed, the micro-credit movement has gathered considerable momentum the world over, with the 1997 Micro Credit Summit anticipating reaching 100 million of the world's poor by the year 2005. This chapter focuses on the role micro-credit programmes can play in enabling women to develop human capital as well as sustainable livelihoods, with a special emphasis on female youth. The development of human capital and sustainable livelihoods are both critical for the well-being of poor women over the long term. The emphasis on female youth is predicated on the grounds that livelihood skills development is a process that must start early and be sustained, and that this, in turn, is critical for determining the status of women in general over the life cycle as well as across generations. This is because of a strong tendency for socio-economic status to be transferred across generations; poor young women who belong to the lowest rung of the socio-economic ladder are more than likely to transfer that status to their female offspring.

The rest of this chapter is organized as follows. The second section discusses the potential of micro-credit programmes for fostering the human capital and livelihoods development of poor female youth in Bangladesh. The third section presents a quantitative analysis, using both descriptive and multivariate methods, of the socio-economic status and empowerment of female youth and adult female participants in the micro-credit programmes of the *Association for Social Advancement* (ASA), a well-known non-governmental organization (NGO) engaged in the provision of micro-credit. The fourth section draws some policy implications.

Micro-credit and the Socio-economic Status of Poor Female Youth in Bangladesh

In spite of significant inter-country differences, it is generally the case that, in the developing countries, women do worse than men, whether one looks at education, nutritional status, wealth or income, mobility, etc. Young women fare even worse, especially in societies such as Bangladesh, where the seclusion ethic, based on the ideology of 'purdah', is an important influence that works to curtail the aspirations and economic and social activities of women early in life. While a slim minority of urban female youth belonging to upper and middle income classes are generally well educated and relatively well placed in the job market (although they are still engaged in 'women's work'), the situation of the vast majority of poor female youth is quite bleak. They lack access to skills development opportunities or to any type of 'capital'– human, social, physical/financial – that would help them to form dynamic livelihoods or achieve autonomy.

Social norms have important implications for both the quantity and quality of human capital that young women can develop. For example, parents typically do not view educating girls as being an act of investment. As a result, often, the type of human capital formed is that which makes them acceptable in the marriage market and is, therefore, usually limited and biased heavily in favour of skills required in traditional home-based activities. Additionally, a bias in favour of males in health care and nutrition (see, for instance, Muhuri and Preston 1991) further degrades the quality of that capital in relation to that of young men. The dominant focus on the marriage potential of a young woman and the widespread practice of providing a dowry, whereby the bride's parents must make payments to the groom and/or his parents (the 'bride price') as a means of securing the marriage, mean that young women are perceived as liabilities and are to be married off at the earliest possible stage. The average age at first marriage is still a low twenty years, although it is up from sixteen years over the past two decades or so. However, the average age in rural areas has not risen as much. These factors suggest that many female youth, especially the poor, do not acquire human capital beyond a rather rudimentary type, and that therefore women have no 'fall-back' in the event of abandonment or abusive relationships once married. To the extent that poor young women acquire some skills, these keep them in low-paying jobs (such as garment factories). Many poor female youth, however, are pushed into prostitution, roadside hawking or domestic service. This is all the more likely for the very poor, where entry into demeaning occupations is simply a matter of survival, and social norms are of secondary importance.

The scarcity of household resources usually means that boys and girls are not able to get an education. However, to the extent that it is still possible to provide an education for children, the incentive is to educate boys. In patriarchal societies such as Bangladesh, there is a strong incentive to educate boys, since they not only command a dowry when they marry, but also provide for their parents in old age. Girls, on the other hand, marry into their husbands' families, and their responsibilities lie there. The opportunity cost of educating girls can be high, because they provide long hours of unpaid work in the home – cleaning, cooking, fetching fuel, looking after siblings and many more chores, while their brothers do not have to bear these responsibilities to the same extent. There can also be a 'psychic cost' in sending adolescent girls to school, because of parental concerns that the moral 'safety' of their daughters, a factor of considerable importance to the honour and status of the family and for the marriage prospects of the girls themselves, might be compromised through social interaction with males (Sharif 2001). In addition, poor female youth will enter the labour market to earn their dowry in order to reduce the financial burden on their parents. Kabeer (1997) found this to be the case among garment-factory workers in Bangladesh. Thus, poverty can combine with conservative social norms to restrict opportunities available to poor female youth, with lasting adverse consequences. Specifically, there is little likelihood that poor female youth will be able to break out of the grip of poverty, develop sustainable livelihoods and transfer an improved economic and social status to their children. What can we expect from micro-credit programmes in this situation?

There has been enormous growth in micro-credit programmes in Bangladesh over the past two decades. At this time, the 'Big Three' – the Grameen Bank, the Association for Social Advancement, and BRAC, the Bangladesh Rural Advancement Committee – now reach millions of individuals.[2] Many of these programmes target poor, married women and, as such, they miss a large number of poor female youth. On the other hand, since the age at marriage has been very low in the country, a sizeable number of female youth can be reached by such programmes, though in relatively smaller numbers than adult females. Micro-credit programmes have the potential to benefit poor female youth in several ways, from enabling them to develop their human capital and livelihood capabilities, and to acquire social capital, to reducing gender inequalities in the household by empowering them in various decision-making contexts.

By participating in micro-credit programmes, poor female youth can develop income-generating activities, which, in turn, could provide a basis for developing sustainable livelihoods. In that event, the amelioration of the household resource constraints might enable their children (especially girls) to go to and stay in school, an alternative that would otherwise not be available. In this way, micro-credit programmes might not only help poor families to climb out of poverty, but also have beneficial, long-term, intergenerational effects on women by enhancing the quantity and quality of human capital. However, a vast majority of poor female youth are neither in school nor participants in micro-credit programmes. Rather, they are often engaged in economic activity at the lowest level, or in home-based activities such as cleaning, cooking and looking after siblings. To the extent that these girls belong to households in which their mothers are engaged in income-generating activities supported by micro-credit, they might be able to develop human capital if household resources enabled them to go to school. Thus, female youth either develop livelihood skills related to their enterprises, if they participate in credit programmes, or benefit indirectly by being able to go to school if their mothers are programme participants. Indeed, the latter impact can be very important, since it provides the opportunity, if not the guarantee, of breaking out of the intergenerational cycle of poverty. The main difficulty is that there is little guarantee that the amelioration of household resource constraints would translate into girls' attending or, more importantly, completing school, if parents choose to educate boys only (for the reasons cited earlier). Indeed, such girls might have to shoulder even greater domestic responsibilities at home if their mothers are busy running micro-enterprises.

Social capital, the actual or virtual resources (trust, friendship, solidarity, support) that individuals have access to through participation in extra-household settings, can also be acquired by women participating in group-credit programmes. This provides additional support for the success of income-generating activities started with financial capital, and can empower women emotionally, an important factor in their well-being. Empowerment can also occur in other contexts. If participating in credit programmes improves the status of female youth, it could reduce gender inequalities in decision-making within the household.

In the Bangladeshi context, there has been a steadily growing literature on the impact of micro-credit programmes. A number of studies show that such programmes lead to improvements in the nutrition and education of children (especially girls), and to an improvement in the income status of households participating in such programmes (see, for instance, Khandker, Alam and Greaney 1995, Chowdhury and Khandker 1995, and the Association for Social Advancement (ASA) 1997), enabling them to climb out of poverty (Khandker and Chowdhury 1995). Some studies also point to the empowering impact on women of credit programmes, along various dimensions of choice (Amin, Becker and Bayes 1998; Hashemi, Schuler and Riley 1996; Schuler, Hashemi and Riley 1997; Chen 1983), and to the reduced likelihood of abandonment and/or physical abuse (Amin and Pebley 1994; Naved 1994). At the same time, there can be negative consequences. First of all, it needs to be borne in mind that, although most micro-credit programmes are purportedly aimed at the very poor, the reality appears to be different. Many of the poorest women have not been reached by credit, as has been noted by the ASA itself (ASA 1997: 17). Additionally, many poor female youth are not in credit programmes; and although they could benefit if they belong to households in which their mothers get credit, this is far from guaranteed, because of inequalities within the household. That is, in the face of overall resource scarcity and the high opportunity costs of young girls outside the home, parents might decide to educate sons rather than daughters. This might be especially reinforced given that investing in a girl's human capital development is not considered worthwhile, as noted above.

If young girls are not able to develop human capital in this context, and continue to do unpaid household work, then one must ask whether women can reap any long-term benefit through participation in micro-credit programmes. Poverty alleviation might occur for credit participants. But, if their children, especially girls, are not able to develop human capital and social capital, and hence sustainable livelihoods, through formal education, then credit programmes would be relatively limited in terms of what they can achieve. It must also be noted that merely providing credit for enterprises without effective education and training in enterprise management does not mean that such activities will provide sustainable livelihoods. Moreover, even among those who do benefit from access to micro-credit, not all female youth are able to (or want to) manage micro-enterprises. Questions should also be raised about the nature of income-generating enterprises that can or should be supported by micro-credit. Indeed, if micro-credit-promoted enterprises simply add to the low-value-added, low-productivity production activities that already saturate the informal sector, it is quite unlikely that they would develop into sustainable livelihoods that offer a chance to break out of poverty permanently. This is a particular danger for the poorest, for whom these enterprises represent a survival strategy. On the other hand, if poor women do succeed with micro-enterprises and poverty reduction does take place, as found in the study by Khandker and Chowdhury (1995), they might still lack the resources to develop more dynamic and livelihood-enhancing enterprises, especially if they possess only rudimentary human capital. Furthermore, that women have access to credit does not guarantee that they have control over its use or the income generated through activities financed by that credit (Goetz and SenGupta 1996), nor that violence against them would decrease. One observer of the programmes of the Grameen Bank even goes so far as to argue that violence against women increases (Rahman 1999). Thus, even if credit programmes do, in fact, fight poverty, there is no guarantee that intra-household inequalities will be significantly changed.

What, then, can we realistically expect from micro-credit programmes as far as female youth are concerned? Can we expect micro-credit to fight poverty and empower women young and old, so that they and their daughters have a chance of developing sustainable livelihoods in the long term? If empowerment comes only slowly because social norms change slowly, it would be unrealistic to expect a programme that provides small loans to have any major impact except, perhaps, over a long period. A sufficiently longer time-frame is needed to be able to assess the long-term evolution of the status and livelihoods of female youth and adults who participated in credit programmes, and, more significantly, those of their children. For, if there are no meaningful intergenerational effects, then micro-credit programmes will not make a dent in poverty, much less empower women in their households and in their communities. If poverty reduction does take place without a reduction in gender inequalities, then some might question why such programmes need to target mostly women.

A Quantitative Analysis of the Socio-economic and Decision-making Status of Female Youth and Adults in ASA Credit Programmes

In this section, our objective is to examine empirically how female youth who participated in the credit programmes of the ASA were affected in important areas of decision-making as compared to adult women in those programmes. The objective is not so much to test for the impacts of credit participation on women's economic and social status. Rather, we seek to determine whether (and to what extent), the decision-making ability of youth participants differs from that of adult participants along various dimensions of choice.

The analysis is conducted in two steps. We look first at the issue largely in descriptive terms, and then turn to multivariate analysis. The data used for our analysis are drawn from a socio-economic survey of households in Bangladesh conducted by the ASA, beginning in the summer of 1997. The ASA is now the third largest credit-granting non-governmental organization in Bangladesh, with the typical loan size in 1997 being small (less than $200) and the rate of interest charged being 25 per cent on average (ASA 1997: ix, 2). In its survey, the ASA took a multi-stage random sampling approach, with the selected households being classified into two groups – the 'treatment' group, consisting of loan participants, and the 'control' group, consisting of non-participants. To be eligible for participation in the ASA credit programme, the woman had to be at least once married and between the ages of eighteen and fifty-five years, and to belong to a household with land ownership of less than half an acre and a maximum monthly income of Taka 3,000. The non-participants consisted of women who would otherwise be eligible for participation. In selecting these women, a wealth ranking of village households was initially done; from those eligible from this ranking, a random selection was made.[3]

Table 13.1 provides some basic summary statistics on the characteristics of the chosen households. Of a total of 483 women in the ASA sample, 368 (76.2 per cent) belong to the treatment group (these are ASA participants). The bulk of participating women are adults (above twenty-four years of age), with only seventy-nine members (21.5 per cent) being female youth. In this chapter, the age bracket for youth is sixteen to twenty-four years, although it is recognized that this range could vary depending upon the cultural setting. The average household has five members, with a minimum of one and a maximum of twelve. The demographic composition suggests that there are relatively more younger members, with the average household having about two minor children of less than sixteen years. Also, households have, on average, at least two members who are not children. The average age of the household head is forty-one years, while that of the spouse (where present) is thirty-one years.

The ASA survey did not ask questions about formal schooling, but ranked women along a six-point scale based on their literacy and numeracy skills. The highest score an individual could get on each category

Table 13.1   Household Characteristics: Summary Statistics

	All Households (N=483)			
	Panel A			
Characteristics	Mean	Standard Deviation	Minimum	Maximum
Household Size	5.0	1.9	1	12
Household Composition				
Adult Sons	0.4	0.8	0	4
Adult Daughters	0.1	0.4	0	3
Minor Males (under 16)	0.9	0.9	0	7
Minor Females (under 16)	1.0	1.0	0	5
Age				
Household Head	40.8	11.2	20	75
Spouse	31.0	9.1	15	60

	Panel B	
	Number	Per cent
Basic Education:		
Household Head[a]		
Yes	175	36.5
No	305	63.5
Spouse		
Yes	87	20.1
No	332	76.9
Other[b]	13	3.0
Primary Occupation:		
Household Head		
Agriculture	94	19.6
Household Work	16	3.3
Non-agriculture	209	43.5
Miscellaneous[c]	161	35.6
Spouse		
Agriculture	6	1.4
Household Work	347	80.3
Non-agriculture	29	6.7
Miscellaneous	50	11.6

Source: Computed from ASA survey data files made available to the author.

Notes: a. The number of household heads reported is 480 not 483, since in three cases non-responses made classification difficult. The number of spouses is 432. Percentages for household head and spouse are expressed with respect to these totals.

b. 'Other' refers to non-responses to the questions on education.

c. The miscellaneous category under primary occupation includes non-responses. Means and variances of household composition variables have been calculated, including zero observations.

was a six. This meant that the individual could read and write a sentence (literacy) and do simple multiplication and division (numeracy). We assumed that an individual had a basic education if she scored a six on each; otherwise, we treated the individual as lacking a basic education. On the basis of this criterion, we found that 36.5 per cent of household heads had a basic education, while only 20 per cent of spouses met that condition. Looking at the occupational patterns in Table 13.1, it can be seen that household heads are primarily engaged in either agricultural (crops, fishing, etc.) activities, or in non-agricultural jobs (government and private service). In contrast, spouses are overwhelmingly engaged in household work. The miscellaneous category is somewhat misleading in that, although it includes retired individuals, invalids, and the un-employed, it also includes all non-responses.

Table 13.2 provides descriptive statistics on various socio-economic variables for female youth and adult participants. In the demographic area, the average age of youth participants is about twenty-one years, while that of adult participants is thirty-five years. As expected, adult participants have larger family sizes with greater numbers in all demo-graphic categories. Note that the households of both adults and youth have an average of more than two other family members – typically, parents of the husband or families of the husbands/wives – reflecting the import-ance of extended families in both cases.

Table 13.2 also provides comparative statistics for the two groups of women in terms of marital and household status, education and occupation. In terms of marital status, it is clear that both groups consist predominantly of married women, the percentage of such women being about two percentage points lower for adult women. This reflects the greater likelihood amongst the latter of widowhood and/or abandonment. The household status variable shows that the vast majority of women, adult or youth, are not household heads. However, the data are suggestive that female youth are less likely to be household heads, with less than 5 per cent of such women reporting such status, while the corresponding number is more than twice that for adult women. Of course, adult women are more likely to be widowed and/or abandoned, and hence more likely to head households.

Basic education, as defined earlier, also appears to show perceptibly larger differences among the two groups of women, with about 80 per cent of adult women reporting that they did not have a basic education, compared to less than 75 per cent of youth. This difference, no doubt, is partly reflective of the greater spread of education among the poor over the past two decades or so. Thus, as is generally true in a number of

Table 13.2 Descriptive Statistics for Female Youth and Adult ASA
Participants

	Panel A							
	Youth Participants (N=79)				Adult Participants (N=289)			
Demographics	Mean	S.D.	Min.	Max.	Mean	S.D.	Min.	Max.
Age (years)	21.0	2.3	15	24	35.1	8.4	25	70
Family Size	3.9	1.4	1	9	5.3	1.8	1	11
Adult Sons	0.1	0.5	0	4	0.6	0.8	0	3
Adult Daughters	0.0	0.0	0	1	0.2	0.4	0	2
Minor Males	0.7	0.7	0	3	1.0	0.9	0	5
Minor Females	0.7	0.7	0	3	1.0	1.0	0	5
Other Members	2.5	1.1	1	7	2.5	1.1	1	9

	Panel B			
	Number	Per cent	Number	Per cent
Marital Status				
Married	74	93.7	265	91.7
Unmarried	2	2.5	1	1.3
Widowed	1	1.3	15	5.2
Other[a]	2	2.5	8	2.8
Household Status				
Full Household Head	2	2.5	30	10.4
Partial Household Head	2	2.5	11	3.8
Not Household Head	75	94.9	247	85.5
Other[a]	0	0.0	1	0.3
Basic Education				
Yes	20	25.3	51	17.6
No	58	73.4	233	80.6
Other[a]	1	1.3	5	1.8
Primary Occupation[b]				
Household Work	66	83.5	219	75.8
Agriculture	1	2.5	2	1.4
Non-agriculture	3	3.8	7	10.4
Professions	0	0.0	2	0.7
Other	9	11.4	34	11.8

Source: Computed from ASA survey data files made available to the author.

Notes: a. 'Other' refers to non responses to questions in the relevant category, except
under Primary Occupation.

b. Under Primary Occupation, 'agriculture' includes fishing; 'non-agriculture'
includes government/private service and trade. 'Professions' includes masonry,
carpentry, pottery; 'other' includes, in addition to non-responses, the
unemployed, invalids, beggars, etc.

developing countries, youth today show lower illiteracy rates compared to adult women. Finally, a look at the occupational patterns suggests that while all women (youth and adults) have their primary occupation in home-based activities, with smaller numbers being engaged in other occupations, the differences between female youth and adults seem to be quite large. Only about 75 per cent of adults are engaged in household work, compared to almost 84 per cent of youth, and substantially greater proportions of the former are in non-agricultural occupations, which include trade and government and private services. It needs to be cautioned, however, that the magnitude of these variations could be different, often quite dramatically, if all the non-responses were known.

One of the more relevant questions pertaining to credit programmes relates to the extent to which women are empowered to make decisions regarding matters that affect their families as well as themselves. For empirical purposes, this requires being able to quantify empowerment. This is not an easy task, since, conceptually, not only are there many dimensions of empowerment, but the concept can mean different things in different cultural settings. My purpose is not so much to look into the question of what values should underlie definitions of empowerment in Bangladesh as to use the ASA's own terms of reference with regard to the survey objectives on gender issues to examine the issues indicated earlier. The survey asked both participant and non-participant women about various aspects of their lives, some clearly more important than others, to ascertain the extent to which they could participate in the decision-making process of the households to which they belonged.

The indicators of empowerment are based on women's ranking of the degree of their participation in decision-making in the following areas:

1. Daily food purchases.
2. Large purchases, which include outlays on housing, furniture, assets and the like.
3. Family size.
4. Health expenditures.
5. Education of children.
6. Marriages (of children) and social events.

For each of these areas of decision-making, the survey asked women to rank, along a five-point scale, the extent to which they could participate in decision-making, with a 1 signifying that she could not participate in decision making at all, a 2 that she could possibly influence her husband on the decision, a 3 that the decision was joint, a 4 that she could take a partial decision on her own, and a 5 that she could make the decision entirely on her own. For purposes of the multivariate analysis we collapsed this scale to a binary scale, with a value of 1 being assigned if a woman selected 3 or more, and a value of 0, if she selected 1 or 2. Thus, a 1 signified that a woman was empowered in decision-making (in any of the above decision categories), while a 0 implied that she was not.[4] The statistics presented in Table 13.3 can be used to compare the decision-making status of female youth and adults.

Given the role that women are traditionally expected to play in Bangladeshi society, a significant factor affecting their empowerment is the restriction on their mobility outside the home. With that restriction, it is difficult for a woman to be economically and socially mobile, and this has an adverse impact on her well-being. In group lending programmes, women must meet weekly with their group members, so one would expect that participation should indeed draw women, youth and adults, out of the home. However, what about women's broader social and economic mobility? If, indeed, participation in credit programmes increases women's mobility, does this extend to mobility in the broader sense, and, more importantly, is this dependent upon age? That is, are female youth more restricted than adults? To study this question, we constructed a mobility index.

The survey asked women on a binary scale, whether they were mobile with respect to seven indicators of mobility – visiting neighbours, going alone to the village market, going alone to a market in another village, attending social events alone in the village, visiting the village doctor alone, visiting a doctor in another village alone and attending a clinic/ hospital alone. In each of these categories, an individual indicated whether she could or could not do each. Since these mobility indicators are not of equal importance, we weighted the responses to each differently to arrive at the final mobility index ranging from 0 (the case of no mobility) to 5 (the case of perfect mobility).[5] If a woman scored 2.5 or more on the index, she was classified as being mobile, and as not mobile otherwise. The summary statistics presented in Table 13.3 can be used to compare female youth and adults.

It is quite clear from Table 13.3 that, in all dimensions of choice, the average score of female youth participants is less than that of their adult counterparts, although the margin of difference varies. The difference is smallest for family size and largest for mobility. In addition, the average score suggests that both youth and adults are most empowered in the daily food purchases category and least empowered with respect to their mobility. On the other hand, adult females appear to be able at least to

Table 13.3 Decision-Making Scores: Descriptive Statistics on Youth and
Adult Participants

Area of Decision-Making	Youth Participants (N=79)	Adult Participants (N=289)
Daily Food Purchases		
Mean Score[a]	4.14	4.26
Standard Deviation	1.31	1.08
Per Cent[b] Not Empowered[c]	10.13	5.19
Large Purchases		
Mean Score	2.95	3.31
Standard Deviation	0.77	0.06
Per Cent Not Empowered	13.92	7.27
Family Size[d]		
Mean Score	2.97	3.02
Standard Deviation	0.23	0.60
Per Cent Not Empowered	3.80	5.43
Education		
Mean Score	3.18	3.35
Standard Deviation	0.66	0.95
Per Cent Not Empowered	1.27	6.23
Health		
Mean Score	3.12	3.29
Standard Deviation	0.95	0.93
Per Cent Not Empowered	11.39	7.61
Marriage		
Mean Score	2.89	3.12
Standard Deviation	0.62	0.79
Per Cent Not Empowered	10.13	7.96
Mobility		
Mean Score	1.50	2.16
Standard Deviation	1.32	1.46
Per Cent Not Empowered	79.75	55.02

Source: Computed from ASA survey data files made available to the author.

Notes: a. The score for each area (except mobility) ranges from 1 (no say in decision-making) to 5 (can make decisions alone), with joint decision-making being denoted by 3. For mobility, the range is from 0 (no mobility) to 5 (complete mobility).

b. Percentages are calculated inclusive of non-responses.

c. The per cent not empowered are those with a score of less than 3, or less than 2.5 for mobility.

d. The totals used to compute all percentages are those shown at head of the table, except for family size, where the sample of adult members is confined to women in the (15–45 years) age group.

make joint decisions in all dimensions of choice (save mobility), while this is only partially true for female youth. At the same time, the mobility of both adult females and youth is low, despite the fact that the former are much more mobile than the latter. For instance, almost 80 per cent of female youth are not mobile (compared to 55 per cent of adult females). Thus, the descriptive evidence does not paint a positive picture for youth participants compared to their adult counterparts. However, one must be cautious in making too much of these differences. First, in some dimensions (such as education), the proportion of non-responses is quite large. More importantly, are the observed differences statistically significant, and can they be attributed to age alone?

As a first step to answering these questions, we tested whether the observed differences in youth and adult mean scores were statistically significant using standard t tests. Our results indicated that the differences in average scores are significant at the 1 per cent level of significance for the large purchases, marriage and mobility dimensions of choice, and at the 10 per cent level of significance for the education and health categories. On the other hand, these differences are statistically insignificant for the remaining categories. Therefore, these tests suggest that adult females do have an advantage over youth, at least with respect to their mobility, as well as in the marriage and large purchase areas of choice. A major problem with this analysis is that no controls are made for individual and household characteristics that might explain the observed youth–adult differences. To address this, we adopted a multivariate approach, using probit regression to test whether youth are indeed more disadvantaged than adults in the each of the dimensions discussed above, controlling for the influence of individual and household characteristics.

We start with the theoretical foundations underlying the probit model used. Conceptually, we can think of empowerment as being a multi-dimensional variable that is not directly observed. Specifically, assume that empowerment is a latent variable y*, which measures the extent to which the individual is empowered. We suppose that this propensity is determined by a set of explanatory variables x_k according to the following stochastic model:

$$y^* = b_0 + \Sigma b_k x_k + u$$

where x_k stands for the explanatory variables (k = 1,2,3,...,m), and u is a random error. Although we have data on the x variables, we do not observe the empowerment variable y*. What we observe, on the other hand, is y = 1 (if the individual is empowered according to some proxy index) and zero if she is not empowered. That is, the dummy variable y can be thought of as the dichotomous realization of the latent variable y*. More specifically, when y*≤c, where c is some unknown threshold value, y = 0, and when y*>c, y = 1. Assuming that the u variable is normally distributed with zero mean and unit variance, the model becomes the probit model, and this can be estimated using maximum-likelihood.

To test whether youth are less likely to be empowered than adults, we use a dummy variable YOUTH = 1 if the participant is under twenty-five years of age, and 0 otherwise. Several other variables are used as control variables. Since one would expect that educated individuals are more likely to be empowered, we use an education variable, measured along the lines outlined in the previous section. It too is a dummy variable, with SCHOOL = 1 if the individual has a basic education and zero otherwise. Asset ownership can be an important determinant of a woman's status within the household and in the community. For instance, evidence shows that where women have rights in land, they also enjoy greater freedoms, and can have greater control over household food stores and the like (Agarwal 1997: 19). We included a dummy variable LAND = 1 if a woman owned land, and zero otherwise to capture differences in empowerment that could be attributed to land ownership. We also controlled for the effects of the primary occupation of women by using a dummy variable OCCUPATION = 1, if the woman's primary occupation did not involve housework (and zero if it did). Women who are engaged in work outside the home are likely to be more empowered to begin with.

The final set of variables used in the empirical analysis reflect the demographics of the household. Specifically, we considered the age–sex composition of the household in which the woman resides. This can have an important impact on the bargaining position (and hence empowerment) of women because of the potential for the formation of coalitions and the nature of a woman's social capital within the household, especially when extended families are quite common and sons and their wives, as well as their parents, live in the same household. Coalitions and a woman's social capital within the household could work either to increase part-icipation in decision-making or to decrease it, via their impact on her bargaining position (Agarwal 1997). For example, the presence of a mother-in-law could weaken a woman's decision-making status unless she can improve her bargaining position through coalitions (say with her children). The presence of co-wives in polygamous households could also go either way. It could easily decrease empowerment, or, in the event of a coalition between the co-wives, increase it. In this study, we considered several variables to incorporate some of these factors.

These are the number of adult sons, adult daughters, minor sons (under sixteen years of age), and minor daughters, the number of other adults (for example, daughters-in-law, mothers-in-law, etc.), and a dummy variable POLYGAMOUS =1 for a polygamous household.[6]

The results for all the probits are reported in Table 13.4. It is clear that the YOUTH coefficient is negative in all probits except one, suggesting that female youth participants are less empowered by micro-credit programmes. The exception is the education probit, but here the coefficient is not statistically significant even at the 10 per cent level, while it is also not statistically significant at the 5 per cent level in the family size and marriage probits. In these three cases then, the evidence does not imply that female youth participants do any worse than adult females. But in all other probits, the YOUTH coefficient is statistically significant at the 5 per cent level (or less), thereby pointing to the lower decision-making ability of female youth, especially with regard to their overall mobility. There is no systematic pattern to the effects of other variables in the probits. However, it seems that the presence of minor children (male or female) reduces the decision-making ability of women participants. This suggests that the least empowered are likely to be female youth with minor children. It seems that despite direct participation in credit programmes, female youth tend to remain at a disadvantage with regard to decision-making when compared to female adult participants. Thus, some empowerment comes with age, and if female youth participants are found to be no more empowered than non-participants, then other means of ensuring that female youth get the chance to develop human capital would be needed.

Conclusion

This chapter has examined the role that micro-credit programmes play in promoting the human capital and sustainable livelihood development of poor female youth in Bangladesh. In a patriarchal society such as Bangladesh, conservative social norms and poverty combine to constrict the opportunities available to poor women (especially youth) for developing human capital and sustainable livelihoods, both of which are needed to break out of the intergenerational cycle of poverty. Social norms also cement intra-household decision-making inequalities. Under these conditions, what can micro-credit programmes achieve? To the extent that they fight poverty and help females who directly get micro-credit to develop sustainable livelihoods, it is possible that daughters are also

Table 13.4 The Probit Estimates of Decision-Making Ability[a]

Control Variables	Daily Food Purchases	Large Purchases	Family Size	Health	Education	Marriage	Mobility
Constant	2.320	1.907	2.559	1.729	1.734	1.594	−0.172
	(6.09)	(6.40)	(5.54)	(6.30)	(5.69)	(5.21)	(−0.82)
Youth[b]	−0.678	−0.663	−0.298	−0.423	0.260	−0.290	−0.803
	(−2.19)	(−2.49)	(−0.87)	(−1.64)	(0.68)	(−1.02)	(−3.97)
School[b]	−0.440	0.152	0.160	0.135	0.312	0.273	0.314
	(−1.80)	(0.57)	(0.51)	(0.55)	(0.89)	(1.00)	(1.77)
Land[b]	0.138	0.066	0.556	0.096	0.394	0.359	0.223
	(0.51)	(0.30)	(2.12)	(0.45)	(1.56)	(1.61)	(1.40)
Adult Son[b]	−0.338	−0.266	0.111	−0.225	−0.355	−0.347	−0.058
	(−2.40)	(−2.12)	(0.50)	(−1.79)	(−2.89)	(−2.43)	(−0.61)
Adult Daughter[b]	−0.034	−0.012	−0.669	0.103	0.130	0.296	−0.008
	(−0.14)	(−0.05)	(−1.98)	(0.43)	(0.44)	(0.89)	(−0.04)
Minor Son[b]	−0.126	−0.124	−0.480	−0.219	−0.219	−0.299	−0.054
	(−1.14)	(−1.34)	(−3.72)	(−2.27)	(−2.00)	(−2.86)	(−0.66)
Minor Daughter[b]	−0.322	−0.255	−0.420	−0.107	−0.226	−0.082	−0.137
	(−2.65)	(−2.30)	(−2.73)	(−1.02)	(−1.98)	(−0.74)	(−1.79)
Other Adult[b]	0.094	−0.026	−0.114	0.089	0.362	0.190	−0.058
	(0.84)	(−0.25)	(−0.86)	(0.64)	(2.01)	(1.39)	(−0.66)
Polygamous[b]	−0.643	−0.397	–	–	–	−0.167	−0.084
	(−1.42)	(−0.85)	–	–	–	(−0.287)	(−0.21)
Occupation[b]	0.382	0.617	–	0.214	0.381	0.325	0.224
	(1.11)	(1.83)	–	(0.81)	(1.15)	(1.09)	(1.35)
Count R^2	0.93	0.91	0.95	0.91	0.94	0.91	0.64

Source: Computed from ASA survey data files made available to the author.

Notes: a. Numbers in parentheses are *t* ratios.

b. YOUTH = 1 if person is under 25 years of age, 0 otherwise; SCHOOL = 1 if person has a basic education, 0 otherwise; LAND = 1 if the person owns some land, 0 otherwise; OCCUPATION = 1 if the person's primary occupation is not household work, 0 if it is. ADULT SON, ADULT DAUGHTER, MINOR SON, MINOR DAUGHTER, and OTHER ADULT are, respectively, the number of adult sons, daughters, minor sons, daughters and other adults; POLYGAMOUS = 1 if household is polygamous, 0 otherwise.

better able to develop human capital, so that, from the long-term perspective, positive intergenerational outcomes for female youth can occur. However, fighting household level poverty does not ensure this if women have little control over the use of household resources (including credit), and this is likely to occur if their general decision-making status is weak. Although some evidence for Bangladesh does point to positive outcomes for children (especially young girls) in the area of nutrition and education, and also suggests that families in which credit is received are lifted out of poverty, it remains to be seen what the longer-term effects, especially for the next generation's livelihood capabilities, are going to be. Since credit programmes often target poor married women, many participants are, in fact, female youth, given that the age at first marriage is low in rural Bangladesh. While credit for this group might enable them to escape poverty, evidence presented in this chapter shows that, independent of whether programme participation helps in general, female youth participants have less control than older participants in household decisions and are significantly less mobile. They are thus less likely to be able to ensure that their daughters will be able to develop human capital. Since the process of human capital development needs to start early in life, advancing credit to female youth might not improve their status nor that of their daughters. More generally, if micro-credit does not reduce intra-household gender inequalities, then one might ask in particular whether targeting women as such serves any purpose.

Perhaps we are demanding too much of micro-credit programmes, and we need to look at broader approaches to empowering women and helping female youth develop human capital and sustainable livelihoods (for instance, state- and community-level initiatives that not only provide better opportunities to female youth for developing human capital, but also work towards changing attitudes in the community and households so that girls would, in fact, be able to take advantage of those opportunities). It is not enough to get female enrolment ratios up if school completion rates are low. It is important that higher enrolment ratios translate into higher educational attainment. This means girls must be able to complete school. In this broader context, micro-credit programmes would probably be more successful in promoting the welfare of female youth over the long term.

It might also be that de-linking micro-credit from micro-enterprises is an idea that needs to be given greater attention. Not all women (youth or adult) want to (or can) run enterprises, and such women are not likely to be reached by such programmes. These groups could also be helped if micro-credit provision were not tied to micro-enterprises. The needs for credit are diverse, and by ameliorating household resource constraints, access to credit which is not tied to micro-enterprise could give poor households greater flexibility in satisfying what they perceive to be their needs. More generally, poor women need access not just to credit, but also to a variety of small savings products that would allow them to accumulate funds (even in tiny amounts) to draw upon in times of hardship. In other words, what is needed is micro-finance and not just micro-credit. Designing micro-finance for meeting the varied needs of poor women in rural areas remains a major challenge.

Notes

1. The author thanks the *Association for Social Advancement* (ASA), Dhaka, Bangladesh, for giving her access to and permission to use their data. The views expressed in this chapter are those of the author and should not be attributed to the ASA.
2. The Grameen Bank has about 2 million clients, while the ASA and BRAC each serve about 1.5 million clients. See Rutherford (1999: 53–4).
3. For further details on the sampling design and related matters, see ASA (1997).
4. These rankings reflect women's perceptions about their decision-making ability within their households, and are thus indicative of the extent to which women feel they have the freedom to make decisions. They are, therefore, different from rankings of decision-making ability that are based on *actual* decisions taken by women.
5. A weight of 0.2 was assigned if a woman could go alone to another village to see a doctor/shop or to a hospital/clinic in the same village, of 0.15 if she could go to see a doctor alone in her own village, of 0.1 if she could go to the market or to social events in the village alone, and of 0.05 if she could visit her neighbours on her own. For a woman who could do each of these, the index would equal one, whereas it would equal zero if she could do none.
6. In the case of family size, the Polygamous and Occupation dummy variables had to be excluded because of convergence problems, while only the former was excluded in the health and education probits for the same reason.

References

Agarwal, B. (1997), '"Bargaining" and Gender Relations: Within and Beyond the Household', *Feminist Economics*, 3: 1–51.
Amin, S. and A. R. Pebley (1994), 'Gender Inequality within Households: The Impact of Women's Development Programme in 36 Bangladeshi Villages', *The Bangladesh Development Studies*, 22: 121–54.

Amin, R., S. Becker and A. Bayes (1998), 'NGO-Promoted Microcredit Programs and Women's Empowerment in Rural Bangladesh: Quantitative and Qualitative Evidence', *The Journal of Developing Areas*, 221–36.

ASA (Association for Social Advancement) (1997), *Impact Assessment of ASA*, Dhaka: Association for Social Advancement.

Chen, M. (1983), *A Quiet Revolution: Women in Transition in Rural Bangladesh*, Cambridge, MA: Schenkman Publishing Company.

Chowdhury, O. H. and S. R. Khandker (1995), 'Do Targeted Credit Programs Improve the Nutritional Status of the Poor', *Credit Programs and the Poor Workshop Paper*, Dhaka: The World Bank and Bangladesh Institute of Development Studies.

Goetz, A.-M. and R. SenGupta (1996), 'Who Takes the Credit: Gender, Power, and Control Over Loan Use in Rural Credit Programs in Bangladesh', *World Development*, 24: 45–63.

Hashemi, S. M., S. R. Schuler and A. P. Riley (1996), 'Rural Credit Programs and Women's Empowerment in Bangladesh', *World Development,* 24: 635–63.

Kabeer, N. (1997), 'Women, Wages and Intra-Household Power Relations in Urban Bangladesh', *Development and Change,* 28: 261–302.

Khandker, S. R. and O. H. Chowdhury (1995), 'Targeted Credit Programs and Rural Poverty in Bangladesh', *Credit Programs and the Poor Workshop Paper*, Dhaka: The World Bank and Bangladesh Institute of Development Studies.

Khandker, S. R., M. Alam and V. Greaney (1995), 'The Determinants and Impact of Basic Skill Attainment: The Role of School and Targeted Programs in Bangladesh', *Credit Programs and the Poor Workshop Paper*, Dhaka: The World Bank and Bangladesh Institute of Development Studies.

Muhuri, P. K. and S. Preston (1991), 'Effects of Family Composition on Mortality Differentials by Sex Among Children in Matlab, Bangladesh', *Population and Development Review*, 17: 415–34.

Naved, R. T. (1994), 'Empowerment of Women: Listening to the Voices of Women', *The Bangladesh Development Studies*, 22: 155–78.

Rahman, A. (1999), 'Micro-credit Initiatives for Equitable and Sustainable Development: Who Pays?', *World Development*, 27: 67–82.

Rutherford, S. (1999), 'The Poor and Their Money', *Working Paper Number 3*, Manchester: Institute for Development Policy and Management, University of Manchester.

Schuler, S. R., S. M. Hashemi and A. P. Riley (1997), 'The Role of Women's Changing Roles and Status in Bangladesh's Fertility Transition: Evidence from a Study of Credit Programs and Contraceptive Use', *World Development*, 25: 563–75.

Sharif, N. R. (2001), 'The Seclusion Ethic and the Educational Attainment and Well-Being of Adolescent Girls', *Briefing Notes in Economics*, forthcoming.

PART V

Policy Perspectives

14

Women's Empowerment Versus Sustainability? Towards a New Paradigm in Micro-finance Programmes[1]

Linda Mayoux

Since the 1990s, funding for micro-finance programmes targeting large numbers of women has increased dramatically as a result of initiatives by the Collective Group to Assist the Poorest (CGAP).[2] Literature prepared for the Micro-credit Summit in Washington, in February 1997, in combination with many donor statements on credit and NGO funding proposals, presents an extremely attractive vision of increasing numbers of expanding, financially self-sustainable micro-finance programmes reaching large numbers of women borrowers and making a significant contribution to global poverty alleviation and women's empowerment. However, parallel to, though to a large extent marginalized by, the current enthusiasm, some researchers have questioned the degree to which micro-finance services in fact benefit women (Everett and Savara 1991; Goetz and Sen Gupta 1996; Mayoux 1995a). Some argue strongly that current models of micro-finance, where the overriding concern is financial sustainability, divert resources from other more effective strategies for empowerment (Ebdon 1995) and/or poverty alleviation (Rogaly 1996).

Current views regarding the potential contribution of micro-finance programmes to women's empowerment fall into four main camps, which are not necessarily mutually exclusive. These camps cross-cut three distinct paradigms of micro-finance, with differing interpretations of both empowerment and sustainability (see Box 14.1). This chapter examines the complex interlinkages between the various dimensions of these differing interpretations. There are inherent tensions between empowerment and the many policies currently implemented to increase short-term financial sustainability. However, evidence indicates that

BOX 14.1. EMPOWERMENT AND SUSTAINABILITY: VIEWS AND PARADIGMS

FOUR VIEWS OF THE RELATIONSHIP BETWEEN EMPOWERMENT AND SUSTAINABILITY:

1. optimism about possible global development of sustainable micro-finance programmes empowering women;
2. recognition of limitations of existing models, but possibility of sustainable strategies, minimizing negative impacts and enhancing contribution to empowerment;
3. provision of financially sustainable micro-finance programmes important as a strategy for poverty alleviation; empowerment as an issue to be addressed by other means; and
4. current emphasis on micro-finance programmes a misplaced diversion of resources from more effective empowerment strategies.

THREE UNDERLYING PARADIGMS:

I – Financial Self-Sustainability Paradigm

Main origins and inspiration: currently dominant within most donor agencies, underlying the models of micro-finance promoted in publications by USAID and CGAP. The dominant inspiration behind many presentations at the 1997 Micro-Credit Summit in Washington, DC (Rhyne and Otero 1994).
Reason for targeting women: efficiency considerations arising from high female repayment rates
Main policy focus: setting up financially self-sustainable micro-finance programmes that increase access to micro-finance services for large numbers of poor people
Empowerment: economic empowerment, expansion of individual choice and capacities for self-reliance
Sustainability: programme financial self-sufficiency.

II – Poverty Alleviation Paradigm

Main origins and inspiration: integrated poverty-targeted community development programmes
Reason for targeting women: higher levels of female poverty and responsibility for household well-being
Main policy focus: micro-finance as part of an integrated programme to alleviate poverty and vulnerability and increase well-being for the poorest households

Empowerment: increased well-being, community development and self-sufficiency
Sustainability: establishment of local-level participatory institutions to ensure long-term community self-reliance and self-determination for the poor

III – Feminist Empowerment Paradigm

Main origins and inspiration: arises from the international women's movement (Sen and Grown 1988) and underlies the gender policies of many NGOs and the perspectives of some of the consultants and researchers looking at gender impact of micro-finance programmes (e.g. Johnson 1997). This paradigm is firmly rooted in the development of some of the earliest micro-finance programmes in the South, particularly SEWA and WWF in India.
Reason for targeting women: gender equity and human rights
Main policy focus: micro-finance as an entry point for women's economic, social and political empowerment
Empowerment: transformation of power relations throughout society
Sustainability: development of self-sustaining participatory women's organizations linked to a wider women's movement for transformation of gender relations.

ignoring empowerment concerns in programme design, as well as having potentially negative affects on women, may prejudice financial sustainability itself (Mayoux 1998, 1999). I argue that a more strategic approach to empowerment is needed, coupled with a wider and more flexible approach to sustainability. First, this would include clear prioritization of the interests of clients/members and a more participatory approach to programme management. Next, it would require greater attention to interorganizational relationships and contexts, considering all facets of micro-finance interventions rather than taking a blueprint programme approach.

Women's Empowerment and Micro-finance: Elements of a Gender Strategy

The concept of empowerment is notoriously contentious. It is a catch-all phrase that has been adopted in discourses with very different underlying understandings of development. In the micro-finance literature it is commonly used with three rather distinct meanings within the different paradigms (see Box 14.1).

Individual Economic Empowerment: Within the financial self-sustainability paradigm it is assumed that increasing women's access to financially sustainable micro-finance programmes will enable women to increase their incomes through micro-enterprise and that this will increase their control over income and resources. This economic empowerment is then assumed to contribute to women's and children's well-being and to enable women to initiate the broader social and political changes they desire. The underlying assumption is that this can happen without explicit support for women within the household or for wider social and political changes in gender or class relations.

Increased Well-being: Within the poverty-alleviation paradigm increasing women's access to micro-finance is seen as increasing their status in the household and community, leading to greater confidence, a share of consumption expenditure and a role in household decision-making. It is assumed, therefore, that women's empowerment and household poverty-alleviation are inherently mutually reinforcing.

Social and Political Empowerment and Ability to Transform and Challenge Gender Subordination: Within the feminist empowerment paradigm gender subordination is seen as a complex, multi-dimensional and all-pervasive process, affecting all aspects of women's lives and embedded at many different mutually reinforcing levels: individual consciousness, the household, work, legislation, state structures and international economic and political systems. Women's empowerment is, therefore, seen as more than economic empowerment and more than well-being benefits, addressing 'strategic gender interests.' It is seen as a process of promoting individual internal change (power within), increasing capacities (power to) and the collective mobilization of women and, where possible, of men (power with) to challenge and change gender subordination (power over). Here it is assumed not only that women have common gender interests and will wish to address these if given sufficient support, but also that micro-finance is a useful entry point into this process.

Firm evidence of gender impact of any sort is limited, and there have been no systematic cross-cultural or interorganizational comparisons of the relative effects of different models or strategies.[3] The data most readily available are financial data on the numbers of loans to women, repayment rates, activities for which loans were given and, in some cases, background information on women and the effectiveness of targeting. Independent academic research on the economic impact or wider social and political empowerment is largely limited to a few studies in Bangladesh and India. Most other documented studies collated in the pilot research are short gender-impact assessments commissioned by Northern NGOs and donors. Other information discussed here is anecdotal, gleaned from impact studies of micro-finance on men and women that have not had a detailed gender focus – for example, papers prepared by Southern NGO staff for the workshops in the pilot research and subsequent correspondence. It is, therefore, not possible at this stage to draw firm conclusions about the relative merits of the different approaches, beyond identification of potential tensions and some possible ways forward.

Nevertheless, despite these shortcomings, the evidence indicates that all the assumed linkages between access and empowerment need to be questioned and are likely to be constrained by the many different and mutually-reinforcing dimensions of gender subordination as indicated in Figure 14.1. Micro-finance programmes can make a contribution to all dimensions of women's empowerment and have done so in some pro-grammes for some women. In some cases this has occurred through women's own strategies for change. In others this has been an outcome of strategic policies for empowerment. The evidence further suggests that men can be important supporters of, as well as significant obstacles to, a process of change.

It is clear that financial indicators of access – women's programme membership, numbers and size of loans and repayment data – cannot be used as definite indicators of actual access or as proxy indicators of empowerment. Registrations of memberships in women's names do not necessarily equate with women's control over loan use or, in some cases, even participation in decisions about loan applications. There is no clear relationship between women's roles in decisions about loan use and whether they choose to use it for their own purposes, or hand it over to men, or whether they are involved in the activity for which it is given and control the income from this. In some instances, increases in incomes have been significant, and there are numerous case studies of successful women entrepreneurs. However, even where levels of repayment are high, the few existing statistical studies of women borrowers (e.g. Everett and Savara 1987, 1991) and men and women borrowers (Hulme and Montgomery 1994; Montgomery *et al.* 1996) find very small increases in income for quite large numbers of borrowers. In only a very small number of cases are there significant increases in income. It is clear that women's choices about activity and their ability to increase their incomes are seriously constrained, in most cases, by a lack of access to other resources for investment. In addition, ongoing responsibility for subsistence, lack of time and low levels of mobility, plus gender-based constraints, limit access to markets in many cultures.

Moreover, increased household income does not ensure that women necessarily benefit or that there is any challenge to gender inequalities within the household. In response to women's increased incomes, men may withdraw more of their own contribution for their own luxury expenditure. Women's expenditure patterns may replicate rather than counter gender inequalities and continue to disadvantage girls. Without substitute care for small children, the elderly and disabled and the provision of services to reduce domestic work, many programmes reported adverse effects from women's outside work on children and the elderly (Mayoux and Johnson 1997). In spite of this, women themselves often value the opportunity to be seen to be making a greater contribution to household well-being, gaining thereby greater confidence and sense of self-worth. But access to even small increases in income may come at the cost of heavier workloads. As a result, some women face considerable hardship in order to meet loan repayments, forgoing food and other consumption expenditure. And although in many cases women's increased contribution to household well-being has considerably improved domestic relations, in other cases it has intensified tensions.

It is important to note that there is no necessary link between micro-finance and social and political empowerment. There have been positive changes in household and community perceptions of women's role, as well as changes at the individual level. There have also been significant changes even in societies where women's roles have been very circumscribed. It is likely also that changes at the individual, household and community levels are interlinked and that individual women who gain respect in their households then serve as role models for others, leading to a wider process of change in community perceptions and male willingness to accept change (Lakshman 1996). However, there is little contextualization of these trends. We do not know for how many women these changes are occurring. In many programmes, particularly in India, micro-finance has formed a basis for organization against other issues such as domestic violence, male alcohol abuse and dowry. At the same time, in most programmes, there is little attempt made to link micro-finance with wider social and political activity. In the absence of specific measures to encourage this trend there is little evidence of any significant contribution of micro-finance to women's empowerment. There is some

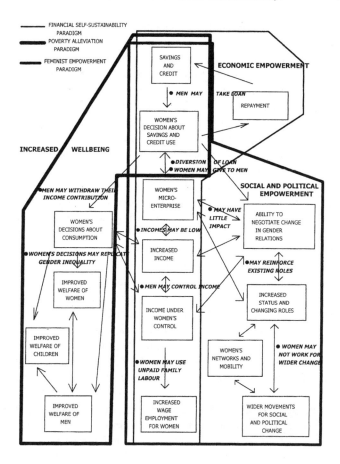

Figure 14.1 Virtuous spirals: questioning assumptions.

evidence to the contrary, that micro-finance and income-earning may take women away from other social and political activities and that micro-finance groups may put severe strains on existing networks if repayment becomes a problem.

Women in different societies face different problems and adopt different strategies, as for example, the women in Vietnam, Bangladesh and Uganda. Equally, there are differences between very poor and not-so-poor women. In many cases contextual constraints at all levels have prevented women from accessing programmes, increasing or controlling incomes or challenging subordination. The contribution of micro-finance alone is likely to be most limited for the poorest and most disadvantaged women. All the evidence suggests these women are the most likely to be explicitly excluded by programmes and peer groups where repayment is the prime consideration and/or where the main emphasis of programmes is on existing micro-entrepreneurs. For some women, micro-finance may be positively disempowering, leading to severe impoverishment or abandonment and putting serious strains on networks with other women. This is particularly the case where explicitly planned support networks have not been set up. This does not mean, however, that micro-finance programmes that take into account the specific needs of these women could not be a very useful development intervention. There is also considerable variation within programmes and within (even very poor) communities that would belie the possibility of predictive modelling based on, for example, household structures or automatic benefits of particular policies.

The inherently complex and potentially conflict-ridden nature of empowerment itself means that total success will never be achieved for all women. Moreover, any gender-based policy is likely to be contested by both women and men. As discussed above, there are trade-offs for individual women, and differences and conflicts of interest between women, as well as resource and power inequalities between women and men at all levels. Nevertheless, despite the inevitable complexities, evidence does suggest significant elements of a gender-based policy that would make micro-finance *more empowering* for *more women* (see Box 14.2 below).

Firstly, gender-based policy requires not only strategies targeting women but a reconsideration of all policies from a gender perspective. This will involve a detailed examination of underlying assumptions about gender differences in rights, responsibilities and roles underlying definitions and policies aimed at the household, community, entrepreneur and farmer, to explicitly include women's concerns in 'malestream' policy. The persistent 'malestream' policy assumptions affect women's access to programmes and the degree to which they are able to benefit. For example, a common inequity occurs when women are required to have their husband's signature for access to a loan while men do not need their wife's signature even when they use her property as collateral.

Gender guidelines are also needed in staff recruitment and promotion. Evidence indicates a clear association between contribution to women's empowerment, and even women's access to micro-finance, and levels of female staff.[4] This is an extremely complex issue that is not necessarily resolved by women-only programmes. Women are not necessarily more gender-aware than men, and also require training to make them aware of

BOX 14.2. ESSENTIAL ELEMENTS OF A GENDER POLICY

INSTITUTIONALIZED GENDER GUIDELINES IN 'MALESTREAM' POLICY: to increase access, enable articulation of women's aspirations and needs and ensure gender equity in overall programme policy

- **examination of all policies from a gender perspective,** in particular concepts of 'household' and 'community' and implicit assumptions about gender differences in rights, responsibilities, roles and consequent gender differences in opportunities and constraints
- **commitment to gender equity in staff recruitment and promotion,** including necessary changes in institutional culture to assist female staff
- **concrete incentives for gender equity in programme implementation** by both male and female staff to ensure that women benefit from programmes

STRATEGIES TARGETING WOMEN: to address women's particular disadvantages

- **conditions of micro-finance delivery** to be flexible to women's aspirations and strategies
- **complementary services** to include explicit attention to gender, in particular: gender training/mutual learning for women to increase skills and networks for challenging gender inequality, services to reduce burden of unpaid domestic work, gender advocacy and lobbying at local, national and international levels
- **structures for participation** by women clients in decision-making and strategies to increase the contribution of groups to empowerment
- **recognition of women's differing needs** and identification of what these might be
- **mechanisms for the representation of very poor women,** women in difficult relationships and younger women in decision-making to ensure that they are not disempowered.

STRATEGIES TARGETING MEN: explicit strategies to redistribute power and resources

- **gender awareness for men** throughout the programme with concrete incentives for 'good practice'
- **incentives to register property and assets** in women's names or in joint names

- **strategies to reinforce and strengthen male responsibilities** for household well-being, including that of their wives and daughters
- **organizing male support for change** in gender relations.

INTER-ORGANIZATIONAL LINKAGES: to increase impact and decrease costs of empowerment strategies

- linking with and supporting women's own networks for change
- working towards institutional consistency on gender in other linked organizations
- working with other organizations to increase potential to challenge gender subordination.

SOME KEY QUESTIONS:

- **'Malestream' Policies:** Can equitable gender relations be encouraged through changes in 'malestream' policies? What does this imply for assumptions about rights, responsibilities and roles within households and communities embedded in all development interventions?
- **Affirmative Action:** Do women need different or preferential treatment from men? How far and in what ways can policies assist women in disadvantaged and vulnerable situations without making negative stereotypical assumptions and creating a 'female ghetto'?
- **Cooperation, Conflict and Change:** How far and in what ways can unnecessary conflict and suffering for individual women be avoided without compromising commitment to change? How far can women themselves be expected to bear the responsibility and costs of challenging gender subordination?
- **Differences Between Women:** Is there any 'female norm' for gender policy? How far and in what ways can the different and possibly conflicting needs of different women be accommodated?
- **Policies Targeting Men:** What are the implications of targeting men through specific gender redistributive policies to encourage men's own support for positive changes in women's access to power and resources and/or to counter male opposition to change?

the perspectives and problems of poor women. Nor is it sufficient to set quotas for numbers of female staff. Although it is obviously the case that male staff may be very gender-aware and supportive, it is generally only where there is a critical mass of women in positions of sufficient authority within organizations that gender issues become fully integrated into 'malestream' programmes and implemented. However, recruiting women to such positions is often difficult given the gender constraints under which female staff as well as clients are operating. Achieving these goals may require changes in organizational culture, recruitment criteria and procedures. A full discussion of what this entails is outside the scope of this chapter, but 'institutionalizing gender' will require resources and commitment. It will not be an easy, cheap or conflict-free process.[5] There is also a need for clear guidelines and concrete incentives for the implementation of gender policy. These would go beyond simply striving to ensure that a proportion of loans or savings are in women's names, ensuring also that women were properly consulted and were aware of strategies, all of which would ensure that they would benefit. These initiatives could also promote the more systematic gathering of information on programme impact.

Strategies targeting women are obviously important in any gender-based policy and have hitherto received the most attention in response to the 'Women in Development' (WID) approach. In thinking about strategies targeting women, however, some tricky questions arise, which are rarely addressed. First, there are questions to be asked about how far and in what ways women need different or preferential treatment from men (in addition to gender equity in 'malestream' programmes). How can programmes address their existing needs without creating female ghettos and stereotypes of expected needs and behaviours? Second, challenging gender subordination cannot be expected to be free from conflict. There are difficult questions to be asked about how far and in what ways unnecessary conflict and suffering can be avoided without compromising commitment to change. Many women may choose strategies that they perceive as strengthening conjugal cooperation; in contrast, some women who choose independence face possible desertion and destitution. Third, in view of differences and potential conflicts of interest between women of different classes, ethnic groups, ages and marital statuses, questions must be asked about which women are to be prioritized or treated as the female norm in considerations of gender needs.

It is clear from the experience of programmes participating in the pilot study that targeting women cannot be used by programmes as a mechanism for overcoming male 'irresponsibility' in savings and loan repayment, while simultaneously assuming this will automatically empower women. Where there is a perception that savings programmes are solely a 'women's affair' this may decrease men's sense of responsibility for the household and increase pressure on women to save any income to which they have access. This leaves men free to use their generally considerably larger incomes for their own luxury consumption. This was the case even in Vietnam, where women had greater levels of control over programmes (Pairaudeau 1996). Where there is a perception that it is easier to get loans for women than for men, evidence from the pilot project indicates that this will lead to men's using women to access loans, creating debt in women's names and making them very vulnerable in cases of marital breakdown (see also Goetz and Sen Gupta 1996). Programmes need to acknowledge the potentially negative effects on gender relations of targeting women. They must also consider ways in which micro-finance provision for men can be a mechanism for challenging gender inequality. This would be one important way of increasing cooperation and decreasing conflict surrounding gender policy, particularly where this actively builds on men's own desire for change. Some men actively support their wives. Male support could be encouraged further through the development of new role models and developing male networks for change. However, this is obviously a difficult balance to achieve without diverting scarce resources and energy from women and women's networks. It must be done alongside reconsideration of 'malestream' policies.

Finally, the degree to which any one programme can achieve significant change is likely to be severely limited in view of the many mutually reinforcing constraints. It is crucial, therefore, that micro-finance programmes link strategically with other forces for change including women's own networks, women's movements and advocacy organizations and gender lobbies within donor agencies.

Empowerment Versus Sustainability? Resolving the Tensions

Increasing women's empowerment requires changes at many levels; it is likely to entail costs and, as mentioned, may generate conflict. In the first instance, policies aimed at women's empowerment will not easily be incorporated into programmes based on financial self-sustainability. Currently, this is the dominant paradigm among most of the donor members of CGAP that provide much of the funding for micro-finance programmes. Here, sustainability is interpreted in strictly financial terms. The aim is to develop financially self-sufficient credit programmes, which cover operating costs (including loan loss reserves), costs of funds and inflation through fees and interest charges. To achieve genuine commercial viability, these programmes must also yield a profit to owners and shareholders. This is to be done by banking mechanisms to maximize income and minimize the costs of financial services: in particular, high interest rates, programme growth, savings mobilization, group liability for repayment and minimalist service provision (see Box 14.3).

However, the evidence indicates emerging contradictions within the financial sustainability paradigm itself, because of insufficient attention to the interests of clients. The underlying assumption is that development costs can be passed on to groups and clients on the further assumption that they will be able and willing to contribute the time, skills and resources to access the services on offer. Targeting women has often been premised on assumptions about their greater docility and submission to pressure from peers and programme staff, leading to higher female repayment rates even where the women themselves do not use the loan. Yet, there is accumulating evidence that women may not be willing (even if they are able) to pay the high interest rates required if they have alternatives. Moreover, they may not remain passive once they are less vulnerable. A number of programmes are experiencing serious difficulties in expansion and high drop-out rates because women proved unwilling to take on the debt burden in their existing situation. Evidence from Grameen Bank indicates that increasing numbers of members may default as their incomes increase and they increase their range of potential credit sources (Wiig 1997). In FINCA, Uganda, it appeared that many women voted with their feet, rejecting high interest rates and forming their own independent participatory groups once they had sufficient capital. In some ways this is evidence of success; but it created serious problems for FINCA's strategy of programme growth to self-sustainability.

Achieving financial sustainability is itself financially costly in both the short and the long term. The rapid growth of micro-finance into large self-sustaining programmes requires professional, and hence costly, banking expertise on a permanent basis. It requires sophisticated management information systems that are expensive to introduce and require skilled staff to maintain. Such systems are only used to collect and manipulate financial data, which are, themselves, difficult to calculate and require close monitoring to ensure reliability. Furthermore, setting up financially self-sustaining systems diverts considerable resources from the institutional capacity-building of staff and client organizations. Moreover, data collected are not necessarily reliable indicators of either poverty-alleviation or empowerment. There are serious questions to be asked. Are such programmes the best use of scarce donor resources in every case? Is it universally the case that setting up such programmes is, in fact, the best use of scarce donor resources?

BOX 14.3. FINANCIAL SUSTAINABILITY: POLICIES, TENSIONS AND POTENTIAL LINKS WITH EMPOWERMENT

FINANCIAL SUSTAINABILITY – DEFINITION

Financial self-sufficiency is achieved in four stages. At the first level, grants for soft loans cover operating expenses and establish a revolving loan fund. However, when programmes are heavily subsidized and performing poorly, the value of the loan fund erodes quickly through delinquency and inflation. At the second level, programmes raise funds by borrowing on terms near, but still below, market rates. Interest income covers the cost of funds and a portion of operating expenses; but grants are still required to finance some aspects of operations. At the third level, most subsidy is eliminated. At the fourth level, programmes are fully financed from the savings of clients; funds are raised at commercial rates from formal financial institutions. Fees and interest income cover the real cost of funds, loan loss reserves, operations and inflation (Otero and Rhyne 1994).

POLICIES IN THE FINANCIAL SELF-SUSTAINABILITY PARADIGM

reducing programme costs:

• programme growth to benefit from economies of scale
• keeping staff costs low through decreasing staff numbers or keeping salary levels down through decentralization
• increasing 'voluntary' contributions of clients and groups
• decreasing transaction costs of services through simplification of procedures and decentralization to locate services near clients
• reducing services

increasing repayment levels for both group and programme sustainability:

• introduction of efficient management information systems to track clients and monitor financial performance
• 'the stick': negative coercion: programme penalties for non-repayment, group peer pressure
• 'the carrot': positive incentives to repay, such as larger repeat loans for good repayment record

increasing programme income:

• increasing interest rates and service charges
• mobilizing savings, leaving significant interest margin between interest on loans and savings

- profitable investment of programme assets
- selling shares to clients and/or private sector

SOME INHERENT TENSIONS WITHIN THE PARADIGM

- keeping programme costs low vs
  - need for professional financial staff in competition with private banking sector
  - staff costs for programme growth
  - providing clients/members with the skills to make a useful contribution to the running of the programme
- willingness/ability of poor female clients to join programme and repay (and hence successful targeting and programme growth) vs
  - high interest rates
  - requirements for voluntary contribution
  - reduction in services

Evidence suggests the need to develop a much more sophisticated model for analysing the interrelationships between different dimensions of sustainability. These points are summarized in Box 14.4. Although access to sustainable micro-finance is the necessary starting-point for all other potential benefits, scarce donor resources must be used in the most cost-effective way possible. There is likely to be a very delicate balance of interests between and within each level of sustainability, depending on client perceptions and motivations as well as financial incentives. It may be that it is only in particular participatory models, with both material and social incentives to repay, that different levels of sustainability can be maintained, as in the SANASA model (Montgomery 1996). The degree to which gender might make a difference to these general findings is also unclear.

At the programme level, financial and institutional sustainability cannot be assumed to be synonymous. As has been noted by critics within the poverty alleviation paradigm (e.g. Johnson and Rogaly 1997), long-term institutional sustainability may be financially costly in the short term. There is a need to look at alternatives to the model of large-scale poverty-targeted banking programmes implicit in most of the CGAP literature, particularly that from the World Bank, USAID and DFID. These alternatives would have a rather different sustainability dynamic but, in many contexts, may make a greater contribution to poverty-alleviation and empowerment. Alternative models already exist. But these have become marginalized in the rush for demonstrable numbers to attract major donors in the wake of the Micro-credit Summit, and by the dominance of very large organizations in this process. The alternatives include programmes that see sustainability in terms of stimulating and supporting many small micro-credit groups, encouraging them to become independent. This is already happening with women's ROSCAs, which are both financially and institutionally sustainable without external support. Such strategies are also particularly useful where there is a receptive formal banking sector, as in India. Arguably, even where the context is less favourable, programmes developing grassroots information exchange systems between women to stimulate the setting up of ROSCAs by women themselves would be more appropriate than setting up separate top-down NGO programmes. NGO and donor efforts could then be focused on lobbying for the reform of the formal banking system and the provision of complementary services rather than providing funds. Again, these strategies are already being promoted and supported, even by donor agencies like DFID UK operating firmly within the financial sustainability paradigm. At the programme level, in many contexts it may be cheaper in the longer term to decentralize and simplify the banking procedures and develop the financial skills of staff committed to poverty-alleviation and women's empowerment; in this case they would potentially be motivated in the longer term by non-financial as well as more modest financial incentives. Setting up systems for client monitoring, together with information exchange on issues useful to them, could also be a cost-effective long-term strategy combining capacity-building and empowerment with sustainability aims.

Nonetheless, these models also need to be examined critically for their contribution to poverty-alleviation and empowerment, rather than their inherent superiority to a 'hard-nosed banking approach'. They also need to be fully integrated into a wider strategy for combining financial and institutional sustainability.

Where a positive contribution to empowerment or poverty alleviation is shown, even within the financial self-sustainability approach itself, there must be room for negotiation regarding the time-scale for sustainability. It must also be determined precisely which costs are to be included in the financial sustainability equation and which are to be treated as ongoing, or one-off, separately funded services. Donors like DFID-UK, committed to the sustainability approach, have also supported complementary services and have a policy commitment to women's empowerment. Micro-finance programmes, like Grameen Bank, seen as 'ideal types' of the sustainability model, have continually explored strategies to empower

BOX 14.4. EMPOWERMENT AND FINANCIAL SUSTAINABILITY: SOME WAYS OF RESOLVING THE TENSIONS

INTERLINKED DIMENSIONS OF A WIDER APPROACH TO SUSTAINABILITY

CRITERIA:

- financial: calculated in economic terms, balancing monetary costs against income
- institutional: assessed in terms of durability of the organizations set up and/or contribution to wider capacity-building of staff and clients

ORGANIZATIONAL LEVEL:

- the programme
- loans and savings groups
- individual members

DYNAMICS:

- maintenance of the programme status quo
- an enduring mechanism for programme growth
- development by a programme of independent grassroots organizations or members
- establishment of links with other institutions for sustainable access to resources and services

POTENTIAL CONTRIBUTIONS OF EMPOWERMENT TO SUSTAINABILITY

- economic empowerment (increased income, control over income and access to resources) decreasing default as women are more able to repay
- increased well-being: women have more skills, time and resources to contribute to programme and groups
- social and political empowerment: enhances economic empowerment and well-being and enables women to be more active in their involvement (e.g. because of decreased restrictions on their movements and contacts with men, greater organizational skill and network contacts)

SOME STRATEGIES FOR RESOLVING THE TENSIONS

conditions of micro-finance delivery

- 'the carrot' approach to repayment: positive incentives to repay (e.g. larger repeat loans, interest rebates, including loans on preferential terms for lucrative non-traditional activities)
- all assets generated formally registered in women's names as condition of the loan
- 'multiple choice' options based on participatory consultation
- creation of sense of ownership and commitment to programme sustainability by giving high savings returns and /or control by women of at least some programme assets
- participatory consultation and transparency about use of programme income and hence 'value for money' generated by high interest rates

groups formed for micro-finance delivery can be developed as:

- an entry point for training
- a forum for information exchange
- a basis for local collective action
- loose network for information exchange/collective
- action beyond the local-level local groups combined into larger federations and movements

reducing costs of complementary services

- fully integrating gender and empowerment issues into all client/member and staff training
- initiating and supporting collective mutual learning and other service provision by clients/members
- cross-subsidy from charging better-off clients for some services
- charging all clients for some services once they have reached a certain level
- inter-organizational collaboration
- applying for separate, ongoing donor funds.

---

women. There may also be contexts where, although micro-finance services could be a very useful contribution to empowerment and poverty alleviation, achieving financial sustainability is very difficult. Impediments to financial sustainability may arise from the distances between populations, problems of developing markets, extreme disadvantage and lack of skills. Although these factors should not be an excuse for relaxing repayment requirements and financial rigour, serious questions need to be asked about the morality of passing all the costs of development on to very poor people. The experience of programmes at the workshops in the pilot phase suggests a range of possible strategies for combining women's empowerment and sustainability objectives (Mayoux 1998, 1999).

A New Sustainability for Empowerment Paradigm: Participatory Programme Management, Interorganizational Collaboration and Continuing Questions

Any conclusions at this stage can only be tentative. The evidence appears, to some extent, to support all four of the contrasting views aimed at developing sustainable micro-finance programmes that empower women. In relation to the first view, there are indeed grounds for optimism. Micro-finance services have significantly increased incomes for some women who have, in turn, improved their positions within their families and communities, even without non-financial interventions. Micro-finance programmes have also been used successfully as an entry point for the wider social and political mobilization of women. However, it appears likely that programmes operating within the strict financial sustainability paradigm have an inherent logic that favours the better-off among the poor and those women who are initially less disadvantaged. In practice, these tendencies are often countered by other poverty-targeted or empowerment strategies; but the latter have hitherto received insufficient attention within mainstream sustainability debates and guidelines for best practice.

In relation to the second view, there are ways in which the contribution to empowerment could be increased. There is, however, an urgent need for more systematic policy-oriented research and a longer-term process of intra- and interorganizational learning to identify and develop strategies for best practice. There are a number of essential elements of a gender strategy that need to be adapted to particular contexts and the needs of members. These are likely to lead to the development of a range of models, which could address potential interlinkages and tensions between poverty alleviation and empowerment in different ways, rather than to the advocacy of one particular universally 'optimum' paradigm or model. Two essential elements of such an optimum paradigm are indicated, however: first, more effective client/member participation and, second, greater collaboration with other institutions to ensure sustainable access to resources and services.

As I indicated at several points, increasing client/member participation can contribute to both empowerment and sustainability. Participation is fundamental in all three paradigms outlined above. However the term 'participation' is used in many different ways, as is summarized in Box 14.5. The particular balance between different aspects of participation may be crucial in increasing sustainability, poverty amelioration and empowerment. Flexibility in meeting women's needs and in determining the best combination of empowerment and sustainability objectives can only be achieved through a process of negotiation between women and development agencies based on extensive consultation with women and research into women's needs and constraints. This requires a more comprehensive framework for programme management. The outcome of increasing client participation in programme design is unlikely to result in one single model chosen by all women in all contexts. Participation has costs as well as benefits for women, and choices would continue to be constrained by sustainability considerations, in combination with the resources and capacities of women and programmes. A 'participation for empowerment' approach would differ from the financial self-sustainability approach in taking a multidimensional view of empowerment. This approach would also prioritize the needs of poor women participants and disadvantaged non-participants over those of programme staff and donors. At the same time, it would have to balance and negotiate, where possible, the demands of donors and women clients within constraints of available donor resources and the need for long-term sustainability.

Macro-level constraints on women's empowerment must also be clarified. So, too, must the limitations of micro-finance programmes and the possibilities of linking with other institutions to address these issues. Interlinkages with other institutions are critical in all three paradigms. In the feminist empowerment paradigm, interorganizational linkages have always been important, particularly the lobbying on gender issues and connecting with the women's and trade union movements. In the poverty alleviation paradigm there is an emphasis on the need for complementary welfare services; but micro-credit is often advocated as an alternative to the more contentious and potentially conflictive mobilization of women around gender issues. Finally, in the financial self-sustainability paradigm there is considerable emphasis on donor pressure to reform the private and government formal banking sector to make it more accessible to women. This has included recommendations on collateral requirements. It has also included changing property laws, as discussed in RESULTS 1997. However, the main emphasis throughout the CGAP literature is on ways to remove competing subsidized credit programmes; micro-credit

---

BOX 14.5. A NEW SUSTAINABILITY FOR EMPOWERMENT PARADIGM: PARTICIPATORY PROGRAMME MANAGEMENT, INTER-ORGANIZATIONAL COLLABORATION AND CONTINUING QUESTIONS

A FRAMEWORK FOR PARTICIPATORY PROGRAMME MANAGEMENT:

an ongoing system of participatory consultation involving the different stakeholders with influence over decision-making to:

- investigate women's aims, needs and strategies and establish possible strategies for enhancing contribution to empowerment that do not unnecessarily increase women's vulnerability
- elucidate the potential conflicts between empowerment and sustainability within the resource and skill constraints of women and development agencies

an institutional framework for participatory decision-making, including:

- grassroots groups for savings and credit (SCGs) of varying composition and structure depending on the needs of the women concerned
- a federation of grassroots groups with wider policy-making powers
- mechanisms for clarifying donor/NGO needs and constraints and negotiating between these and the demands of grassroots groups

INTER-ORGANIZATION COLLABORATION:

- profitable ethical investment of programme assets, particularly in enterprises that empower women
- selling shares to ethical private-sector concerns
- stimulation of self-expansion of self-funding grassroots groups through mutual learning
- lobbying and advocacy to increase access for poor women and to change regulations on e.g. collateral and asset ownership in formal government and private-sector financial services
- linking with providers of complementary services, including gender awareness and gender advocacy expertise
- lobbying to ensure continuity of donor funds for necessary complementary services

---

CONTINUING QUESTIONS FOR A NEW PARADIGM:

- What are the remaining trade-offs between financial sustainability and empowerment and poverty alleviation?
- Where empowerment and poverty alleviation are shown to conflict with financial sustainability, how might this affect the time-scale for achieving financial sustainability; and, which costs should be treated as ongoing social services to be met from separate funds?
- Are there any contexts or target groups where micro-finance services make a useful contribution to empowerment and poverty alleviation but could not be financially sustainable?
- Answers to these questions will determine the outcomes of future micro-credit initiatives and the lives of the women and men they affect.

---

is often presented as a poverty-alleviation solution in the context of wider economic reform that reduces access to welfare services.

In relation to the third and fourth views, there is evidence that micro-finance *per se* is not a panacea, and that other empowerment strategies are also needed. The pilot study covering evidence from the South Asia region and Africa reinforces earlier critical conclusions from Bangladesh about the potentially negative impacts of micro-finance on some women (Goetz and Sen Gupta 1996). At the same time, however, it also indicates the need to challenge the third view, currently prevalent in some donor and NGO circles, which contends that micro-finance need not concern itself with empowerment. For many women, poverty-alleviation, even in its narrow definition of increased incomes, cannot take place without wider social and political empowerment. Serious questions need to be asked about the use of development funds for programmes that may be potentially disempowering in some contexts for some women. Evidence indicates that micro-finance can be empowering. It is important, therefore, to consider how its contribution can be increased, particularly if this can be done cost-effectively and in ways that enhance programme sustainability.

In relation to the fourth view, despite the potential contributions of micro-finance programmes to women's empowerment, this outcome is dependent on, rather than a substitute for, adequate welfare provision and feminist mobilization. Where adequate welfare provision and strong women's organizations exist, women themselves are more likely to use micro-finance services for empowerment; furthermore, there are then more avenues for programme linkages without using programme funds. It is imperative, therefore, that donors do not divert funds from social service provision and support for women's mobilization around gender issues. What is particularly worrying about the current situation is that financially sustainable minimalist micro-finance is being promoted as the key strategy for poverty-alleviation and empowerment in response to ever-decreasing Northern aid budgets. This is happening in the context of structural adjustment policies that seriously disadvantage women and decrease the availability of complementary services. Unfortunately, in this climate, even the basic funding for micro-finance programmes themselves appears haphazard and uncertain (Scully and Wysham 1997).

Notes

1. This chapter is based on the findings of a pilot research project funded by the Small Enterprise Development Fund, DFID-UK and coordinated by Action Aid and a steering committee of UK-based NGOs including ACORD, CAFOD, CARE-International, Christian Aid, Friends of ASSEFA, Oxfam, Opportunity Trust, Save the Children, WOMANKIND and World Vision. It summarizes a longer paper (Mayoux 1998).
2. Consultative Group to Assist the Poorest is a major international collaborative initiative arising from the 1993 International Conference on Actions to Reduce Global Hunger and was formally constituted in 1995. The nine founding members are Canada, France, the Netherlands, the United States, the African Development Bank, the Asian Development Bank, the International Fund for Agricultural Development, the United Nations Development Program/United Nations Capital Development Fund and the World Bank, later followed by Australia, Finland, Norway, the United Kingdom and Inter-American Development Bank. Approximately US $200 million (including existing budget commitments) was pledged to micro-finance programmes for the poorest groups in low-income countries, particularly women. Actual amounts disbursed by individual CGAP members are considerably higher.
3. Detailed discussion of the evidence with an annotated bibliography is given in Mayoux 1998. See also Mayoux 1999 for a specific African perspective.
4. The low level of success of AKRSP was attributed to failure to employ and adequately to train female extension staff (Harper 1995). A reduction in female staff in ACORD-Sudan also appears to have led to a dramatic decrease in women's participation (Stallard 1996).
5. For a discussion of the issues see Goetz 1992; Macdonald, Sprenger, Dubel, and Field 1998.

References

Unpublished Sources

Harper, A. (1995), 'Providing Women in Baltistan with Access to Loans – Potential and Problems', AKRSP Pakistan.

Johnson, S. (1997), 'Gender and Microfinance: Guidelines for Best Practice', Action Aid, UK.

Lakshman, M. T. (1996), 'Participatory Assessment of the Benefits of Self-Help Income Generating Activities of the Sucharita Women Society on Families and Children', Save the Children Fund-UK.

Mayoux, L. and S. Johnson (1997), 'Micro-Finance and Women's Empowerment: Strategies for Increasing Impact', Report of workshop held 13–15 January, Addis Ababa, Ethiopia. London: Action Aid.

Pairaudeau, N. (1996), 'Savings and Loan Use Survey and Gender Impact Assessment of Uong Bi savings and Credit Scheme', Action Aid Vietnam.

Scully, N. D. and D. Wysham (1997), 'The World Bank's Consultative Group to Assist the Poorest: Opportunity or Liability for the World's Poorest Women? A Policy Critique', Washington: Institute for Policy Studies.

Stallard, D. (1996), 'Institutionalizing Gender: Observations on ACORD's Port Sudan Small-Scale Enterprise Project, Sudan', Unpublished Report.

Wiig, A. (1997), 'Credit Expansion in Micro-credit Programmes: Dilemmas and Feasible Methods of Studying Them', Unpublished paper presented to CGAP Working Group on Impact Assessment Methodologies, April.

Published Sources

Ebdon, R. (1995), 'NGO Expansion and the Fight to Research the Poor: Gender Implications of NGO Scaling-Up in Bangladesh', *IDS Bulletin*, 26: 49–55.

Everett, J. and M. Savara (1987), 'Institutional Credit as a Strategy Toward Self-Reliance for Petty Commodity Producers in India', in A. M. Singh and A. Kelles-Viitanen (eds), *Invisible Hands: Women in Home-based Production*, Newbury Park, CA: Sage Publications.

—— and —— (1991), 'Institutional Credit as a Strategy Toward Self-reliance for Petty Commodity Producers in India: A Critical Evaluation', in H. Afshar (ed.), *Women, Development and Survival in the Third World*, Harlow: Longman Group.

Goetz, A. M. (1992), 'Gender and Administration', *IDS Bulletin*, 23: 6.

Goetz, A. M. and R. Sen Gupta (1996), 'Who Takes The Credit? Gender, Power and Control over Loan Use in Rural Credit Programmes in Bangladesh', *World Development*, 24: 45-63.

Hulme, D. and R. Montgomery (1994), 'Cooperatives, Credit and the Poor: Private Interest, Public Choice and Collective Action in Sri Lanka', *Savings and Development*, 18: 359–82.

Johnson, S. and B. Rogaly (1997), *Microfinance and Poverty Reduction*, Oxford: Oxfam Publishing.

Macdonald, M., E. Sprenger, I. Dubel, S. Field (1998), 'Gender and Organizational Change: Bridging the Gap between Policy and Practice', *Development in Practice*, 8: 247–8.

Mayoux, L. (1995a), 'From Vicious to Virtuous Circles? Gender and Micro-Enterprise Development', *UNRISD Occasional Paper*, No. 3, Geneva: UNRISD.

—— (1998), 'Participatory Learning for Women's Empowerment in Micro-finance Programmes: Negotiating Complexity, Conflict and Change', *IDS Bulletin*, 29: 39–50.

—— (1999), 'Questioning Virtuous Spirals: Micro-finance and Women's Empowerment in Africa', *Journal of International Development*, 11: 957–84.

Montgomery, R. (1996), 'Disciplining or Protecting the Poor? Avoiding the Social Costs of Peer Pressure in Micro-Credit Schemes', *Journal of International Development*, 8: 289–305.

Montgomery, R., D. Bhattacharya and D. Hulme (1996), 'Credit for the Poor in Bangladesh', in D. Hulme and P. Mosley (eds), *Finance Against Poverty*, London: Routledge.

Otero, M. and E. Rhyne (eds) (1994), *The New World of Microenterprise Finance: Building Healthy Financial Institutions for the Poor*, London: IT Publications.

RESULTS (1997), 'The Micro-credit Summit February 2–4, 1997 Declaration and Plan of Action', Washington DC: RESULTS.

Rhyne, E. and M. Otero (1994), 'Financial Services for Micro-enterprises: Principles and Institutions', in M. Otero and E. Rhyne (eds), *The New World of Microenterprise Finance: Building Healthy Financial Institutions for the Poor*, London: IT Publications.

Rogaly, B. (1996), 'Micro-finance Evangelism, "Destitute Women", and the Hard Selling of a New Anti-poverty Formula', *Development in Practice*, 6: 100–12.

Sen, G. and C. Grown (1988), *Development, Crises and Alternative Visions: Third World Women's Perspectives*, New York: Monthly Review Press.

Singh, A. M. and A. Kelles-Viitanen (eds) (1987), *Invisible Hands: Women in Home-based Production*, Newbury Park, CA: Sage Publications.

15

Linking Formal and Informal Financial Intermediaries in Ghana: A Way To Increase Women's Access to Financial Services?

J. Howard M. Jones and *Owuraka Sakyi-Dawson*

This chapter has its origins in a DFID-funded research project that examined the scope for enhancing the role of the informal financial sector in renewable natural resources development (RNR) in Ghana.[1] The initial premiss was that while financial service demands from small-scale operators in the RNR sector are largely unmet by formal financial institutions, the informal financial agents that do serve the sector's needs operate under capital constraints that limit the scale and term of their operations. Bringing together the capital and resources of the formal financial sector with the knowledge and outreach of the informal financial sector could offer one way to help bridge the gap between clients' financial service needs and financial service provision.

Initial research concentrated on identifying financial service needs and the extent of financial service provision for clients in the RNR sector in three research locations.[2] Subsequent research identified existing linkages between formal and informal financial intermediaries and examined recent examples of formal linkage arrangements between selected financial intermediaries. During these investigations, the gender implications of linking formal and informal financial intermediaries proved very striking, and we concentrate on this aspect of the project in this chapter.

We first consider the general arguments in favour of linking formal and informal financial intermediaries and then examine Ghanaian women's access to financial services. We then outline the major players in the financial services sector in Ghana and the most recent financial sector reforms. A brief overview of existing linkages between financial

271

intermediaries sets the stage for a detailed examination of the formal links that three different types of formal financial institutions have established with two kinds of informal financial intermediaries. The chapter ends by identifying unresolved issues regarding the linkages of informal and formal financial intermediaries.

Linking Formal and Informal Financial Intermediaries

Establishing and/or enhancing links between formal and informal financial intermediaries is seen as a way to build upon each other's comparative advantages and mitigate the effects of each other's comparative disadvantages (Germidis 1990; Ghate 1992; Zeller *et al.* 1997).

On the plus side, the banks have their own particular strengths. They are able to mediate funds between surplus and deficit units that are widely separated. Their interest charges are usually substantially below those demanded by informal lenders. They have the resources to support large-scale investment over a long period of time. In many countries the banks have a physical network enabling the introduction of many potential clients to mainstream capital markets.

However, banks' reluctance to provide small-scale savings and lending facilities to small-scale primary producers in rural areas and slum dwellers in urban areas demonstrates the negative side of formal financial sector operations. Just 15 per cent of farmers in Asia and Latin America, and only 5 per cent of farmers in Africa are reported to obtain finance from formal sources (Braverman and Huppi 1991), a situation explained by general perceptions of a remote and geographically dispersed clientele, seasonal peak-load demand for speedy disbursement, high transaction costs, high administrative and monitoring costs, and high risks.

Moreover, access to banks by small-scale borrowers and lenders can be inhibited by the nature, characteristics and requirements of these formal financial institutions. Poor physical and social access, low literacy and numeracy skills, inflexible and time-consuming procedures, restricted hours of opening and non-provision of consumption and emergency credit act as powerful disincentives for the small-scale rural and urban operator. Many of these are particular barriers for poor women with multiple work obligations in the household and informal economy (Berger 1989; Holt and Ribe 1991; Jiggins 1985).

In many cases the more positive features of informal financial intermediaries and agents mirror the disadvantages of the formal financial institutions. To varying degrees these positive features include easy physical and social access to the rural and urban poor (including women), small-loan and small-deposit provision, multiple loan provision, low non-interest borrowing costs, flexibility in loan use, rapid processing, locally suited collateral requirements and high repayment rates. Similarly, the more negative features of informal financial agents mirror the more positive features of formal financial institutions. Moneylender interest charges tend to be relatively high, loans are limited in size and duration and operations are often highly localized, limiting the ability to deal with covariate risks. Informal savings services often lack monetary savings options with real returns (Zeller *et al.* 1997).

Even so, as a result of their embeddedness in the local economy and society, and the nature of their operations and products, informal financial agents overcome the information asymmetries that banks typically face when dealing with physically and socially distant clients. The informal financial agents are thus better able to mitigate the resulting problems of moral hazard, adverse selection and enforcement (Bell 1993: 195) compared to the banks, and at much lower transaction costs compared to those of these formal financial institutions (Zeller *et al.* 1997).

Linking formal sector financial institutions with informal financial agents is therefore a way to bring together the capital and resources of the former with the knowledge and outreach of the latter. Taking advantage of existing informal agents and their client base entails few marginal costs for the formal financial institutions (Quainoo 1998). Market integration is facilitated through greater flows of funds between formal and informal financial agents (Aryeetey 1994), and society is saved the costly inter-mediation resources devoted to unsuccessful attempts by formal financial institutions to reach resource-poor borrowers (Ghate, 1997). However, care must be taken not to jeopardize the essential informality of informal operations and, for some, enhancing the role of individual informal lenders poses an unacceptable risk of reinforcing and perpetuating an unsatis-factory status quo (Singh 1990).

Another, and perhaps less contentious, option is for the formal financial institutions to identify the more positive operations of the informal financial agents and incorporate these into their products and services (Germidis 1990; Ghate 1992; Zeller *et al.* 1997). Some believe this can increase women's access to financial services, with Berger (1989: 1029), for example, noting 'Experience teaches that if state or private lenders are to reach poor women, they must adopt some of the features of the informal credit sources to which they now turn'.

Women's Access to Financial Services in Ghana

Women's access to formal financial services is poor, although access to financial resources for low-income women is a key factor in human development (UNDP 1995). This is the case in Ghana, where credit received by women rarely comes from the formal sector, and particularly the case for women working in the informal sector of the economy (Holt and Ribe 1991; Bortei-Doku Aryeetey and Aryeetey 1996; Quainoo 1999). A study by Duncan (1997), in the Volta, Ashanti, Brong Ahafo and Eastern Regions shows that between 77 and 98 per cent of women taking loans sourced these loans from the informal financial sector. Only in regions with special credit programmes targeting women, such as the IFAD-SCIMP Schemes with the Agricultural Development Bank and Rural Banks in the Ashanti and Brong Ahafo Regions, did relatively higher proportions of women use formal sources of credit.

The Financial Services Sector in Ghana

There is certainly no shortage of potential linkage partners within the financial services sector in Ghana, which includes a wide and diverse range of players, both formal and informal. The formal financial institutions operating in Ghana are shown in Box 15.1. The banking sector comprises the Bank of Ghana (The Central Bank), eight commercial banks, three development banks, three merchant banks and 133 unit rural banks. The Ghana Commercial Bank (GCB), Barclays Bank of Ghana (BBG), Standard Chartered Bank of Ghana (SCB), Ghana Cooperative Bank, Meridian Biao Bank and the Social Security Bank (SSB) dominate the commercial banking sector. The three development banks are the National Investment Bank, the Agricultural Development Bank (ADB) and the Bank for Housing and Construction (BHC).

Urban and southern concentrations of these formal financial institutions are very evident. Of the 180 branches of the three main commercial banks (GCB, BBG, and SCB), 28 per cent are located in rural areas. Fifty-six per cent of the 32 ADB branches are located in rural areas. Although the headquarters of all 133 Rural Banks are sited in rural areas, they commonly have multiple agencies in urban areas. Although banks are present in all ten regions of Ghana, there is a relative dearth of formal financial institutions in northern Ghana: seven out of the thirteen districts in the Northern Region have no banks and the ratio of clients to banks in northern Ghana is much higher (100,000:1) compared to that in the country as a whole (16,000–26,000:1) (Nass and O'Dowd 1997).

BOX 15.1. FORMAL FINANCIAL INSTITUTIONS OPERATING IN GHANA (DECEMBER, 1998)

BANKS

Bank of Ghana (Central Bank)
8 Commercial Banks
3 Development Banks
3 Merchant Banks
1 Co-operative Bank
133 Unit Rural Banks

NON-BANK FINANCIAL INSTITUTIONS

21 Insurance Companies
Stock Exchange
264 Forex Bureaux
13 Finance Companies
7 Savings and Loans Companies
6 Leasing Companies
3 Discount Houses
2 Building Societies
1 Venture Capital Company
1 Mortgage Finance Company

The semi-formal and informal financial intermediaries and agents operating in Ghana are shown in Box 15.2. The first credit union in Africa was formed in the Upper West Region of Ghana in 1955. At present there are a total of 203 credit unions, half of them located in urban areas, and just 27 of them are located in the three northern regions. A national credit union association was formed in 1968 and, since 1971, has been known as the Ghana Co-operative Credit Union Association. Savings and credit cooperatives are registered cooperative organizations whose main activity is lending to a limited number of members from regular dues. A review of fourteen NGOs operating in Ghana showed the wide variety of potential roles such organizations can play in the financial services sector. Although NGOs in Ghana are actively involved in providing and/or facilitating savings and credit facilities, their operations tend to be localized and they continue to meet only a 'minuscule' amount of the total unmet demand for financial services in rural areas (Reed *et al.* 1994).

BOX 15.2. SEMI-FORMAL AND INFORMAL FINANCIAL INTERMEDIARIES AND AGENTS IN GHANA

SEMI-FORMAL
Credit Unions
Savings and Credit Cooperatives
Non-Government Organizations (NGOs)

INFORMAL
Moneylenders
Susu collectors (savings mobilizers)
Traders/suppliers/middlemen
Agricultural produce processors and input distributors
Susu Groups/ROSCAs (Rotating Savings and Credit Associations)
Family, relatives, friends and neighbours

The informal financial sector in Ghana in itself comprises a very diverse range of players. In addition to moneylenders and *susu* collectors (savings mobilizers) financial services are provided by a number of operators engaged in related upstream and downstream activities (input distributors, traders, processors), personal informal sources of credit (friends, family, relatives, work colleagues), and the formation of self-help groups based on kinship, age set, or dominant economic activity (Jones *et al.* 1999). Moreover, for certain RNR activities, different sets of operators alternate in the role of creditor and debtor depending on the season and stage of the enterprise life-cycle.

Broadly speaking there are two categories of moneylenders: those who operate under licence and those without official sanction. The latter group are prevalent in farming communities, and rely, to a large extent, on personal knowledge of clients to guarantee their money in the absence of collateral. Often they are rich cocoa farmers or businessmen whose cash is generated from other activities. Traders often give suppliers' credit or an advance payment against farm produce. Similarly, processors and input suppliers prefinance customers' activities, usually for a specific cash crop.

As informal financial agents, the *susu* collectors are unusual in having an apex organization to represent them. Excluding northern Ghana, 850 *susu* collectors are registered with the Ghana Cooperative *Susu* Collectors'

Association (GCSCA). A high proportion of *susu* collectors operate in urban areas, usually working as individual operators, sometimes with assistance. Although *susu* collectors are generally known as savings mobilizers, some of them also provide 'advances' to their regular clients. In Ghana, ROSCAs, popularly known as *susu*, have a long-standing tradition, having appeared in the country probably in the early 1900s. Initially thought to be an urban phenomenon, ROSCAs are currently widespread in rural areas, especially among traders (Bortei-Doku Aryeetey and Aryeetey 1996).

As individual savings mobilizers, the banks are characterized by a large client base, large deposits and a high annual value of deposits. To varying degrees, the converse applies to credit unions, to *susu* collectors and ROSCAs. Nationally, the Rural Banks have an average of 12,000 accounts and the ADBs an average of 4,324 accounts, while the credit unions have an average of 253 members and the *susu* collectors an average of 300 clients. Of the nineteen ROSCAs surveyed in northern Ghana, membership ranged from five to forty persons, with 63 per cent of these groups having between ten and twenty members.

Salaried workers and traders are the favoured clients of the rural banks and the ADBs. In terms of occupation, ethnicity and gender, membership profiles of the credit unions in the three research areas are relatively homogeneous, with an active involvement in the RNR sector. The *susu* collectors provide savings facilities to individuals involved in a wide variety of informal income-generating activities: traders, cart pushers, apprentices, mechanics, drivers and sometimes farmers and fishermen. Most of the ROSCA members in the North are engaged in processing and marketing.

In only one of the three research areas did the ADB and a Rural Bank give some indication of the gender composition of accounts: around 70 per cent of savings and fixed deposit accounts are held by men. In contrast, the majority of members in the credit unions are women, as are the clients of the *susu* collectors.[3] Women's jobs as processors and/or traders are more likely to bring them in a daily income as compared to men. Of the nineteen Northern ROSCAs, sixteen are all-women groups, and women form the majority of members in the other three groups.

On the credit side the banks are characterized by relatively high-value and longer-duration loans, which require physical collateral and/or salaried workers acting as guarantors, and are advanced after a formal and relatively long application procedure. Advances made by the *susu* collectors are usually low-value, very short-term (less than one month), provided on an interest-free basis without collateral, and are disbursed immediately if the money is to hand. In contrast to the *susu* collectors, the moneylenders advance loans on interest (higher than the banks), and for rather longer periods (though shorter than the banks) but, as in the case of the *susu* collectors, these loans are provided without collateral and are disbursed very quickly if funds are available and the client is known to the moneylender. Of the nineteen Northern ROSCAs, seven (37 per cent) provide just savings mobilization and rotation, and eight (42 per cent) also provide welfare facilities to members, while four (21 per cent) provide credit to members in addition to rotated savings and welfare facilities.

Thus the opportunities offered by combining the banks' capital with the intrinsic advantages of the informal agents (small savings and loan provision, physical and social access, simple procedures, reliance on social capital and collateral, quick withdrawal and disbursement and high proportions of women clients) are one argument for linking the formal and the informal financial intermediaries. Another argument derives from the views clients have of the financial services they require and the perceptions they have of the relative advantages and disadvantages of the various financial service providers.

Clients want financial service providers to provide services such as reliability, trustworthiness, flexible hours, outreach, physical and cultural accessibility, provision of a range of financial services, speedy procedures, understanding clients' businesses and the ability to communicate with clients. More specifically, for credit, clients also want discretion, transparency, seasonally sensitive products and terms, timeliness, procedures tailored to clients' needs, fair interest rates, money available at short notice, sufficient capital for clients' needs and repayment in cash or kind; while for savings, desired features include physical security, acceptance of small denomination notes, collection at place of work, simple withdrawal procedures, investment opportunities, use as future collateral and flexible deposit terms (Jones *et al.* 1999).

Clients also have clear views on the relative advantages and disadvantages of using different financial service providers. These are shown in Table 15.1, with reference to client perceptions of selected formal and informal financial intermediaries in the three research areas. From the table it is clear that, by themselves, the individual financial service providers do not encompass all the features desired by clients, but that, in combination, possibly through linkage arrangements, they may be in a better position to do so.

Table 15.1 Clients' Perceptions of Selected Formal and Informal Financial Intermediaries

Financial intermediaries	Advantages	Disadvantages
Banks	Lower interest charges Larger amounts available Good for expanding business when timing not so crucial and collateral available	Physical collateral required Intimidating form filling Slow disbursement of loans Untimeliness of loans Rent seeking by officials Delays in withdrawing funds Mistrust when banks fail/ officials abscond Distance to travel Depreciation of deposits with high inflation
Credit Unions	Relatively low interest rate Quicker than bank Cheaper than bank Facilitate loans	For members only Not so quick as friends and market women
Moneylenders	Money available Quick and easy processing Security through guarantor	High interest charges
Susu collectors	Encourages savings habits Money can be used for personal expenditures Easy withdrawal	Some untrustworthy Need a regular source of income to use Vulnerability of savings Credit advances very short-term

Financial Sector Reforms in Ghana

In 1988 the Government of Ghana initiated the Financial Sector Adjustment Programme (FINSAP) as part of the Economic Recovery Programme (ERP) introduced in 1983. The Programme sought to provide support particularly to the productive sectors, and has been addressing the institutional and structural weaknesses of the financial sector. Credit ceilings were phased out by early 1988 and the agricultural credit target was removed in 1991. Interest rates had been allowed to rise in line with inflation, and ceilings were removed in 1987.

The Financial Institutions (Non-Banking) Law, passed in 1993, is being supported by the Non-Bank Financial Institutions (NBFI) Assistance Project, which provides wide-ranging support to NBFIs, such as capital market institutions, contractual savings institutions, mortgage financing institutions and others to promote the growth of an efficient, competitive, well-regulated non-bank financial sector. A total of thirty-three NBFIs had been registered by the end of 1998 (ISSER 1999). A Rural Finance Project has aimed to strengthen credit unions and restructure rural banks, numbering 133 by 1998, of which however only sixty-one are classified as performing satisfactorily by the Bank of Ghana (ISSER 1999).

The main objectives of financial sector reform include (i) increasing the mobilization of domestic savings in formal and informal financial sectors, facilitating the flow of international capital into Ghana through better financial intermediation and supplying financial services competitively to the economy; and (ii) creating an environment conducive to greater private sector activity and ensuring the successful implementation of the privatization programme for state-owned enterprises and the three largest state-owned banks. Bank density has increased to 323 branches from 313 (twelve new branches and two closures). In addition, there has been an alarming trend in the spatial distribution of bank branches in recent years, with banks retreating from rural to urban areas – a situation that conflicts with the financial authorities' objective of bringing banking to the doorstep of the rural people to enhance monetization and stimulate the development of those areas (ISSER 1999). To avoid diverting resources from rural areas to urban areas, rural banks with branches in urban areas were given directives to close all such branches in 1998. In general there has been a heightened competition in the banking industry. To attract customers, competitive advertising offers various attractive packages with favourable returns for special deposits.

Until recently, FINSAP was wholly concerned with the formal banking system except for the NBFI provision. The linkage in deposit mobilization that already occurred between formal and informal banking sectors had no formal recognition. Nor did government financial policy encompass the role of NGOs in financial service delivery. However, the Ministry of Finance has recently focused greater attention on rural and micro-finance delivery in an effort to integrate financial markets and bring micro-finance closer to small entrepreneurs. An explicit recognition of the critical role of linkages, in improving the efficiency of the financial system, has stimulated greater interest in and understanding of the informal financial sector and NGOs. The main planks of the Rural and Micro-Finance Initiative (RMFI) policy include incentive structures, regulatory policies, development of a national strategic framework for rural and micro-finance and institutional strengthening and capacity-building (Siriboe 1998).

Existing Linkages between Financial Intermediaries in Ghana

In our initial exploration of policy options for linking formal and informal financial intermediaries, a first step was to identify existing linkages between the different players in the financial services sector and to determine what advantages and disadvantages they attached to these arrangements. In terms of flows of funds there are significant linkages between financial institutions in the three research areas. Some of these are regular (for instance, traders depositing funds with *susu* collectors, *susu* collectors depositing mobilized savings with banks) while others are more sporadic and more localized (for instance, moneylenders receiving loans from banks). For banks, the main motivation to link with informal agents such as the *susu* collectors is increased and less costly deposit mobilization, while the informal agents value the security of bank deposits and see deposits as a route to accessing bank loans.

In addition to these 'institutional' linkages, it is clear that there are also important credit relations at the community level between different actors in particular economic sub-sectors: for example, between boat-builders, fishing gear sellers, fishermen crew, traders, processors and salt-sellers within the inland fishing communities (Jones *et al.* 1999). In our analysis of such linkages we concentrate on recent formal linkage arrangements that have been established between three different types of formal financial institutions and two kinds of informal operations. In addition, we also examine the adoption of a particular informal operation by one of the formal financial institutions.

Table 15.2 provides some background information on the three formal financial institutions: (i) CITI Savings and Loan Company (CITI), a non-bank financial institution; (ii) Metropolitan and Allied Bank (M&A), a private commercial bank; and (iii) the Ahantaman Rural Bank (ARB). Both CITI and the M&A bank are relatively recent financial institutions, established in the 1990s, while the Ahantaman Rural Bank has been operating since the mid-1980s. Whereas the first two formal financial institutions each operate in the Greater Accra area, each with a Head Office and three branches, the ARB, with its head office and seven agencies, is

Table 15.2 Background to Three Formal Financial Institutions with Links to Informal Groups/Agents

Features	CITI	M & A Bank	Ahantaman RB
Date established	1992	1995	1984
Number of branches agencies	HO + 3 branches	HO + 3 branches	HO + 7
Location	Greater Accra	Greater Accra	Western Region
Number of staff	54	102	104
Gender of staff	47% female	28% female	33% female
Number of accounts	15,785[a]	6,876[b]	26,623
% of accounts by gender	41% of individual customers=female	n.a.	45% of individual accounts held by women

Notes:
n.a. not available
[a] Includes 1,679 (11%) company accounts, but excludes number of fixed deposit accounts.
[b] Includes 1,967 (27%) corporate accounts.

located along the coast in the Western Region. The M&A bank and the ARB each have about twice as many staff as CITI, but CITI has the highest proportion of female staff (47 per cent). The number of accounts they hold ranges from nearly 7,000 (M&A) to just over 26,000 for the ARB, with quite high proportions of these accounts held by women: 41 per cent for CITI and 45 per cent for the ARB.

However, from Table 15.3 we can see that, with linkage to *susu* groups and *susu* collectors, the potential for reaching even more women clients is very considerable. The left-hand side of Table 15.3, as with Tables 15.4 to 15.6, provides details on the links the three financial institutions have established with *susu* groups: sixteen, seven and seventeen groups for CITI, M&A and ARB respectively. In contrast, the right-hand side of Table 15.3, again as with Tables 15.4 to 15.6, shows two different kinds of links: first, those that CITI has established with sixty-three individual *susu* collectors, sixteen of whom also take loans from CITI to on-lend to their own clients; second, details of the employment of twenty-six *susu* clerks by the ARB to operate as *susu* collectors for the bank, an interesting

Table 15.3 Members of *Susu* Groups and Clients of *Susu* Collectors Linked to Three Formal Financial Institutions

Features *Susu* Groups	CITI Savings & Loan Co.	M & A Bank	Ahantaman RB	Features *Susu* collector/ clerks	CITI Savings & Loan Co.	Ahantaman RB
No. of groups linked with	16	7	17	No. *Susu* Collectors/ clerks linked	63 saving, 16 also taking loans	26
				Gender Collectors/ clerks	61 men, 2 women	25 women, 1 man
Total members	4,634	929	1,260	No. of clients	25,000	6,000
Members' Occupations	Traders, artisans	Mainly traders	Farmers, traders, artisans	Clients' Occupations	Traders, artisans, market labour	Women= traders, men= artisans
Average membership	289	133	74	Average no. clients	400	255
% women members	82% (8–94%)	77% (41–90%)	70%	% women clients	never<70%	60%
% women committee members	63% (17–100%)	45% (0–83%)	n.a.			

Notes: n.a.= not available.

example of a formal financial institution's adopting an informal savings practice for its own purposes. Thus, in Tables 15.3–15.6, there are three kinds of comparisons: links with informal groups, links with individual *susu* collectors and adoption of informal operations.

When we consider the membership of the linked *susu* groups and the number of clients of the linked *susu* collectors / clerks, the outreach potential of linkage for the formal financial institutions is very apparent. The total numbers of indirect clients through linkage with the *susu* groups varies from 929 for the M&A bank to as many as over 4,500 clients for CITI. In addition, the sixty-three *susu* collectors linked to CITI have themselves 25,000 clients, while the twenty-six *susu* clerks employed by the ARB service a total of 6,000 clients. From Table 15.3 we can see that many group members and clients of the *susu* collectors/clerks are traders and artisans, with the ARB noting that the traders tend to be women and the artisans men.

Not only does linkage with *susu* groups and *susu* collectors have the potential to reach very large numbers of clients, but a high proportion of these clients are women: from between 70 and 82 per cent for membership of the *susu* groups, 60 per cent for the clients of the *susu* clerks and never less than 70 per cent for clients of the *susu* collectors linked to CITI. Does high female membership in the groups translate into control of these groups? Some indication of this is given by a comparison of the percentage of female members in *susu* groups linked to CITI (82 per cent) and the M&A bank (77 per cent) with the percentage of female committee members in these groups (63 per cent for CITI and 45 per cent for M&A). Although the percentage of female committee members can vary greatly from group to group, the overall percentage of women committee members is less than their membership profile.

From Table 15.4 we can see that the links between the three formal financial institutions and the *susu* groups and *susu* collectors/clerks are a relatively recent phenomenon. CITI has established relations with the sixteen groups over a four-year period, 1994 to 1998, the M&A Bank with the seven groups between 1997 and 1999, while the ARB has established links with the seventeen groups from 1996. A minority of the *susu* groups had already been established for a long period by the time they became linked to their formal partners: between fourteen to twenty years for three groups linked to CITI and twenty-one years for one of the groups linked to the M&A Bank. Ten of the remaining groups linked to these two institutions had been established between one and six years before linking, and a further ten groups had just been established or were less than a year old when links were initiated. All the groups linked to the ARB were between one and three years old when links to this bank were established. Bank requirements for linkage variously relate to prior savings, registration and organization of the group in terms of having an executive. All the groups meet weekly and interact with the banks on a weekly or fortnightly basis.

It is important to consider the changes that have taken place within the groups as a result of these formal linkage arrangements. The links CITI has established with the individual *susu* collectors have been in operation since 1994, and the ARB started to employ the *susu* clerks a year later, in 1995. The *susu* collectors are required to be registered with the Greater Accra Susu Collectors' Association before they can be linked to CITI, while the *susu* clerks need two guarantors and, in terms of education, at

Table 15.4 Background to Linkage Arrangements with *Susu* Groups and *Susu* Collectors/Clerks

Features Susu Groups	CITI Savings & Loan Co. (16 groups)	M & A Bank (7 groups)	Ahantaman RB (17 groups)	*Features Susu collector/ clerks*	CITI Savings & Loan Co. (63 SCs)	Ahantaman RB (26 SClks)
When linked	1994–1998	1997–1999	From 1996	When linked	Since 1994	Since 1995
Age when linked	3:14–20 yrs 7: 1–5 yrs 6:inception	1:21 yrs 3: 3–6 yrs 4:< 1 yr	1-3 yrs			
Requirements for linkage	Prior savings Registered joint & several guarantee	Registered limited by guarantee	Properly organized with executives/ even registered	Requirements for linkage	Certified by GASCA[a]	2 guarantors insured O levels
Frequency of meetings	Weekly	Weekly	Weekly			
Frequency of interaction	Weekly	Fortnightly	Fortnightly			
Changes in leadership	More literate leaders replaced illiterate leaders	In one[b] group an additional man and women	Some withdraw/ others join			

Notes:

[a] Greater Accra Susu Collectors' Association

[b] The women to take mobilized savings to the bank, the man to do the bookkeeping.

least two 'O' levels to be employed by the ARB. In the case of CITI, more literate group leaders have replaced illiterate leaders, while for the M&A Bank in one of the seven *susu* groups a man had been added to the executive to deal with the bookkeeping.

From Table 15.5, the advantages of linkage for the three formal financial institutions are very apparent. For CITI in particular, the amount of weekly savings mobilized through the sixteen groups is very considerable: ¢262 million[4] on a weekly basis, with an average of ¢16 million per group, accounting for over a quarter (26 per cent) of CITI's deposit liability. The M&A Bank and the ARB mobilize similar amounts of deposits through their groups on a weekly basis: ¢26 million and ¢24 million respectively. Although CITI does not have figures for weekly savings mobilized through the sixty-three *susu* collectors, they reckon that such savings account for a further 3 per cent of the company's deposit liability, while the savings mobilized by the twenty-six *susu* clerks account for as much as 18 per cent of deposit liability of the ARB.

Some indication of savings mobilized by individual members of the *susu* groups and clients of the *susu* collectors/clerks is also given in Table 15.5. For CITI and the M&A Bank the weekly individual savings are similar: ¢5,500 to ¢330,000 for the former and ¢3,000 to ¢300,000 for the latter. The rather lower range of ¢12,500 to ¢25,000 for groups linked to the ARB no doubt reflects the more rural location of this financial institution. Clients of the *susu* collectors linked to CITI deposit between ¢500 and ¢10,000 with these informal agents on a daily basis. The interest earnings on deposits for group savings are similar for CITI and the ARB: between 15 and 20 per cent for the former and 21 per cent for the latter. The M&A bank pays either no interest or 15 per cent on deposited group savings, depending on subsequent loan arrangements (i.e. zero interest on deposits can lead to an interest charge of 65 per cent of market rates on a loan). The *susu* collectors linked to CITI receive between 13 and 21 per cent on the savings they mobilize from their clients, depending on the type of account they use for depositing these funds. The clients of the *susu* collectors receive no interest from the *susu* collector, and, as with traditional *susu* operations, pay one day's saving to the *susu* collector as commission. In this respect there is a difference from the operations of the *susu* clerks employed by the ARB. In contrast to traditional *susu* clients, the clients of these clerks do not have to pay a day's savings as commission and can, in fact, earn interest on their accumulated savings if these are put into a savings account at the bank.

The advantages of linkage for both the formal financial institutions and the informal groups/agents are also apparent with respect to lending arrangements. These are shown in Table 15.6. First, let us consider loans advanced by the three formal financial institutions through the *susu* groups. What are the advantages for these three institutions? They can advance loans in a cost-effective manner by advancing loans to many individuals using the mechanisms of the groups themselves. CITI advances between ¢2 million and ¢679 million to each group on a weekly basis, with an average of ¢160 million. Such lending now accounts for as much as 70 per cent of this institution's loan portfolio. The M&A Bank advances between ¢30 million and ¢750 million to each group over a complete cycle. The ARB advances much lower figures to its groups, between ¢300,000 and ¢1 million, again reflecting the more rural nature of this institution and its groups. In turn, these loans translate into loans

Table 15.5   Savings Mobilized Through Informal Groups/Agents

Links with *Susu* Groups	CITI 16 groups 4634 members	M & A Bank 7 groups 929 members	Ahantaman RB 17 groups 1260 members	Links with *Susu* collectors/ clerks	CITI 63 SCs 25,200 clients	Ahantaman RB 26 SClks 6,000 clients
Savings mobilized by groups	¢262m weekly	¢26m weekly	¢24m weekly	Savings mobilized by *susu* collectors/ clerks	n.a.	¢750,000 daily ¢300m monthly
Average savings mobilized by groups	¢16m weekly	¢3.7m weekly	¢1.4m			
Savings mobilized by members	¢5,500– ¢330,000 weekly	¢3,000– ¢300,000 weekly	¢12,500– ¢25,000 weekly	Savings mobilized by clients of SCs/SClks	¢500– ¢10,000 daily	n.a.
Interest paid on deposits	15–20%	0% or 15% depending on loan arrangements	21%	Interest paid on deposits	13–21% to SC	Yes, if transferred to savings account
% Deposit liability	26%	n.a.	2.4%	% Deposit Liability	3%	18%

Notes:
n.a. = not available
¢: In March 1998 £1 = 3,846 cedis.

to group members of between ¢0.5 million and ¢30 million for CITI, between ¢300,000 to ¢5 million for the M&A Bank and a lower figure of ¢100,000 for the ARB.

Three further benefits accrue to these three formal institutions. They earn interest on the loans advanced to the groups (38 to 42 per cent for CITI and 65 per cent of the market rate for M&A); they achieve very high repayment rates, with the M&A Bank noting that these rates are higher than for corporate customers; and high proportions of group members have 'graduated' to direct relations with the financial institutions. In the case of CITI, it is mandatory for all group members to open an individual account with this institution. Forty-nine per cent of members in groups linked to the M&A Bank have opened individual accounts with the bank, and this is the case for 90 per cent of the members of groups linked with the ARB.

Table 15.6 Loans Advanced through Informal Groups/Agents

Links with *Susu* Groups	CITI 16 groups 4634 members	M & A Bank 7 groups 929 members	Ahantaman RB 17 groups 1260 members	Links with *Susu* collectors/ clerks	CITI 63 (16) SCs	Ahantaman RB 26 SClks
Loans from FI to groups	Min. ¢2m Max. ¢679m aver. ¢160m Weekly	¢30m–¢750m per cycle	¢300,000 to ¢1m			
Loans from groups to members	Min. ¢0.5m Max. ¢30m Aver. ¢2m	¢300,000 to ¢5m[a]	¢100,000	Loans from SCs/SClks to clients	RS: ¢20,000 to ¢750,000 ES: ¢90,000 to ¢1m[b]	¢0.5m to ¢1m
				Average	n.a.	¢0.5m
				No.clients receiving loans	10–30 at a time	approx. 100 monthly
				Gender of clients	80% female	60% female
Interest charges	CITI to group 38–42%[c] Group to members 20–25%[d]	65% of market rate	n.a.	Interest charges	RS: 0% ES: CITI to SCs 3.5% mth SCs to clients 3.5–5% month	40%
Loan duration	2-year cycle	1-year cycle	FI to group: 9–12 months Group to member: 1–3 months.	Loan duration	RS: 1 month ES: 3–6 months	9–12 months
Criteria for loan	Savings record; Guarantors	Savings/atten. record	n.a.	Criteria for loan	Savings record	Savings record
Repayment rate	98%	100% better than corporate customers	95% to ARB 99% to groups	Repayment rate	98%	95%
% Grad. to direct relations with FI	Mandatory for all members to have a/cs	49%	90%	% Grad. to direct relations with FI	Occurs, but no figures available	90%

Notes:

n.a. = not available.

[a] Based on figures for three groups and depending on value of weekly contributions

[b] RS=regular *susu*, ES=extended *susu*: for explanation see text.

[c] On reducing balance

[d] Flat rate.

What are the potential advantages and disadvantages of linkage for the group members? For members of groups linked to CITI and the M&A Bank, a major advantage is that a greater number of members receive their loans earlier in the cycle compared to a traditional rotation system. For example, let us take a group of 100 members, each contributing ¢11,000 on a weekly basis over a two-year period. Under CITI's arrangements, twenty-five members would receive a loan in week ten compared to ten clients under simple rotation. The figures for weeks twenty-four, fifty and seventy-five are 50/24, 75/50 and 100/75 respectively. Moreover, given the very high proportions of women members of these groups, large numbers of women clients are able to get access to these group-mediated bank loans. However, there is a price to pay for this advantage. Whereas under system rotation no interest is charged, under CITI's arrangements members pay a flat rate interest charge of 21 per cent for the loan they receive. Moreover, continuing with this example, under the linkage arrangements the loans members receive are rather smaller than they would be under simple rotation (¢1.0 million compared to ¢1.1 million) and no members receive any loan until week ten, compared to traditional ROSCA operations, where members would start to distribute rotating savings from the first week. Nonetheless, the possibility of graduating to direct relations with the financial institutions through building up a credit history in group transactions is a further advantage of the linkage arrangements for the members.

As with group finance, the advantage to CITI of links to the *susu* collectors is the access such linkage provides for cost-effective loan provision to large numbers of 'indirect' clients. In Table 15.6 a distinction is made between regular *susu* and extended *susu*. The former refers to *susu* collectors who operate in the traditional manner and use CITI to deposit their mobilized savings, while the latter refers to *susu* collectors (sixteen of the sixty-three) who, on the basis of accumulated savings deposited with CITI, also take loans from CITI that they on-lend to their clients. *Susu* collectors operating regular *susu* do provide 'advances' to their clients, but these are very short-term (less than one month), though they have the major advantage of being interest-free. The advances provided under extended *susu* are of higher value and longer duration compared to regular *susu* advances; however, they do have a major disadvantage for the *susu* collectors' clients of being interest-bearing: 3.5 to 5 per cent a month.

A similar situation exists for lending to the clients of the *susu* clerks employed by the ARB. In this case, such clients can receive overdraft facilities from the bank on the basis of savings mobilized through the *susu* clerks. The value of these (¢0.5 to ¢1.0 million) is higher than advances provided under traditional *susu* and of longer duration (between nine and twelve months), but, again, interest is charged (40 per cent annually) compared to the non-interest-bearing advances provided by traditional *susu* collectors. In the case of both *susu* collectors linked to CITI and *susu* clerks employed by the ARB, high proportions of clients receiving loans are women (60 to 80 per cent), repayment rates are very high (95 to 98 per cent), and, in the case of the ARB, 90 per cent of the *susu* clerks' clients have 'graduated' to direct relations with the bank.

Conclusions

As with any policy proposals, there are arguments for and against linking formal and informal financial intermediaries. Bringing together the resources of the formal banking system with the knowledge and outreach of the informal agents and groups is seen as a way to increase access to financial services for those normally excluded from direct relations with formal financial institutions. At the same time, lingering perceptions of the exploitative nature of some informal financial agents and operations, on the one hand, and the risks of destroying the essential informality of informal financial service providers, on the other hand, are reasons for leaving the informal financial sector well alone.

The financial services sector in Ghana is very dynamic, with many different kinds of formal and informal financial service providers. In terms of deposit and loan flows, many interactions between the different financial intermediaries have developed in the normal course of business transactions. However, in recent years there have been a growing number of bank and non-bank financial institutions that have sought to formalize their relations with informal financial agents and groups. Although financial sector policy to date has not explicitly incorporated provision for the informal financial sector, there is a growing official recognition of this sector's role and the need to facilitate linkages between formal and informal financial intermediaries. Although the informal financial sector in Ghana itself comprises a very diverse set of players, formal financial institutions have tended to concentrate on establishing links with *susu* groups and *susu* collectors: groups and agents that have the potential to channel large amounts of informal savings into the formal financial sector.

In this chapter we have examined the links three different kinds of formal financial institutions (two urban, one rural) have established with

Jones, J. H. M., O. Sakyi-Dawson, N. Harford and A. Sey (1999), 'Improving Financial Services for Renewable Natural Resources Development in Ghana: Establishing Policy Guideline for the Informal Sector', Report to the Policy Research Programme, Natural Resources Policy and Advisory Department, Department For International Development, Reading: AERDD, The University of Reading and Department of Agricultural Extension, University of Ghana.

Quainoo, A. (1998), 'Ghana Micro-finance Institutions Action Research Network. Overview of MFI Activities since Formation of Network', Accra: Consultancy Report.

—— (1999), 'Financial Services for Women Entrepreneurs in the Informal Sector of Ghana', Accra: Report to the Ghana Micro-finance Institutions Action Research Network.

Published Sources

Aryeetey, E. (1994), *Financial Integration and Development in Sub-Saharan Africa: A Study of Informal Finance in Ghana*, London: ODI Working Paper 78.

—— (1996), *The Formal Financial Sector in Ghana after the Reforms*, London: ODI Working Paper 86.

Bell, C. (1993), 'Interactions between Institutional and Informal Credit Agencies in India', in K. Hoff, A. Braverman, and J. E. Stiglitz (eds), *The Economics of Rural Organization. Theory, Practice and Policy,* New York: Oxford University Press.

Berger, M. (1989), 'Giving Women Credit: The Strengths and Limitations of Credit as a Tool for Alleviating Poverty', *World Development*, Vol. 17, No. 7: 1017–32.

Bortei-Doku Aryeetey, E. and E. Aryeetey (1996), *Operation, Utilization and Change in Rotating Susu Savings in Ghana*, Technical Publication No. 59, Legon: Institute of Statistical, Social and Economic Research, University of Ghana.

Braverman, A. and M. Huppi (1991), 'Improving Rural Finance in Developing Countries', *Finance and Development*, March: 42–4.

Duncan, B. A. (1997), *Women in Agriculture in Ghana*, Accra: Friedrich Ebert Stiftung.

Germidis, D. (1990), 'Interlinking the Formal and Informal Financial Sectors in Developing Countries', *Savings and Development XIV* (1): 5–21.

Ghate, P. (1992), *Informal Finance: Some Findings from Asia*, Hong Kong: Oxford University Press.

Holt, S. L. and H. Ribe (1991), *Developing Financial Institutions for the Poor and Reducing Barriers to Access for Women*, Washington, DC: World Bank Discussion Paper 117.

ISSER (1999), *The State of the Ghanaian Economy in 1998*, Legon: The Institute of Statistical, Social and Economic Research, University of Ghana.

Jiggins, J. (1985), 'Rural Women, Money and Financial Services', *Community Development Journal*, Vol. 20, No. 3: 163–75.

Nass, L. and S. O'Dowd (1997), *Micro-financing and Poverty Alleviation in Northern Ghana: Pointers to Development of Sustainable Financial Services: The Cases of Upper West Region, Northern Region and Upper East Region of Ghana,* Tamale, Ghana: ISODEC.

Reed, L. *et al.* (1994), *The Role of NGOs in Rural Financial Intermediation in Ghana,* Accra: OPPORTUNITY International and TechnoServe.

Singh, I. (1990), *The Great Ascent. The Rural Poor in South Asia,* Baltimore, MD: The Johns Hopkins University Press, The World Bank.

Siriboe, J. B. (1998), 'Towards Improved Micro-finance Service Delivery: The View of the Government of Ghana', in N. Harford et al. (eds), *Improving Financial Services for the Renewable Natural Resource Sector in Ghana: Policy Guidelines for Enhancing the Role of the Informal Financial Sector,* Reading: Report of a workshop held in Sunyani, Brong Ahafo Region, Ghana, April 1998.

UNDP (1995), *Human Development Report,* New York: Oxford University Press.

Zeller, M., G. Schrieder, J. von Braun and F. Heidhues (1997), *Rural Finance for Food Security for the Poor. Implications for Research and Policy,* Washington DC: International Food Policy Research Institute.

16

Financial Arrangements Across Borders: Women's Predominant Participation in Popular Finance, from Thilogne and Dakar to Paris. A Senegalese Case Study[1]

Abdoulaye Kane

This chapter focuses on women's prominent role in the savings and credit practices common to most Senegalese households in recent times. Tontines, which the Senegalese call *natt*, *tegg*, *piye*, *boukari*, *sani diamra* or *mbotaay*, are omnipresent in the residential neighbourhoods, markets and workplaces of rural and urban areas. My field study shows that they also exist among Senegalese immigrants, particularly women, in Paris. In the literature on informal finance, these organizations are referred to by the generic names of Rotating Savings and Credit Associations (ROSCAs) or Accumulating Savings and Credit Associations (ASCRAs).[2] However, these two categories do not fully reflect the wide diversity of African mutual aid efforts, particularly in Senegal. I therefore suggest use of the more inclusive term, 'popular socio-financial arrangements'. These can be defined as associations with members who agree to pool their resources, such as money, goods or labour, making regular or occasional contributions to a fund that is given, in whole or in part, to each contributor in turn. The order of allocation may be determined by chance (drawing of lots or organization of a family ceremony), by auction or by general agreement on the relative urgency of the different members' needs.

The present chapter will examine popular socio-financial arrangements of the contractual and monetary type – the Rotating Savings and Credit Associations and the Accumulating Savings and Credit Associations. In French-speaking African countries like Senegal, the term *tontine* is used to denote both the ROSCAs and the ASCRAs. F. J. A. Bouman (1995)

Table 16.1 Configuration of Financial Operations in a Six-Member Tontine[3]

Position	A	B	C	D	E	F	Fund	Credit	Savings	Period
1	**100**	**100**	**100**	**100**	**100**	**100**	**600**	500	100	January
2	100	**100**	**100**	**100**	**100**	**100**	**600**	400	200	February
3	100	100	**100**	**100**	**100**	**100**	**600**	300	300	March
4	100	100	100	**100**	**100**	**100**	**600**	200	400	April
5	100	100	100	100	**100**	**100**	**600**	100	500	May
6	100	100	100	100	100	**100**	**600**	0	600	June
Total	**600**	**600**	**600**	**600**	**600**	**600**	**3600**	**1500**	**2100**	**6 months**

documents their existence in almost eighty countries, and lists the terms used in the various cultural regions. Tontines are found in almost all African countries, notably in Cameroon (Henry *et al.* 1991; Rowlands 1995; Niger-Thomas 1995), in Benin (Lelart 1990) and in South Africa (Bähre 1998), but also in Asia (Lelart 1993; Smets 1998; Lont 2001), in Latin America (Bijnaar 1998) and in the Caribbean. In all settings scholars noted the prominent participation of women, as compared to that of men, in these informal financing organizations (Ardener and Burman 1995). The question thus arises: why do women in general, and Senegalese women in particular, prefer the tontines to other formal or informal financial intermediaries?

Historical Survey, or The Search for Origins

Tontines date back to pre-colonial times, but they did not attract significant attention from researchers until the early 1960s (Geertz 1962; Ardener 1964; Bouman 1979). The more recent explosion of interest in popular financial arrangements followed the debt crisis of the early 1980s, which prompted a search for alternative models of development financing. The devastating failure of external financing schemes gave rise to a new discourse and financial methods emphasizing the mobilization of internal resources. Rather than acknowledge the banking system's inability to adapt to different socio-cultural environments, some specialists chose to explore the duality of African financial systems (Hugon 1990). They discovered an informal financial system side-by-side with the informal economic sector and operating in response to the same logical imperatives.

To understand the dynamism that characterizes tontines in contemporary African communities, one must explore their roots in reciprocity and sociability practices built on familial and neighbourhood ties. Gift-giving during major social events, such as marriages, religious celebrations, funerals and baptisms, is key to the social bond in Africa. Some scholars argue that the pre-colonial tontine was an integral part of a reciprocity system that favoured the circulation of labour, agricultural and artisanal products or precious metal jewellery, over that of money (Lelart 1995: 93). Other authors suggest that these village-level community solidarity mechanisms were the ancestors of contemporary monetary tontines (Henry *et al* 1991; Essombe Edimo 1995; Mayoukou 1994). In their view, pre-colonial labour tontines were gradually transformed into monetary tontines following the introduction of currency. However, some historical studies reveal the early existence of very complex monetary systems in some West African societies (Jones 1958; Hopkins 1966; Johnson 1970; Adebayo 1994). The introduction of Western currency following colonization would result in far more dramatic changes in African economic and social life.

As Bouman underlines, the introduction of taxation, manufactured products, and education, along with the broader revenue and currency culture, had a profound impact on African societies. Reciprocal practices featuring the exchange of material goods gave way, little by little, to new forms of reciprocity where money increasingly served as the essential medium of exchange. The gradual monetization of reciprocal relations was reflected in the mixed nature of offerings during family ceremonies in both rural and urban areas. Before the introduction of currency, agricultural and artisanal products dominated exchanges and reciprocal relations. The arrival of modern currency meant that female organizers of family events received cash as well as agricultural, artisanal and manufactured products. The *mbotaay* and the *piye woudere* – social solidarity practices associated with family ceremonies in the *Wolof*[4] and *haal pulaar*[5] communities – today prefer cash to payments in kind, with the exception of highly valued manufactured goods. This change in reciprocal relations is linked to the practical nature of money as a medium that fosters balanced reciprocity.

Gender relations have been manifested in these reciprocal relationships through the sexual division of labour in the organization of ceremonies. While men assume responsibility for all aspects of the religious ritual, women are assigned duties involving customs and practical organization. In the case of marriage, for example, it is the men who build the alliance between the two families based on Islamic principles and rules in the

Mosque, while the women welcome guests and prepare meals. In addition to these tasks, women play a pivotal role in reciprocal relationships. They exchange gifts, donations and offerings at this type of ceremony, although they must rely on financial contributions from men in order to fulfil their social obligations. The essential role played by Senegalese women during family ceremonies may contribute to their predominance in mutual types of popular financial arrangements.

Tontines may be seen as an adapted form of reciprocal relations shaped by monetization. This hypothesis appears plausible, since tontines look to traditional modes of reciprocity for their organizational model and their operating procedures, as well as their notions of trust and social control. Tontines embrace the principles of rotation and chance, while offering the regular social meetings that still today characterize the *mbotaay* and the *piye woudere*. Moreover, women often organize tontines to deal specifically with social events in the same way as the *mbotaay* and the *piye woudere*.

Contemporary popular financial practices are thus rooted in a very long history of reciprocity and mutual aid on social occasions. Marriages, baptisms, funerals, religious celebrations and other rites of passage are special occasions during which the solidarity of kin, neighbours or co-worshippers is translated into collective responsibility for the financial and material requirements of the ritual. Two major differences, however, distinguish the traditional forms of mutual aid from the rotating savings and credit associations. On the one hand, the former do not ensure equality of rewards and sacrifices for each participant, while the latter provide a relative balance between contributions and benefits for each member at the end of the tontine cycle. In addition, traditional mutual aid initiatives arise from social obligations inherent in family or neighbourhood bonds, while modern tontines are based on contractual or voluntary principles.

Typology of Senegalese Tontines

The wide diversity of tontines makes any attempt at classification hazard-ous. Indeed, each tontine is a unique arrangement fashioned to suit the means and needs of its members. Tontines, in fact, resemble chameleons, always assuming the colour of their environment. Thilognese tontines adopt structures inspired by a caste-based social hierarchy, while Dakar's tontines encourage the integration within urban society of ethnically and religiously diverse individuals. At the same time, the tontines organized by Senegalese women in France help their members combat loneliness and adapt to their new social and institutional environment. Variations in contribution rates and order of rotation further illustrate the extreme adaptability of tontines. Daily contributions reflect the rhythm of economic activity in market tontines, while monthly contributions are required of salaried members of workplace tontines. Frequency of payment in neighbourhood tontines ranges from a week to a month, depending on the nature of activities and the regularity of members' revenues.

Such variations notwithstanding, informal financial specialists propose classification schemes for these popular financial arrangements. Thus, Bouman (1994) distinguishes the ROSCAs from the ASCRAs on the basis of distribution modes. In the ROSCAs, the lump sum available at the end of each period is given in whole or in part to one of the participants, most often chosen by lot. In the ASCRAs, by contrast, an accumulation phase precedes the rotation among members of reimbursable credit with interest. The fund can also be loaned to non-members, on the condition of repayment, at a higher interest rate. At the end of a fixed period, the members may decide to share equally the entire fund and the accumulated profits.

Other authors, like Claude Dupuy (1990), distinguish between different types of savings mobilization. He emphasizes community savings efforts, where individuals club together to solve their financial problems. However, such a classification fails to consider that credit is as important as savings in this kind of arrangement, at least for the associative-type groups. Moreover, in market tontines, where members need cash to purchase merchandise, the main objective is to obtain low-cost credit.

On closer examination, the categories presented by Bouman and Dupuy appear to overlap. Village or religious community-type tontines, like ASCRAs, encourage accumulation. However, unlike ASCRAs, the mobilized amounts are not designated for interest-bearing credit distribution, but are earmarked for community projects or members experiencing difficulties. Associative tontines are also very similar to ROSCAs, at least in their rotation of savings and/or credit pay-outs. According to Dupuy, associative tontines include ROSCAs as well as ASCRAs. In fact, the term 'tontine' is used not only for ROSCAs and ASCRAs but also for other types of mutual financial arrangements, such as the solidarity funds commonly found in emigrant communities.

Overall, these classification efforts are unsatisfactory, for they fail to consider the actors and their relationships with one another. Too much attention has been devoted to the way in which money circulates – rotation or accumulation – while neglecting the social links between members. The present study proposes a typology that overturns this perspective,

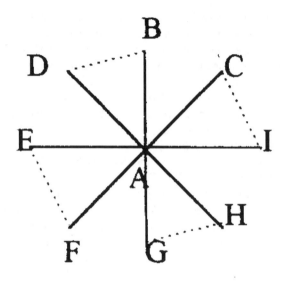

Figure 16.1 Structure of Relationships in a Mutual Tontine

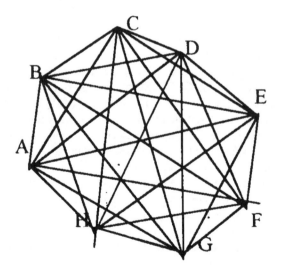

Figure 16.2 Structure of Relationships in a Commercial or Financial Tontine

placing the actors and the social connections they have forged at the centre of these financial arrangements. This reorientation is essential, since the success of this type of financial intermediation relies heavily on participants' ability to build relationships based on trust, solidarity and social control that are sufficiently strong to prevent default.

Tontines can thus be divided into two categories according to the nature of the relationships that exist among the participants, as illustrated in the above figures. First, there are mutual tontines based on sociability. For the most part, these are exclusively female organizations, found in residential neighbourhoods, in workplaces or among immigrants from the same village. In such associations, members know one other and are expected to attend meetings at which contributions and pay-outs are made. Absent and late members pay fines into a contingency fund that covers missing contributions on distribution day. In this type of tontine, social aspects, such as meetings, educational discussions and mutual aid, are as important as the money that circulates. Moreover, principles and procedures are largely modelled on reciprocal practices associated with family ceremonies such as the *mbotaay*[6] and the *piye woudere*.[7]

Second, there are commercial tontines that feature an organizer who serves as an intermediary between the participants. The members therefore do not need to know each other. The organizer collects contributions by making periodic visits to members' houses and market stalls. When the fund is complete, the organizer selects the recipient by considering factors including trustworthiness, urgency of need, affinity or family ties. Unlike the leaders of the mutual tontines, the commercial tontine organizer is paid for fulfilling administrative duties. In some cases, the organizer and members agree from the outset on the terms of payment. Most organizers ask each fund recipient for the equivalent of one contribution. But the advantages enjoyed by commercial tontine organizers, as compared to ordinary participants, must not be exaggerated. The organizer must assume full responsibility for any defaults that may occur during the tontine cycle. In cases of failure to make payments, the organizer must complete the fund and negotiate to recover debts. The remuneration received, therefore, not only compensates organizers for their fund-raising work, but also for the risks assumed.

The large markets of Dakar, Sandaga and Tilène boast special commercial tontines that promote the accumulation of small savings rather than the rotation of credit and/or savings pay-outs. They are run by market tontine managers, men or women possessing a solid, trustworthy reputation. These managers are itinerant bankers, commonly serving hundreds of clients who daily deposit their small savings (between 100 CFA F and

Table 16.2   Variation of Market Tontine Managers' Remuneration

Daily payment	1 month	3 months	6 months	9 months	12 months
1,000 CFA F	1,000 CFA F	2,500 CFA F	5,000 CFA F	7,500 CFA F	10,000 CFA F

Source: Kane 1997–8.

10,000 CFA F). Like the organizers of commercial tontines, they tour the markets collecting dues from their clients.

A. N. is one of Sandaga's market tontine managers. In a large notebook, he keeps track of 275 clients who are involved in diverse market activities: from fabric merchants and vegetable- and fish-sellers, to street hawkers and restaurant operators. Each morning, he visits his clients, who pay him a sum agreed upon in advance, ranging from 250 to 10,000 CFA F. As soon as the collection is complete, A. N. deposits the money in his local bank account. The duration of the savings process, like the amount, depends on the client, ranging from one month to a year. For his intermediation work, A. N. receives payment based on the duration of the savings process. In concrete terms, the remuneration based on a daily contribution of 1,000 CFA F is indicated in Table 16.2.

A. N. grants credit to some of his loyal clients at a 10 per cent interest rate. Considering that clients may at any time demand their deposits, he uses only one-third of his cash for his credit services. In the light of this constraint, the payment deadlines are also very short, varying from three- to nine-month terms. In addition to money earned through his savings and credit services, A. N. receives substantial interest on his bank account. These advantages led him to abandon his first job, selling chickens, in order to devote himself exclusively to his financial intermediary role.

The categorization presented here applies only to Senegal. This classification also reveals that mutual tontines are exclusively female, while commercial tontines have a mixed membership. In all cases, however, women participate in greater numbers than men. What are the factors that may account for women's predominance in tontines?

Factors Accounting for Women's Predominance in Senegalese Tontines

Women are prominent in mutual and commercial tontines in Thilogne (a rural area in the north of Senegal), in Dakar (an urban area and capital of Senegal) and among Senegalese immigrants in France. Mutual tontines, which represent a little more than two-thirds of all the neighbourhood

Table 16.3   Classification of tontines according to the sex of the participants

Place	Tontines – Total	Male Tontines	Female Tontines	Mixed Tontines
Thilogne	**16**	**0**	**11**	**5**
Neighbourhood	10	0	10	0
Market	6	0	1	5
Dakar	**242**	**4**	**153**	**85**
Neighbourhood	136	0	125	11
Market	96	4	26	66
Workplace	10	0	2	8
Paris	**10**	**0**	**8**	**2**
Total	**268**	**4**	**172**	**92**

Source: Kane 1997–8.

tontines examined, are female-only associations. The other one-third is made up of mixed-membership commercial tontines in which women dominate. Earlier studies of Senegalese tontines came to the same conclusion. Dromain (1990:172), for example, estimated that women represent 73.67 per cent of Senegalese tontine members. Table 16.3 presents the gender distribution for the 268 tontines in my sample.

All the exclusively female tontines (172 of 268) are mutual tontines composed of participants who know one another. Female-only tontines are prevalent in both Thilogne, with 11 out of 16, or 68 per cent of tontines, and Dakar, where they account for 153 out of 242, or 63 per cent of tontines. Among Senegalese immigrants in Paris, exclusively female tontines are even more widespread, representing four-fifths of all tontines. In both Thilogne and Dakar, most of the female-only tontines are located in residential neighbourhoods. No mixed or male neighbourhood tontines exist in Thilogne, where 10 out of 11 female-only tontines are neighbourhood ones. In Dakar, 125 tontines out of 153 female-only tontines are in neighbourhoods, along with 11 mixed tontines, but no exclusively male ones. Moreover, women far outnumber men in the mixed tontines, by a ratio of three to one in the market tontines and six to one in the commercial neighbourhood tontines. Three factors may account for this massive female membership.

First, mutual tontines provide their female participants with a forum for discussion and the sharing of information. Despite meagre resources, the members' ultimate goal is not only financial accumulation for consumption or investment purposes. Even more than financial rewards, participants are seeking practical knowledge from their fellow members. Moreover, this type of tontine fosters the growth of a social aid and support network. In difficult times, members can rely on group solidarity. The majority of women interviewed, in fact, participate in several tontines at the same time in order to expand their social contacts.

Women value the social aspects, like regular meetings, discussions and sharing of experiences, rather than just the purely financial benefits of savings, credit and insurance. This factor is key to understanding their participation in mutual tontines (Rowlands 1995: 118–19). In some cases, where the fund does not even cover the expenses incurred in organizing meetings, the tontine provides an excuse for women to get together. In most mutual tontines, meetings are organized at each of the participants' homes in turn. Before starting the contributions, socialization and animated discussion on subjects of common interest allow the participants to gain useful information on matters such as married life, child-rearing, reproductive health, hygiene and economic opportunities.

Second, women's preference for mutual tontines is a product of a particular socio-cultural and religious context that favours distinctively female and male spaces. Senegalese society has been profoundly shaped by the legacy of patrilineal social structures and the Muslim religion, which assigns women primacy in the domestic sphere and men the dominant role in the public sphere. Men are no more welcome in neighbourhood mutual tontines than women are in mosques or cemeteries. This spatial differentiation helps explain the female presence in rural and urban-based neighbourhood mutual tontines. These female-run associations represent, above all, socially acceptable spaces where women may freely join together, without male interference, to resolve common problems.

Women's economic and financial dependence on men is a third contributing factor. The division of labour associated with the gendered differentiation of social space results in an unequal sharing of authority, responsibilities and obligations between men and women. In the vast majority of Senegalese households, the husband is expected to be the family breadwinner, while the wife is responsible for child care, housework and management of the family budget (Dromain 1990). In rural areas, however, women are actively involved in the production process in addition to the heavy domestic tasks they perform, such as drawing water from wells, collecting wood, washing clothes, crushing millet grains and cooking. While electric appliances and urban services somewhat lighten the load of city women, they, like their rural counterparts, are still confined to the household.

Most women who participate in neighbourhood tontines draw their contributions from the household budget, funds given them by their husbands. Women, therefore, have a vested interest in keeping their husbands out of the tontines, where they would learn about female accumulating strategies. This is especially important in polygamous families, where each wife attempts to draw maximum advantage from the family budget for the needs of her children.

Women's exclusion from paid labour inevitably leads to their dependence on men. Without access to revenues, other than those of their husbands, and marginalized in inheritance arrangements, women have great difficulty in gaining ownership of land or real estate, resources most often required by banks as collateral for loans. In theory, only men work for wages and must provide for the material needs of their wives.

In fact, more and more women participate actively in the building of family revenues. During Dakar's economic crisis of the 1980s and its aftermath, women came to the aid of husbands who were laid off or whose earnings were insufficient to support their families. These women have made their mark in all areas of the informal economy. From dyeing to sewing to hairdressing, from small retailers to food service to import–export, they demonstrate a vigorous entrepreneurial spirit and strong managerial skills. At the same time, Dakar's women began to break out of their domestic confines and are gradually freeing themselves from economic dependence on men. As for widows or single mothers, they have long assumed sole responsibility for their family's needs as female heads of households (Bop 1995).

Unfortunately, this female dynamism is not recognized within the formal financial system, where financing conditions exclude from the outset the overwhelming majority of women. However, limited means notwithstanding, women forge ahead to create innovative financial arrangements tailored to their needs.

The Functions of Senegalese Tontines

Senegalese tontines offer their members a compulsory savings scheme, access to interest-free credit and an extensive social network they can turn to in times of need. Of course, certain conditions must be met in order to carry out these functions. First, it is essential that members build mutual trust-based relationships. Second, there must be deterrent measures to prevent any breach of trust; this entails an effective social control system to prevent and penalize default. Finally, it is vital that members maintain

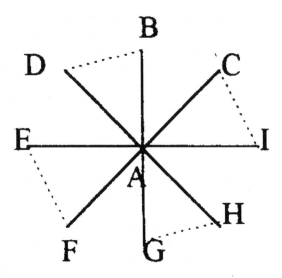

Figure 16.3 The Double Triangulation of Tontine Foundations and Functions

solidarity relations, to ensure continued access to free credit and to mobilize adequate savings for their personal projects. Figure 16.3 presents the triangular nature of tontine foundations and functions.

Trust, solidarity and social control are the foundations of tontine success. All three elements are the products of painstaking social construction in an environment characterized by the proximity of social actors and personalized relationships. In an earlier study (Kane 2001), I analysed the different strategies implemented by tontine participants to avoid breach of trust, to reinforce social control methods and to perpetuate solidarity relations. The three functions of the Senegalese tontines will now be examined in more detail.

a. Savings

The most obvious function of tontines is the creation of small savings. Several researchers have concluded that one of the main motivations of female tontine participants is to build up compulsory savings with group support (Dromain 1990; Lelart 1995; Bortei-Doku and Aryeetey 1995). Saving is difficult in a society in which familial and social obligations require the redistribution of revenues within the extended family and neighbourhood. Tontine participation offers the individual a means of acquiring capital that would otherwise be difficult to accumulate.

Senegalese women can choose from a variety of compulsory savings schemes. The *condamne* is a widely-used instrument for limiting spending. It consists of a hermetically-sealed box with a hole to receive change or bank notes. The individual who drops money into the *condamne* creates a barrier that can only be bridged by proudly destroying the box once the savings goal is reached. Because it relies only on individual willpower, however, the *condamne* has serious limitations as a savings tool. Self-control may not be enough when faced with an overwhelming desire to spend or circumstantial social obligations.

Far more effective than the *condamne* is a second type of self-regulation, involving an external source of constraint. Savings are handed over to a reliable individual with a solid reputation in the community, such as the money-holders or market tontine managers. Savers may request that their deposits be withheld for a fixed period, or until spending or investment planning is complete. In this case, the money-holder or market tontine manager is a financial counsellor as well as a savings collector. Yet this financial arrangement also has its limitations. Faced with emergencies or family or religious-based social obligations, the individual may request the return of savings before the scheduled deadlines.

The tontine's advantage lies in its collective form of restraint, making it more effective than either self-control or the controlling agency of an isolated individual (De Swaan 1995). The tontine member commits at the outset to make regular, fixed contributions throughout the entire duration of the cycle. With group support, the participant follows through by mobilizing savings for consumption, investment and social security purposes. Social pressure to practise self-restraint, to adopt Elias's expression, seems to be what many tontine participants are seeking (Elias 1994).

The mobilization of significant savings through small periodic contributions is the main attraction of the tontine model. This is summed up in the oft-repeated words of field study participants: '*tu cotise peu et tu lève beaucoup*'.[8] Indeed, saving usually involves sacrifice or delayed gratification. In the case of female tontine participants, the sacrifices are offset by the modest amount of contributions and the significant anticipated benefits.

Tontine savings do not necessarily represent, as economists have argued, only that portion of revenue not devoted to consumer spending. Such savings, in fact, involve long-term plans for consumption, investment or social security needs. This distinction is important, for it helps dispel misapprehensions concerning the poorer social classes' propensity to save. If we accept that savings capacity is linked to revenue levels, and that the higher the revenue the more likely one is to save, the poor will have great difficulty in saving, since they may well earmark their entire revenue for consumption purposes. The very existence of tontines, however, demonstrates that the poorer social classes are able to set aside significant savings, however low their revenues may be.

b. Credit

Like many southern-hemisphere countries, Senegal faces the critical problem of financing its development. Access to credit and the mobilization of savings are major problem areas in the formal financial intermediation framework. Moreover, Senegalese banks systematically deny credit to the vast majority of citizens. Two deterrent factors are at work here: on the one hand, credit-granting conditions make the poorer social classes ineligible for loans and, on the other, complex banking procedures alienate a population with an illiteracy rate of more than 70 per cent.

In fact, the refusal of credit affects not only the poorest segments of the population, but also most of the informal sector entrepreneurs, who are categorized as potentially high-risk clients. The bank's lack of confidence in most citizens is reflected in weighty collateral and personal contribution requirements, as well as exorbitant interest rates of 15 to 20 per cent. Women are particularly hard hit. Economic dependence on men means that women do not possess the property essential for loan collateral. Moreover, women's higher illiteracy rate hampers their understanding of banking procedures.

This combination of factors accounts for the massive female membership in the Rotating Savings and Credit Associations (ROSCAs), through which they mobilize savings and obtain credit. Thus, the neighbourhood ROSCAs most often meet consumer needs, while the market and workplace associations mobilize savings for investment in revenue-generating activities.

Table 16.4 presents the results of a survey conducted among 31 participants in Thilogne and 318 participants in Dakar, as well as 20 Senegalese immigrants in Paris. Participants were asked how they used the tontine money and responses were divided into four categories – consumption, investment, foresight and prestige – based on the type of expenditures made by fund recipients. Significantly, meeting investment needs was reported as the main priority, particularly in the Thilogne and Dakar market tontines, as well as among Senegalese immigrants in France.

Table 16.4 Financing Needs Met by Participants

Place	Consumption	Investment	Foresight	Prestige	Respondents
Thilogne	**8**	**15**	**6**	**2**	**31**
Neighbourhoods	7	2	4	2	15
Markets	1	13	2	0	16
Dakar	**106**	**156**	**46**	**10**	**318**
Neighbourhoods	77	69	22	5	173
Markets	26	81	18	2	127
Workplaces	3	6	6	3	18
Paris	**5**	**7**	**2**	**6**	**20**
Total	**119**	**178**	**54**	**18**	**369**

Source: Kane 1997–8.

Thus 48.23 per cent of the 369 respondents, particularly those in market tontines, reinvested the tontine money in their revenue-generating activities. The financing of investment needs was reported by 86.4 per cent and 63 per cent respectively of the Thilogne and Dakar market tontine members, as compared to just 13.3 per cent and 39.8 per cent respectively in the same neighbourhood associations. Consumption came in second place overall, as reported by 32.24 per cent of the respondents. Consumer spending appears especially important for members of the neighbourhood tontines, as reported by 87.5 per cent and 72.6 per cent respectively of the Thilogne and Dakar neighbourhood tontine members, while only 12.5 per cent and 24.5 per cent respectively of the Thilogne and Dakar market tontine members said they used the fund for this purpose. Only 14.63 per cent and 4.87 per cent of all respondents used the pay-out for foresight and prestige-related needs.

Some tontines do seek to provide their members with specific goods or services valued by married women. In this case, the initial agreement between members requires that the lump sum must be spent on particular items. Almost 20 per cent of the sample of 268 tontines, including approximately 32 per cent of the Dakar and Thilogne neighbourhood tontines, fall into this category. Some help their members to acquire household and kitchen appliances, furniture, entertainment devices and kitchen utensils, or to purchase a range of beauty products, or to buy fashionable clothes and shoes for important social occasions. An example of one ROSCA is composed of thirty women from the same neighbourhood. Each member contributes 2,500 CFA F every fifteen days and eventually receives 75,000 CFA F in credit or savings. The women agreed at the outset to use the tontine money to each purchase a gold chain and earrings. The fund recipient is chosen by lot at each meeting and visits the jeweller accompanied by the tontine organizer. At the end of fifteen months, benefiting from a jeweller's discount, each participant will have acquired the jewellery. This type of tontine reflects gender and cultural priorities and is consumer- and status-oriented, providing goods to meet those needs.

We should not conclude, however, that tontines have a negligible economic impact because they often focus on social status and prestige-related consumption. In fact, the boundaries between consumption and investment are often blurred. A refrigerator may be considered a consumer item when used to store family food, but when, as is often the case, it is used to make ice cream destined for sale, it may become an investment. Moreover, Thilogne and Dakar market and workplace tontines exist primarily to finance informal economic activities. The women who participate in these tontines seek to obtain credit either to purchase essential business items, or to invest in the expansion of their micro-enterprises. Such tontines serve as true financial instruments for informal businesses.

The key role played by tontines in the informal economic sector is illustrated by two market tontines based in Thilogne and Dakar. Thilogne boasts a forty-member market tontine, including twenty-eight women. All participants make daily contributions of 2,500 CFA F, accumulated over a period of five days before allocation of the lump sum of 500,000 CFA F. One of the first fund recipients purchased an oil pump, a peanut-crushing machine and merchandise for her small business. On her last turn, she used the credit granted to acquire a freezer and a new scale. For this member, the market tontine serves as an important financial tool, providing interest-free business capital.

The tontine organized by A. N. at Dakar's Colobane market is composed of twenty-five female members, mainly restaurant operators. Members' daily contributions of 3,000 CFA F are distributed as a lump sum at week's end to one of the participants chosen by lot. The recipient obtains just 500,000 CFA F of the 515,000 CFA F lump sum, with the remaining amount deposited in a contingency fund. Thanks to the tontine money, A. N. was able gradually to acquire the equipment necessary to transform an outdoor diner into a restaurant housed in a small rented building, with new tables and benches, plates and soup spoons. For small business people, the tontine is a flexible arrangement that helps meet their financing needs in a way unmatched by formal financial institutions.

c. Social Security Through Mutual Aid

Tontine members can also count on group solidarity to help in difficult times. Social networks in mutual neighbourhood tontines provide a social safety net, and it is not uncommon for members to fund one of their counterparts who is facing particular problems. Mutual tontine members also demonstrate their support on various social occasions.

The relationships forged within tontines may indeed outlive the associations themselves. When one of the participants faces a happy event (marriage or baptism) or a sad occurrence (theft, accident or death), the tontine group makes voluntary contributions when it does not already have a solidarity fund for this purpose. Group visits offer moral support as well as financial aid. Furthermore, at the end of each tontine cycle, members organize a party during which they are paired up with one another by lot. Each woman develops a relationship based on reciprocal obligation with her 'twin' or *ndeydikke* both within and beyond the tontine. For tontines in operation for some twenty years with more or less the same members, this pairing system serves to reinforce group solidarity, since almost all the women maintain favoured relations with one another.

Linkages Between Tontines, Micro-credit Organizations and Banks

Theories of financial duality in developing countries suggest that popular financial arrangements and formal financial institutions are basically incompatible. In fact, despite their theoretical and concrete differences, I find that the two are not mutually exclusive. The existence of tontines in Dakar's commercial banks, in the heart of the formal financial system, shows that economic actors may use both systems simultaneously.

Informal economic agents, especially women, deliberately build bridges between their tontines and the micro-credit organizations or banks. In many cases, where the pay-out is preceded by a lengthy accumulation phase, savings are deposited in a bank account opened in the name of the tontine leader. Moreover, as mentioned above, most tontine organizers or market tontine managers in Dakar have a bank account to safeguard the sums collected. The market tontine managers play an essential role by channelling small savings towards the commercial banks. Of course, banks certainly prefer big clients to small ones, given the cost of transactions. And small savers, for their part, are discouraged by minimum deposit conditions and by the real transaction costs, which include transportation and lost time. They turn instead to tontine leaders, or to market tontine managers, who tour the market to collect their savings. Transaction costs are thus kept low owing to the personalized trust relationships that exist between small savers, on the one hand, and mutual tontine leaders, commercial tontine organizers and market tontine managers on the other. The geographical and psycho-social proximity in which they operate facilitates risk evaluation. Mutual trust and closeness also aid in the creation of effective social control mechanisms for prevention of default or the imposition of social sanctions, often much more effective than institutional penalties. From this point of view, tontine intermediation between small savers and banks significantly reduces the transaction costs for both parties. Banks should develop this double intermediation in order to tap more fully the largely unknown or neglected savings potential in popular financial arrangements. The estimates presented in the following table provide a clear indication of earnings presently sacrificed by formal financial institutions. During a two-year period, on average, a sum of 2,817,348,867 CFA F circulates within 232 market and neighbourhood tontines examined in Dakar. If we assume that the number of tontines in the four neighbourhoods (thirty-four tontines per neighbourhood) and six markets (sixteen tontines per market) as well as their monetary value as reported in my field study are representative of other city neighbourhoods and markets, the total number of tontines in Dakar and their circulating monetary mass (for an average duration of two years) may be estimated respectively at 6,220 and 55,661,560,379 CFA F.

Micro-credit organizations and procedures occupy a middle ground between formal financial methods and popular financial practices. The micro-credit approach is original in that it draws both on banking

Table 16.5   Estimated Number of Tontines and Circulating Monetary Mass in Dakar's Neighbourhoods and Markets

Place	Number of tontines in the study	Estimated number of tontines, Dakar	CMM[9] in the tontines	Estimated CMM in Dakar's tontines
Neighbourhoods(4)	136	5100[10]	899,703,567	33,289,031,879
Markets (6)	96	1120[11]	1,917,645,300	22,372,528,500
Total	232	6220	2,817,348,867	55,661,560,379

Source: Kane 1997–8.

management methods and on the proximity-based trust and social control modes that characterize popular financial arrangements. This facilitates joint initiatives involving tontines and savings and loan societies or the micro-credit organizations.

The links established between a Tilène market tontine and the *Femmes Développement Entreprises en Afrique* micro-credit programme (FDEA) offers an example of successful interaction between a micro-credit organization and popular financial arrangements. Like most micro-credit organizations, the FDEA offers modest amounts of financing at the outset, with increased credit following on successful repayment of debts. The start-up financing granted to this ten-member female tontine was 300,000 CFA F, or 30,000 CFA F per woman, for a six-month term at an interest rate of 5 per cent. The women adopted the principle of the group guarantee, committing to make the payment on behalf of any of their members who might default on the loan.

The ten women also organized an accumulating tontine to help them respect the FDEA repayment schedule, with daily contributions pegged to the size of the loans. After five months of daily payments of 250 CFA F, each participant had accumulated 45,000 CFA F, 15,000 CFA F more than the amount received from the FDEA. The credit now repaid with interest, the FDEA granted a second loan of 450,000 CFA F, or 45,000 CFA F per woman. Tontine members increased their daily contribution to 300 CFA F, and repaid their debt after six months, when each of the members had accumulated 54,000 CFA F. Satisfied by these results, the FDEA then doubled its credit, granting a loan of 900,000 CFA F, or 90,000 CFA F for each woman. Daily contributions were set at 600 F CFA and, in six months' time, each member had mobilized 108,000 CFA F. This highlights the productive results that may be achieved by combining popular financial practices and institutional financing. The articulation of tontines and financial institutions is, moreover, not only a group-based phenomenon. Indeed, persons who receive credit on an individual basis can also use the tontines in order better to meet their commitments to the savings and loan societies or to the banks.

Conclusion

This chapter sheds light on the historical roots of mutual aid practices in Africa. It also explains the reasons for women's predominant role in the Senegalese tontines, which evolved from the gradual monetization of social relationships. The prevailing system of gender relations in Senegal and the gendered differentiation of space favours a strict separation between male and female mutual aid initiatives. The economic dependence of women on men, as prescribed by the patrilineal social structures and Islam, prevents women from owning material goods or from engaging in salaried labour that might provide collateral for bank loans. Tontines are, in fact, the only tools available to most women seeking access to a modest level of credit. In the absence of viable financing alternatives, tontines serve as indispensable financial instruments adapted to the financial needs of the majority of women. Tontines also offer highly-valued social benefits. It is easy to understand, therefore, why Senegalese women prefer these associations to all other forms of financial intermediation. Ultimately, the system of mutual guarantees may replace the collateral required by formal financial institutions and facilitate the repayment of bank or micro-credit organization loans.

Fostering linkages between tontines and formal financial institutions appears a promising strategy in the campaign to improve women's access to credit. Tontines must be accepted as financial instruments on an equal footing with banks or micro-credit organizations. Furthermore, it is essential that the bridge-building process respect the principles and procedures underpinning tontine success and originality. All those committed to increasing women's access to credit in the developing countries should work to promote the highly creative combinations of informal and formal financing strategies developed by the economic actors in this study.

Notes

1. I would like to thank Wendy Johnston for translating this text.
2. The French names are, respectively, *Associations Rotatives d'Épargne et de Crédit* (AREC) and *Associations Accumulatives d'Épargne et de Crédit* (AAEC).
3. This is a theoretical example designed to show those unfamiliar with the tontine phenomenon how a simple tontine works. In fact, there are a variety of complex tontine forms. The regulations concerning frequency of payment, operating rules, contribution rates and order of rotation vary from one to another, adapting to the means and the needs of its members.
4. The Wolof constitute the dominant ethnic group in Senegal, representing 43.3 per cent of the population. They are prominent in the large cities like Dakar and in some rural areas such as the Baol, the Djolof and the Walo.
5. The *haal pulaar* are Senegal's second major ethnic group, representing 23.8 per cent of the population. They are found mainly in the middle valley of the

Senegal River. My field study in Thilogne and among the Senegalese emigrants in France focused mainly on this group.
6. The *mbotaay* is an association of married women who agree to exchange gifts or money at family events.
7. The *piye woudere* are a version of the *mbotaay* in the *haal pulaar* community.
8. 'You contribute little and receive much' (translation).
9. CMM is the Circulating Monetary Mass in the tontines for the duration of a cycle, which varies from one tontine to another. For estimate purposes, I have presented the duration of cycles in months and adapted the statistics to an average duration of two years. The CMM is obtained by multiplying the fund amount by the number of participants.
10. This figure is extrapolated from my study of four neighbourhoods, on which basis there are an estimated thirty-four tontines in each of Dakar's 150 neighbourhoods. The estimate of the number of tontines in the markets follows the same method, assuming that at least sixteen tontines exist in each of the seventy Dakar markets, as revealed by my study of six markets.
11. The estimate of the number of tontines per market is extrapolated from my study of six markets.

References

Unpublished Sources

Bähre, E. (1998), Doctoral Research on Popular Financial Arrangements in South Africa, University of Amsterdam, Amsterdam School for Social Science Research.

Bijnaar, A. (1998), Doctoral Research on the Kasmoni or Tontines in Surinam and among Surinamians living in Amsterdam, University of Amsterdam, Amsterdam School for Social Science Research.

Kane, A. 1997–8. Field study.

—— (2001), 'Les caméléons de la finance populaire au Sénégal et dans la diaspora, Dynamique des tontines et des caisses villageoises entre Thilogne, Dakar et la France', unpublished Ph.D. thesis, University of Amsterdam, ASSR.

Lont, H. (2001), 'Juggling with Money: Adversities and Financial Self-help Organisations in Urban Yogyakarta', unpublished Ph.D. thesis, University of Amsterdam, ASSR.

Smets, P. (1998), Doctoral Research on the Chits Funds in India, University of Amsterdam, ASSR.

Published Sources

Adebayo, A. G. (1994), 'Money, Credit and Banking in Precolonial Africa. The Yoruba Experience', *Anthropos* 89: 379–400.

Ardener, S. (1964), 'The Comparative Study of Rotating Credit Associations', *Journal of the Royal Anthropological Institute* 94(1): 201–29.

—— and S. Burman (eds) (1995), *Money-Go-Rounds: The Importance of Rotating Savings and Credit Associations for Women*, Oxford: Berg Publishers.

Bop, C. (1995), 'Les femmes chef de famille à Dakar', *Africa Development*, XX, 4: 51–67.

Bortei-Doku, E. and E. Aryeetey (1995), 'Mobilizing Cash for Business: Women in Rotating Susu clubs in Ghana', in S. Ardener and S. Burman (eds), *Money-Go-Rounds: The Importance of Rotating Savings and Credit Associations for Women*, Oxford: Berg Publishers.

Bouman F. J. A. (1979), 'The ROSCA, Financial Technology of an Informal Savings and Credit Institution in Developing Economies', *Savings and Development* 3(4).

—— (1994), 'ROSCA and ASCRA: Beyond the Financial Landscape', in F. J. A. Bouman and O. Hospes (eds), *Financial Landscapes Reconstructed: The Fine Art of Mapping Development*, Boulder, CO: Westview Press.

—— (1995), 'ROSCA: On the Origin of the Species', *Savings and Development*, XIX, 2: 117–45.

—— and O. Hospes (1994), *Financial Landscapes Reconstructed: The Fine Art of Mapping Development,* Boulder, CO: Westview Press.

De Swaan, A. (1995), *Sous l'aile protectrice de l'État*, Paris: PUF.

Dromain, M. (1990), 'L'épargne ignorée et negligée: les resultats d'une enquête sur les tontines au Sénégal', in M. Lelart (ed.), *La Tontine*, Paris: AUPELF-UREF/ John Libey Eurotext.

Dupuy, C. (1990), 'Les comportements d'épargne dans la société africaine: études sénégalaises', in M. Lelart (ed.), *La Tontine*, Paris: AUPELF-UREF/John Libey Eurotext.

Elias, N. (1994), *The Civilizing Process*, Vol. 1, Oxford: Basil Blackwell.

Essombe Edimo, J.-R. (1995), *Quel Avenir pour l'Afrique? Financement et Développement*, Paris: Ed. Silex/Nouvelles du Sud.

Geertz, C. (1962), 'The Rotating Credit Association: A "Middle Rung" in Development', *Economic Development and Cultural Change*, vol. 1, no. 2: 241–63.

Henry, A., G. H. Tchente and P. Guillerme-Diumegard (1991), *Tontines et banques au Cameroun. Les principes de la société des amis*, Paris: Karthala.

Hopkins, A. G. (1966), 'The Currency Revolution in South-West Nigeria in the Late Nineteenth Century', *Journal of the Historical Society of Nigeria* 3(3): 471–83.

Hugon, P. (1990), 'La finance non-institutionnelle: expression de la crise du développement ou de nouvelles formes de développement', in M. Lelart (ed.), *La Tontine*, Paris: AUPELF-UREF/John Libey Eurotext.

Johnson, M. (1970), 'The Cowrie Currencies of West Africa', *The Journal of African History*, 11: 17–49, 331–53.

Jones, G. I. (1958), 'Native and Trade Currencies in Southern Nigeria during the Eighteenth and Nineteenth Century', *Africa*, 28: 43–54.

Lelart, M. (1990), 'Une tontine mutuelle dans l'administration béninoise', in M. Lelart (ed.), *La Tontine*. Paris: AUPELF-UREF/John Libey Eurotext.

—— (ed.) (1990), *La Tontine*. Paris: AUPELF-UREF/John Libey Eurotext.

—— (1993), Les systèmes parallèles de mobilisation de l'èpargne', *Epargne sans frontière*, No. 30 (March): 30–5.

—— (1995), 'Les pratiques informelles d'épargne et de crédit: une approche économique', in J.-M. Servet (ed.), *Epargne et Liens Sociaux. Etudes Comparées d'Informalités Financières*, pp. 85–104. Paris: Association d'Economie Financière.

Mayoukou, C. (1994), *Le système des Tontines en Afrique. Un système Bancaire Informel*, Paris: Ed. L'Hartmattan.

Niger-Thomas, M. (1995), 'Women's Access to and Control of Credit in Cameroon: The Mamfe Case', in S. Ardener and S. Burman (eds), *Money-Go-Rounds: The Importance of Rotating Savings and Credit Associations for Women*, Oxford: Berg Publishers.

Rowlands, M. (1995), 'Looking at Financial Landscapes: A Contextual Analysis of ROSCAs in Cameroon', in S. Ardener and S. Burman (eds), *Money-Go-Rounds: The Importance of Rotating Savings and Credit Associations for Women*, Oxford: Berg Publishers.

Continuity and Change – Towards a Conclusion

Ruth Pearson

This volume demonstrates the long relationship between women and credit in a variety of different economic, political and social contexts. It might lead some to a preliminary conclusion that women have always been involved in commercial activity and, that, in spite of obstacles to accessing whatever forms of financial credit were available in particular times and places, women used their ingenuity and creativity to obtain the financial resources demanded either by necessity or by commercial ambition. Indeed, the accounts in this volume do point to historical continuities. In considering and assessing those continuities there are four main points which arise from these case studies.

First, in spite of the current enthusiasm in development circles for supplying women with small amounts of credit in order to facilitate an increase in entrepreneurial activity which will raise household income, the ways in which women use financial resources underline the intricate connection between productive and reproductive activities rather than the separation between them. Although many administrators of micro-credit projects see it as a failure if women use credit intended for commercial purposes to meet family expenditures – such as medicines, school fees, food needs or even repayment of other consumption credit – women are often aware of the integral link between their reproductive responsibilities and productive ends. Secondly, it is also clear that as economies pass through a transition from a situation where the majority of consumption and reproductive necessities are met outside the cash nexus to a situation where even basic reproductive needs – such as food, housing and, in more modern economies, access to education, health care and transport – have to be paid for with currency, women's demand for money very legit-imately increases for reproductive needs as well as for productive activities. This is often the reason why there has been such a strong response from very poor communities to the financial services offered by micro-credit and micro-savings initiatives which extend below the cut off level for formal financial services. There have been other points in history – in the proto-industrialization period in Western Europe and in the transition to a modern economy in Ireland, for example – when women's demand for money responded to similar catalysts.

The third continuity demonstrated by a comparative analysis is that although most women are embedded in the institution of marriage and the household is the main unit of both production and consumption, husbands and husbands' networks are not the primary source for women who access money credit. Some women find it necessary to explore other avenues because their husbands are absent, travelling on business, migrating for employment, or missing as a result of desertion or death. But whether husbands are present or absent, the historical examples from seventeenth-century France to twentieth-century South Africa indicate the centrality of other women in the community – both inside and outside extended families – for the provision of credit for women. The final point to be emphasized is that very often it has been informal sources of credit, often community based and accessed through a range of kin and social networks, that have been the primary means through which women accessed credit, not only because their demand for credit comes out of their responsibility for family survival and reproduction, as we noted above, but also because their networks are embedded in circuits of reproduction rather than in productive activities.

Clearly, there are strong points of continuity. Yet it also essential to avoid complacent conclusions which assume a homogeneity in credit activities among all women both over time and in different societies; it is essential to identify and understand the differences in women's relations to credit that result from their particular temporal, cultural and social contexts, differences that are highlighted by historical and comparative contemporary analyses. Many studies have examined women's exper-iences with credit primarily through an analysis of their connections with commercial activities. Their experiences have been reassessed and even celebrated – as, for example, in the case of those widows in eighteenth-century England or nineteenth-century France who successfully took on the business mantels of their late husbands. Among the contemporary women whose success has been celebrated are those who start with a minuscule loan from an organization like the Grameen Bank or SEWA and are able to build enterprises which lift them and their families out of poverty. However it is also interesting to view women's financial relation-ships through the lens of social policy, asking the question: who takes responsibility for household survival and how is this responsibility mediated via the state, the community and individual families and households? As noted above, in developing countries it is clear that much of the demand by poor women for money credit originates from the increasing necessity for cash in order to meet basic needs of household members. This demand has intensified from the 1980s onwards as developing countries have experienced the dismantling of whatever infrastructure had existed to provide reproductive services, such as health and education, as public goods free at the point of consumption. This dismantling of social programs came in response to neo-liberal economic policies imposed by the Washington-based financial agencies on poor countries unable to meet their international debt obligation and translated into enforced Structural Adjustment policies. Increasingly, even the poorest families have had to pay user charges – for primary school materials, for medicines in health centres – at the same time as subsidies on other services, such as transport and electricity, have been abolished, leading to a sharp increase in the need for money income to survive.

A parallel experience was faced by many households in the Former Soviet Union and eastern Europe where people lived through a period of transition which involved not only a shift from a centrally planned to a private capitalist economy, but also from a system where a range of basic needs and social programs – including housing, education, health and child care, as well as old age and sickness pensions – were met by the state, to one in which the responsibility for basic services and for survival outside the wage labour market fell to individuals and households rather than the collectivity. This is the context which propelled many Western donors to offer credit to women, often the first causalities of labour shedding by former state enterprises. This credit is designed to help women start small businesses to provide a basic income for household survival. Although this experience is in many ways parallel to what is happening in low income developing countries, the nature of the transition is very different; these women's experiences of financial services and of enterprise is of a qualitatively different nature. Moreover, as the chapters on Senegal, India and South Africa indicate, in developing countries there are well established informal institutions organizing money credit for poor households – a resource not available in pre-1989 Eastern Europe and the Former Soviet Union. It is therefore not surprising that micro-credit for women has been relatively less successful in Eastern Europe and the former Soviet Union than similar provision for men, or for both women and men in Sub-Saharan Africa or in South and South East Asia.

A quite different analysis is required to understand what has propelled the development of credit schemes for women in North America and Western Europe. Such an analysis is also facilitated by using the lens of organization and responsibility for household welfare and survival. Since the Micro-Credit Summit in 1997, endorsed by both Hillary and Bill Clinton as the route to economic self-sufficiency for marginalized groups in the United States, there has been an explosion in what is known as the 'micro-credit' industry in North America, as well as a growing number of initiatives in the UK and Northern and Western Europe. However, it is noteworthy that the growth and acceptance of such programmes both by people living in poverty and by policy makers have been much more muted in comparison with the enthusiasm in government circles in the South and the East. This is because until the recent trends towards the dismantling of the welfare state there had been a consensus in the North that the responsibility for household survival and the provision of safety nets for those unable to work – through age, infirmity or lack of opportunity – should be met through the public purse. In recent years, in both the USA and the UK, this consensus has been modified; in both countries the poor are required to demonstrate their entitlement to public subsidies through demonstrating a willingness to work in the wage labour market. And in the absence of regular employment opportunities, this generally means 'make work' initiatives such as the Blair government's 'New Deal' schemes. Both countries are moving towards a situation where access to benefit depends on participation in these quasi-labour markets, with the USA imposing a five year total limit on accessing any benefits at all. Both countries have shifted their policies towards the support of lone parents (overwhelmingly mothers). In the UK, there is a 'New Deal for Lone Parents' which encourages women to rejoin the labour market after their children enter primary school; in the US, benefits are withdrawn from single mothers (though not from children) after five years of public support. Both these examples point to a transformation in the orientation of social and welfare policies in these countries. Rather than the state taking on the responsibility for household survival, individuals are expected to meet these needs through the labour market. Women with children are now discouraged from what has been termed 'dependency' on the state and expected instead to be independent – through the labour market – as well as to seek financial support directly from the fathers of their children. This latter policy resulted in the establishment of the Child Support Agency in the UK in the 1990s, a state body whose only function was to retrieve child maintenance from absent fathers. Given the historic struggle by feminists to establish women's independent entitlements to state support for bringing up children, the notion of independence based solely on labour market participation has to be seen as contradictory.

In this context, encouraging the poor to use the micro-credit model to initiate small enterprises which would directly provide for household subsistence is seen as another route towards independence for the poor rather than a continuing reliance on public funds. However, for women raised in a society in which they expected family maintenance to come through either men or the state, many of whom have settled into poorly paid part time work as a supplement to rather than a main element in household survival and have no entrepreneurial history or experience, the very real risks in borrowing to provide an uncertain income stream are, from their perspective, simply too great. And their perspectives explain their limited involvement in many micro-credit programs. Interestingly where women's credit schemes and small business have flourished is in situations such as the Norwich Full Circle project, where credit is part of a package which includes training and support for women, consolidating existing or initiating new entrepreneurial activities whereby the project is able to mediate against the risk averseness and unfamiliarity of this group with financial or business activities.

In the USA the experience has been somewhat different. Credit for poor women and men has been most successful amongst relatively recent immigrant groups – from Central America or South East Asia – who bring with them both the experience of using money in trade for survival and also familiarity with a range of informal credit networks. But amongst long settled economically excluded groups, such as African Americans, there has been little enthusiasm for pursuing access to new forms of credit, often soberly judged as an increase in indebtedness unlikely to provide the basis for successful business activities in marginalized ghetto neighbourhoods and localities.

In other countries in the North the residue of historically organized welfare benefits has also militated against the attractiveness of borrowing for poor groups. Unlike the experience from pre-welfare state eras or of regions in the global South and East, the existence of a system of welfare entitlements in the West means that the State requires vigilance to ensure that people are not both participating in economic activity and at the same time claiming benefits on the basis of the absence of such activities and incomes. In general governments and government agencies have been suspicious of people from welfare dependency groups who are assumed to be welfare cheaters rather than proto-entrepreneurs. As Connolly (1985: 62) succinctly observed: 'unlike the positions emanating from the First World, where the informal sector is seen as employment disguised as unemployment, the informal sector in the Third World is unemployment disguised as employment.' Yet the informal unregulated sector is where the poor of the South and increasingly the Eastern regions of the world are being forced to make their living, without the expectation of government assistance, vigilance or regulation. In the North, however, in spite of successive employment crises and policy realignments, the normal view of most policy makers is that the labour market is regulated and formal and that activities outside this are suspect and potentially problematic.

What this comparative analysis tells us is that at the beginning of the twenty-first century we are in an era where women from poor communities have very limited economic entitlements to welfare benefits and are being (half-heartedly) encouraged to access financial services as a way to supplement direct assistance from the state. While women are now becoming the majority of the employed labour force in the industrialized economy, this has coincided with the contraction of the provisions of the welfare state and the expectation people have of it – hence the current enthusiasm for private insurance for pensions, health care and education costs. If the alternative presented to mothers is the push to dependency on men and the labour market rather than the state, it is unsurprising that feminists have welcomed the provision of credit for women as an empowering strategy leading to independence and self reliance. But, as we can see from the historical and comparative analyses presented in this volume, the ability of women to use credit in an empowering way depends very much on the economic and social context in which it is offered and in which it can be deployed to take advantage of economic activities.

The studies presented here should, therefore, raise a note of caution to those who would be inclined to stress too strongly the continuity in women's use of credit over time and in different countries. While the chapters strongly illustrate the fact that in many contexts women as well as men needed to access funds for household necessities and for business activities, the risks, the benefits and the implications of such credit vary enormously. Highlighted in some of the historical studies is the role of middle class women from trading communities whose access to credit is important in comparison with men of their class. However, lessons from other historical examples and from more recent times, in both developing and industrialized countries, illustrate how women from the poorer classes have employed credit as means of survival rather than to enhance growth. The contrasts serve both to demonstrate the importance of comparative analyses and the dangers of one-size-fits-all perspectives and policies.

References

Connolly, P. (1985), 'The Politics of the informal sector: A critique', in N. Redclift and E. Mingione (eds), *Beyond Employment: Household, Gender and Subsistence*, Oxford: Blackwell.

Index